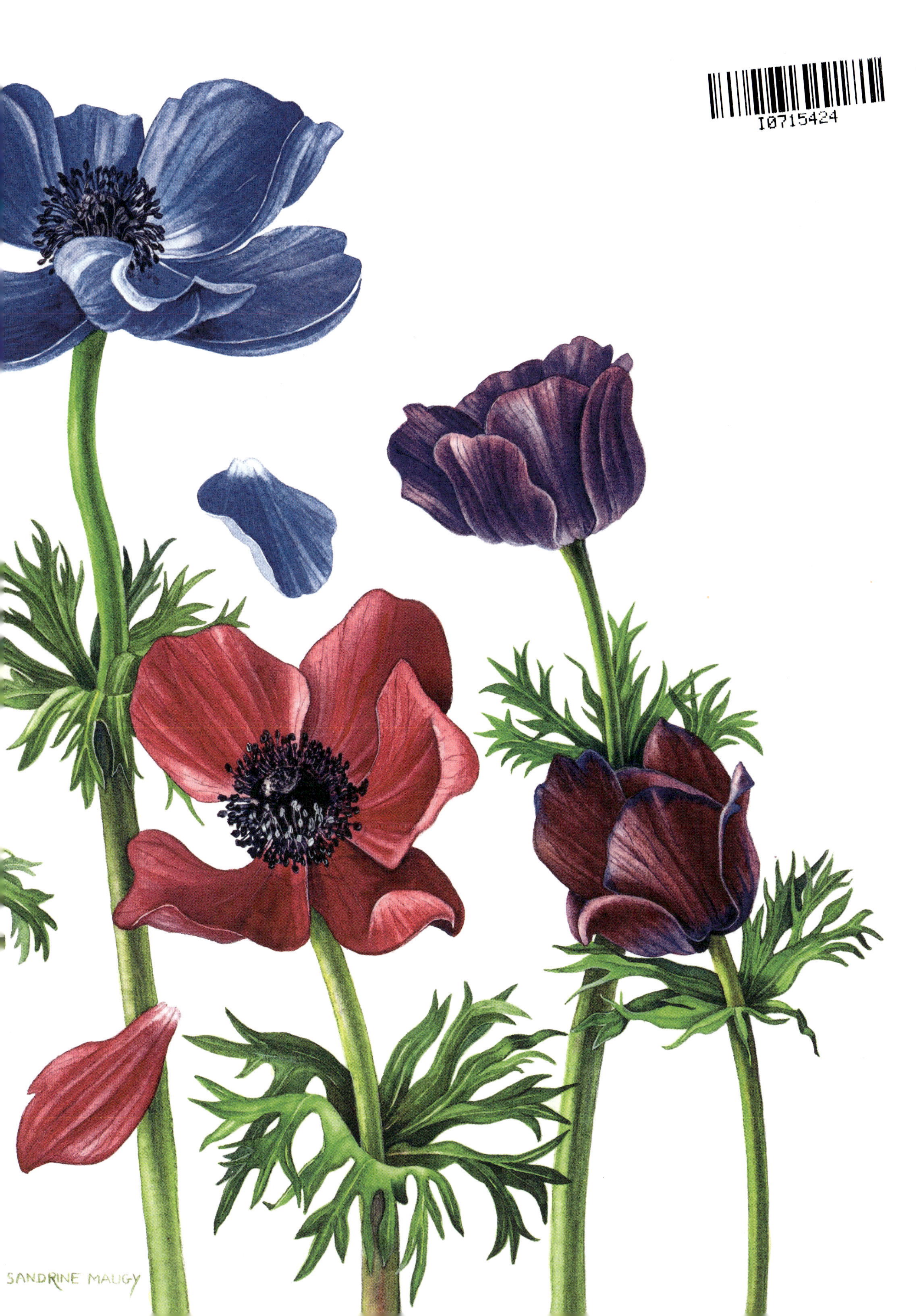

I0715424
SANDRINE MAUGY

BOTANICAL WATERCOLOURS
through the seasons

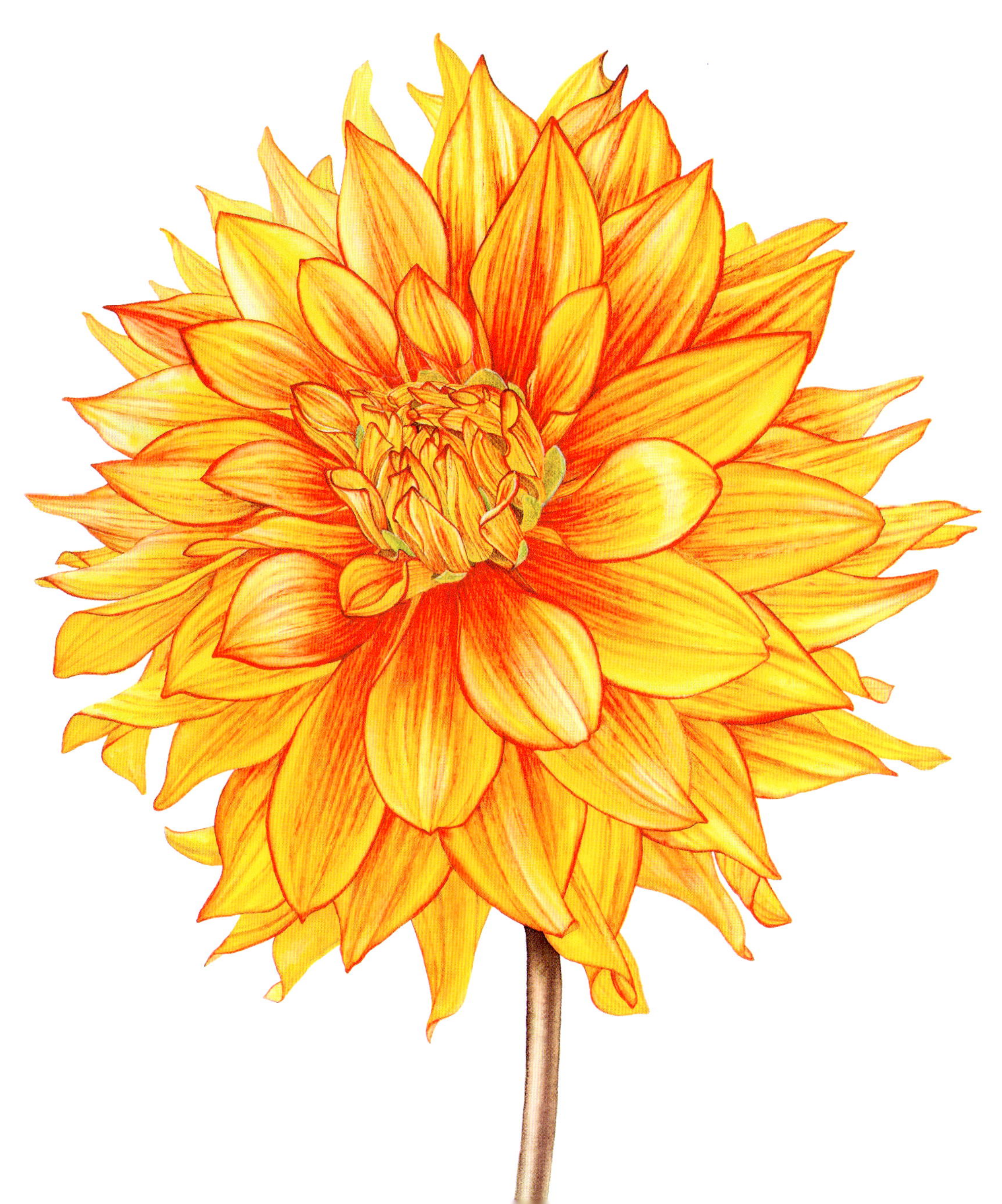

Dedication

Botanical Watercolours through the seasons is dedicated to my mum, who would have loved it. Maman didn't share my love for all seasons and always struggled with the fading light of Autumn... She left this world in November 2013.

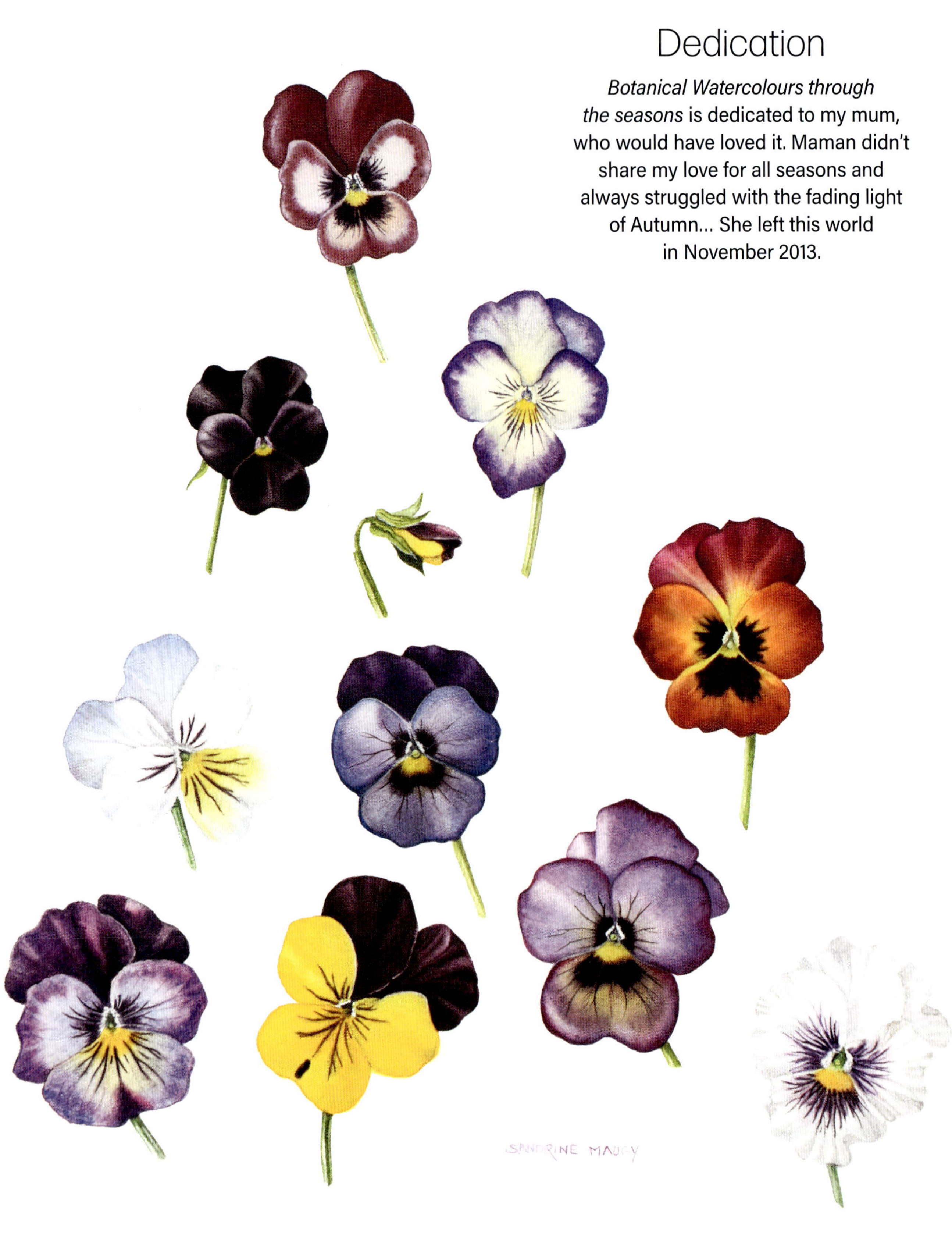

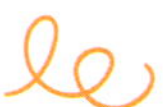

BOTANICAL WATERCOLOURS
through the seasons

An all-year-round guide to painting flowers and plants

Sandrine Maugy

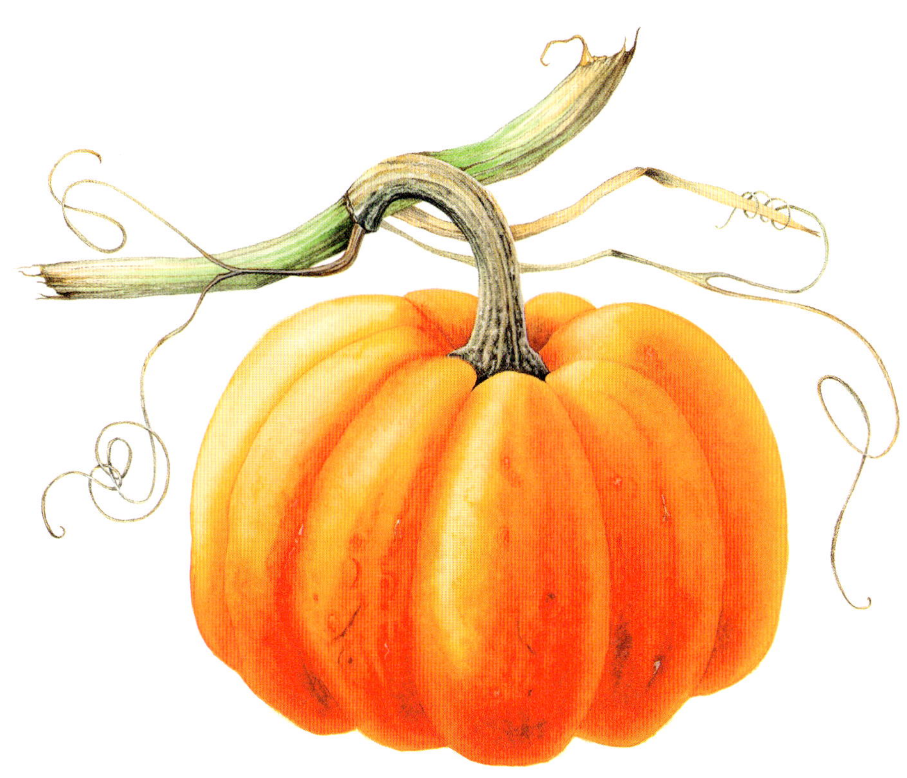

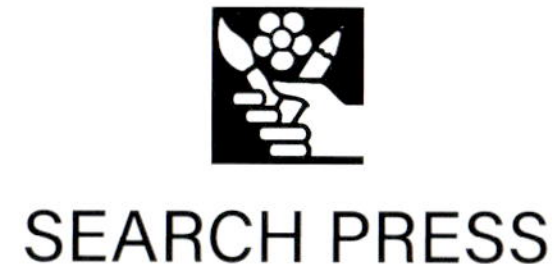

SEARCH PRESS

First published in 2022

Search Press Limited
Wellwood, North Farm Road,
Tunbridge Wells, Kent TN2 3DR

Text copyright © Sandrine Maugy, 2022
Photographs by Sandrine Maugy and Mark Davison
Photographs and design copyright © Search Press Ltd. 2022

ISBN: 978-1-78221-943-9
ebook ISBN: 978-1-78126-937-4

Suppliers
If you have difficulty in obtaining any of the materials and equipment mentioned in this book, then please visit the Search Press website for details of suppliers:
www.searchpress.com

Discover bonus video tutorials by Sandrine Maugy via the Bookmarked Hub: www.bookmarkedhub.com

You are invited to visit the author's:
Website: www.sandrinemaugy.com
YouTube channel: @AtelierSandrineMaugy
Patreon: www.patreon.com/SMaugy
Instagram: @sandrinemaugy
Etsy shop: www.etsy.com/uk/shop/FlorasPatch

Publishers' note
All the step-by-step photographs in this book feature the author, Sandrine Maugy, demonstrating how to paint botanical watercolours. No models have been used.

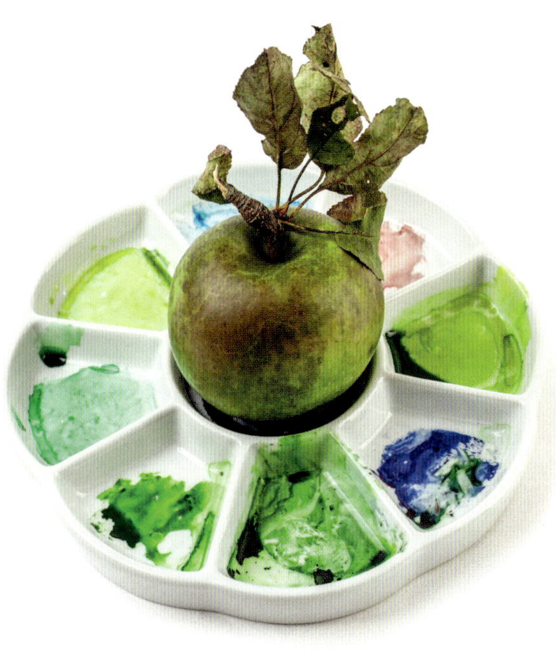

Page 1
Dahlia 'Dazzling Magic', from West Dean Gardens.

Page 2
Viola collection
Shown also on page 145.

Page 3
Pumpkin, watercolour
Shown also on page 108.

Page 5
Echeveria, watercolour
Demonstrated on pages 152–161.

Contents

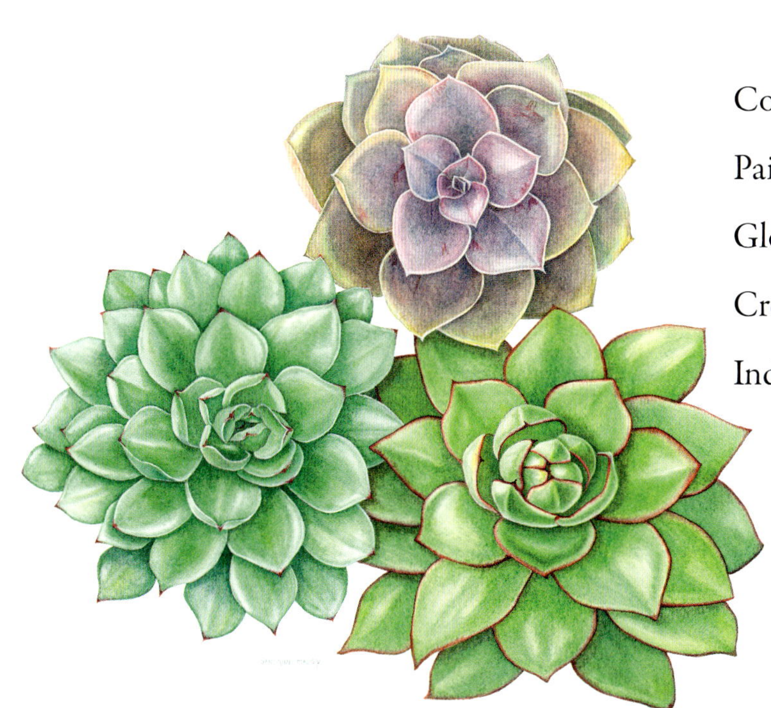

FOREWORD

Tom Brown, Head Gardener at West Dean College, West Sussex; Journalist and Broadcaster

Over recent years, the world has slowed down enough for people to stop and learn to appreciate the natural world around them. Botanical painting optimizes the process of understanding and interpreting those beautiful intricacies of nature through art. Sandrine's book allows us to develop our creativity through her step-by-step tuition which I enjoy whilst she teaches at West Dean College. Through Sandrine's guidance we can learn to celebrate and document the natural rhythms of our green spaces around us, from our gardens and courtyards to nearby forests and fields.

Sandrine has been teaching at West Dean College since 2005. On each of Sandrine's visits to West Dean, she is very engaged with the garden and landscape, selecting flowers and subjects that optimize the time of year and encouraging her students to get out into the environment to study and indulge in the horticulture around them. As Head Gardener of this 90-acre garden, I have assisted Sandrine's classes by providing a range of fruits, flowers and vegetables for her students to study and paint. I revel in the opportunity to look at my surroundings from another perspective, taking time to value the subtle blushes on a ripe pear and a composition of the fleeting delicacy of a tulip as I gather materials for classes.

The gardens at West Dean and, indeed, our own gardens allow us to completely immerse ourselves in the dynamic of the seasons, witnessing the eruption of life in Spring and the balmy Summer heat, influencing our interpretation of the botanical subjects around us. It is Sandrine's botanical knowledge that sets her apart; through her observation and expertise, Sandrine's interpretation of natural forms is heightened.

Botanical painting gives us an insight into the subtle language of flowers – how they attract pollinators or invite fertilization on the lightest of breezes. All of these faint or inconspicuous processes are, in their own way, profound and need to be honoured through informed art. Colour is a vital component of this book – there is a kaleidoscope of tones of each and every colour, which is celebrated in botanical art. Nothing in nature is superfluous or unnecessary: each facet of botany is in place for a purpose, and botanical art reveres this.

In many aspects of our lives, we hurtle through day after day, missing the wonderful intricacies all around us. Let's take some time, each and every one of us, to listen to the sounds of nature, feel the rhythm of the seasons and observe and interpret the wonders of plant life through botanical painting.

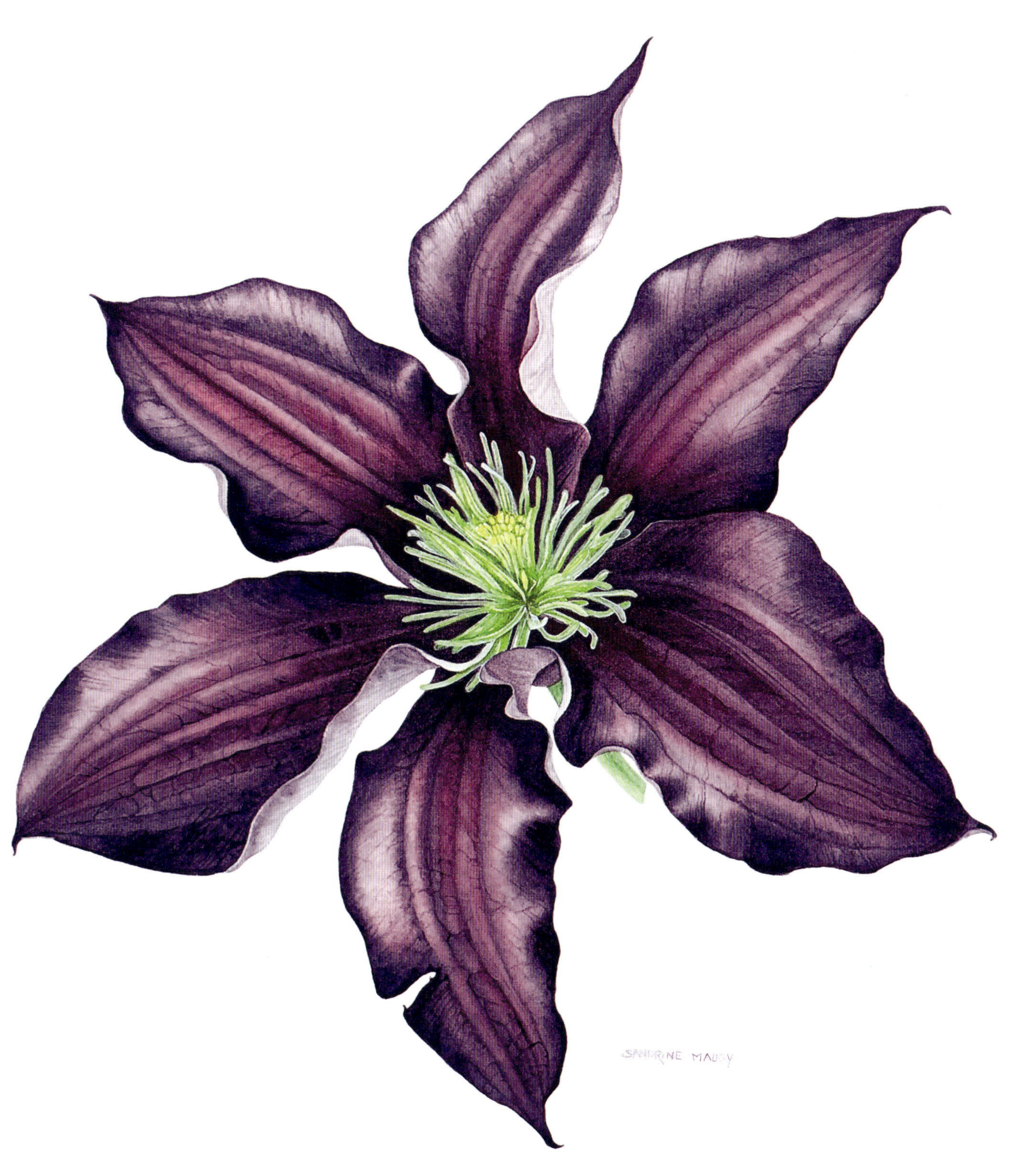

SANDRINE MAUGY

INTRODUCTION

I have always loved the passing of the seasons. It gives a rhythm to life that I find at times soothing and at other times stimulating, but always welcome and most enjoyable.

Spring brings the joyful waking-up of nature, displaying arrays of yellow-greens and bright colours while the birds regale us with their dawn chorus. The luscious Summer carries intense blues in the sky and in the flower borders, inviting us to temporarily move our painting studio to the garden for a spell of *plein air* painting, sheltering from the dazzling sun in the generous shade of the placid trees. Soon the silent mists of early Autumn mornings appear, to be vanquished and lifted by a weakening sun, revealing branches laden with colourful leaves. The storms take them out one by one and our walks turn crunchy underfoot. Finally, the naked garden of Winter shivers under low skies that have me waiting and yearning for the snow that will hush the world and turn the landscape into a dreamy, monochrome picture. Then the birds get noisy again, waking us up at dawn with their antics, and it starts all over again…

Being a botanical artist has added another dimension to this rhythm. Each season yields a bounty of new subjects to paint and brings another reason to anticipate the changes. The palette adapts to nature's transforming colours and textures, and the inspiration follows. I would find it difficult to paint a dead leaf in July or blossom in September, but I look forward to portraying them when they are in season.

In *Botanical Watercolours through the seasons*, I have explored the subjects offered along the year, starting with the awakening of Spring and ending with the festive holly, choosing different textures and colours while offering a choice of difficulty levels. Each of the seasonal chapters contains three tutorials. The first one is for beginners, the second one for intermediates and the last one for more advanced painters. The subjects reflect the varied types found in botanical art, demonstrating a selection of flowers, leaves and fruit.

Initially, following the tutorials step-by-step should give you the confidence to pick your own subject and adapt them, using them as an inspiration and a guide with your own drawings and palettes.

The opening section gives advice about which materials to use, tone and shadows, colour theory, and the techniques I use in my work. When choosing materials and paints I strive to run an ethical art practice, using environmentally-friendly and cruelty-free products. At the end of the book you will find a useful colour-conversion chart that will allow you to follow the tutorials even if your palette differs from mine.

Starting with a sunny daffodil, I invite you to join me on this journey through the seasons and enjoy the plants, blooms and fruit that Nature is bestowing upon us for inspiration.

Happy painting!

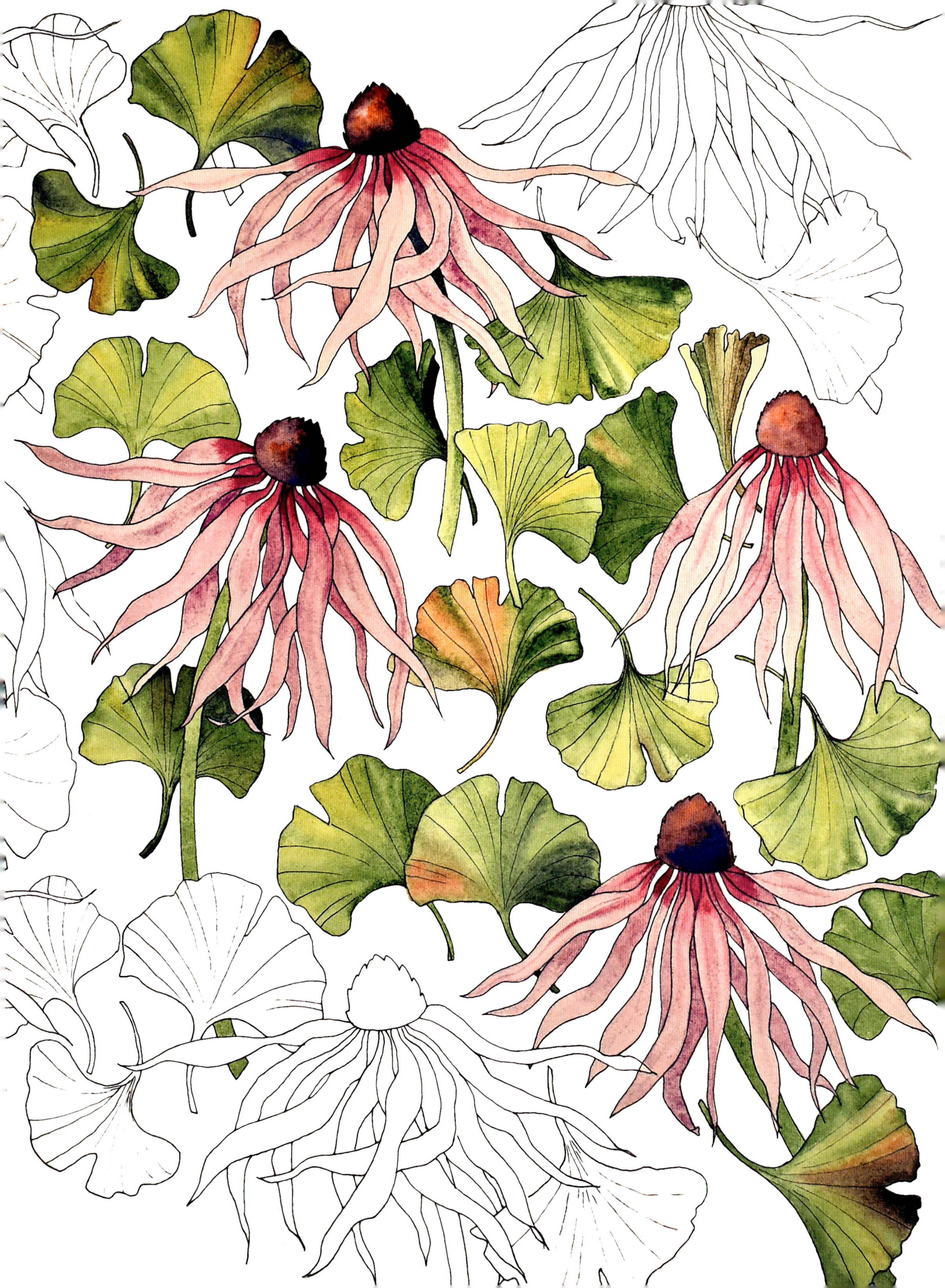

MY ETHICAL STUDIO

Do you sometimes wonder where your art materials come from and what impact your art has on the environment? My endeavours to run my life and my home in an ethical way have naturally spilled into the art studio and as a result my art practice has evolved over the years to be as ethical as possible.

Whether you would like your art to be cruelty-free or respectful of human rights; your art materials to be in line with your vegan lifestyle; or whether you simply care about the environment, here are a few tips that should help you towards your ethical goals.

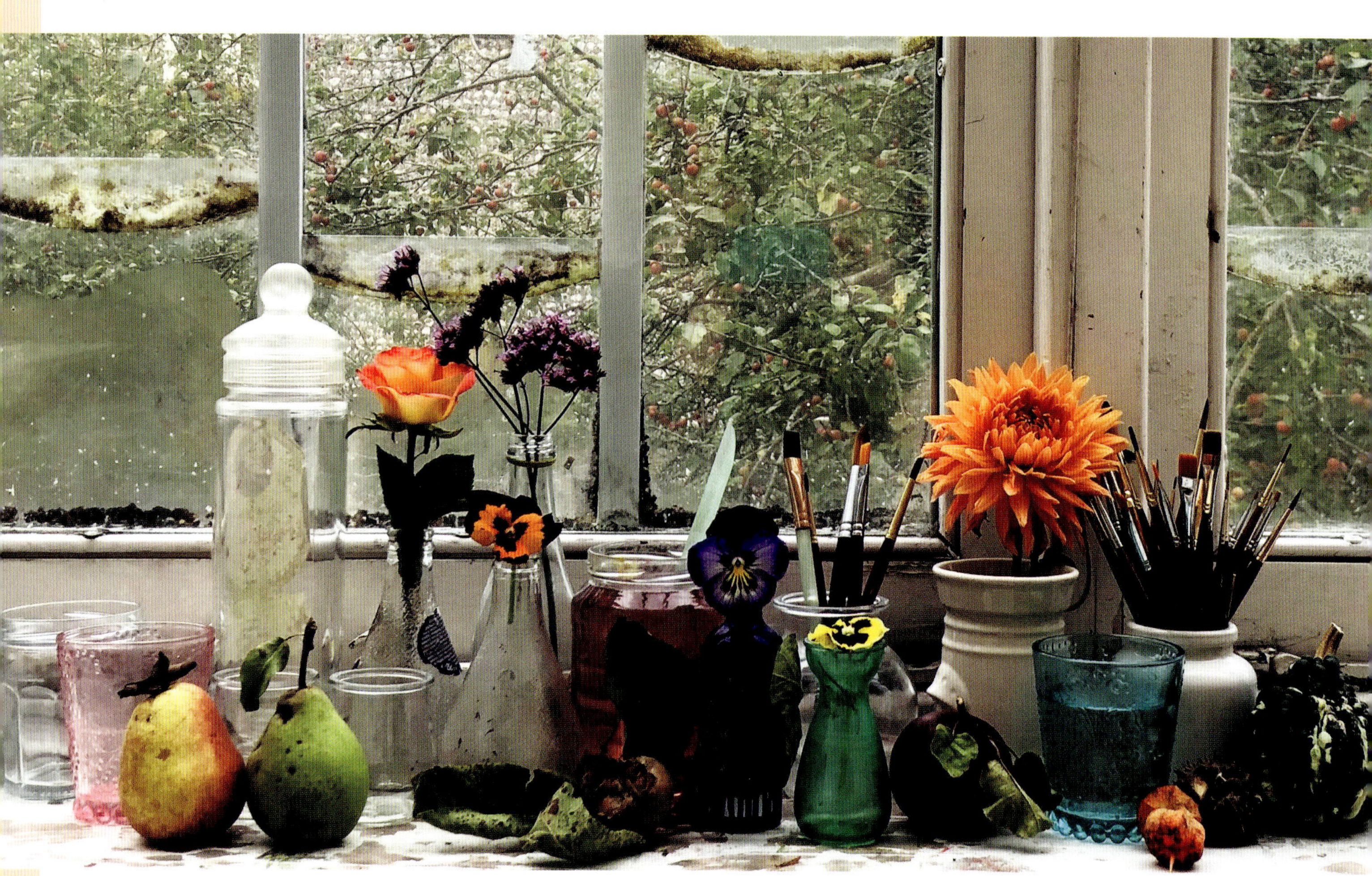

Paints   If the environment is your main concern, water-based paints are more environmentally friendly than oil-based media. Watercolour and gouache are less polluting than acrylics, which are adding to the plastic waste contaminating the oceans.

The main thing to watch out for is the pigment type. Some are non-toxic but some are bad for the environment. The most notorious is cadmium, which is radioactive. As a botanical artist, it does not make sense to me to take my inspiration from nature and then pour cadmium-contaminated water down the sink. We also have to think that although the paint manufacturers in Europe have strict contaminated-waste-disposal guidelines, the pigments themselves are made in countries where environmental laws and rules protecting workers and villages near toxic factories are almost inexistent. While cadmiums were once desirable colours, I think that their toxicity now outweighs their usefulness. These days, there are some excellent cadmium substitutes available – some brands such as Daniel Smith have removed cadmiums completely from their range and I am sure that eventually other paint manufacturers will follow their lead.

Regarding pigments, there is also an ethical issue when it comes to lightfastness. Using a fading paint such as Opera Rose and then selling a painting that will degrade rapidly is not the most ethical thing to do. Picking your pigments carefully will ensure that people who love your art enough to buy a painting will enjoy it for a longer time.

Paper   Some cartridge-paper pads are made from recycled paper, and bamboo watercolour paper appeared a few years ago, being marketed as more environmentally friendly than cotton paper because bamboo requires less water to grow. Many watercolour papers are sized with animal-derived gelatine: Arches and most Saunders Waterford papers are the most prestigious examples. Fabriano Artistico and most Fabriano papers use a plant-based size and Bockingford paper is also gelatine-free.

Brushes   When I first started to learn how to paint, I used sable brushes because that is what my tutors told me to do. The idea was that synthetic brushes were for amateurs and that real artists used animal bristles. Kolinsky sable brushes were the best in the world, because the sables living in Siberia were so cold that their tails were bushier as a result. I would have been horrified at the suggestion that I should wear a real fur coat but never gave a second thought to the idea of using sable hair. And yet... Sables are raised on fur farms where they live in unnatural and often cruel conditions and are killed exclusively for their fur. Years ago it was a hopeless mission to find a synthetic brush that would perform as well as sable. These days, though, some synthetics are so good that I could easily be tricked into thinking that they are natural hair.

I have recently been testing dozens of models from different brands. If you want to retain the feeling of animal hair without the ethical dilemma, I recommend the da Vinci Casaneo series 5598.

I personally prefer a slightly stiffer brush, as natural hair is a bit too 'floppy' for me. I like Pro Arte Prolene Plus Series 007, and Jackson's Studio Synthetics series 505 collections. The Princeton Neptune synthetic squirrel is a wonderful brush. At a fraction of the cost of real animal hair and without the cruelty, all these are definitely worth a try.

Plastic   Plastic is less insidious than other environmentally unfriendly substances (such as pigments); however, swapping plastic water pots for old jam or mustard jars, using a wooden or metal paintbox and carrying brushes in a wooden brush case can be easily done. My plastic eraser has been replaced with the Fabriano rubber eraser. There are still little things like watercolour pans that defy my determination to eliminate all plastic. However, as I use Daniel Smith watercolours, the pans are infinitely refillable.

And if you are vegan...?   If you are vegan, the art world is as much a minefield as the rest of your life, but by now you are probably used to it. Most watercolour paints contain either ox gall or honey; many papers are sized with animal gelatine; some pigments, like Bone Black, are made from charred bones and even cruelty-free brushes can have shellac-varnished handles. Obviously Egg Tempera is not an option...

On the following pages you can find the materials and equipment I use for drawing and painting, all of which are vegan-friendly.

I am not suggesting that you throw away all your paints and art supplies and replace them all at once. But when you finish your next watercolour tube or your current paper pad, perhaps you can think about how you choose to replace it.

I hope that this information will help you select the best-quality art materials while following your choice of ethical lifestyle.

WORKING SPACE

The first thing to do when embarking on your artistic endeavours is to set up
a working space that is practical, inspiring and that reflects your personality.

My painting desk is installed in a bay window that faces west. By setting up a potter's stand in
front of the right window, I allow the main light source to come from the left, flowing through
the left and main front windows.

I have set up a bird feeder in the *Magnolia grandiflora* that grows outside the window, so
I always have many feathered companions to keep me entertained while I work. It can be
maddeningly distracting but never fails to lift my spirits. The sparrows are especially bossy,
landing on the window frame and staring at me until I give in and fill the feeder. It never takes
more than a couple of minutes – and I suspect mind control.

I don't work well in artificial light, so this setup also ensures I have plenty of natural light to
work with. It also means that my painting days are longer in the Summer than in the Winter.

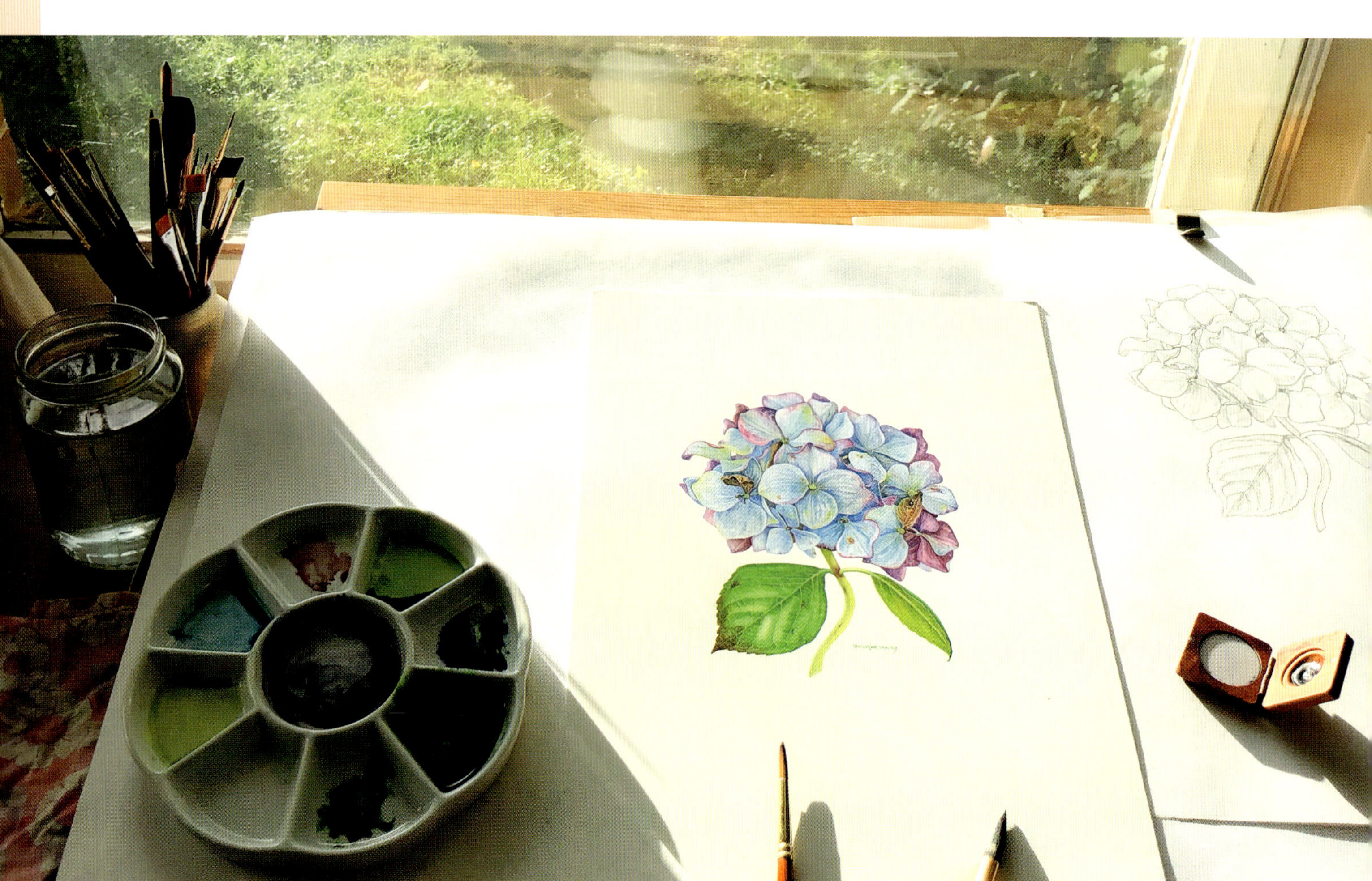

PAINTING FROM LIFE

Whenever possible, try to work from real flowers and fruit rather than from photographs. Photographs are cold and flat, which can make it difficult to inject life into a painting. A live subject will instil your work with its vitality.

I find that working from live subjects is a lot more inspiring than working from photographs. Apart from the fact that photographs never show the true colours of flowers, I need to be able to touch the subjects, feel their textures, see their colours with my own eyes and smell their perfume. You can learn a lot about the top of a leaf if you are able to turn it over and see what is happening on the underside. You can find out which colour to use as the base for a petal by checking what colour it is on the reverse side.

In addition, I don't wish my paintings to look like photographs: I want them to look like paintings. I find this easier to achieve when the subject is right there in front of me. Get to know your subjects, talk to them, and they will in turn talk to you, giving you inspiration and infusing your work with life.

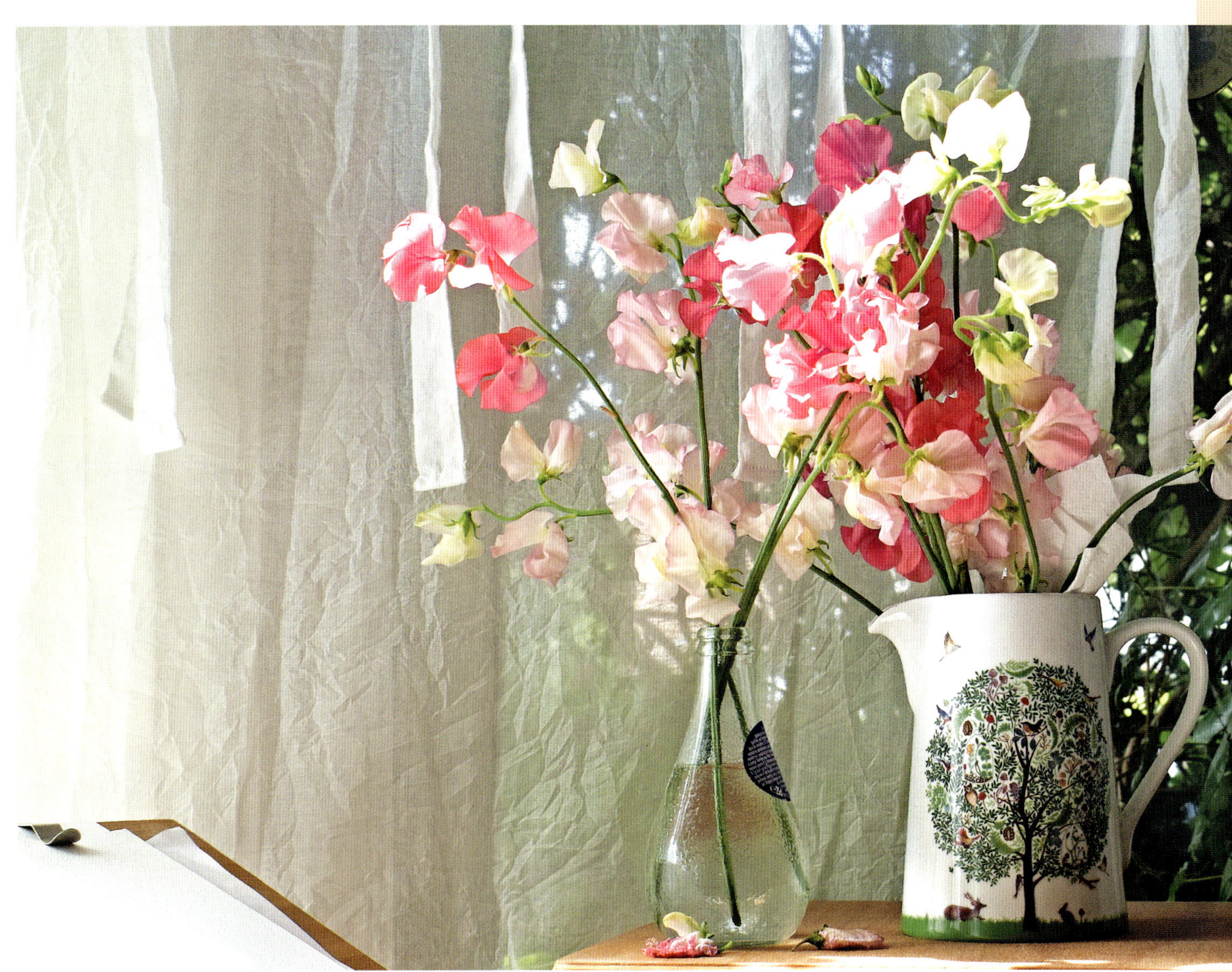

DRAWING KIT

Papers

Cartridge paper   I use Fabriano cartridge paper, in different weights and sizes. I like their White Ecological Artist Paper, which is sustainably produced using hydro-power and is 100 per cent recycled.

Tracing paper and Tracedown transfer paper   I use tracing paper to trace my sketches and transfer them to the watercolour paper. The lighter the weight, the better. To transfer, I use a red coloured pencil with Tracedown transfer paper, which is similar to carbon paper but grease- and wax-free. This method allows me to be as loose and messy as I need to be, as the finished transferred drawing will always be immaculate regardless of what happened in the sketchbook.

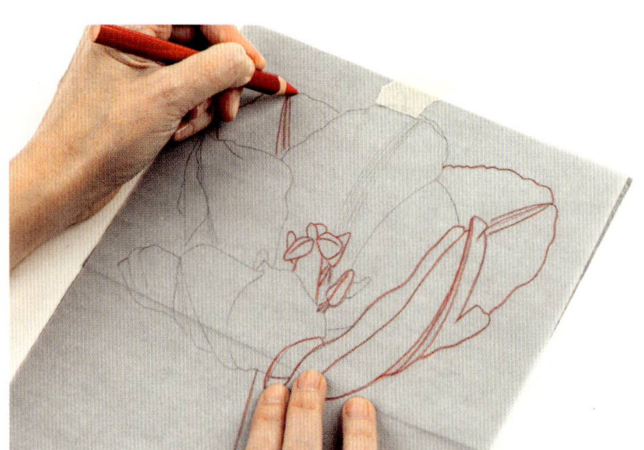

Sketchbooks

I love sketchbooks. Rather than having piles of unrelated sketches in various drawers, I like the way a sketchbook tells a story. When I draw in a sketchbook, I tend to write notes not directly related to my subject, like what the birds are doing outside the window, or which music I am listening to while drawing. Reading these years later brings back memories that would otherwise be forgotten.

My favourites sketchbooks are the Atoma system and the Frisk layflat sketchpad (shown right). The Atoma is a clever system that allows any kind of paper to be perforated and added to a ring-binding system, whatever the weight. This means I can add watercolour paper as well as cartridge paper to the binding. The pages can be removed, repositioned and added multiple times. The covers are bought separately and come in card as well as washable 'vegan leather' paper.

The Frisk pad is very handy when taking my drawing kit on trips. The A4 format (297 x 210mm/8¼ x 11½in) lays flat to become A3 (297 x 420mm/11¾ x 16½in). The paper is white and smooth and the 290gsm (135lb) weight takes a light wash.

Pencils

I prefer mechanical pencils to traditional ones because I don't like to break the flow of drawing with the need to sharpen. I use mechanical and clutch pencils made of wood with a metallic mechanism to avoid using plastic.

I have a 2mm 2B that I use for the initial loose drawing and a 0.5mm B that I use to refine the drawing once I have the main lines.

I sometimes also use a Derwent Dark Wash sketching pencil for quick tone studies (shown opposite, next to the red pencil).

Erasers

My main eraser is a Fabriano rubber eraser and I also use a putty eraser to lift off excess graphite if the transfer paper gets too heavy.

Geometry equipment

I like to have a ruler and even sometimes a pair of compasses to work out my composition. They help to keep things balanced and within the right shapes without the need for measuring everything, which again helps with keeping the drawing loose.

For the 'Holly Star' tutorial (see pages 164–169), I also used a protractor to calculate the positions of the five branches of the star.

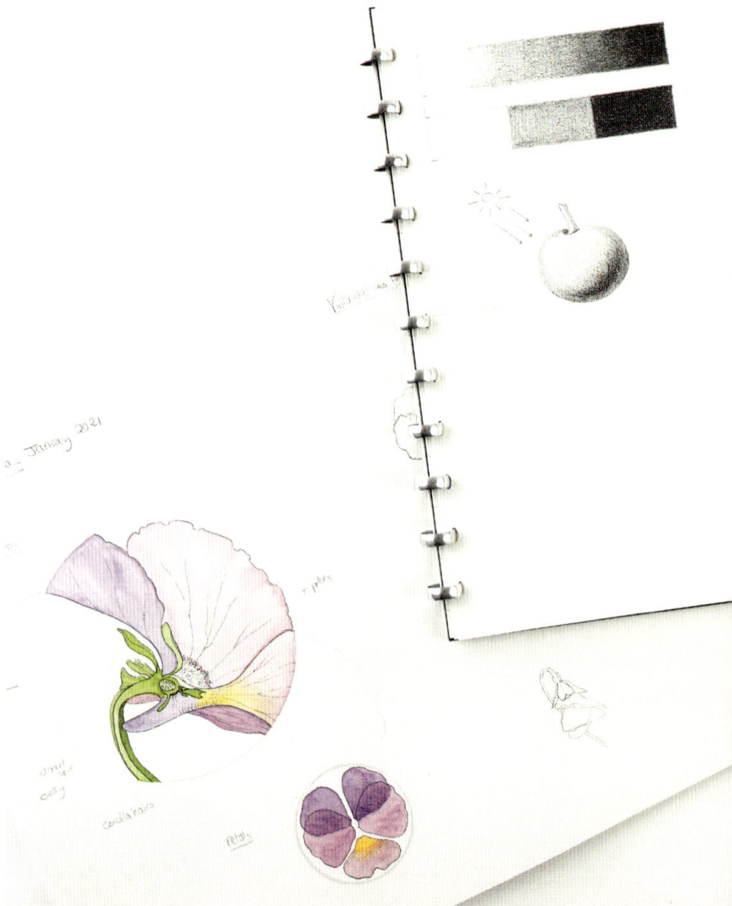

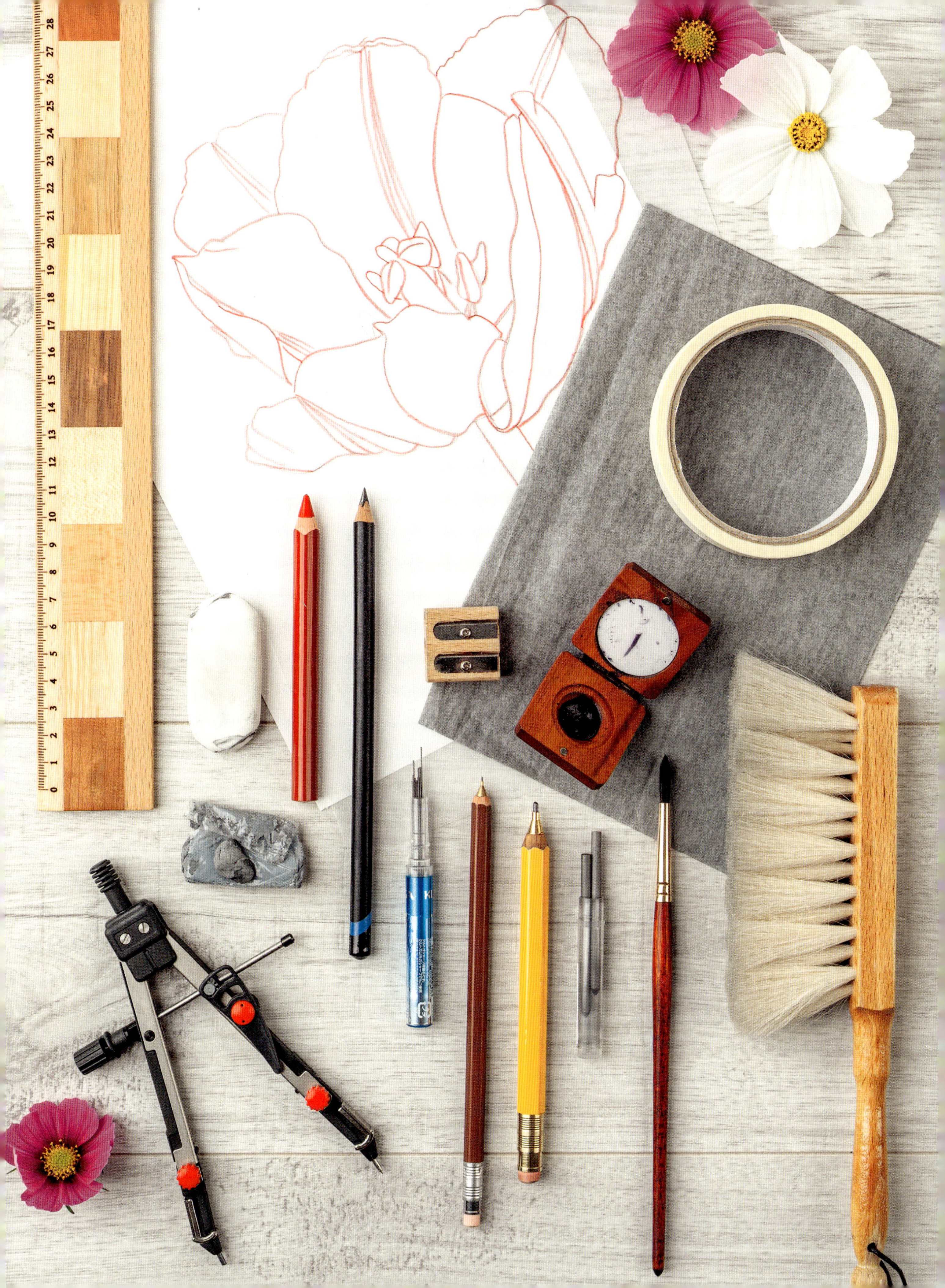

PAINTING KIT

Having the right materials and working with the best pigments is crucial. Watercolour is not a particularly easy medium and working with poor-quality pigments, brushes and paper will not make it any easier. The same is true of your equipment: working with a ceramic palette and having a double pot of water is a good start.

Palette

Ceramic palettes are much more pleasant to work with than plastic ones. The paints glide beautifully on them and don't crackle as they do on plastic. Ceramic or porcelain palettes also show truer colours. Plastic palettes become stained but ceramic ones can go in the dishwasher and come out as clean as new.

Painting cloths

It is best to use a cotton cloth to wipe brushes. Kitchen paper or tissues are coated in chemicals to make them more absorbent and more resistant to tearing. These chemicals get picked up by the brush and interfere with the washes. Suitable cotton cloths include old handkerchiefs, face cloths, old cotton bedsheets or tea towels. They can be washed in the washing machine using laundry balls (eco balls), but avoid using fabric softeners, which may leave an undesirable residue on the cloths.

Water pots

In order to keep the water clean and the washes bright, I use two water pots: one for the initial rinsing of the brush, in which the water gets dirty quite quickly, and the other for a final dip to make the brush completely clean. I use old glass food jars, such as cornichon (pickle) jars, which are easy to wash.

Brushes

I use only synthetic brushes (see page 11). Apart from the cruelty-free aspect, the fact that they have better spring and tend to carry less water are two factors that suit my very wet approach to washes. My favourites are Pro Arte Prolene Plus Series 007 for general purposes and Princeton Neptune for softer glazes. I also use a small Major Brushes flat ⅛in (3mm) brush to lift veins and details.

Paper

After years of trying different papers in different weights, I now exclusively use Fabriano Artistico Hot-pressed (HP) Extra White, 640gsm (300lb). It is the most beautiful paper and is perfectly suited to my style and technique.

Paints

I have a lot of paints – definitely more than is strictly necessary. The reason is that when I wrote my first book, *Colours of Nature*, about paints, colours and pigments, I discovered a whole new wonderful world. I went from minimalist palette artist to playful and curious watercolourist. My long-standing minimalist palette suddenly seemed a tad boring.

My paintbox contains a few unmovable classics such as French Ultramarine but it is also in constant mutation. Some colours come and go, some stay a while, some shoot directly to the favourite colours section and demand a permanent place (Perylene Violet), and some disappear forever after new research reveals that they were not as good as we once thought (Aureolin Yellow)…

I have both pans in a box (shown right) and a tin of tubes. The paintbox is a French antique wooden box given to me by my parents as a present years ago and it is one of my most valued possessions. It contains colours that have proven themselves and have earned a long-term place in my palette. The tin is for tubes of paints that are still in the testing stage and for colours I use a lot on larger pieces of work when working from a tiny half-pan would be inconvenient.

When I travel, I have a smaller metal tin with pans of my 12 essential colours – these are shown on page 23.

Painting materials for all projects

PAPERS

Cartridge paper or sketchbook
Tracing paper
Transfer paper

WATERCOLOUR PAPER

Fabriano Artistico HP Extra White, 640gsm (300lb)

WATERCOLOUR BRUSHES

Pro Arte Prolene Plus Series 007 in sizes 3/0, 0, 2, 4 and 6; Princeton Neptune synthetic squirrel round brush series in sizes 0, 2, 4, 6 and 10; Major Brushes ⅛in (3mm) flat brush
Glass jars and cotton painting cloth
Ceramic palette

PAINTS

Range of artists' watercolour paints (see individual project for colours).

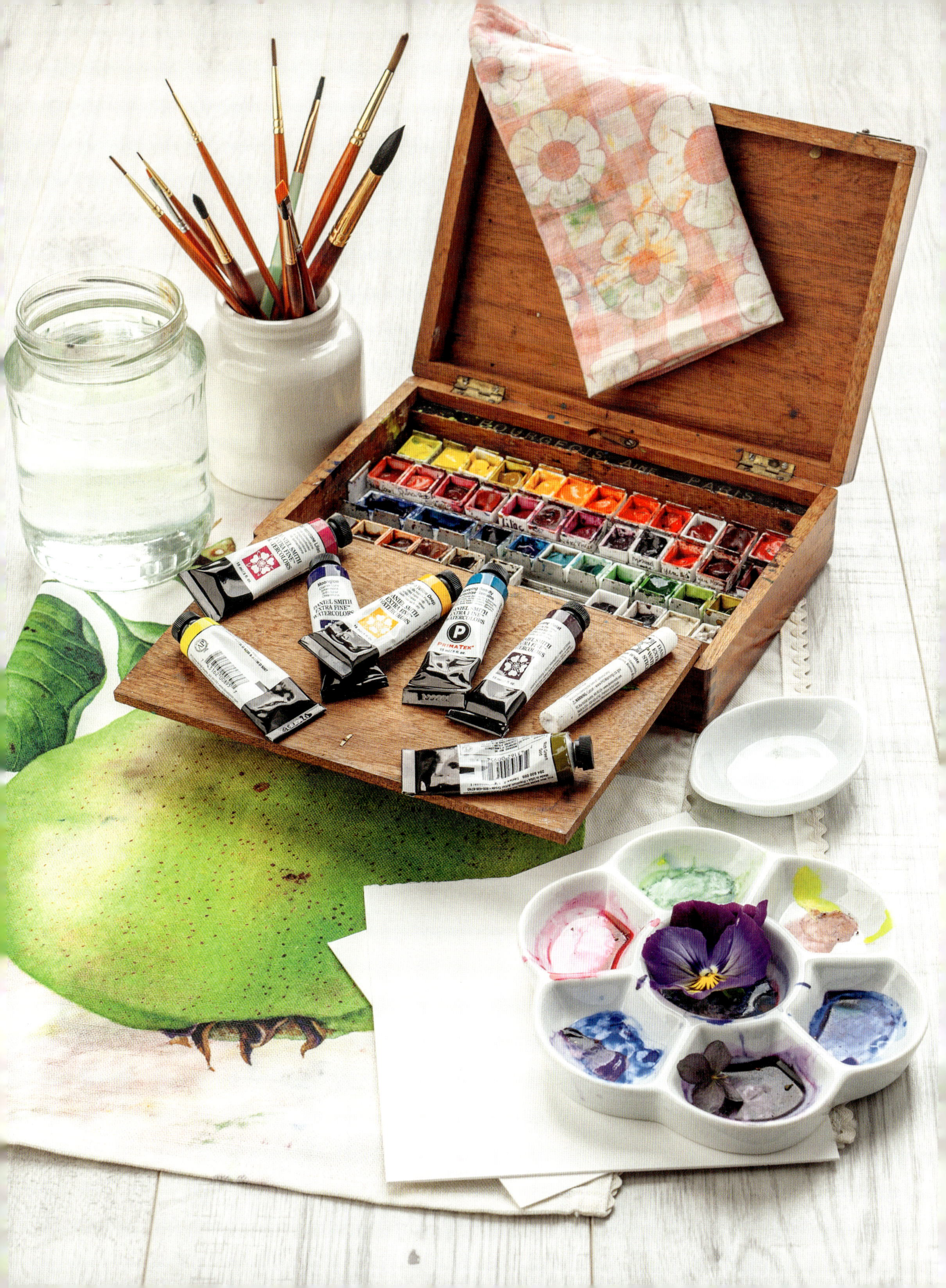

PAINTS AND PIGMENTS

The main ingredient of watercolour paints is the pigment, which gives them
their colour. They also contain gum Arabic, glycerine, sometimes honey or
ox gall and sometimes a filler. Fillers are cheap ingredients that are used to fill
the tube, making the paints more affordable. One side effect of less expensive
ingredients is a dilution of the pigment and sometimes even an opacifying
of the paint.

What to look for in a paint

Transparency   Watercolour is a delicate medium that looks
its best when painted in transparent washes. Opaque colours tend
to get muddy and to overwhelm more fragile colours. They also
inhibit the layering process: a layer of opaque paint will cover any
previous layers and will stop subsequent layers reaching the bright
white paper under the paint. The effect is a matte finish rather than
a glowing one. In the illustration below, you can see how transparent
or opaque paint layers interact with light.

Layering of transparent and opaque paints
T: transparent; O: opaque.

Lightfastness   If you create a work of art you want it to
last, especially if you sell your work. All the colours in your palette
should be lightfast and resist fading, with no exception (that means
you, Opera Rose). Lightfastness ratings are usually indicated on
watercolour tubes.

Single pigment   Some paints are mixes of pigments, and
some are made with a single pigment. Using a single pigment is
preferable, as it reduces the chances of getting muddy washes when
doing your own mixes. It also gives more saturated colours. Pigment
names are written on paint tubes: if the tube lists several pigments
numbers or names, the paint is best avoided in favour of another
containing a single pigment.

Artists' quality   Students' quality paints are cheaper
but they contain fillers in order to save money on ingredients.
These fillers dilute the paints, which are less saturated as a result.
It is impossible to paint bright, glowing subjects with students'
colours. Beware also of cheaper brands that call themselves 'artists'
watercolours'. There is no international standard for this kind of
appellation but usually the low price is a reliable clue as to its quality.

Granulation   Some pigments are coarser than others and
instead of giving a smooth texture, they granulate. Examples include
French Ultramarine, Cerulean Blue and Burnt Umber. Sometimes
this is troublesome because the desired effect is smoothness and
shine, for example when painting a tulip or a physalis. However,
sometimes granulation is an advantage because it adds texture and
helps create a velvety finish, for example, when painting a pansy or
a medlar. It is important to be aware of granulating pigments and
to use them when they can help as well as avoid them when they
might hinder the required finish.

Staining   Some pigments can be easily lifted after drying
(Phthalo Blue) while others are staining; once they are on the paper,
they stubbornly stay there (Permanent Rose).

Toxicity   A toxic pigment is not only harmful to the artist's
health, it is also damaging to the environment. Toxic paints usually
have a health-hazard label on the tubes. The main offenders are the
cadmiums, which are radioactive and have a devastating impact
on watercourses, especially around the factories where they are
produced. Some manufacturers have started phasing them out and
Daniel Smith stopped using them a few years ago. Also avoid cobalt,
which is a heavy metal.

Pigment families

Some pigments come as a one-off, being the result of a chemical reaction or having a unique component. Other pigments come in families, with a range of colours created from the same source. Here are some of the most common, desirable or notorious pigment families:

Quinacridones   These are relatively new to the painting world, having first been introduced in artists' paints by Daniel Smith in the 1970s. They are lightfast, very saturated, transparent, non-toxic and smooth. Their range goes from pink to magenta to golden and reddish browns.

Phthalocyanines (or Phthalos)   These were created accidentally when a worker found blue residue at the bottom of a pot during a mining process. The blue residue was sent to a laboratory for analysis and found to be very saturated in colour and highly staining. As a result, it was developed into a pigment. Phthalos are lightfast, transparent, non-toxic and smooth. Their range is limited to blues and greens.

Cadmiums   Cadmiums were originally used to replace the deadly arsenic colours. They are lightfast, saturated, opaque, toxic and environmentally unfriendly, dense and smooth. Their range covers yellows, oranges and reds.

Perylenes   These are a recent addition to the artist's palette. They are lightfast, not very saturated, transparent, non-toxic and smooth. They have a limited range of maroons, from a muted red to a deep violet.

Pyrrol(e)s   This family comprises a couple of reds that are very useful to replace the fugitive scarlets and vermilions as well as substitutes for the toxic cadmium reds. They are lightfast, saturated, semi-transparent, non-toxic and smooth. They have a very limited range of orange-bias and mid-reds.

Earth colours   The most ancient pigments known to mankind, with their use dating back to cave paintings. This pigment family includes the pigments extracted from soil and mining, mostly issued from iron ore, such as Raw Umber, Burnt Umber, Raw Sienna, Burnt Sienna, Yellow Ochre, Red Ochre and Red Earth. They are lightfast, with varied degrees of saturation and transparency, non-toxic and granulating. They cover a range of neutral colours, from yellow-brown to orange-brown and greenish to reddish brown.

Members of the Quinacridone family

- Quinacridone Gold
- Quinacridone Fuchsia
- Quinacridone Coral
- Quinacridone Red
- Quinacridone Pink
- Quinacridone Rose
- Quinacridone Lilac
- Quinacridone Violet

Members of the Phthalocyanine family

- Phthalo Blue Red Shade
- Phthalo Blue Green Shade
- Phthalo Green Blue Shade
- Phthalo Green Yellow Shade

Members of the Perylene family

- Perylene Red
- Perylene Maroon
- Perylene Violet

COLOUR-MIXING THEORY

The first principles of colour theory were introduced by Italian humanist and artist
Leon Battista Alberti circa 1435, in his treatise, *Della Pittura*
('On Painting'). Leonardo da Vinci developed the work further, followed by
other artists, until Sir Isaac Newton created the first colour wheel in 1706. The
wheel continued to evolve, sometimes involving unexpected contributors such as
German philosopher Johann Wolfgang von Goethe in 1809, who added another
dimension by attributing different feelings to colours. In 1861, a French chemist,
Michel Eugène Chevreul, published what I see as the ultimate colour wheel, which
comprises 72 colours beautifully graduated around the disc.
Let's explore how these colourful wheels relate to colour mixing today and what
principles we can extract from them in order to help us with our petals and blooms.

The bias colour wheel

The most popular colour-mixing theory is based on a wheel that
comprises three primary colours (yellow, red and blue) alternating
with three secondary colours (orange, violet and green). This system
however, has its limitations. Mix the wrong blue with the wrong red
and the violet looks more maroon than purple. This is where the bias
system comes in.

The core principle is that there is no such thing as a pure primary
colour. Let's take yellow as an example. On one side of yellow is
green, on the other side is orange. There is no pure, mid-yellow
that will mix an equally vivid green and a saturated orange. It
will do one or the other. If the yellow leans towards green (with
a green bias, like Lemon Yellow), it will make a vivid green but a
muted orange. If the yellow leans towards orange (with an orange
bias, like New Gamboge), it will make a bright orange but a more
muted green.

The same principle applies to red, with its orange bias on one side
and violet bias on the other side.

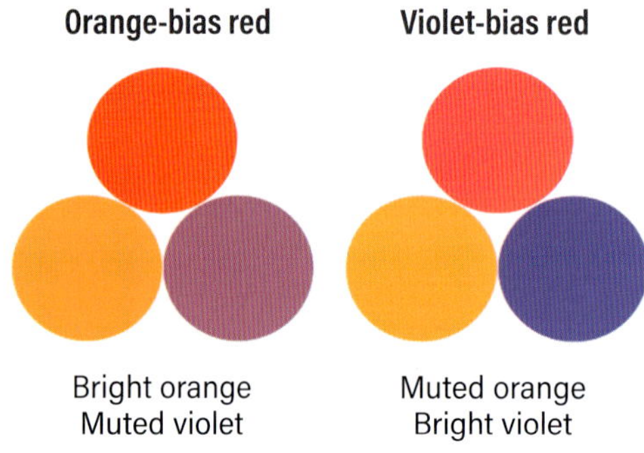

Bright orange
Muted violet

Muted orange
Bright violet

Finally, it applies in the same way to the third primary colour blue,
with violet on one side and back to green on the other side.

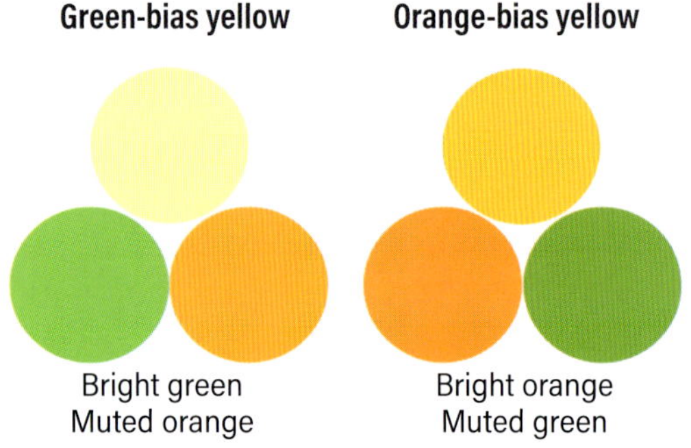

Bright green
Muted orange

Bright orange
Muted green

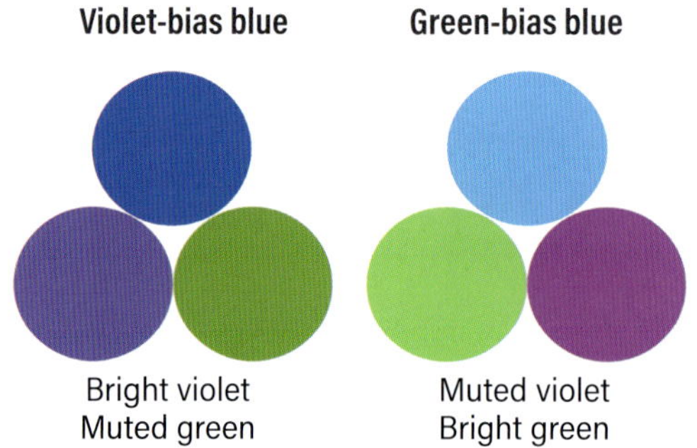

Bright violet
Muted green

Muted violet
Bright green

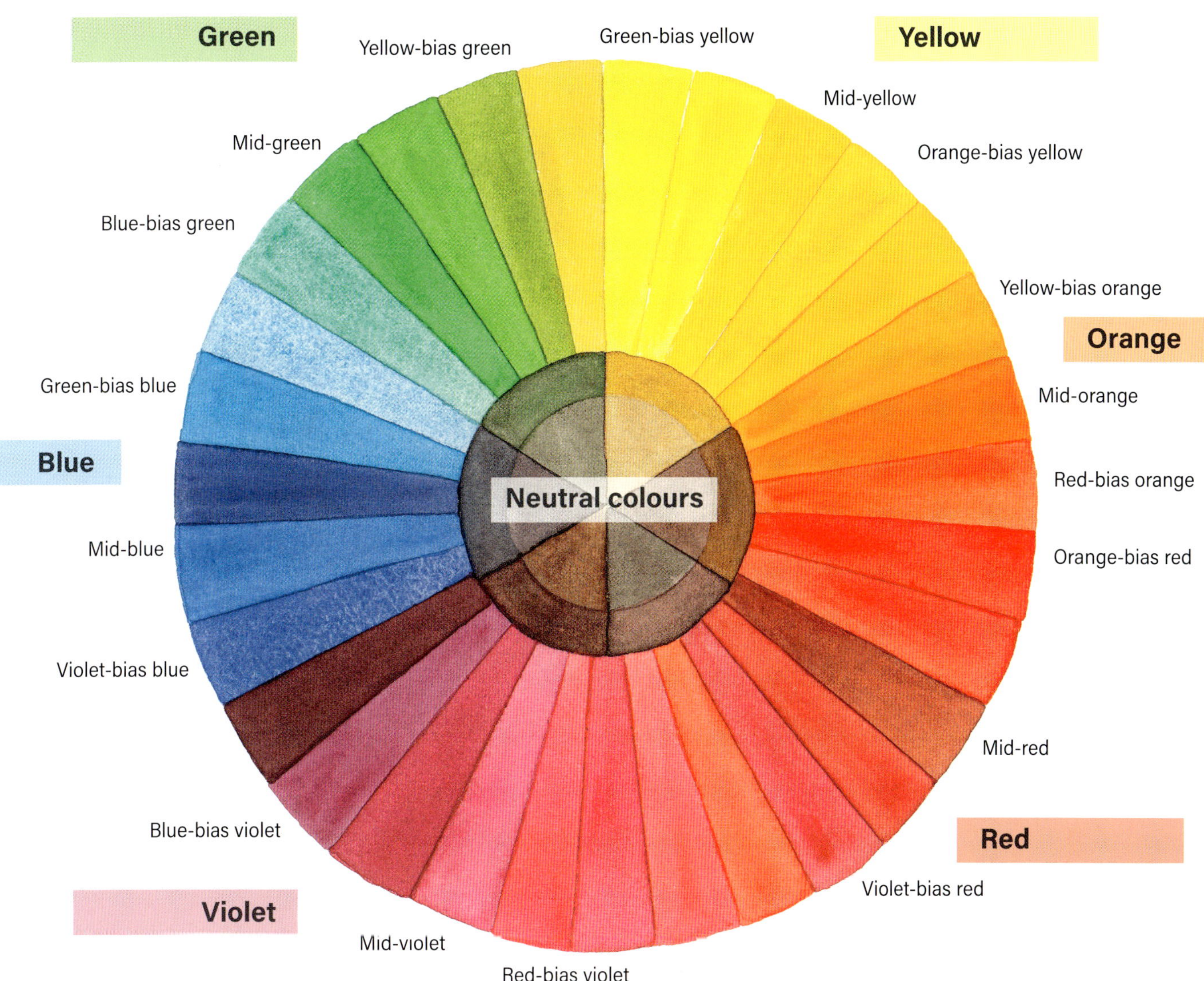

This is the bias colour wheel, inspired by Chevreul's Chromatic Circle, with many variations of the primary and secondary colours, which are situated on the outer ring. The inner ring shows the neutral colours (browns and greys): these are made by mixing complementary colours that sit directly opposite on the wheel.

How many paints do I need?

In order to be able to mix saturated secondary colours, the minimum requirement would be two of each primary (one for each-bias) plus a proper pink, which is necessary for flower painters. However, as long as they fit all the criteria outlined in 'Paints and pigments' (see pages 18–19), there is no limit to the number of paints you can have. I love to play with pigments and mixes, so I have between 40 and 50 different colours.

MY PALETTE

A paintbox is a living entity. As some pigments become obsolete and others are discovered or invented, an artist's palette should evolve accordingly. Arsenic colours were once all the rage, but when the extent of their toxicity became known, their popularity decreased until they were eventually banned. I believe that cadmiums will be the next ones to go. At the other end of the scale, new pigments emerge all the time. Some stay in relative obscurity – such as the wonderful Quinophthalone Yellow – while others quickly rise to celebrity status, like the bright and saturated quinacridones.

Yellow and orange

Hansa Yellow Light
Green-bias yellow

Quinophthalone Yellow
Bright mid-yellow

Mayan Yellow
Less saturated mid-yellow

Nickel Azo Yellow
Golden yellow

Hansa Yellow Deep
Orange-bias yellow

Permanent Orange
Yellow-bias orange

Pyrrol Orange
Red-bias orange

Red

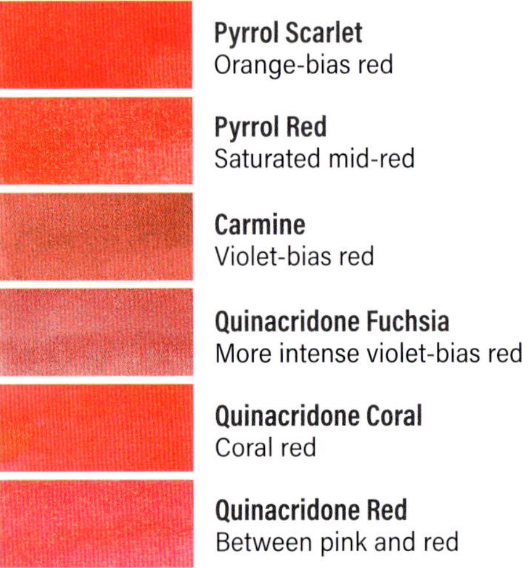

Pyrrol Scarlet
Orange-bias red

Pyrrol Red
Saturated mid-red

Carmine
Violet-bias red

Quinacridone Fuchsia
More intense violet-bias red

Quinacridone Coral
Coral red

Quinacridone Red
Between pink and red

Pink

Quinacridone Pink
True pink

Quinacridone Rose
More intense pink

Magenta

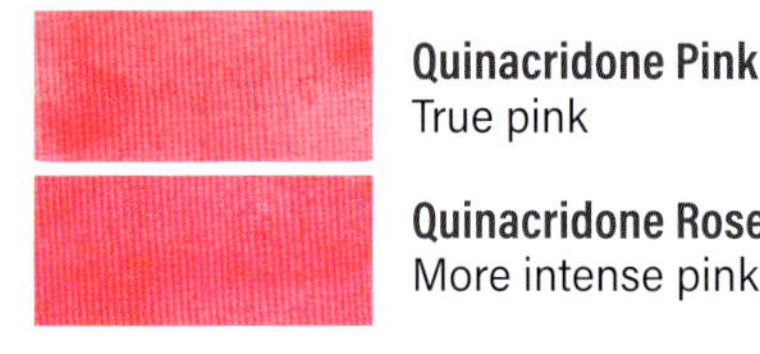

Quinacridone Lilac
Pink magenta

Quinacridone Violet
Violet-bias magenta

Perylene

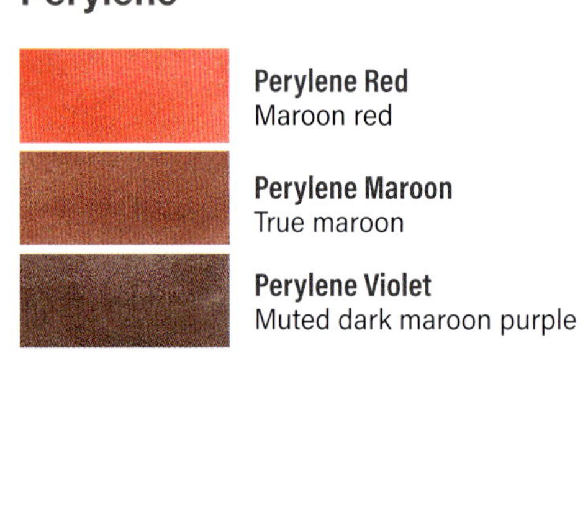

Perylene Red
Maroon red

Perylene Maroon
True maroon

Perylene Violet
Muted dark maroon purple

My 12 essential colours

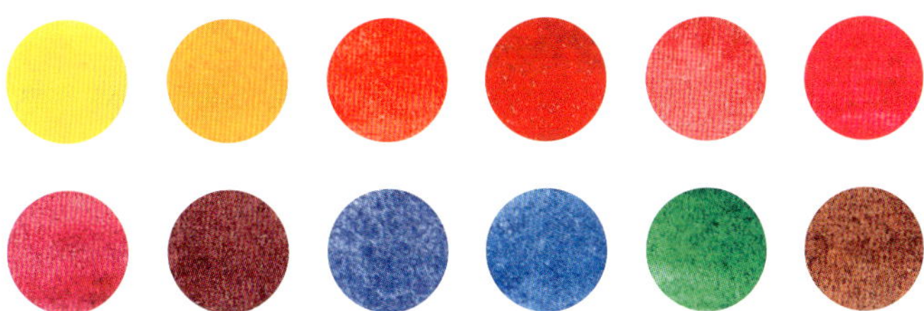

This is a snapshot of what my paintbox looks like in 2022. Since my first book came out, I have gradually moved to using Daniel Smith paints. I love their saturated colours, pure pigments and range of colours. I also like their environmental policies and the fact that they are striving to be an ethical company. I enjoy having all these colours to play with, but I use only up to half a dozen for each painting.

If I had to choose 12 essential colours, this would be my selection: Hansa Yellow Light, Hansa Yellow Deep, Pyrrol Scarlet, Pyrrol Red, Carmine, Quinacridone Pink, Quinacridone Lilac, Perylene Violet, French Ultramarine, Phthalo Blue Red Shade, Phthalo Green Yellow Shade and Burnt Umber. As not all my readers use the same brand, I am including a description of each colour. You can find equivalents in other brands and alternative mixes, whenever there are any, in the Paint-Conversion Table on pages 172–173.

Blue

French Ultramarine
Granulating violet-bias blue

Phthalo Blue Red Shade
Bright mid-blue

Indanthrone (Indanthrene) Blue
Very dark blue

Phthalo Blue Green Shade
Green-bias blue

Cerulean Blue
Granulating opaque light blue

Sleeping Beauty Turquoise Genuine
Green-bias blue

Green

Viridian
Blue-bias green

Phthalo Green Yellow Shade
Mid-green

Sap Green
Muted Sap Green

Rich Green Gold
Muted bronze green

Neutral colours

Quinacridone Gold
Discontinued transparent gold

Quinacridone Burnt Orange
Golden brown

Quinacridone Burnt Scarlet
Bright reddish brown

Burnt Sienna
Muted reddish brown

Burnt Umber
Mid-brown

Raw Umber
Green-bias brown

Moonglow
Convenience mix of purple-grey, which I use for quick sketchbook tone studies

Buff Titanium
Muted creamy white for painting details, when white is too bright

Pearlescent Shimmer
For glazing on insect wings or some seedpods

Titanium White (pigment stick)
Opaque white for details

TONE

A well-placed and wide tonal range is an essential ingredient that will give your painting depth and the realistic three-dimensional quality we are looking for in botanical art. The placement of tonal variations is dictated by the light source. The range of tonal values, from the brightest highlight to the darkest shadows, depends on the light level, the colour of the subject and its texture. To paint the right tones in the right place, we have to rely first on observation, but we can also add a pinch of logic and a sprinkle of artistic licence.

Light direction

This is the main influence on the placement of tone. Parts directly exposed to the light will show the brightest highlights while the parts furthest from the light will be in the shadows. The light direction needs to be consistent on all parts of a subject and on all subjects included in the same painting. A light source from the side is the optimal position, as it creates the most varied areas of light and shade. Moving this lateral light up helps to create a natural look, as if the subject were outdoors and lit by the sun.

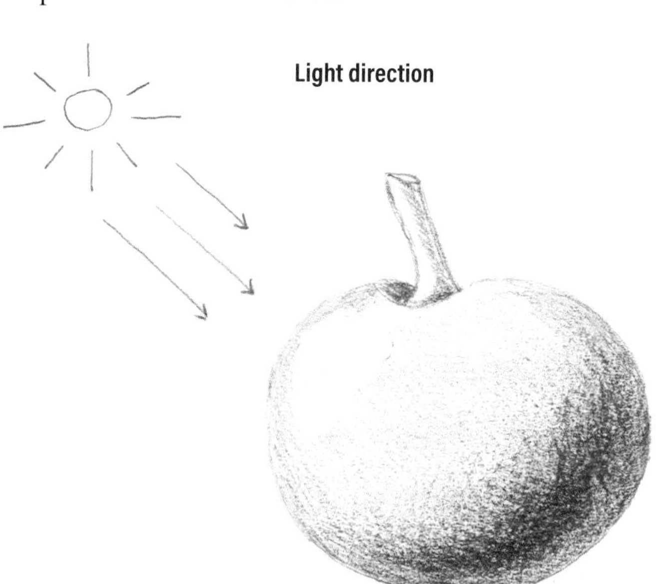

Range of tones

Between the brightest light and the darkest shadows, there is an infinity of tonal values. Shown in continuous tone (top line, below), the values merge into each other seamlessly. This is the best and most accurate way to depict tone in a pencil drawing.

However, when the pencilwork is only a quick study created as a source of information for a painting, separating the tonal values into three zones of highlights, mid-tones and shadows is sufficient and quicker (bottom line, below). When painted wet-in-wet on the watercolour piece, these three zones will merge and create seamless tonal changes on their own.

Range of tones
Top, continuous tone;
Bottom: separated tonal values.

Highlights   Mid-tones   Shadows

Reflected light and cast shadows

The light direction and the texture and colour of the subject are the direct factors affecting the range of tones: a dark subject has darker shadows than a light one, while a velvety texture shows subdued highlights compared to a glossy surface.

There are also some secondary factors coming into play and using them can help create a painting that has more depth and more interest. Two of these secondary factors I often use are reflected light and cast shadows.

No subject exists in isolation. A flower will be surrounded by other flowers, or a piece of fruit hanging in the tree will nest amongst foliage. All these other components, whether painted into the picture or not, can be used to our advantage. Light hitting them will reflect off their surface and add some **reflected light** to the shadow side of the main subject, helping to create form. Please note that the reflected light is never as bright as the main highlight, as only part of the light is reflected.

Cast shadows happen when a part of a subject is casting a shadow on another part that would otherwise be in the light or the mid-tones, such as a leaf over an apple. Again, this helps to create depth by showing that parts of the subjects are in front of each other.

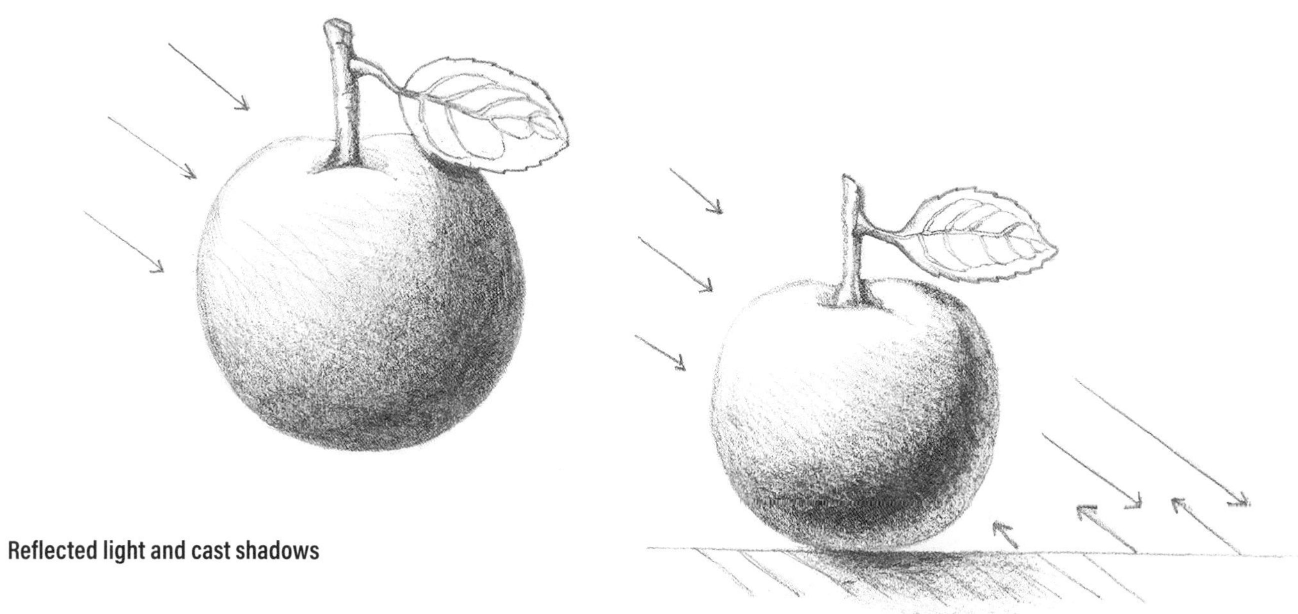

Reflected light and cast shadows

Conclusion

A wide tonal range and carefully placed shadows and highlights are crucial to achieve a good painting. Some people can see tone well while others struggle to make sense of it. This is determined by biology and the way each individual *sees*. But don't despair: even if you have trouble seeing tone, you can practise your observational skills and learn how to work with experience and logic. There is a silver lining: if tone gives you trouble, it means that you are likely to be astute at seeing colours.

Harmonic Shadows

Giving form and depth to a painting is always a challenge. There are many
ways to render tone, but not all of them work for the delicacy and vibrant
colours of botanical art. After experimenting with different methods
to impart form and depth in my botanical paintings while preserving
luminosity, I came up with the concept of Harmonic Shadows.

Leonardo da Vinci's *grisaille*

In order to give depth to his paintings, Leonardo da Vinci used to paint his shadows first,
using a technique called *grisaille*, which consists of painting a monochrome underlayer. He
would then paint the colours on top of that *grisaille* layer, with transparent pigments, letting
the tonal painting show through the colours. However, da Vinci was painting with oils, not
watercolours. After ruling out black and white paints, I also dismissed all ready-made greys,
as they all contain a black pigment. Even Neutral Tint is a mixture of violet and black.

The myth of botanical grey

The quest for a botanical grey is never-ending. Different artists have different recipes,
choosing their pigments carefully to produce a neutral and universal grey that will suit all
subjects. I have tried several versions, but I have always been disappointed: I cannot find
one single recipe to fit all. How can the heavy dark grey doing justice to a black viola respect
the delicacy of a pale daffodil, or the smooth shadow of a silky poppy give enough texture to
a rough quince? Through these experiments, I became convinced that botanical grey is
a myth and that each subject needs a bespoke shadow mix.

The concept of Harmonic Shadows

How to mix a grey without involving black, white, or ready-made greys? One solution is
to mix the three primary colours. Any blue mixed with any red and any yellow will
always make a grey. How to mix a grey that is not clashing with the subject's
colours and respects its tonal range and texture? The answer is to use three
primaries that are already in this subject and that will work in harmony
with it. This is how I came up with the concept of Harmonic Shadows.

Colour is not the only criteria to take into account when selecting
the three primary colours. Some pigments granulate and create
heavy texture while some others are very fine and blend smoothly
with other pigments (see page 18). Selecting the right primaries is
essential to create a successful Harmonic Shadow.

Tips

- Select the three primary colours
carefully, as the whole picture will be
affected by the shadow mix.
- Don't forget to consider texture as
well as colour.
- If one of the colours is not obvious in the
bloom, try to use the foliage to find it.
- If the grey looks too brown, it needs
more blue in the mix.

Selecting the colours

Selecting the three primaries is a process of observation. The subject needs to be scrutinized for colour, texture, intensity, delicacy, depth of tone and transparency. For example, French Ultramarine will give a granulating effect suitable for heavily textured subjects while Phthalo Blue Red Shade, also a red-bias blue, will give a smooth finish.

Here are some examples of shadow mixes to suit a range of botanical subjects:

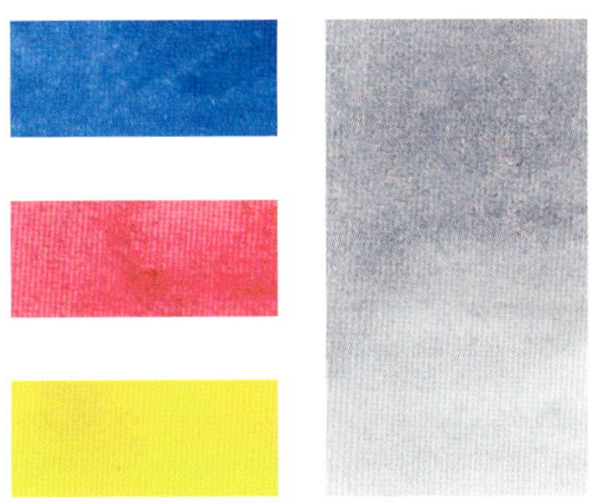

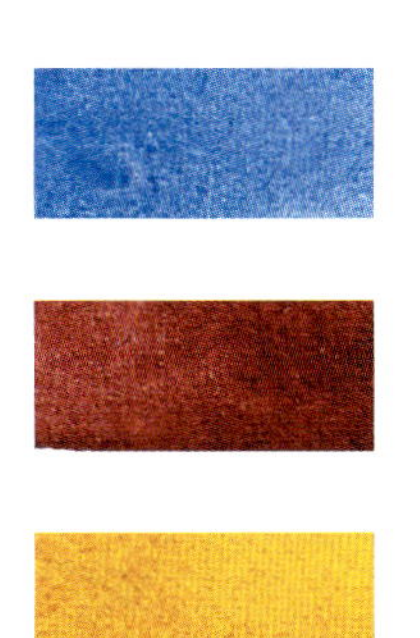

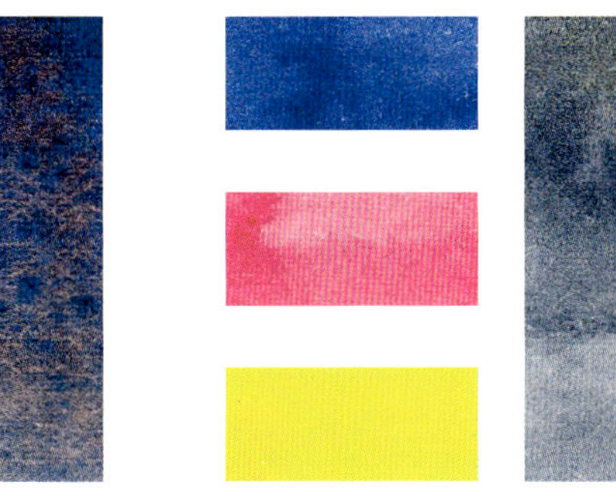

Mix 1
Phthalo Blue Red Shade
+ Quinacridone Pink
+ Hansa Yellow Light
For smooth, delicate, pale subjects such as daffodils, pale roses and pears.

Mix 2
French Ultramarine
+ Perylene Violet
+ Nickel Azo Yellow
For textured, heavier, darker subjects such as a velvety pansy, a dark sweet pea or a chunky quince.

Mix 3
Indanthrone Blue
+ Quinacridone Lilac
+ Hansa Yellow Deep
For smooth, dark subjects, such as holly leaves, a black tulip or an aubergine.

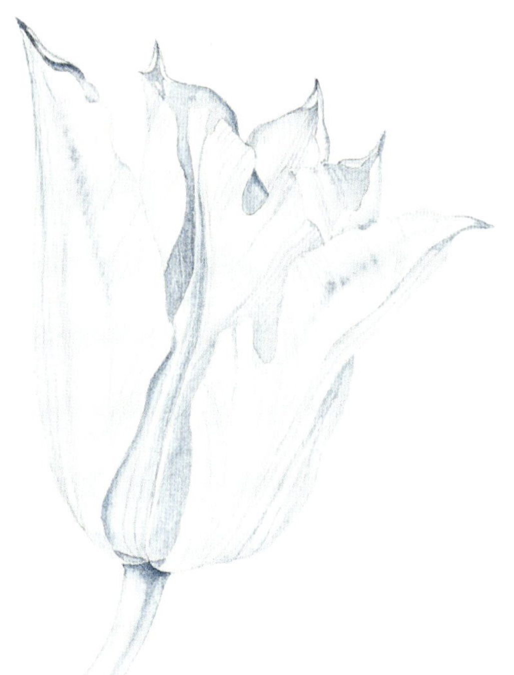

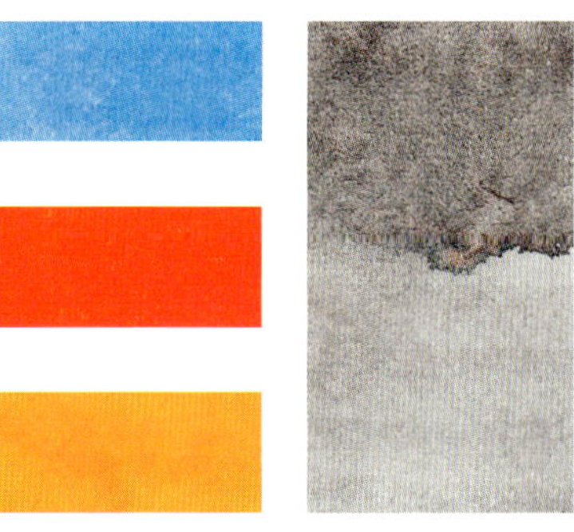

For the shadows on the *Tulipa* 'Ballerina' on the left (shown also on page 57), I used Phthalo Blue Green Shade (because the foliage showed a hint of turquoise suited to this green-bias blue) + Pyrrol Scarlet (an orange-bias red for a bright orange mix) + Hansa Yellow Deep (an orange-bias yellow for a bright orange mix).

TECHNIQUES
Working with washes

What I love most about watercolours is their liveliness. Other media do as they're told but watercolours, when given the opportunity, have a mind of their own. In order to make the most of their dynamic nature, most of my work is painted wet-in-wet, giving the paint some space to surprise me.

Wet-in-wet wash

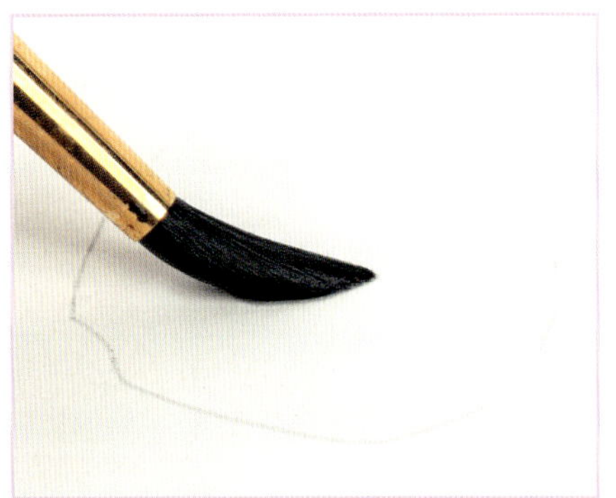

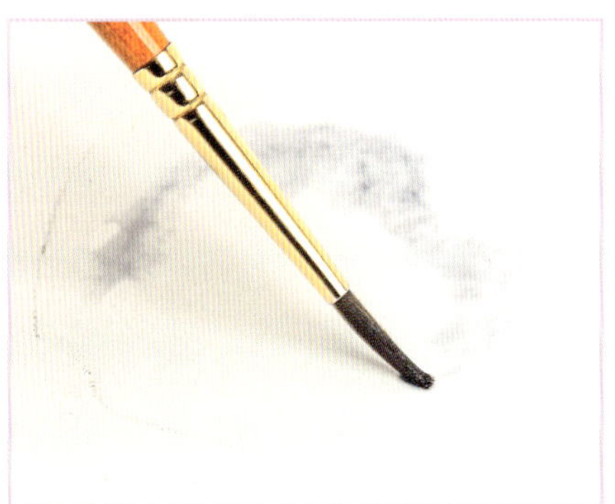

Wet an area of the painting following the outline. Make sure the area is evenly wet, with no dry patch and no puddle.

Load a brush with paint (here the shadow mix) and drop it on the wet paper. Channel where you want the paint to be but don't try to control it too much.

Graded wash

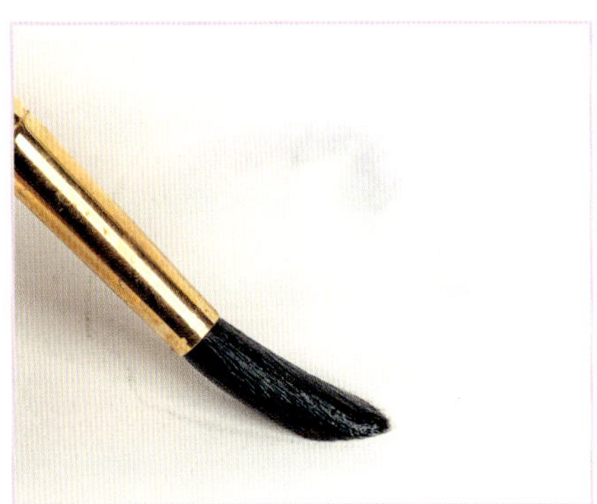

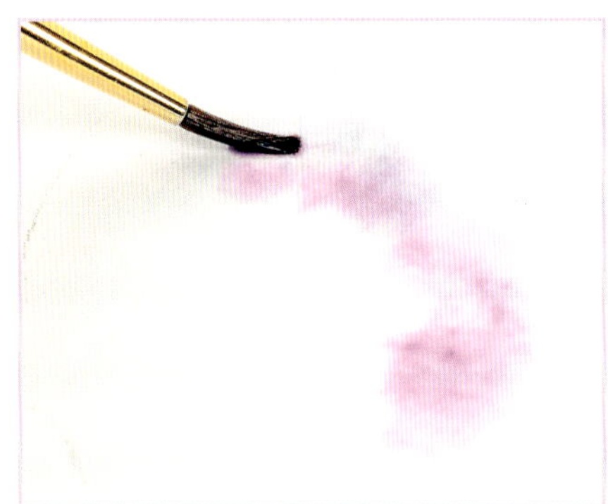

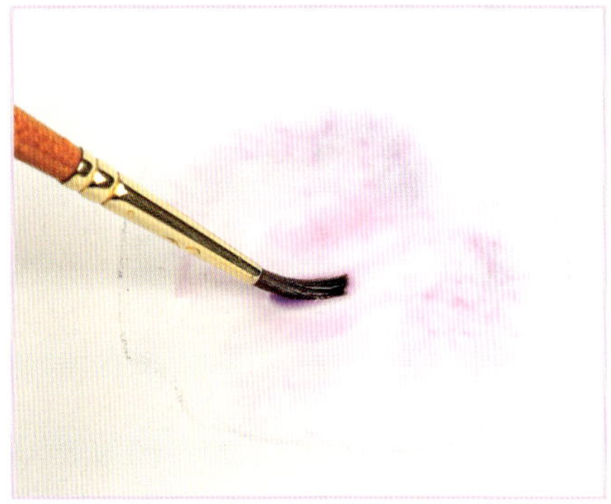

After the area has dried, wet it again in the same way as before.

Load a brush with paint and drop it on the paper, starting over the darkest parts. This is a graded wash, meaning that the paint is not applied evenly everywhere as it would be in a flat wash.

Here, the colour is applied on top of the shadows and over the mid-tones but not over the highlights.

Lifting on wet paper

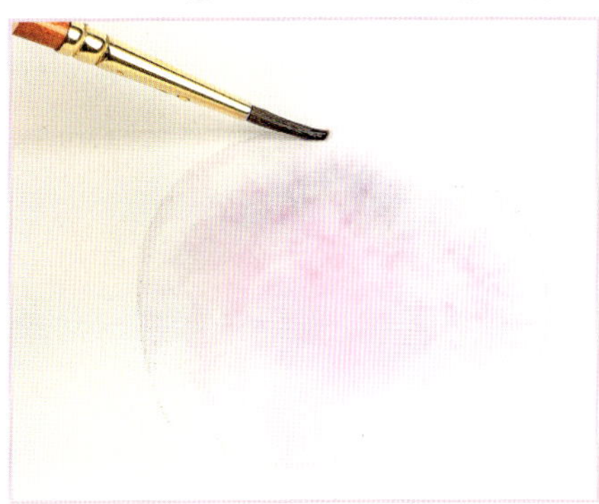

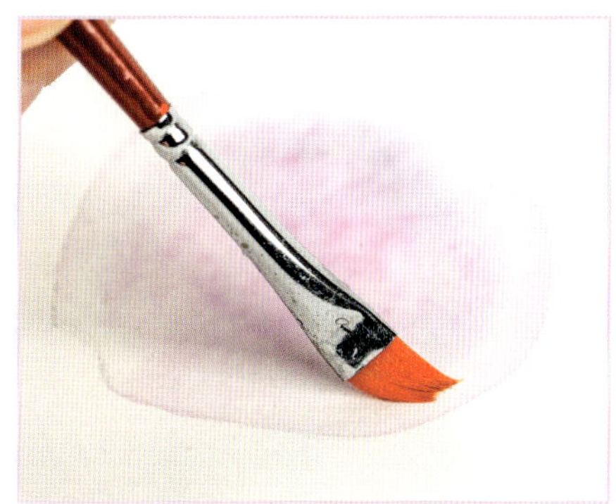

While the wash is still wet, it is possible to lift some paint if it has strayed over a highlight.

If more paint needs to be lifted, a flat brush works more efficiently than a round one.

On-paper mixing

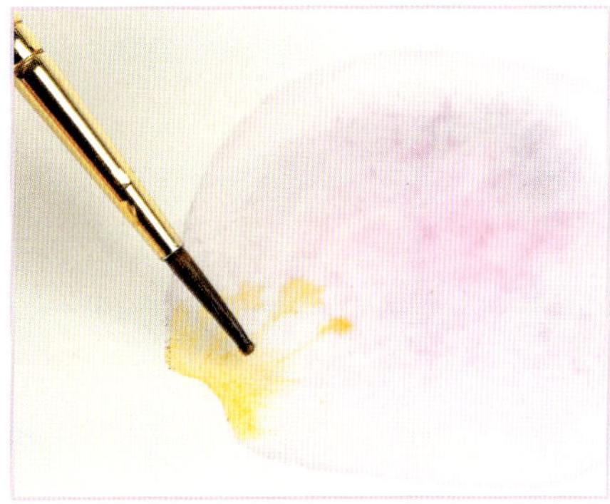

A technique I love using is mixing colours straight on the paper in the same wash. Wet the area again and drop in your first colour, containing it within a specific area. Here I am using yellow at the base of the petal.

While this is still wet, drop in another colour. Here I am using more of the lilac mix over the rest of the petal. The two colours merge where they meet, creating an uneven, natural-looking colour rather than the flat appearance of a premixed colour.

Wet-on-dry

Glazes

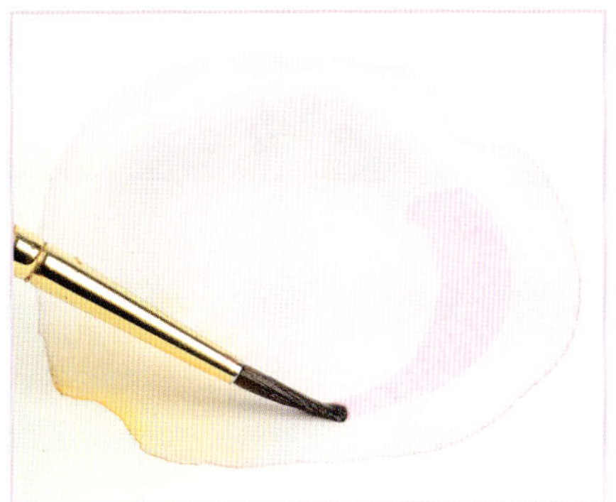

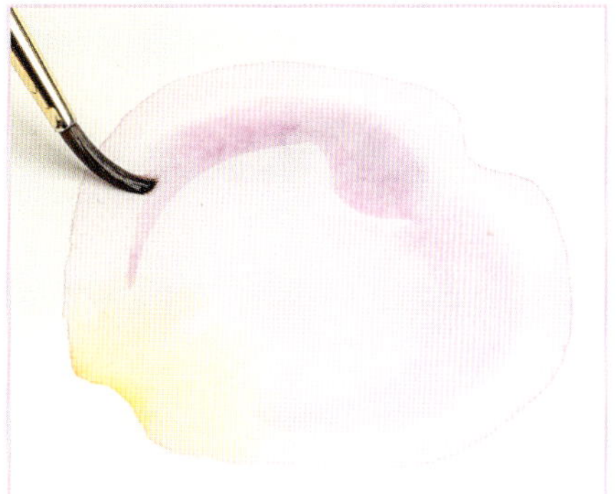

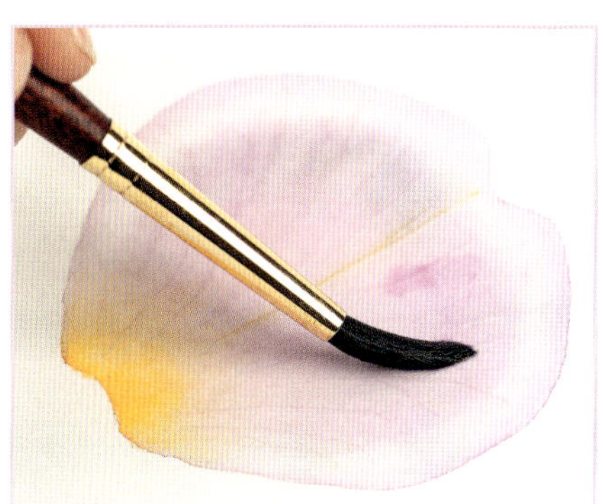

Using a diluted wash, it is possible to build up more colour by adding paint on dry paper.

In order to avoid getting hard edges, it is crucial to blend the edges of the wash straight away using a damp brush.

Towards the end of the painting process, you might want to modify some of the colours or intensify others with a few glazes. These are watery washes applied in a thin layer either on wet or dry paper.

TECHNIQUES
Working on dry paper

After the wet-in-wet washes have laid the foundation and built up enough tone
and colour, the dry-brush work comes in to refine the details that will give
more life to the painting, such as veins, patterns and blemishes. These details
are there to add to the washes, not hide them, so they have to stay unobtrusive,
complementing rather than upstaging.

Dry-brushed colour

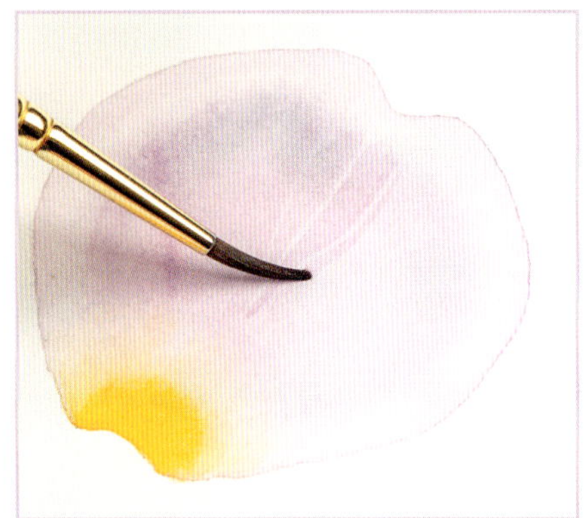

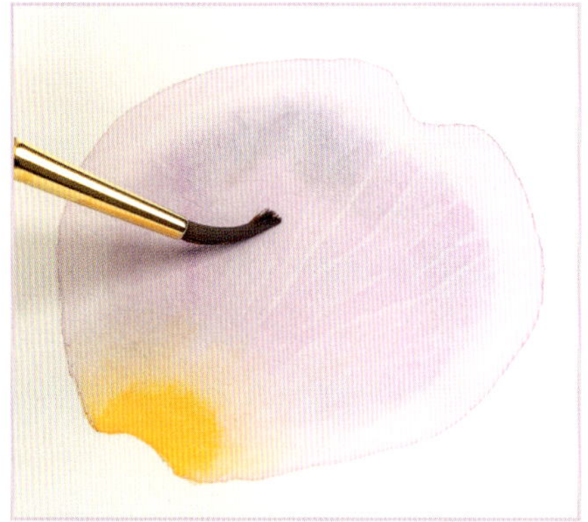

If the colour needs deepening in some
specific places rather than all over, dry-
brush work can be used.

Make sure to blend in with a clean, damp
brush to avoid dry brush marks that would
compromise the softness achieved with the
wet-in-wet work.

Details

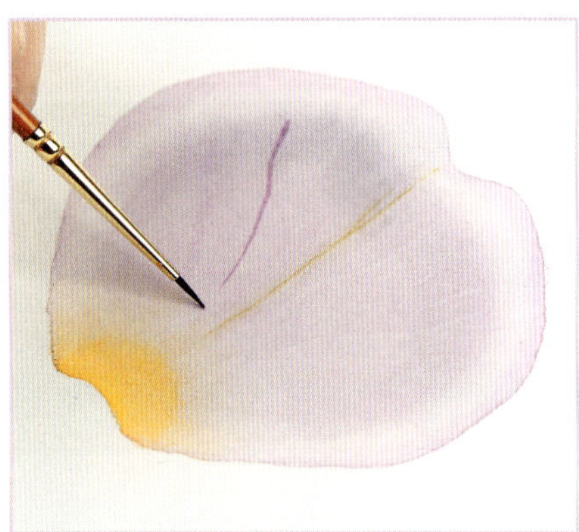

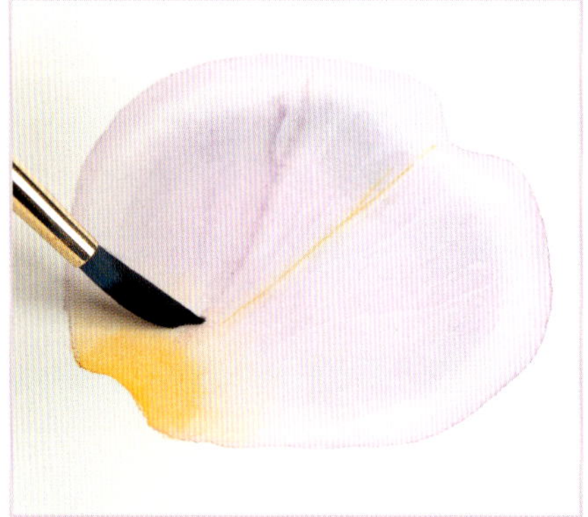

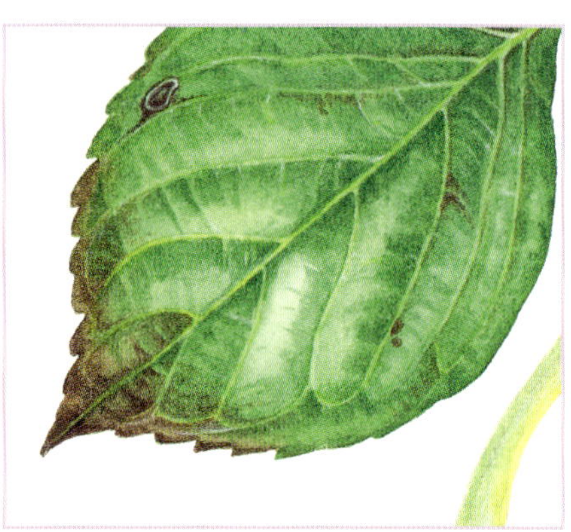

Small details such as veins, markings, folds
or blemishes are added with a tiny brush
loaded with paint that is thick enough to
leave a mark.

Once again, these details are blended into
the texture of the subject with a damp,
soft brush.

Blemishes are also added with a dry brush.
They tend to stand out more than texture or
veins, so they only need to be blended on
their edges.

Lifting on dry paper

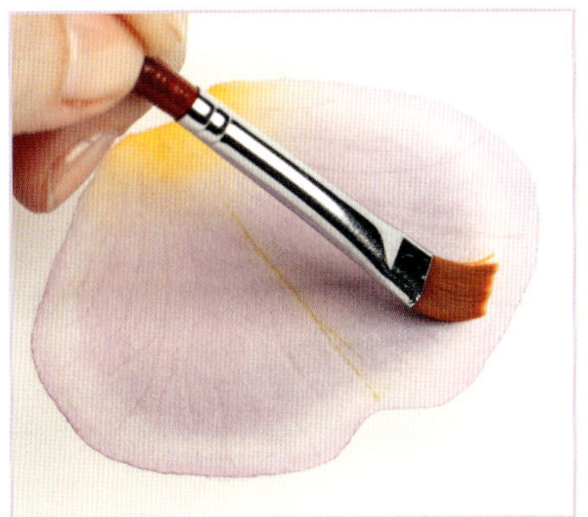

Lifting can be done on dry paper as well as wet paper. However, as some colours are staining, potentially less colour is lifted with this technique compared with when the wash is fresh and still wet.

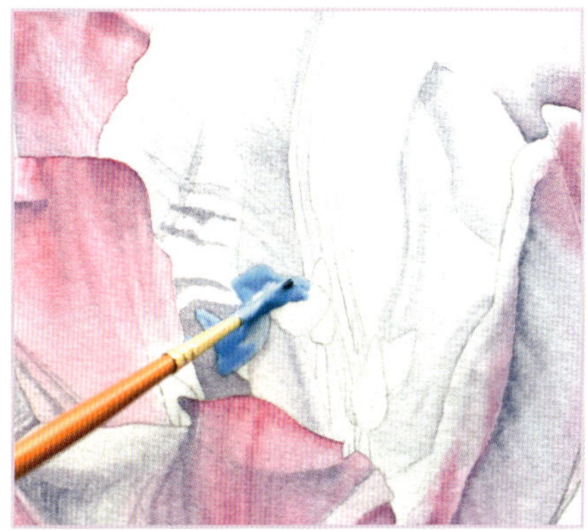

Veins can be lifted with a damp flat brush used on its side, almost like a blade. A low-quality synthetic brush is a good choice, as it is stiff and tough.

Masking

Some details are lighter than the washes behind them. If these details are large enough, it is possible to use masking fluid – blue here – to mask them, paint the washes around them, unmask them and then paint them. See page 90 for more on using masking fluid.

Using white paint

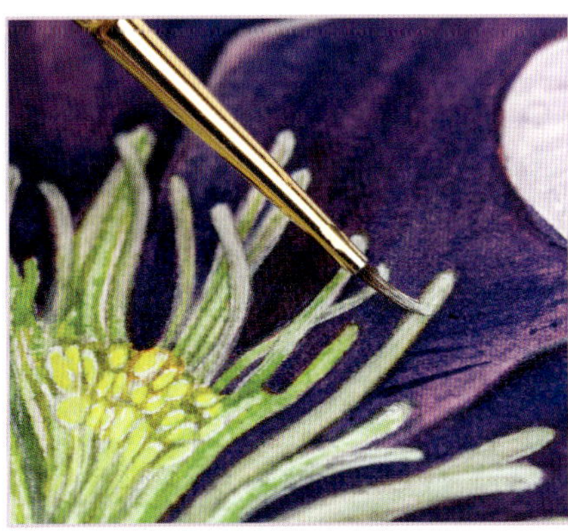

Some details are too small to use masking fluid in a way that will look neat enough. Using white paint is then the best alternative.

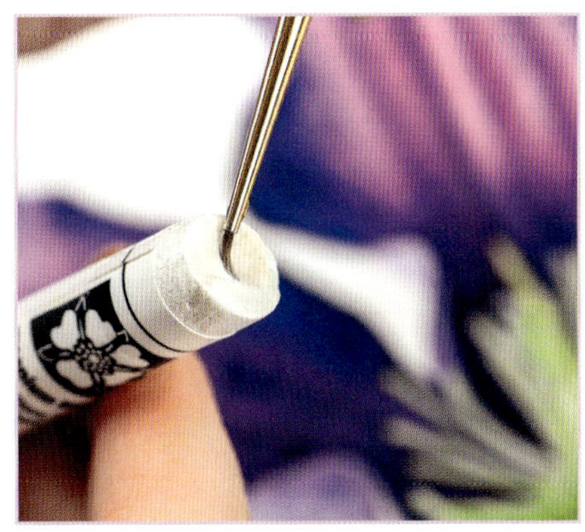

Pigment sticks are my favourite option when using white. They are made of concentrated pigments, meaning that they offer better coverage. They also tend to stay cleaner than a watercolour pan. Titanium White is the most opaque and can cover the darkest washes.

Spring

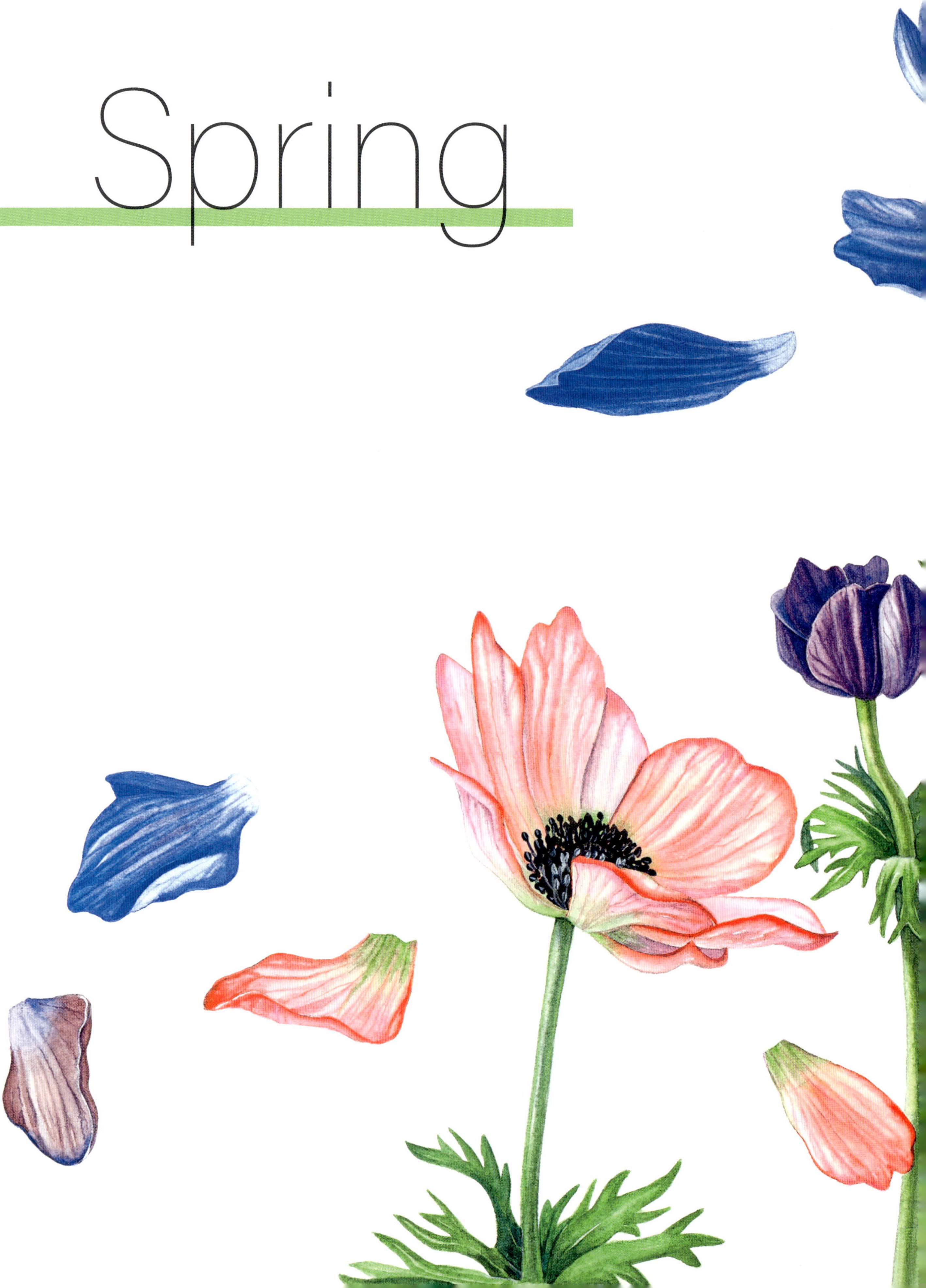

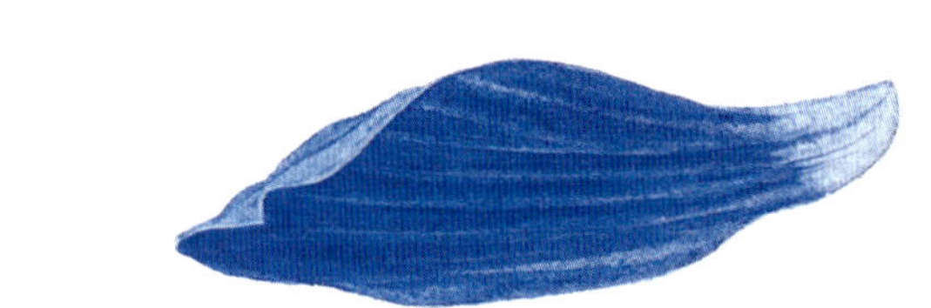

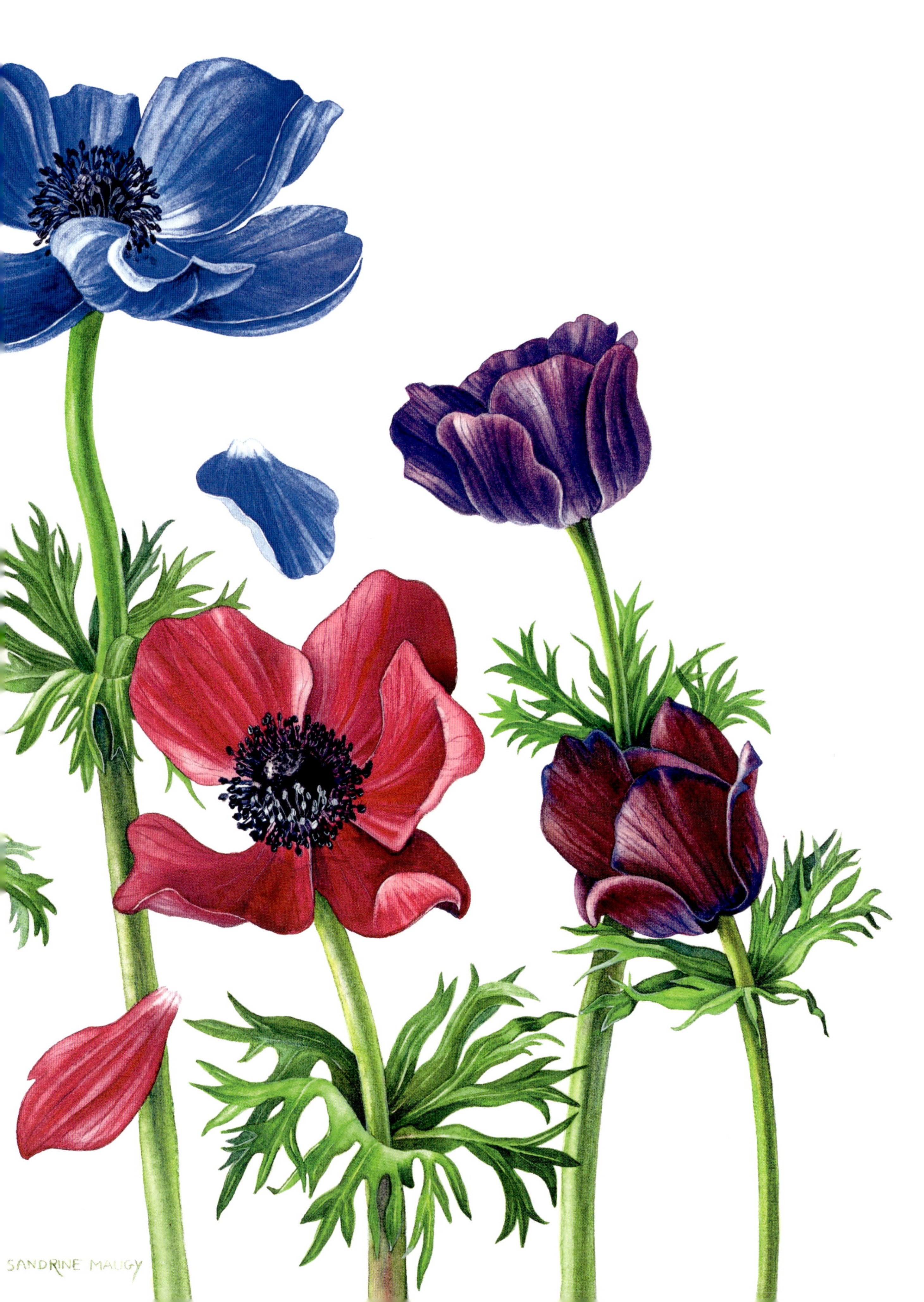
SANDRINE MAUGY

SPRING SUBJECTS
and their palette

Spring is finally here and nature awakes to greet the sun and the lengthening days. The birds voice their delight by waking us up at dawn with their cheerful songs. They start touring the birdhouses in the garden to see which one they fancy the most for their planned family… The birdhouse in the ivy has a better view of the rose bed but the honeysuckle offers more shelter from the wind. Like the birds, the plants are gaining in confidence and start poking their shoots out of the ground and unfolding their foliage. As they have to face these yet uncertain conditions, what are the characteristics of these daring Spring flowers?

Waxy petals and fleshy leaves

There is nothing quite like the sight of a crocus poking its head out of a fresh, thin carpet of snow to lift the spirits of a morose painter. Like the crocus and the daffodil, many Spring flowers have thick, waxy petals (or tepals) and fleshy leaves that have evolved to withstand late snowfalls and morning frosts. A way to render this is to paint the edge of the petals and leaves a slightly different shade of the main colour, thereby showing their thickness. If painted from the side, and the petals or leaves are overlapping each other, this thick edge will also help to create depth. On this waxy texture, highlights appear whenever a surface curves towards the light, forming a jagged line of bright light just inside the edge.

Fleshy leaves tend to be rather stiff, which is a challenge for composition. It is tricky to create an elegant, flowing picture when facing a hyacinth that looks ready for a military parade. Put an emphasis on any movement you can find.

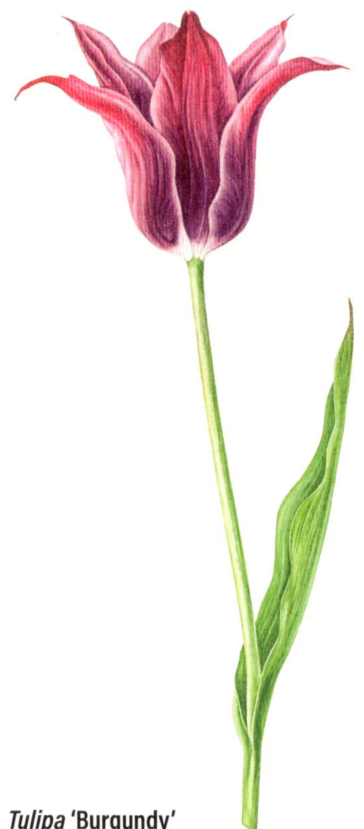

Tulipa 'Burgundy'

Bulbs

Quite a few Spring flowers come out of bulbs, in which their energy can lay dormant and protected during the Winter months. Including the bulb in a painting is a nice touch. You can also add a bit of fluffy moss or crunchy soil to contrast with the crispiness of the bulb skin.

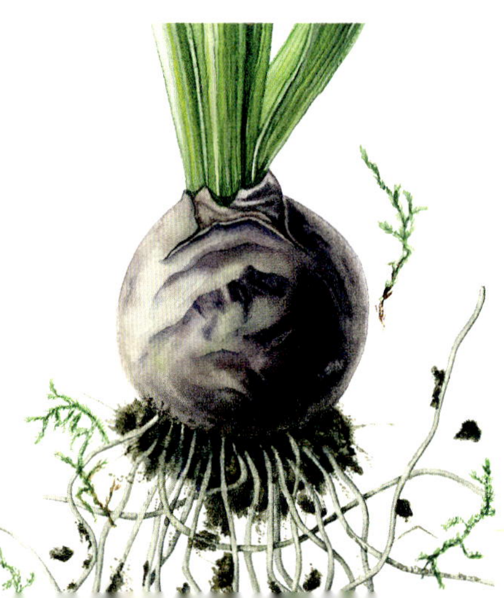

Fresh colours

The first striking aspect of the Spring garden is the freshness. The tender greens, clear blues and vivid yellows of Spring must be treated differently from the richer, deeper colours of Summer and Autumn or the duller shades of Winter. Coming out of hibernation after a few weeks spent painting dead leaves and seed heads, I am wholeheartedly swapping my collection of neutral colours for the vivid hues of brand new-nature.

Some long leaves with parallel veining, such as tulip or daffodil leaves, show a hint of turquoise that looks beautiful with yellow, white or pink flower heads.

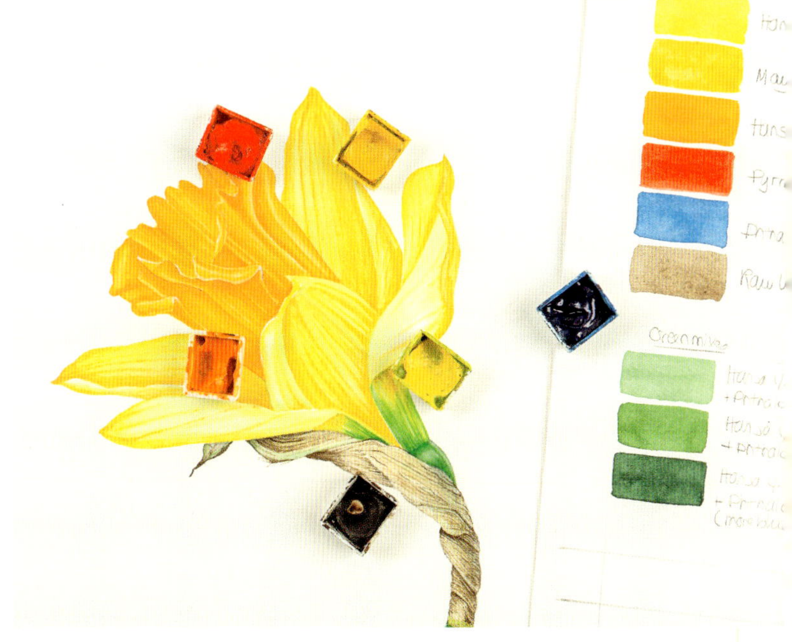

Palette

Other colours appear in the three tutorials, but if you would like a basic palette from which to mix all your colours, the list below is a good starting point for Spring subjects.

Hansa Yellow Light   Green-bias yellow – luminous yellow for glowing petals and fresh greens.
Subjects: Sunny daffodils and pale wild primroses.

Hansa Yellow Deep   Orange-bias yellow – a deeper yellow for mixing saturated orange hues.
Subjects: *Narcissus corona* and saffron-loaded croci.

Pyrrol Scarlet   Orange-bias red – for bright reds and for mixing saturated orange hues.
Subjects: Stratified *Ranunculus* and extravagant tulips.

Pyrrol Red   Mid-red – for the strongest red petals.
Subjects: Original wild tulip and camellia.

Quinacridone Pink   True pink – anything from pale pink to cerise.
Subjects: Delicate blossom and architectural magnolia.

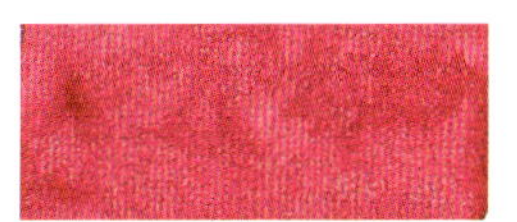

Quinacridone Lilac   Violet-bias red – when pink goes blue and turns to violet.
Subjects: Magenta tulips and, of course, lilac.

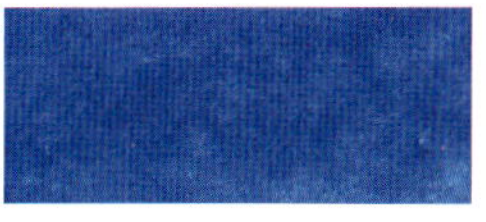

Phthalo Blue Red Shade   Violet-bias blue – for mixing true purples.
Subjects: Violets and the darkest tulips.

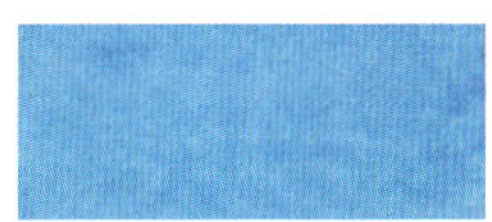

Phthalo Blue Green Shade   Green-bias blue – for turquoise hints in foliage and the undersides of some leaves.
Subjects: Long fleshy leaves and the underside of apple-tree foliage.

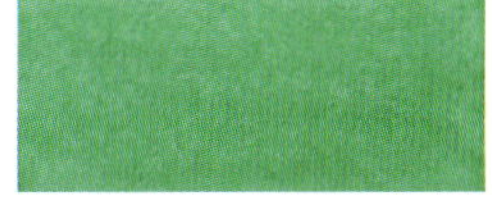

Phthalo Green Yellow Shade
Bright pure green – to be used as a base for fresh greenery.
Subjects: Any foliage.

DAFFODIL

Common name Daffodil	**Flowering** Spring	**Hardiness** Fully hardy
Botanical name *Narcissus*	**Planting time** October to November	**Propagation** Division or seed
Group Bulbous perennial	**Aspect** Full sun	**Native** Southern Europe to North Africa

Daffodil section

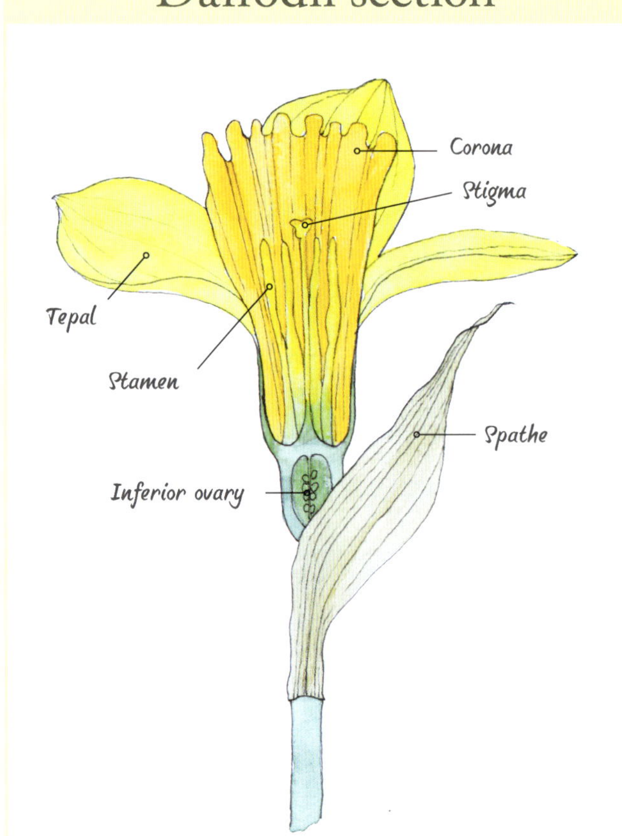

Botanically speaking…

- Daffodils have tepals, which are a cross between petals and sepals.

- The original varieties have six tepals (three inner petals and three outer sepals that look alike). Three tepals are on the inside and three are on the outside, arranged in an alternate pattern.

- The trumpet shape in the centre is called the corona.

- Daffodil colours range from white to different shades of yellow, orange or even pink or green in some garden varieties.

- The stigma at the top of the style is split in three parts.

- There are six stamens arranged around the style.

- The anthers are basifixed (that is, attached by their base).

- Daffodils bear one flower per leafless stem, although some varieties can carry several flowers on a single stem, forming an umbel with up to twenty blooms.

- The leaves are covered with a polymer called cutin, which gives them a waxy appearance.

- The veining pattern on the leaves is parallel, meaning that all the veins run from the base to the tip of the leaf, covering the whole width, with no side veins.

- Buds are protected by a papery membrane called a spathe (singular bract), which stays wrapped around the stem after the buds open.

- Height varies from 5cm (2in) for dwarf varieties to 80cm (31½in) for the tallest ones.

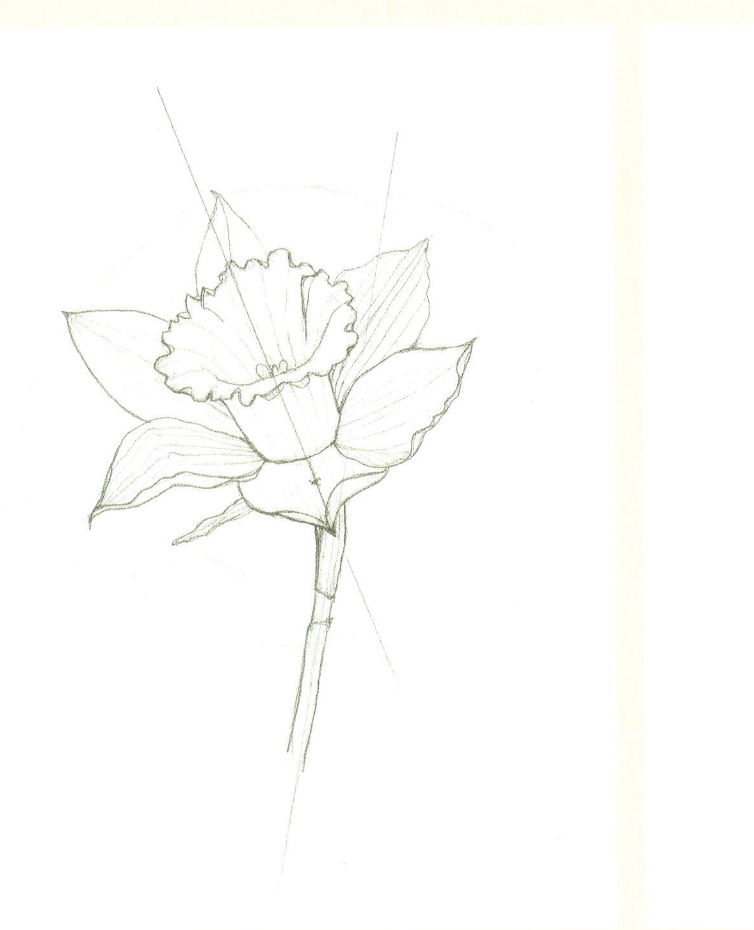

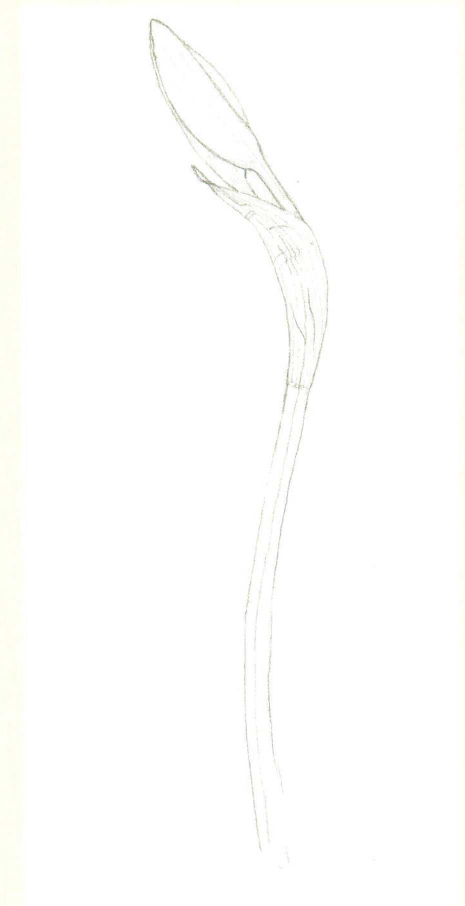

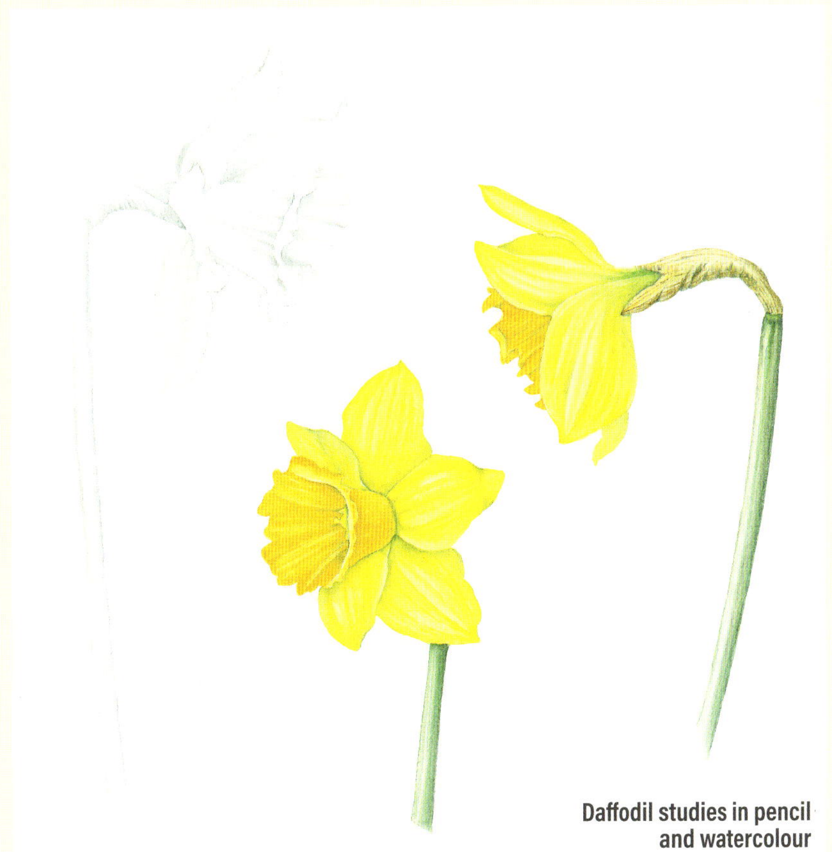

Daffodil studies in pencil
and watercolour

Level 1

DAFFODIL
Sketch and tone study

Daffodils are the harbinger of Spring, the real sunny hope that the Winter is coming to an end and the longer days will prevail. Their bright yellow colours would cheer anybody up. This bright yellow is also what makes them such a challenge to paint: not enough shadows and they look flat, too many, and they look grey and dirty. The key to success is a clean pale grey in strategic places and pure pigments to keep the yellow sunny and glowing.

Materials list

PAPERS

Cartridge paper or sketchbook
Tracing paper
Transfer paper
Watercolour paper: Fabriano Artistico HP Extra White, 640gsm (300lb)

DRAWING

Pencils: 6B for sketch; 0.5mm with an HB lead; 2mm clutch with a 2B lead

PAINTING

Brushes: Pro Arte Prolene Plus Series 007 in sizes 6, 4 , 2, 0 and 3/0

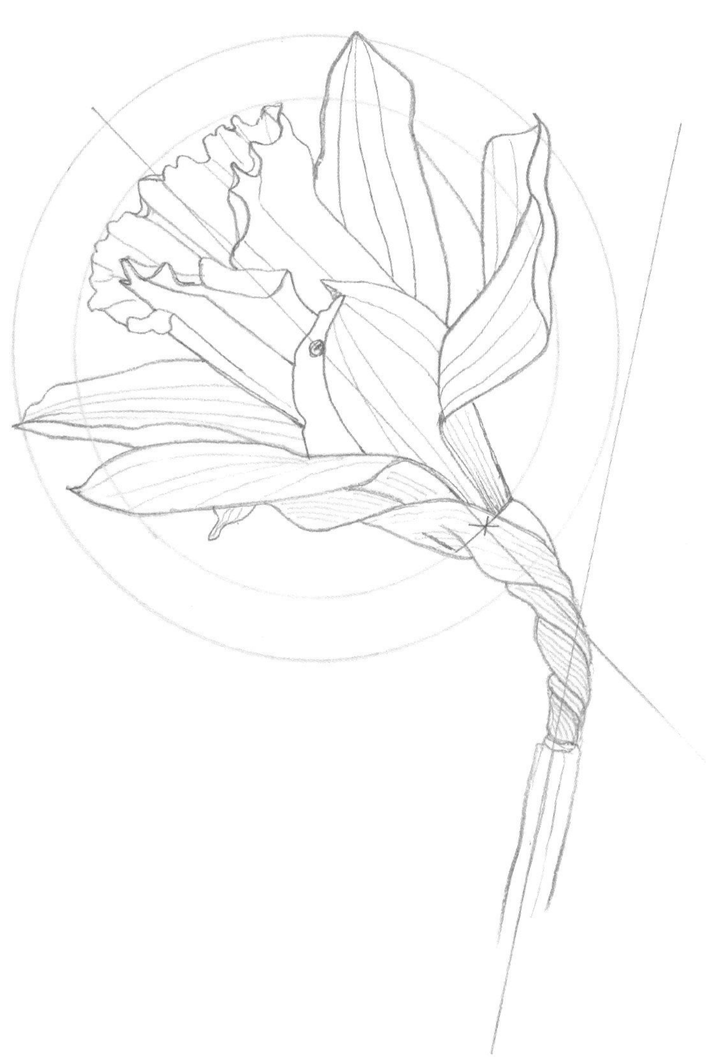

Drawing

Step 1 Start with the construction lines that outline the shapes and directions of the daffodil's main features: a diagonal line goes from the top of the stem through the centre of the corona, separating the tepals into two balanced sections; another diagonal prolongs the stem, paying particular attention to the angle with the other diagonal. A large circle gives an idea of where the tepals are reaching, while a smaller circle encompasses the corona. A small cross at the anchor point (where all the parts join) is a reminder of which direction the central veins, stem and spathe should aim for.

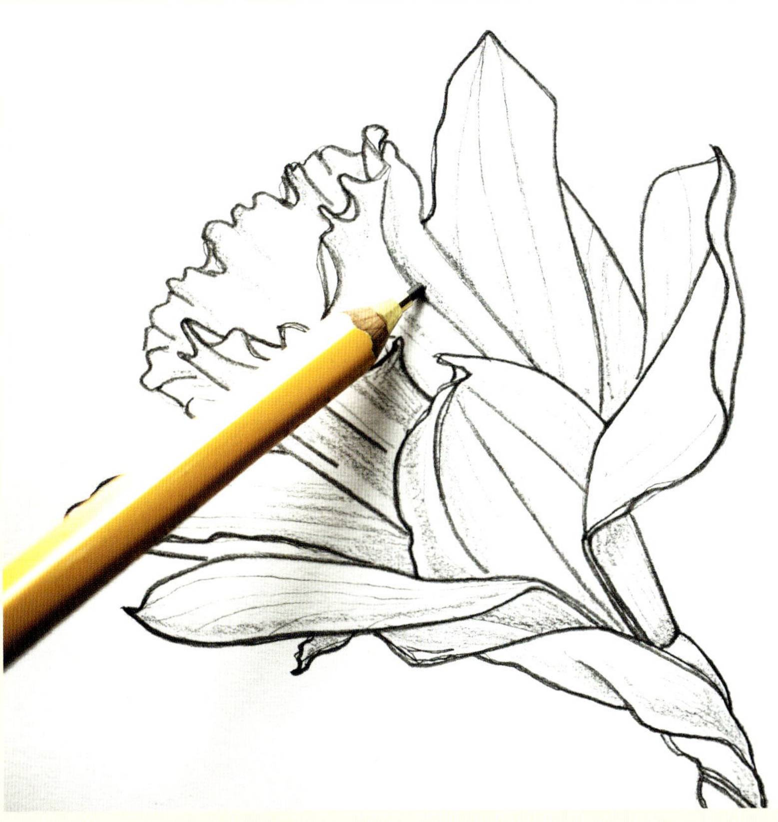

Step 2 Once the drawing is ready, trace it with a low-weight tracing paper and transfer it to the watercolour paper using the transfer paper. It is better to do this before the tone study because the thick markings of the 2B pencil could interfere with the clarity of the lines. You can keep the tracing as a 'master copy' of the drawing, should the painting take a bad turn and you wish to start it again – at this stage, starting again will not take much time.

Tone study

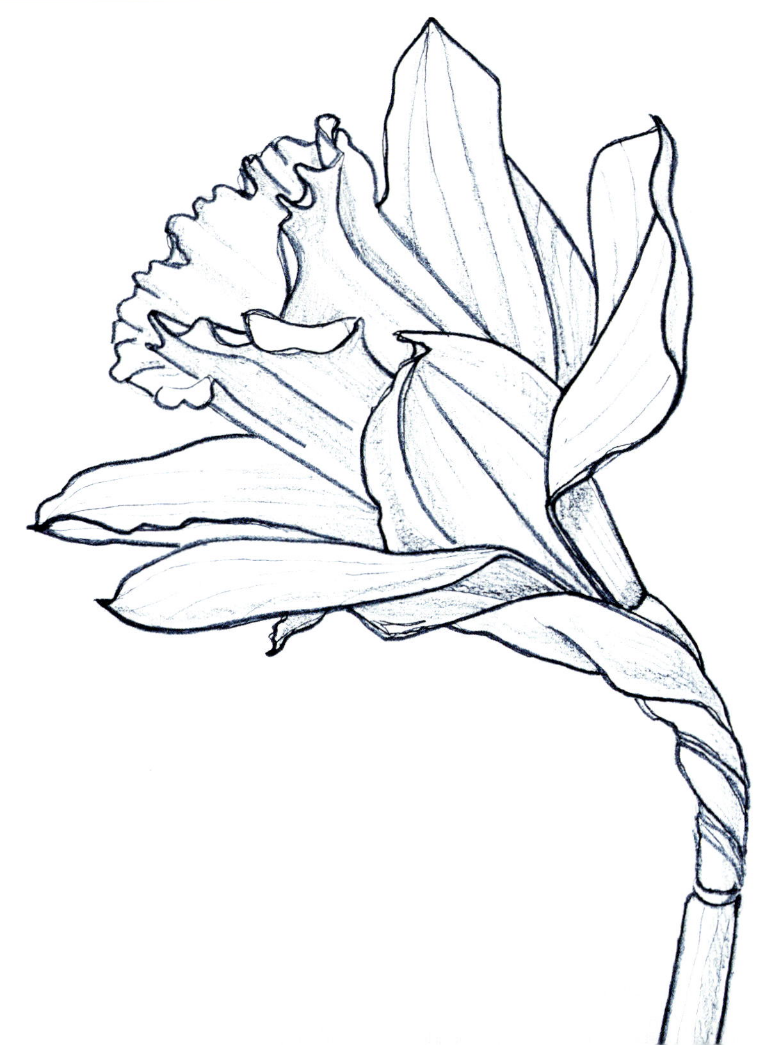

Step 3 Using a thick pencil (here I am using a 2mm clutch pencil with a 2B lead), draw a tone study that you will later use as a reference when painting the shadows on the watercolour version of the daffodil. Light changes quickly and it is important to capture the tone in a 'snapshot', using a medium with which you can work quickly and accurately.

Because daffodils are yellow, it is better to reduce the areas of shadows rather than draw attention to them by making them too large. They need to be there to create form, but too many could make the daffodil look dirty. Yellow is a fragile colour that needs to be treated carefully.

Palette and shadows

Now that the drawing is transferred to the watercolour paper, we are
ready to select our palette. As daffodils are mainly yellow, the focus will
be on that colour. The other pigments will be chosen to complement
the dominant yellow ones.

Palette

Hansa Yellow Light   Green-bias
yellow – the main colour of the tepals
and underlayer for the corona.

Mayan Yellow   Mid-yellow with a
cloudy texture – gives a bit of depth
to the tepals and strengthens the
veins, providing a bit of contrast to the
Hansa Yellow Light. It can be replaced
with a mix of Hansa Yellow Light and
Hansa Yellow Deep.

Hansa Yellow Deep – Orange-bias
yellow – the main colour of the corona.

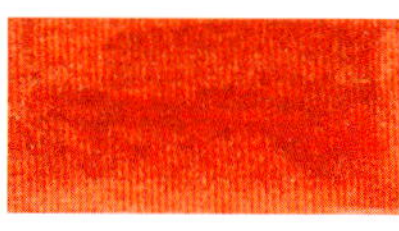

Pyrrol Scarlet   Orange-bias red – can
be added to the orange-bias yellow to
deepen it if needed.

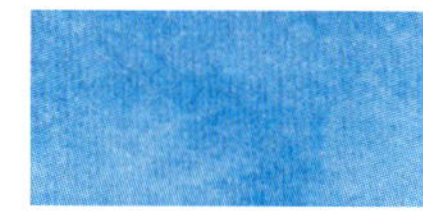

Phthalo Blue Green Shade   Green-
bias blue – Daffodil foliage has a hint
of turquoise so this green-bias blue
is a good choice to mix and darken
the green.

Raw Umber   Green-bias brown – the
base colour of the spathe.

Green mixes

The brightest green, for the base of the tepals and the length of the stem
that is exposed to the light, is a mix of **Phthalo Blue Green Shade** +
Hansa Yellow Light.

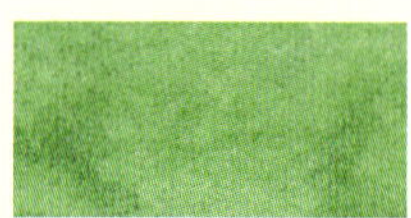

The medium muted green, for the edges of the spathe, is a mix of
Phthalo Blue Green Shade + **Hansa Yellow Deep**.

The dark green, for the stem, is a mix of **Phthalo Blue Green Shade** +
Hansa Yellow Light. The mix is the same as for the bright green, but the
proportion is different. In this version, there is more blue. If the mix is still
too bright, you can add a touch of **Pyrrol Scarlet** to mute it and darken
it further.

Brown mixes

Raw Umber is the base colour for the spathe. In some places, the spathe shows undertones of yellowish-green, while in others, it shows reddish tints. You can modify the **Raw Umber** with **Hansa Yellow Light** for the former and with **Hansa Yellow Deep** for the latter.

Harmonic Shadows

The Harmonic Shadow mix, which consists of three primary colours already present in the painting, is **Hansa Yellow Light + Phthalo Blue Green Shade + Pyrrol Red**. The blue and red are a simple choice because there are only one blue and one red in the palette. For the yellow, I had a choice of three. I selected Hansa Yellow Light because it is the finest pigment and tends to make smooth mixes. Yellow is a fragile colour and it is important to have a smooth, delicate mix for the shadows, so that they don't overpower the subject.

Harmonic Shadows

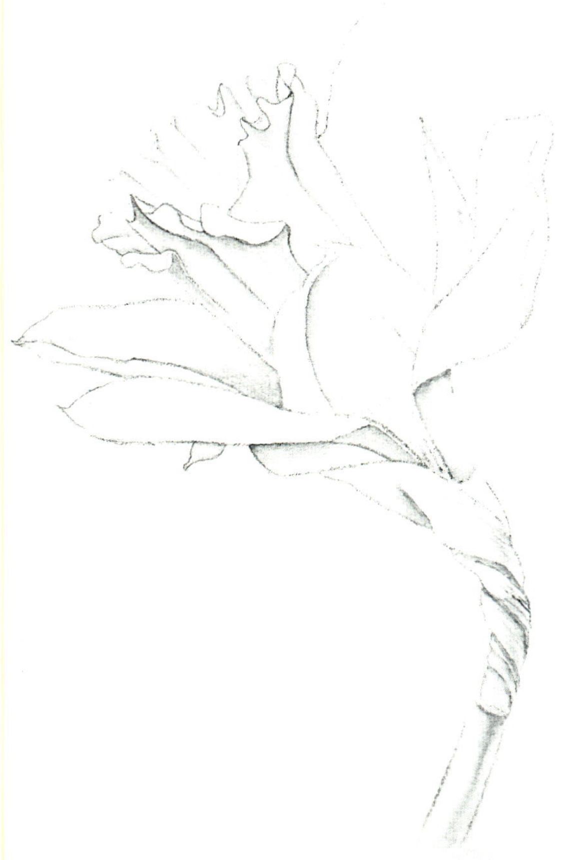

The shadows are painted in two steps. First a wet-in-wet wash on the whole subject, one area at a time, making sure to keep the shadows restricted to the darkest tones. The mid-tones and highlights must remain free of grey in order to achieve the required level of saturation desired for the intense daffodil yellow. Each part is wetted in its entirety and the diluted shadow mix is dropped in with a size 2 brush in the darkest parts. Any new area must be surrounded by dry paper before the water is applied, to avoid the different parts merging into each other.

The second wave of shadows is painted with a dry brush and a size 0 brush, with tiny darker areas accentuating the fold of the spathe and the overlappings and folds of the corona.

Tip

Make sure you erase the transfer lines as soon as is practical, as it is not always possible to erase through a layer of paint.

Wet-in-wet work

The first washes on the daffodil are painted wet-in-wet, giving a smooth colour background to the tepals and corona. Even the spathe has an underlayer of wet work, before the drier markings are painted on top.

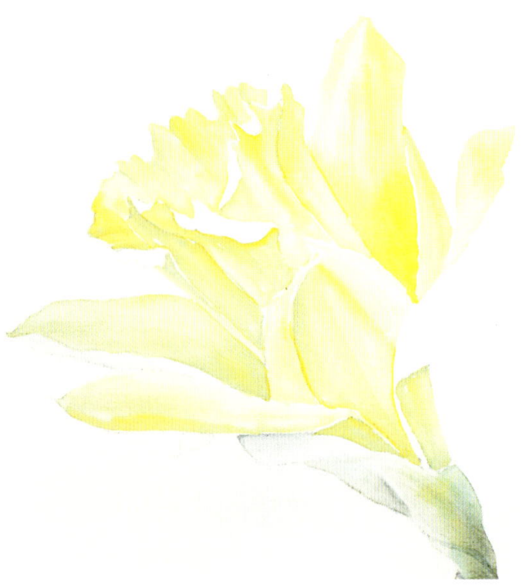

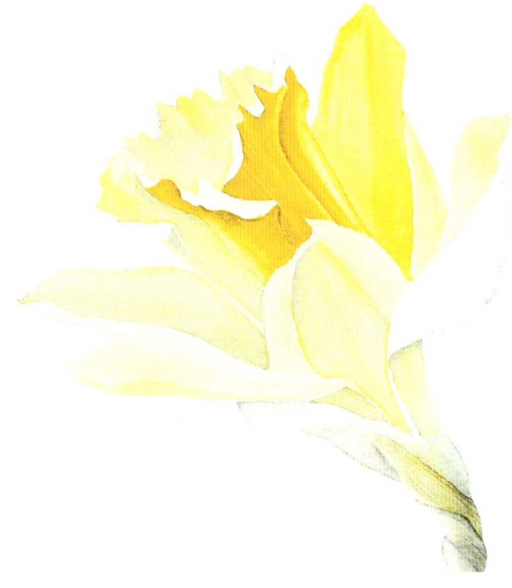

Step 1 The first wash all over the flower head is painted with Hansa Yellow Light. This is the main colour for the tepals, but is also used as an underlayer for the corona, giving a glow to the following, more orange-bias washes.

Step 2 The next colour on the corona is Hansa Yellow Deep, which is the main colour for this part. It is painted wet-in-wet, in sections, covering the shadows first and bleeding into the mid-tones. The sections are dictated by the folds created with the shadow colour.

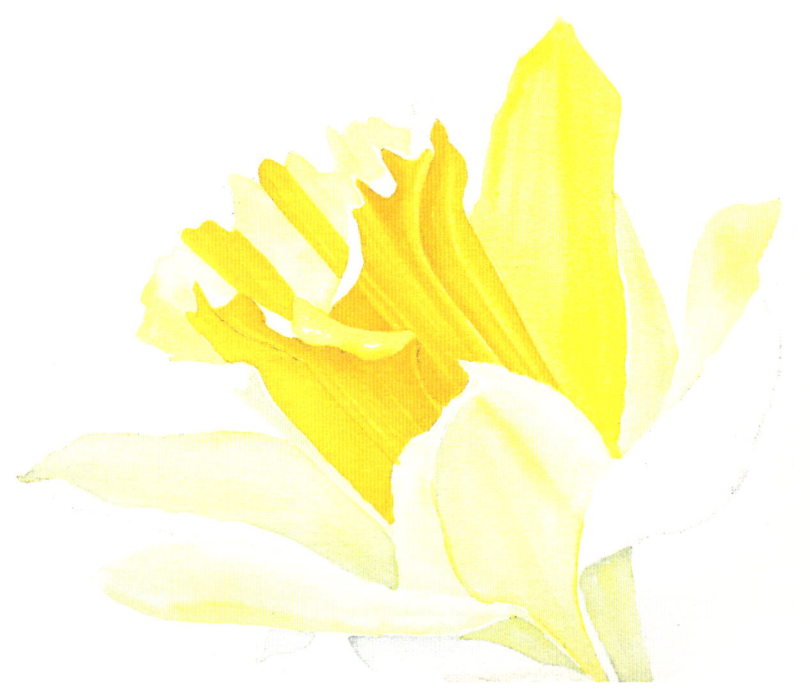

Step 3 Work your way around the corona, one section at a time. If the orange-bias yellow in your palette is not orange enough, you can add a small touch of Pyrrol Scarlet to it.

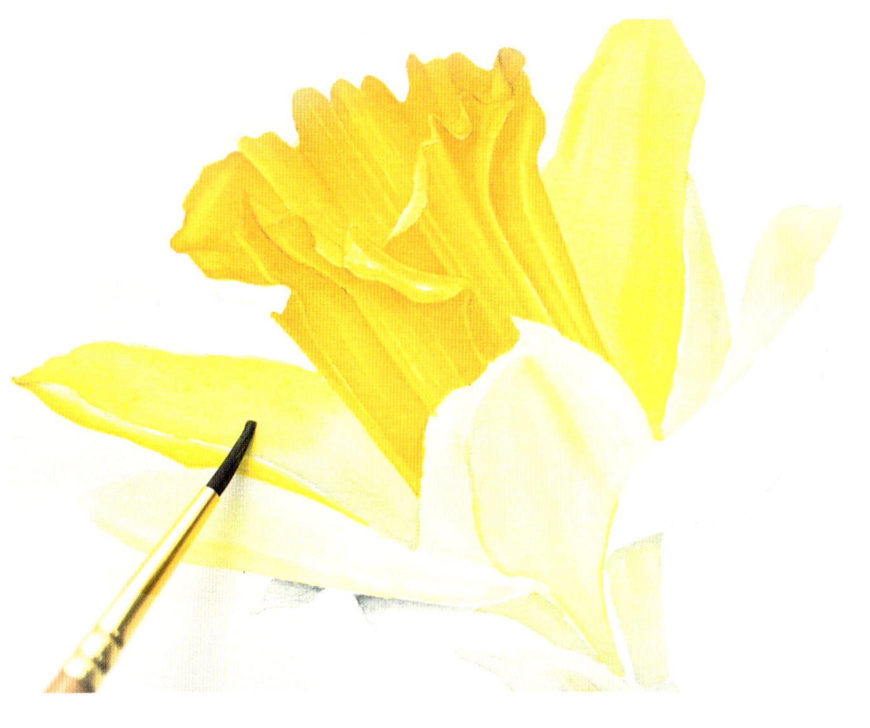

Step 4 The tepal washes are straightforward, painted with pure Hansa Yellow Light. The highlights don't need to be reserved entirely because the texture is not glossy. Each tepal is wetted in turn, dropping in Hansa Yellow Light over the shadows and into the mid-tones. The brush is then softly run over the highlights once most of the paint is unloaded, so that the highlights, although not reserved, have less colour than the rest.

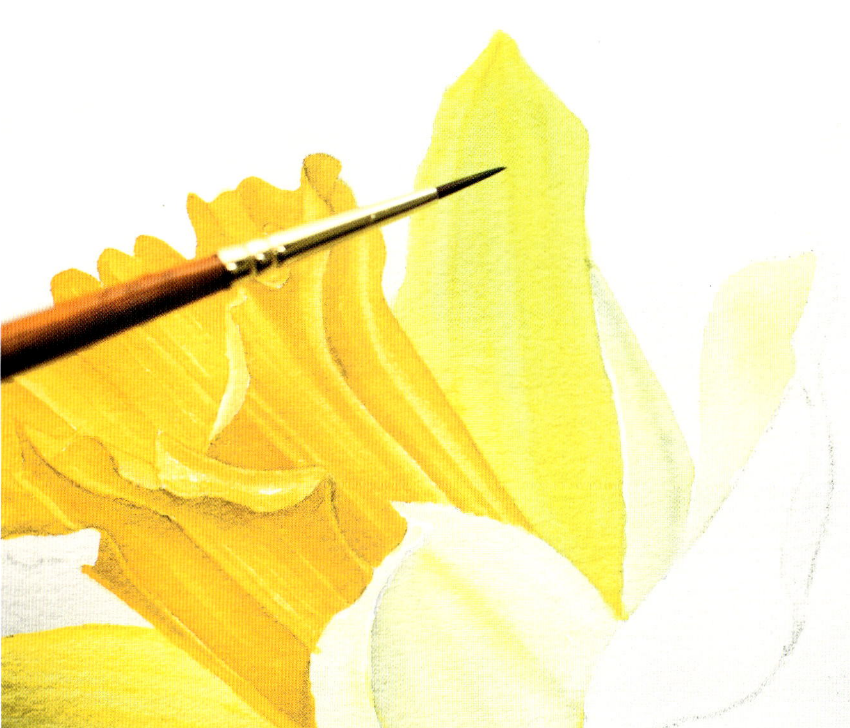

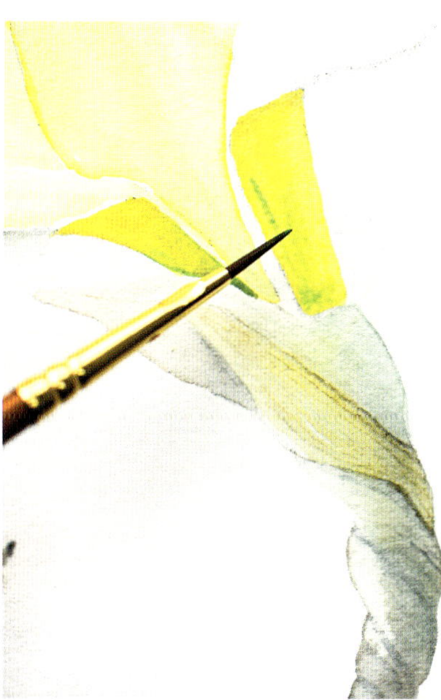

Step 5 In another wash, emphasis can be added to the veins, first with more Hansa Yellow Light and then with Mayan Yellow. The brush is loaded with thicker paint and dragged over the wet paper, creating a line that blends a little but not too far into the wash.

Step 6 The same process is repeated with the green at the base of the tepals, this time with a smaller brush so that the veins stay separated. Doing this wet-in-wet ensures that the lines stay soft. The spathe needs a very light wash of green where it covers the stem, to give a feel of transparency. After this initial green wash, it is painted in Raw Umber with a little Hansa Yellow Light added.

Dry-brush details

Once all the wet-in-wet washes are done (which, for as pale a subject as this, means only two or three washes), dry-brush work can be used to reinforce details and make the spathe look more crispy.

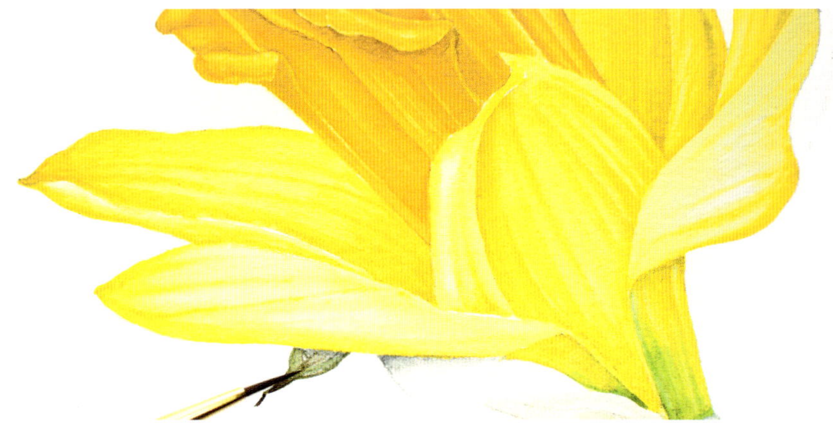

Step 1 To add structure to the sepals, you can add some veins with a damp brush on dry paper, using Mayan Yellow. These should be blended straight away with a damp, clean brush to sink them into the texture. The texture on the corona can be treated the same way by reinforcing the folds.

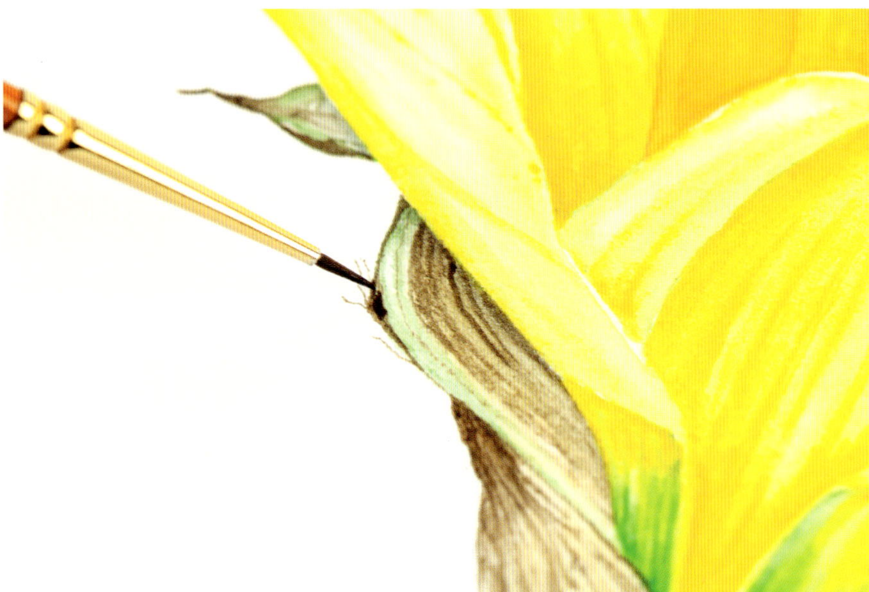

Step 2 My daffodil's spathe had a border of green towards the tip. However, most of it is painted with a dry brush, painting the thin lines that run along its length with a 3/0 brush. A light glaze of Raw Umber can be added to blend them in a little, but this needs to be done after they are thoroughly dry or they will disappear. I would wait for at least a couple of hours.

Tidy up any loose ends and the daffodil is done!

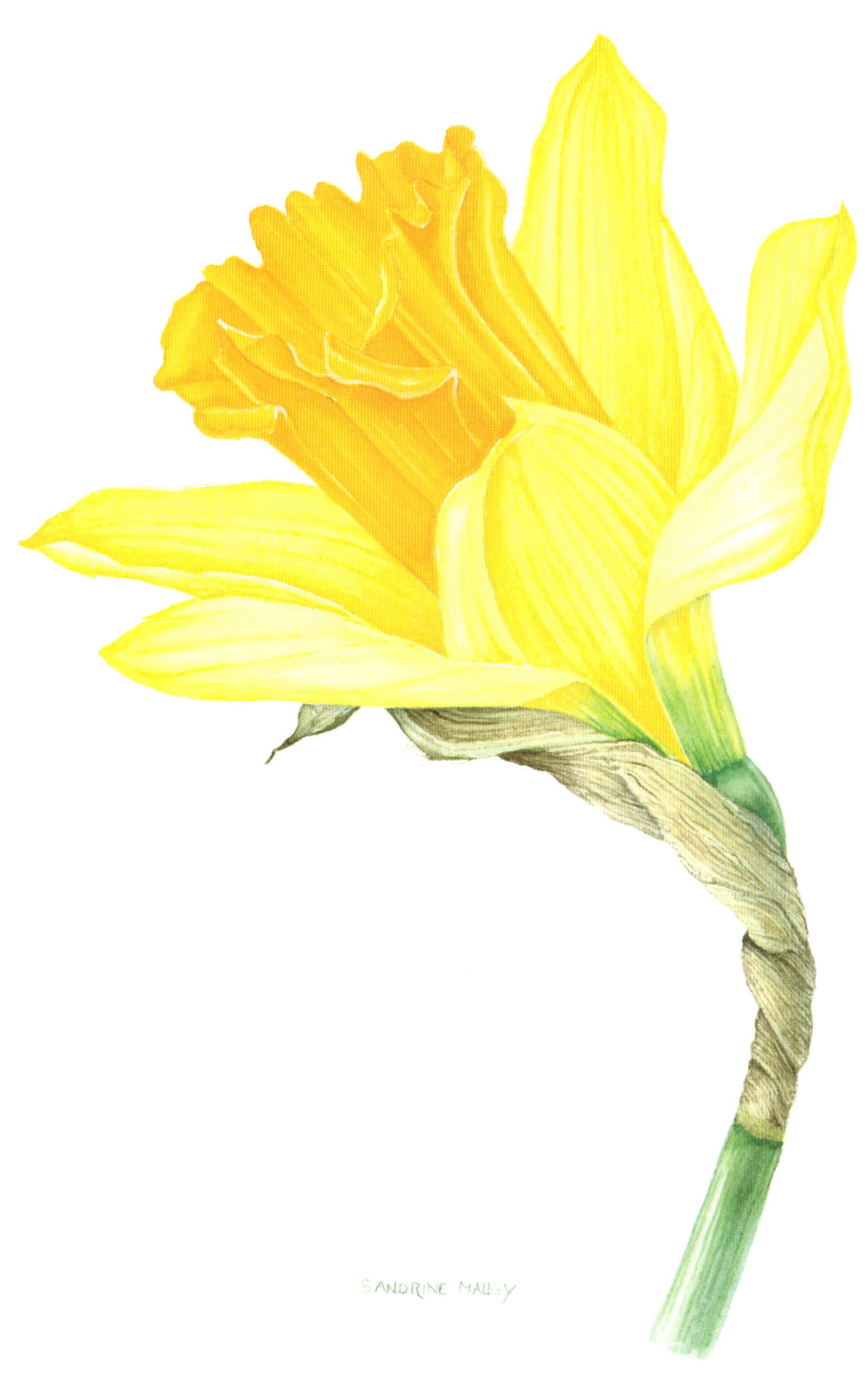

Daffodil
Watercolour on paper.

Anatomy of an

ANEMONE

Common name Anemone de Caen	**Planting time** Autumn in greenhouses	**Propagation** Seed or separation
Botanical name *Anemone coronaria*	or outside in Spring	**Native** Mediterranean region
Family Ranunculaceae	**Aspect** Full sun to partial shade	
Flowering April to June	**Hardiness** Hardy	

Anemone

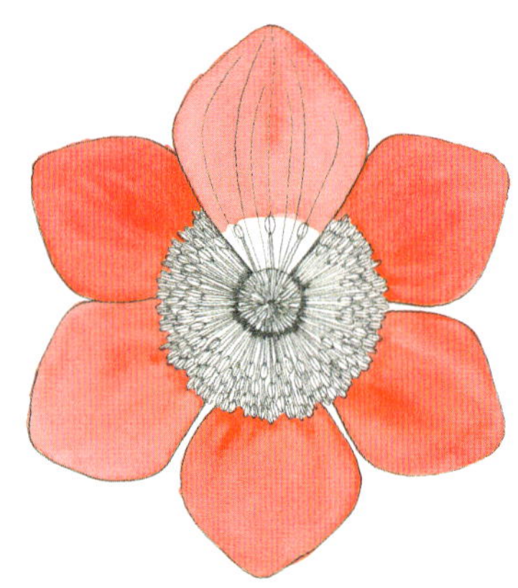

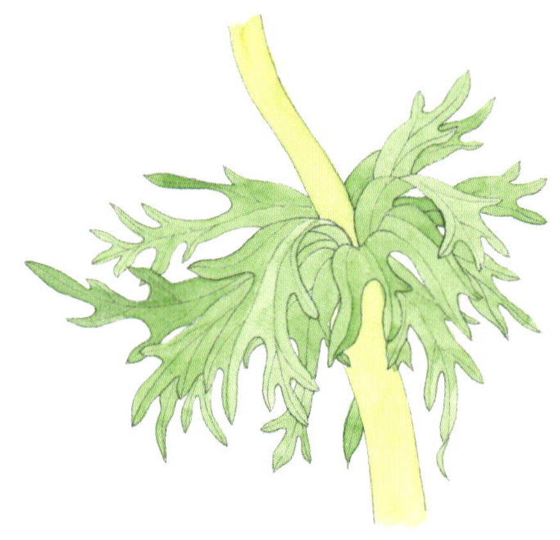

Botanically speaking…

- Anemones come in a range of colours: white, cream, green, blue, violet, magenta, pink and all shades of red.

- Anemones have petal-like tepals surrounding the centre.

- The original wild flower is red and has six tepals. *Anemone coronaria* has five to eight tepals.

- Some hybrids have double flowers and can have many tepals.

- The flowers are 3–8cm (1¼–3⅛in) in diameter. Some modern cultivars have flowers up to 10cm (4in) in diameter.

- The base of the tepal is often a different colour from the rest: for example, white on a red anemone or blue on a purple one. If the base is paler than the rest, it is wise to paint it first so that it doesn't get lost in the deeper colour.

- Anemones carry one flower per stem, which is 20–50cm (8–19¾in) long.

- Each stem carries a basal rosette of deeply lobed leaves that can be right under the flower or a few centimetres below.

- The flower centre is a mound that contains tightly packed pistils surrounded by dozens of stamens in the form of a crown. It is this crown shape that gives the name to *Anemone coronaria*.

- The stamens are almost black.

- Mature anthers are deep purple-black while immature anthers, having no pollen grains, are beige in colour.

- According to a Greek myth, red anemones sprang from Adonis' blood after he died. In his honour, red anemones are also known as 'Adonis flowers'.

- Pliny in his writings observed that anemones are opened by the wind, so they are also called windflowers.

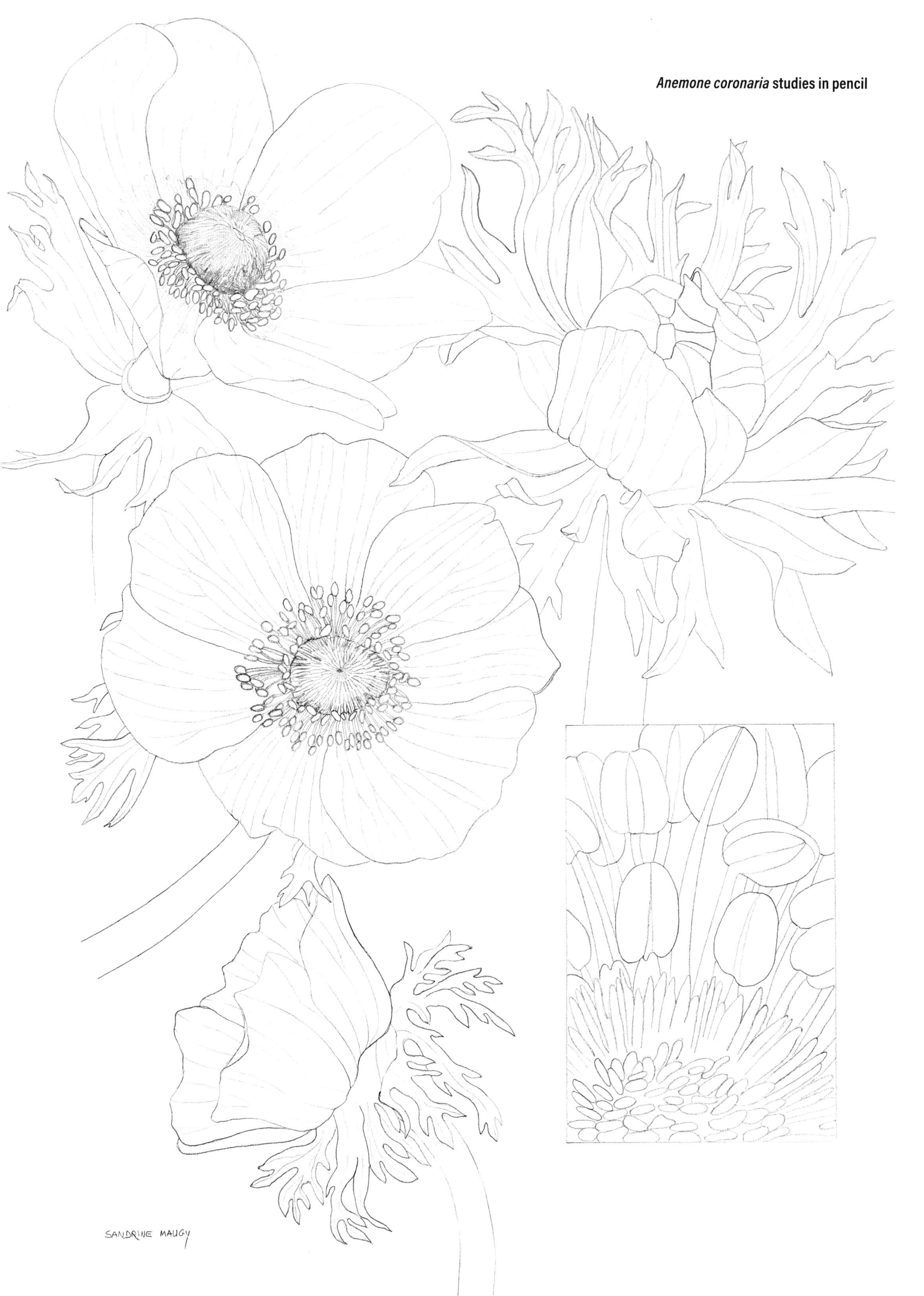

Anemone coronaria studies in pencil
SANDRINE MAUGY

Level 2

ANEMONE
Sketch and palette

Blue anemones are amongst my favourite Spring flowers. Their violet-blue colour, counterpoised with their black centres and vivid green frilly foliage, offers a vision that is irresistible to me. Elegantly perched on top of their twirling stems, they are like blue ballerinas balancing *en pointe*, wearing cellulose and chlorophyl tutus.

For this composition of *Anemone coronaria*, I wanted to portray a flower at three different stages of its life: as a bud, as an opening bloom, and a full, open flower starting to shed its petals.

Drawing

The starting point is to place the flower heads: everything else will be arranged around these main focal points. I placed the three flower heads in a triangle shape at different levels to create a rhythm in the picture. I drew three circles with a compass and sketched the flowers within these circles. The foliage was drawn from life, from a bunch of anemones in front of me, allowing me to 'borrow' from several flowers in order to get the shapes that I wanted for my composition. I added a fallen petal from a fading flower, to give a sense of the cycle of life to the image, and placed it within the bottom-left of the composition, to balance out the strong, black centre of the flower on the right.

Materials list

PAPERS

Cartridge paper or sketchbook
Tracing paper
Transfer paper
Watercolour paper: Fabriano Artistico HP Extra White, 640gsm (300lb)

DRAWING

Pencils: 6B for initial sketch; 0.5mm with an HB lead to refine the drawing
Pair of compasses
Eraser

PAINTING

Brushes: Pro Arte Prolene Plus Series 007 in sizes 4 , 2, 1, 0 and 3/0; Princeton Neptune size 4
Daniel Smith Moonglow for tone study
Titanium White pigment stick (optional)

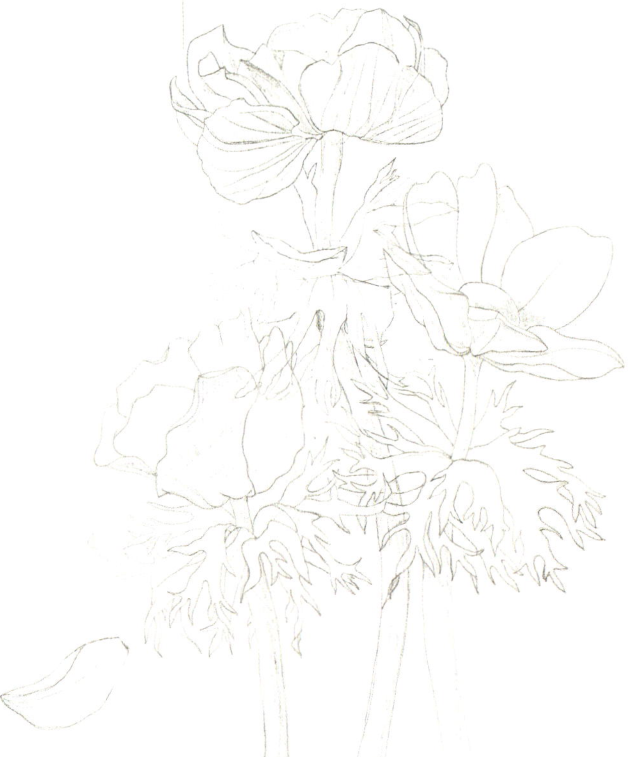

Once happy with the composition, it is time to trace the drawing and transfer it using transfer paper to the watercolour paper. Then put the watercolour aside for now and come back to the drawing for a tone study and for selecting the palette.

The quick tone study is a snapshot of the subject with the light coming from the top left of a west-facing window. Using Daniel Smith Moonglow and a large brush, I painted the tone quickly to make sure there would be no change of light while I was completing the study.

Palette

Hansa Yellow Light   Green-bias yellow – for the palest greens and the shadow colour.

Quinacridone Lilac   Red-bias violet (magenta) – to give a hint of purple to the petals and the stems, and for the shadow colour.

Phthalo Blue Red Shade   Mid-blue with a slight violet bias – the main colour of the petals, and for the shadow colour.

Phthalo Green Yellow Shade   Mid-green – as a base for all the green mixes.

Rich Green Gold   Muted yellow-bias green – for the stems, the veins on the leaves and some of the foliage.

Harmonic Shadows

Hansa Yellow Light + Quinacridone Lilac + Phthalo Blue Red Shade.

Green mixes

Phthalo Green Yellow Shade + Hansa Yellow Light (to lighten) **+ Quinacridone Lilac** (to mute) **+ Phthalo Blue Red Shade** (to darken) **+ Rich Green Gold** (to lighten and mute) in varying combinations and different proportions.

Blue-purple mixes

Quinacridone Lilac + Phthalo Blue Red Shade in varying proportions.

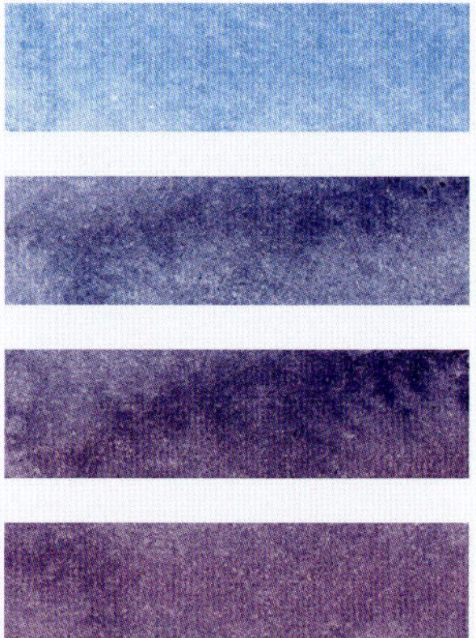

Shadows and underlayer

The drawing has been transferred to the watercolour paper and we are ready to start painting the shadow layer, followed by the underlayer of colour. The drawing is quite intricate, especially the foliage, but the washes are still painted wet-in-wet to keep them soft.

Step 1 To paint the shadows wet-in-wet, select an area covering a single petal or a strand of leaf and wet this area throughly. Drop the shadow mix onto the wet paper, covering the shadow sections, staying away from the mid-tones and, even more importantly, the highlights.

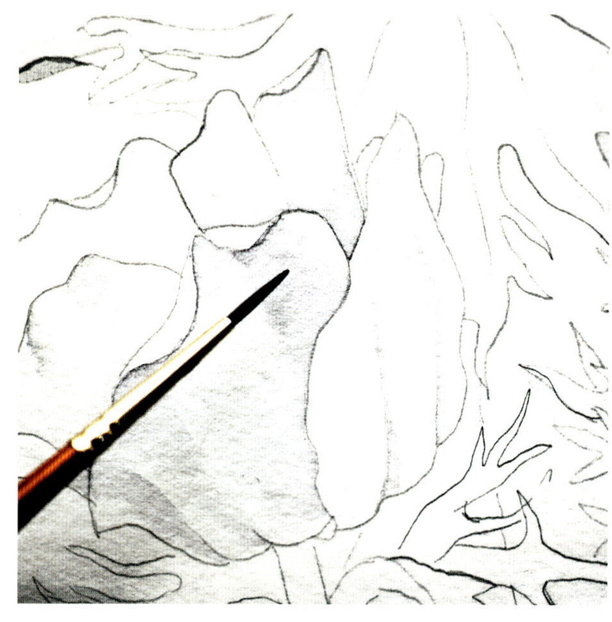

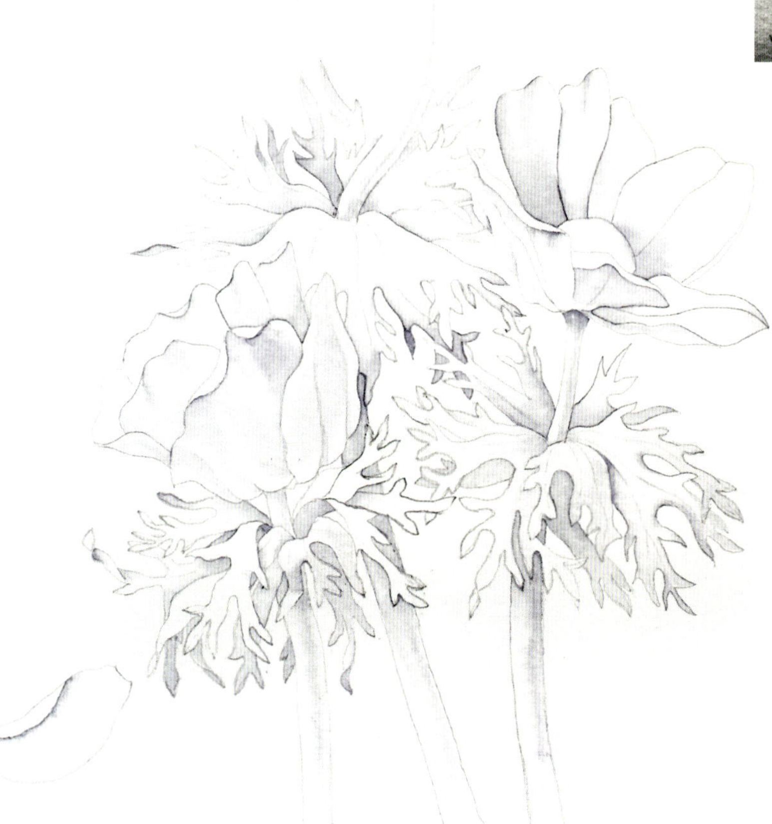

Step 2 The technique is the same whether you are working on a tiny foliage area, a larger petal or a narrow, long stem. The only difference is the size of the brush. A large brush carries a lot of paint, which will spread further. A tiny brush will carry just a small amount of paint, reducing the chance of flooding the wet paper too much. I used a range of brushes, from 0 for the smallest areas to 4 for the largest ones. The shadows are painted over the whole picture before we can start on the colour.

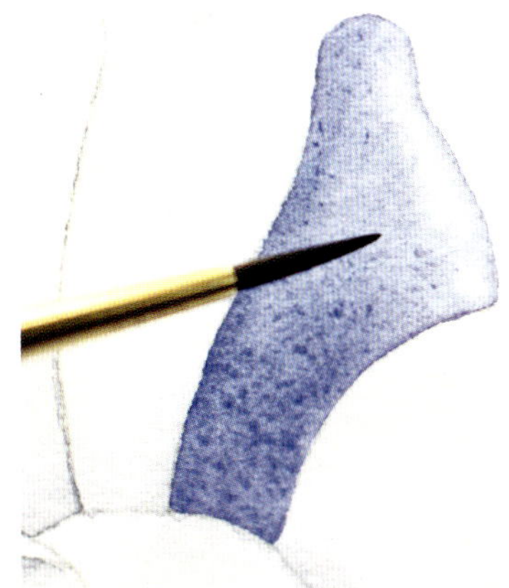

Step 3 The first wash on the petals is a mix of Phthalo Blue Red Shade with a touch of Quinacridone Lilac, to give a more pronounced violet bias to the blue.

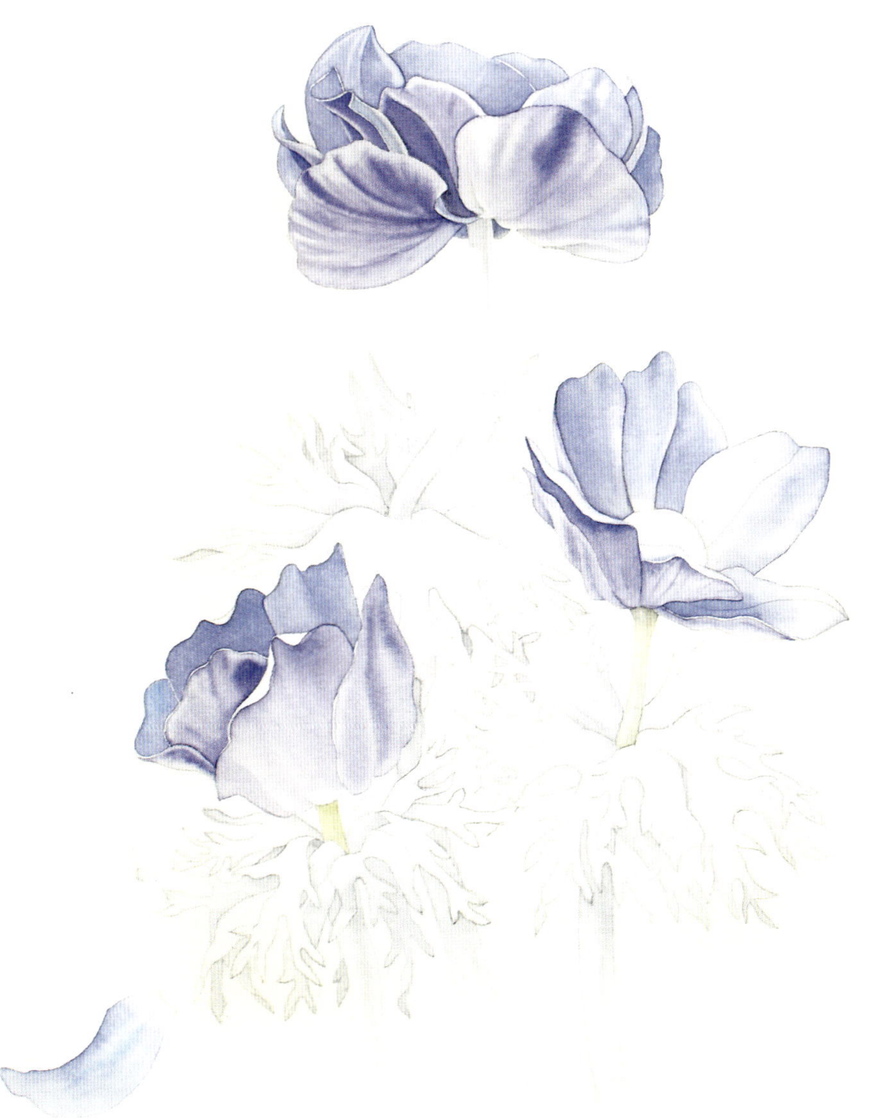

Step 4 The underlayer is painted over all the flowers before we move on to the foliage. The back of the petals is a bluer hue than their top side, which has a stronger violet bias. The same mix of Phthalo Blue Red Shade + Quinacridone Lilac is used for both, but in slightly different proportions.

Colour

There are many variations in the blues of an anemone. The vivid green foliage, itself comprising many hues, will help to bring out the blues while keeping them balanced. Work on the green foliage should start quite early in the painting process, to introduce that balance as soon as possible.

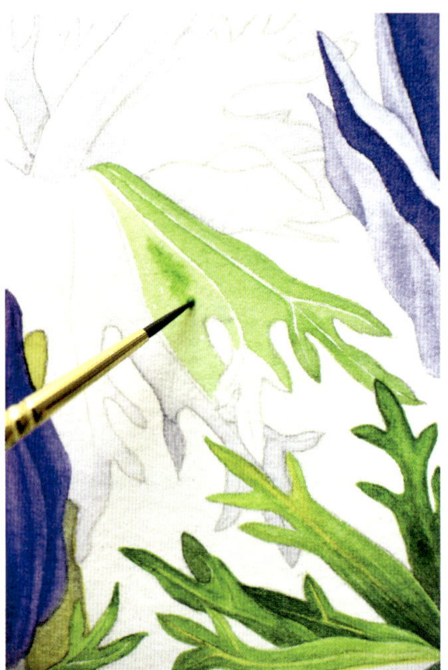

Step 1 The first layer on the foliage is painted wet-in-wet, working on one section at a time. An easy way to border a section is to work between the edge of a leaf and up to the central vein. The green mix is Phthalo Green Yellow Shade + Hansa Yellow Light. A touch of Quinacridone Lilac can be added if the mix feels too bright. It is important to wait until an area has dried before painting an adjacent section. A fine unpainted line is left between the two halves of the leaves, leaving space for the central veins.

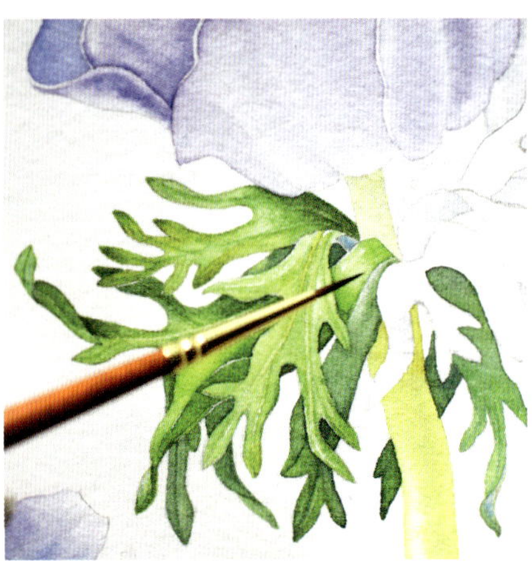

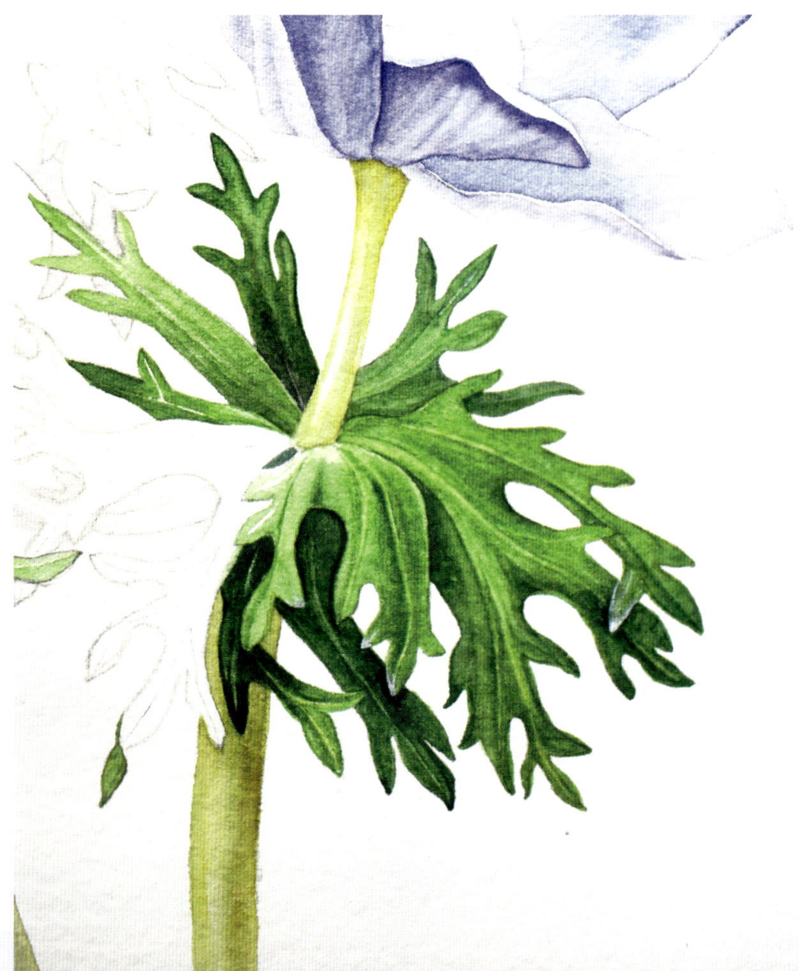

Step 2 Because the foliage is so intricate, it makes sense to work it to a further stage quite soon rather than painting single layers all over and then coming back to it later. Using a size 1 brush and working on the lacy leaves, you can move from wet-in-wet underwashes to damp washes on dry paper sooner than on the larger areas.

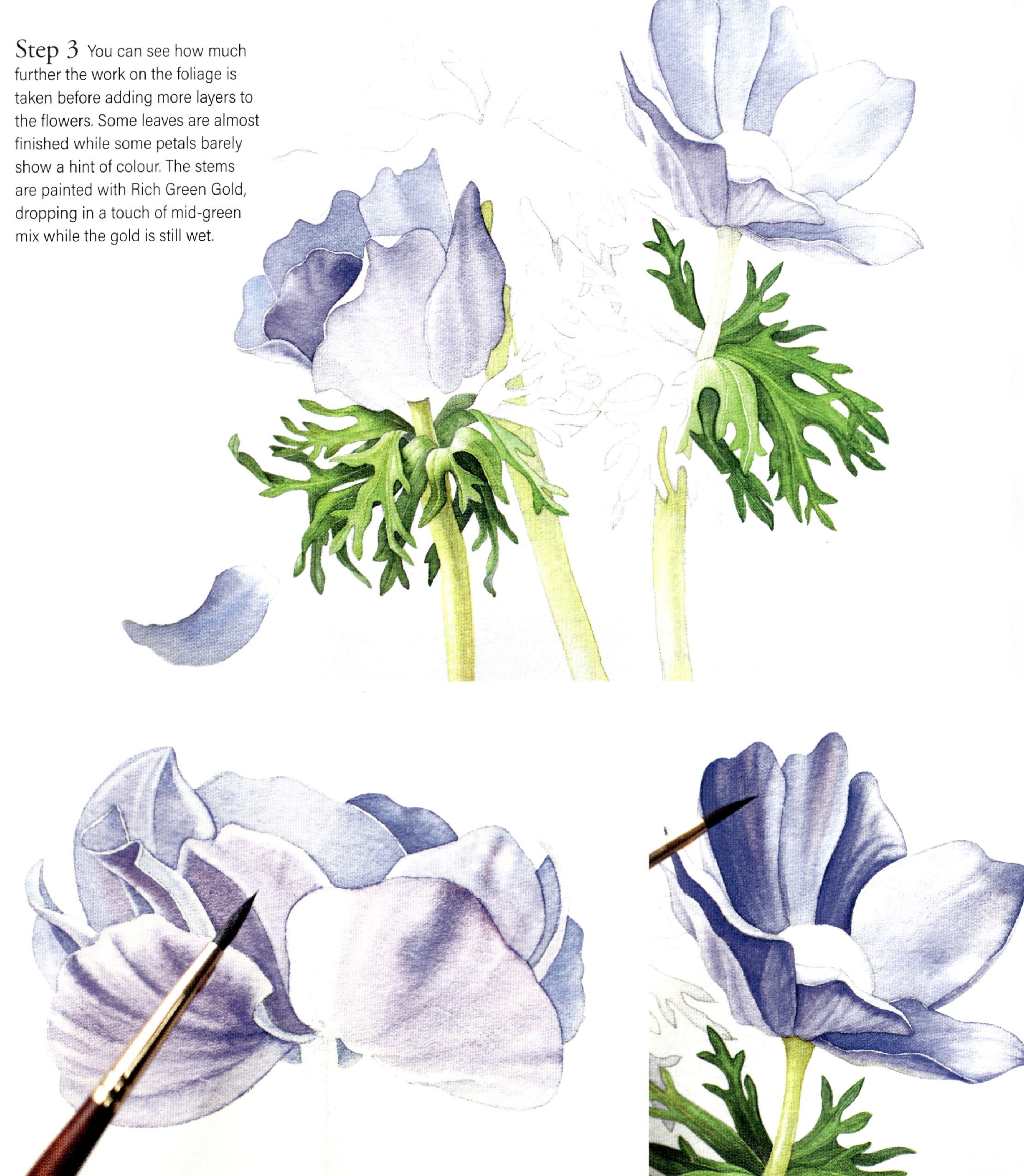

Step 3 You can see how much further the work on the foliage is taken before adding more layers to the flowers. Some leaves are almost finished while some petals barely show a hint of colour. The stems are painted with Rich Green Gold, dropping in a touch of mid-green mix while the gold is still wet.

Step 4 In order to introduce more natural variations in the colour, it is possible to introduce single-colour glazes in between washes of violet-bias blue. Here we have a thin glaze of pure Quinacridone Lilac. This process can be used throughout the painting whenever you feel the colour needs shifting towards violet or towards blue, or to give more depth of colour.

Step 5 A hint of texture and veining can be introduced into the wet-in-wet washes early into the process. This happens naturally as you brush the paint onto the wet surface following the texture of the petals.

Dry brush and finish

The wet-in-wet work is finished and the details can be sharpened up with some dry-brush work, including the busy, minute structure at the centre of the open flower.

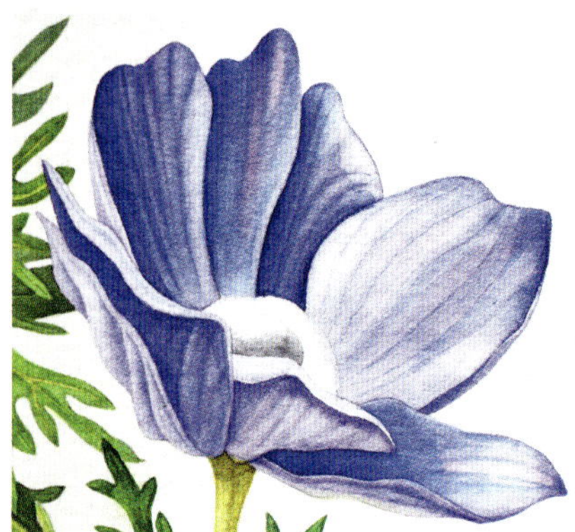

Step 1 The direction of the veins and their pattern is already faintly established with the wet-in-wet work, but more precision and definition are required. To sharpen these veins, paint them with a small 3/0 brush loaded with blue paint, running it gently along the veins and blending the paint straight away with a soft damp brush. The Princeton Neptune brush is good for this, as it is extremely soft and won't disturb the underlying washes.

Centre of open bloom

The centre might at first look complicated and feel a bit daunting. However, an important fact makes it easier to paint than it would at first seem: being near-black, the stamens are much darker than the petals sitting behind them. This means that they can be painted on top of the otherwise finished flower, without having to mask or paint around.

Step 2 Use a tiny 3/0 brush with a good spring (the Pro Arte Prolene Plus Series 007 is good for this), loaded with undiluted paint and painting on dry paper. Effectively, this is drawing with a brush in the same way you would a pencil. If you feel daunted, you can draw the stamens first with a faint pencil line to make sure they are in the right place.

Step 3 The centre mound is first painted with a wet-in-wet layer to place in the shadows, then with a wash of Hansa Yellow Light as an underlying colour.

Step 4 Some stamens partly disappear behind the mound, giving depth to the centre.

Step 5 The gaps are gradually filled with more stamens, including the filaments. A few minute highlights can be added with Titanium White, if necessary, to stand out against the darker blues.

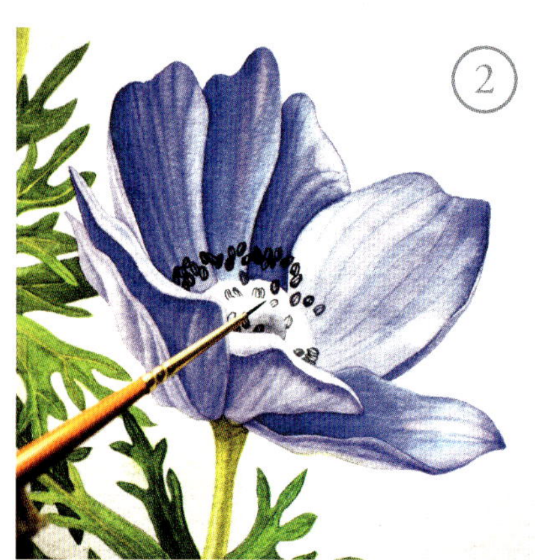
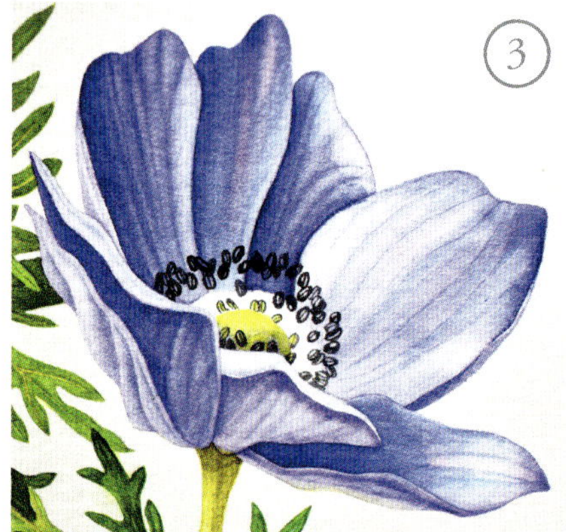
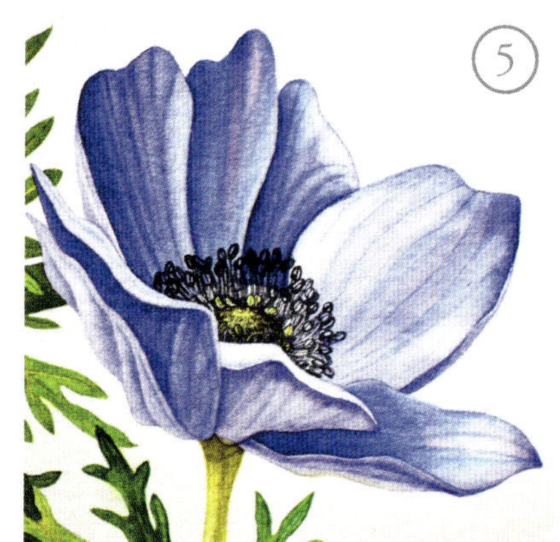

Anemone
Watercolour on paper.

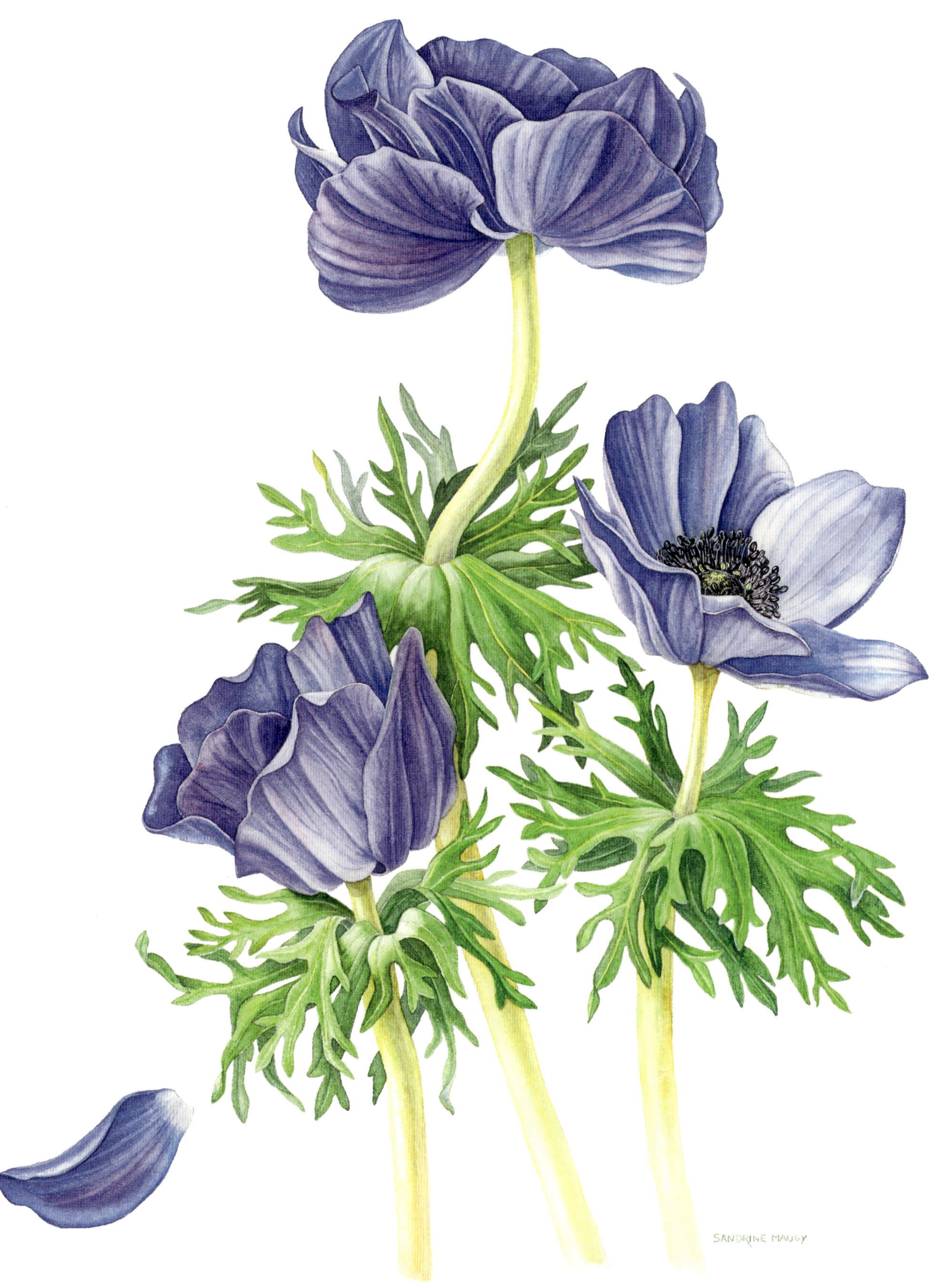

Anatomy of a
TULIP

Common name Tulip	**Flowering** March to May	**Hardiness** Fully hardy
Botanical name *Tulipa*	**Planting time** October to November	**Propagation** Division or seed
Group Bulbous perennial	**Aspect** Full sun	**Native** Southern Europe to Central Asia

Tulip section

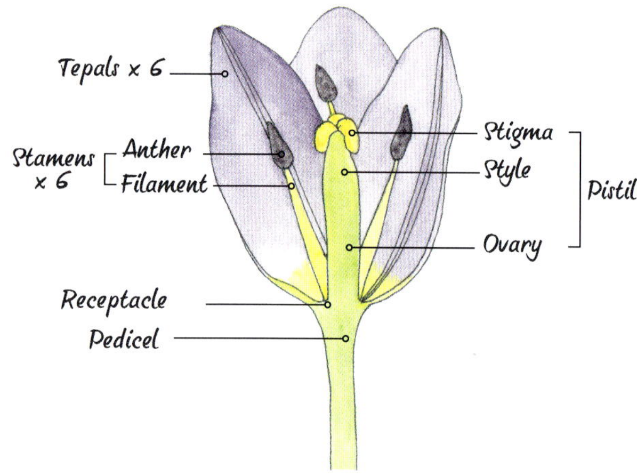

- The base of the tepal is usually a different colour from the rest: for example, yellow on a red tulip or white on a purple one. If the base is paler than the rest, it is wise to paint it first so that it doesn't get lost in the deeper colour.

- The veining pattern on the tepals is unusual: there is one central vein running from base to tip, then a few veins parallel to the central one on either side, then side veins curving from the central veins to the margins.

- The veining pattern on the leaves is parallel, meaning that all the veins run from the base to the tip of the leaf, covering the whole width, with no side veins.

Botanically speaking…

- Tulip petals are too thick and waxy to qualify as petals but they are too colourful and close to the gynoecium (female parts) to be sepals. They are somewhere in between and are called tepals.

- Tulips have a very characteristic texture to their tepals: whatever the colour or shape of the flower, the tepals are built for resistance to potential harsh late frosts and strong winds rather than for delicacy.

- The original varieties have six tepals (three petals and three sepals) but after centuries of breeding hybrids, the number of petals can be anything… When your subject has up to a dozen tepals it is important to draw the right number but for more than that, mistakes are less noticeable.

- When there are six tepals, three are on the inside (the petals) and three are on the outside (the sepals that look like petals), arranged in an alternate pattern. The inner tepals are usually more delicate in texture than the outer ones. The tips are also different.

- The pistil is centred and the style is usually quite thick.

- The stigma at the top of the style is split in three parts.

- There are six stamens arranged around the pistil, but hybrid varieties with more tepals might also have more stamens.

- The anthers are basifixed (attached by their base).

- Tulips have one flower per stem, although some varieties (for example, *Tulipa turkestanica*) can carry several flowers on a single stem – this is uncommon.

Studies of *Tulipa* 'Ballerina'

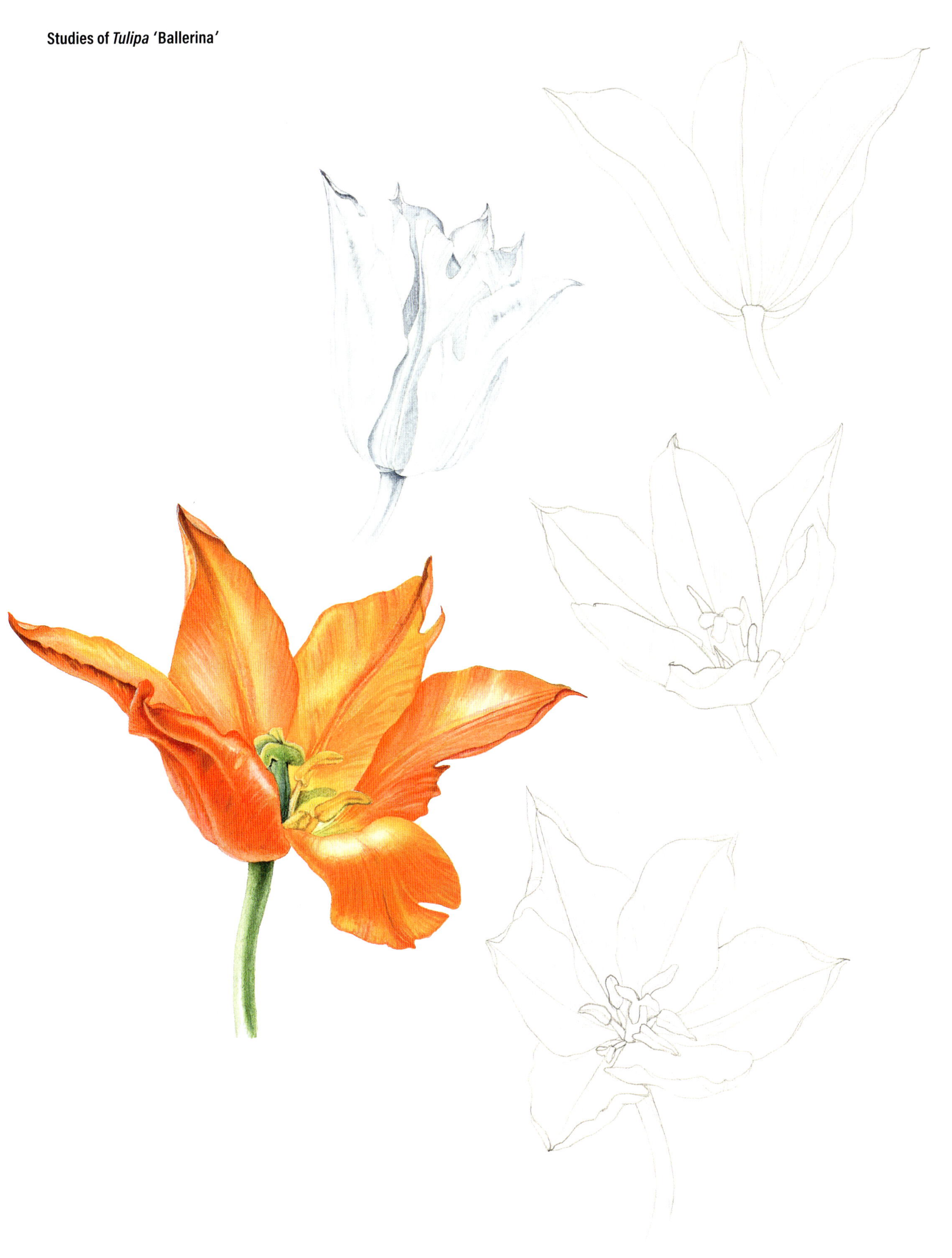

TULIP 'QUEEN OF NIGHT'
Palette and first washes

Of all the tulips that appear regularly in my garden, 'Queen of Night' is definitely queen of the borders. With her deep, almost black petals, she appeals to my Gothic side. She likes to share her bed by the front porch with a 'Black Parrot' and a 'Ballerina' for a touch of complementary colour. Swaying together in the breeze or shining their waxy petals in the full sun, they look stunning under the wisteria.

Palette

Hansa Yellow Light   Green-bias pale yellow – for the centre of the tulip and the stem.

Quinacridone Lilac   Magenta – the petals show a lot of magenta in the lighter parts.

Perylene Violet   Deep violet – the main colour of the flower is almost black with some deep purple hues.

Phthalo Blue Red Shade   Mid- to violet-bias blue with a smooth texture.

Harmonic Shadows

The Harmonic Shadow mix for a black flower needs to be strong and dark enough to show through the subsequent layers of dark paint. However, because the petals are glossy, it is better to use non-granulating pigments, as granulating pigments would give some unwanted texture. For my shadow mix, I used **Perylene Violet + Phthalo Blue Red Shade + Hansa Yellow Light**.

The dark colour that will be used for most of the tulip is a neutral, deep purple mix of **Perylene Violet** with **Phthalo Blue**.

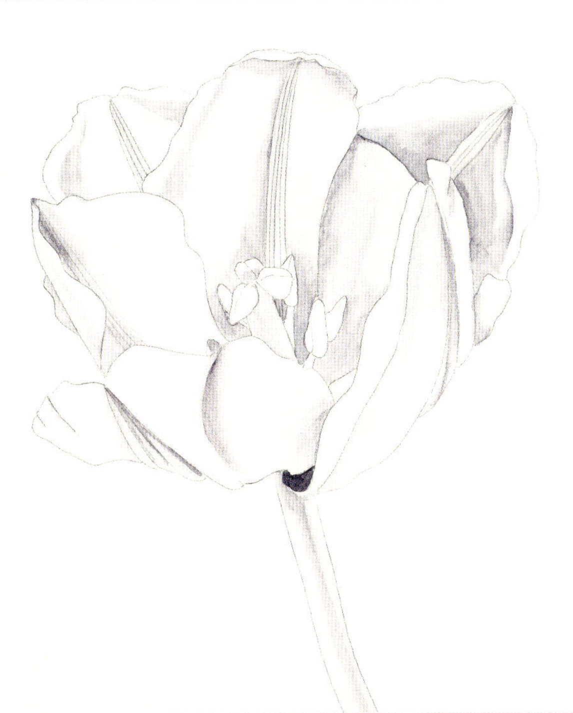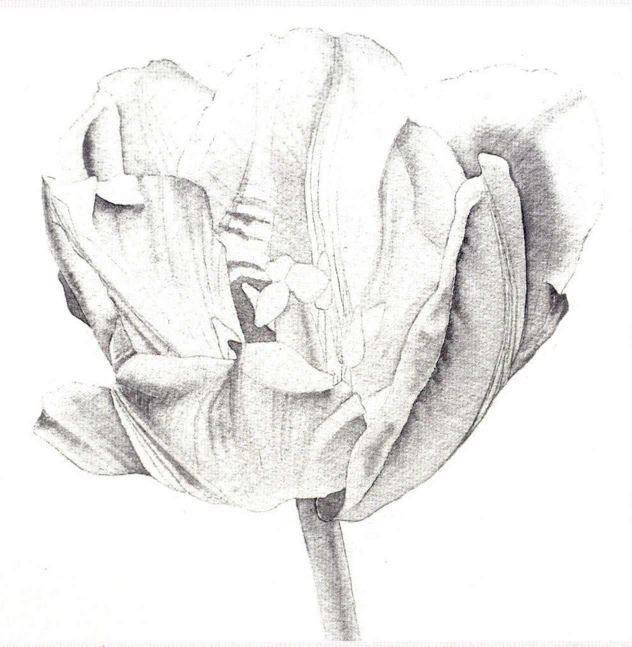

Step 1 Start by sketching the tulip in your sketchbook or on a piece of cartridge paper, marking the veins as well as the outlines of the petals. Veins are visible and give texture to the tulip petals, so it is important to get them right. Trace the drawing and transfer to the watercolour paper. You can then go back to the sketch for a quick tone study. Daniel Smith Moonglow is a good colour to use for this.

Step 2 Once the line drawing is transferred to the watercolour paper, paint the shadows wet-in-wet, brushing following the pattern created by the veining, along the straight central veins and the curved side ones. You need to keep some shine on those petals, so make sure you mark the strong highlights on the sketch and reserve them carefully.

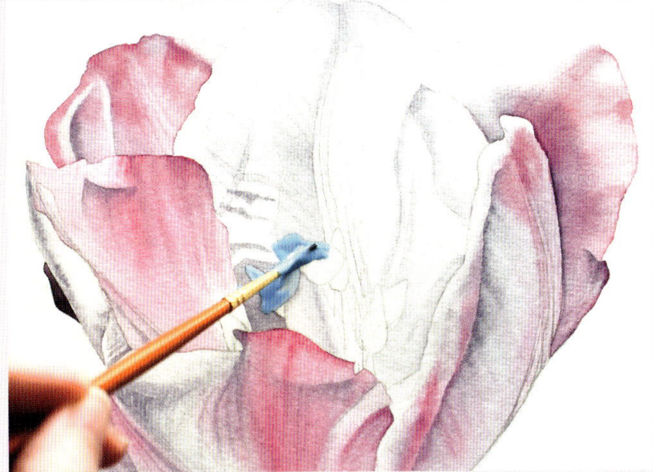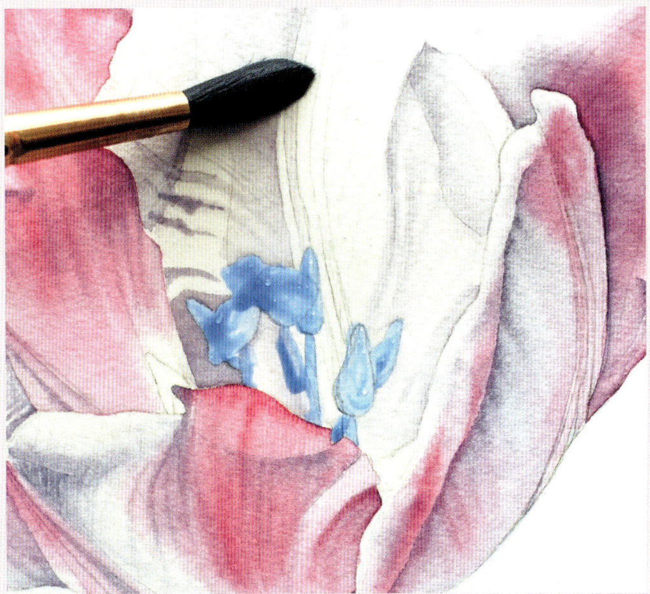

Step 3 The first colour to go down after the shadows is the magenta, or Quinacridone Lilac. This bright colour will shine through the subsequent dark layers of paint, giving light and life to the painting and stopping the dark mix looking flat. Before painting the back petals, mask the pistil with masking fluid to make sure that the area stays clean, ready for the pale yellow.

Step 4 Now that the masking fluid is protecting the pale centre, you can bring out the big brush to paint wet-in-wet washes more loosely and quickly. This is a size 12 soft synthetic brush that carries a lot of water and paint. Continue to add the magenta colour until every petal has an underlayer.

More wet-in-wet work

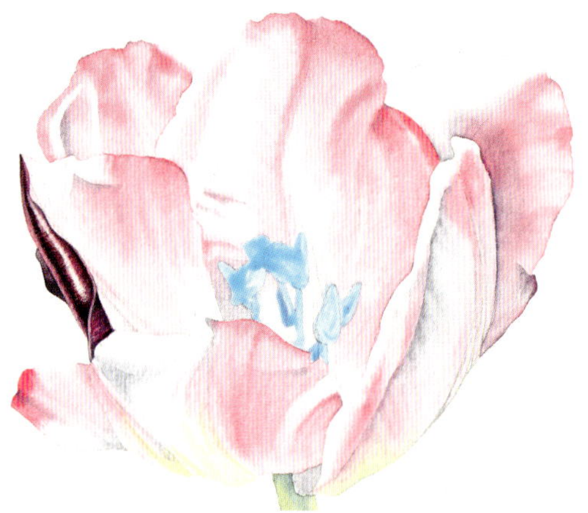

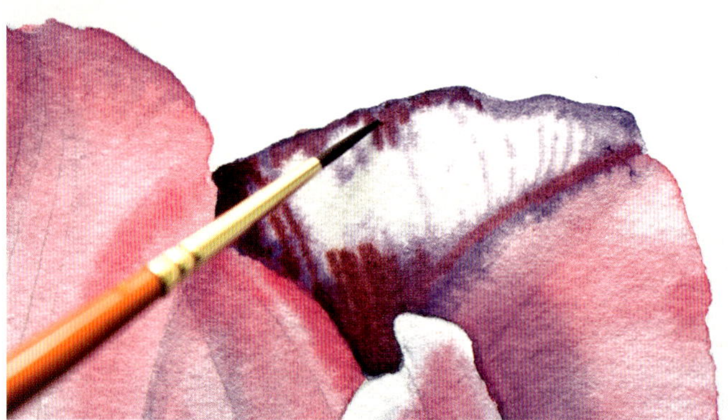

Step 1 I chose the small tepal on the left to test my dark purple mix. At the same time I made sure that my chosen method for creating the highlights gave the result I wanted: working wet-in-wet, painting with a strong colour and leaving a slice of wet but unpainted paper.

Step 2 When you are satisfied with the highlight and colour, it is time to work with the same technique on a larger scale, starting with the tepals at the back. Use a large brush to apply water and a small brush to drop in the colour so that it doesn't spread too far. First add the purple mix, then Perylene Violet while the purple mix is still wet.

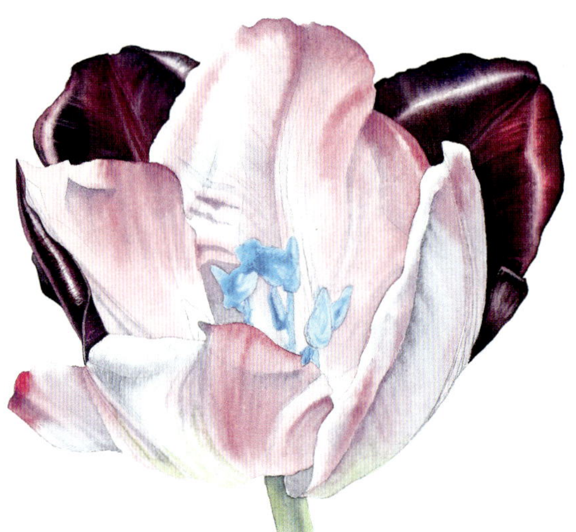

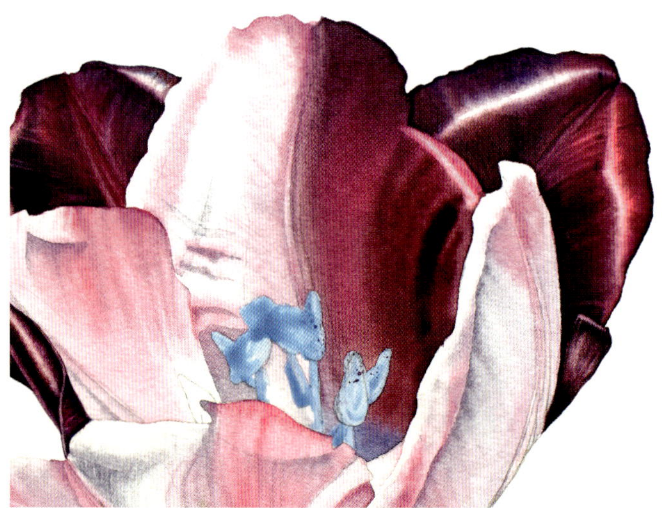

Step 3 Usually I would paint the same number of washes on all the tepals, working in a balanced way through the painting. Because the colour of the tulip is so dark, the layering of multiple washes of dark paint is likely to encroach on the petals in front. In order to minimize the amount of paint lifting to tidy this up, I decided to almost finish the back tepals before starting on the other ones.

Step 4 Still working from back to front, the next tepal is the middle one. If you have a large tepal in your flower, paint it in two parts, using the central veins as a separation. This will give you more time to work the wet-in-wet washes before the paint starts to dry. The first wash on the right half is more magenta with some Perylene Violet and some of the deep purple mix in the darkest parts, all dropped in while the paper is still wet.

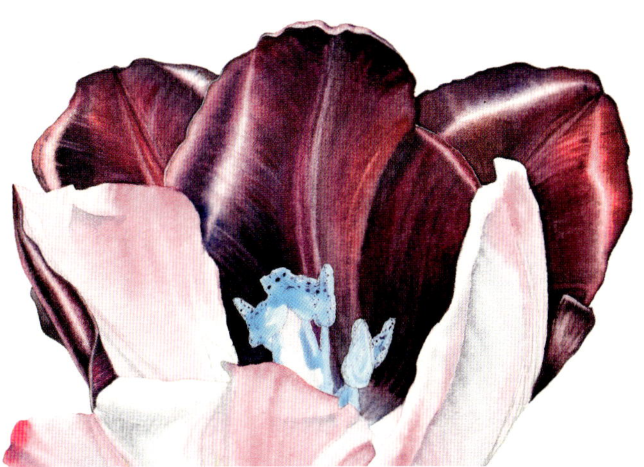

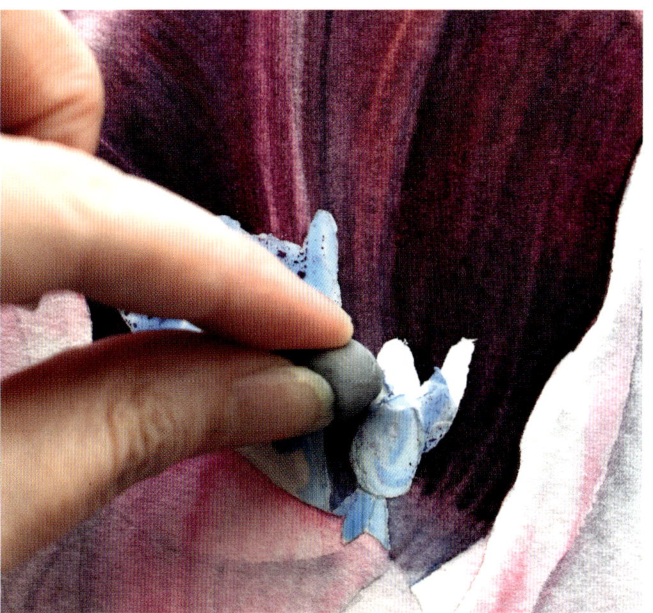

Step 5 The left half is darker towards the bottom. To get the darkness while keeping some intensity, wet the paper (including the highlight) then drop in some pure Phthalo Blue in the darkest areas and some magenta in the lightest. Leave this wash to dry, re-wet the paper and add the purple mix with some extra Perylene Violet added. Make sure you reserve the strong highlights all along the tepals.

Step 6 The tepals behind the masked area won't require any more wet-in-wet work. If they need more details or if more darkening is required, it will be with a dry brush. More wet-in-wet work now would risk lifting the previous washes. So, it is time to remove the masking fluid. Using a putty eraser to gently lift the fluid is a good way to do so without damaging the paper.

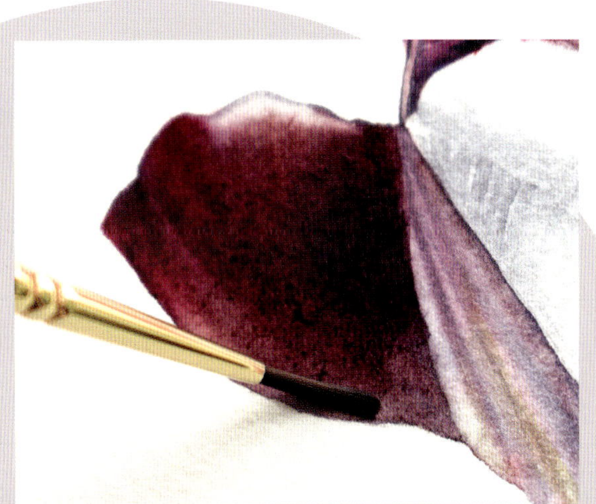

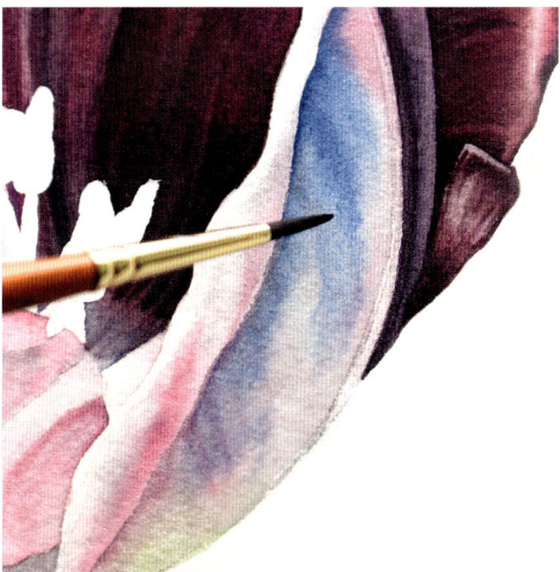

Tip

Make sure that the veins match on either side of the reserved highlights. To achieve this, paint each vein in one sweep, lifting the brush as it goes across the highlight.

Step 7 The reflected light at the bottom of the tepals does not require reserving the highlights in the same way as the main light does. This is because reflected light is never as bright as direct light. Lifting the paint while the wash is still wet is sufficient.

A wet-in-wet wash of pure blue under the main colour allows you to get a dark wash without losing intensity.

Damp and dry-brush work

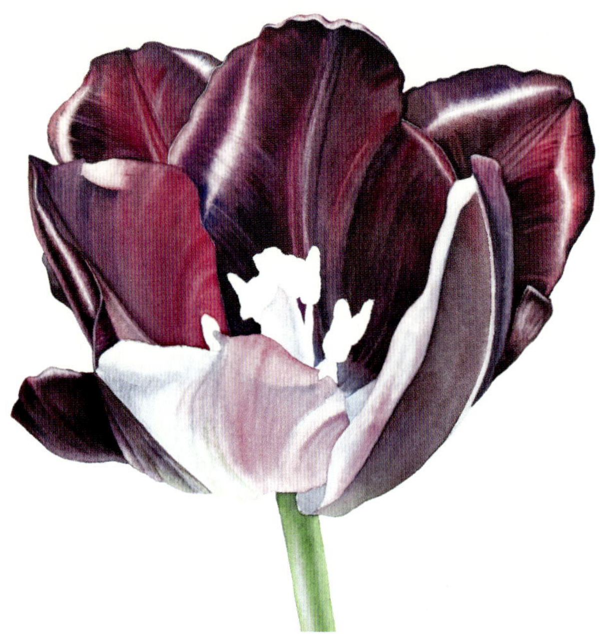

At this stage, wet-in-wet washes are finished on the three back tepals, the masking fluid is gone and the centre is ready to be painted; the tepal on the right has three washes on top of the shadows, the stem has two wet-in-wet washes of a green mixed from the yellow and the blue used in the shadows, and the petal at the front is finished on the left but has only one wash of colour on its right side.

Painting the centre

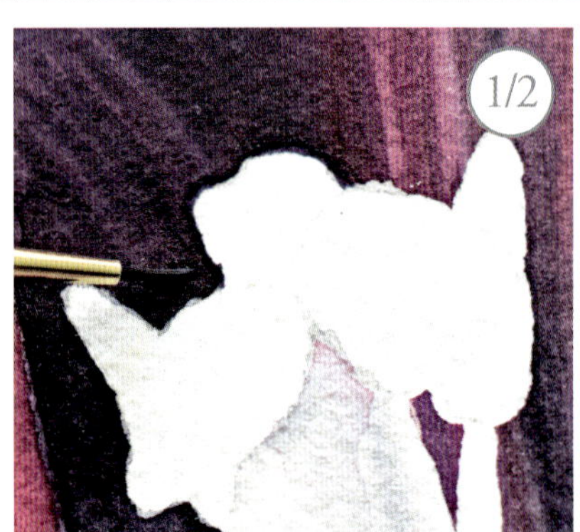

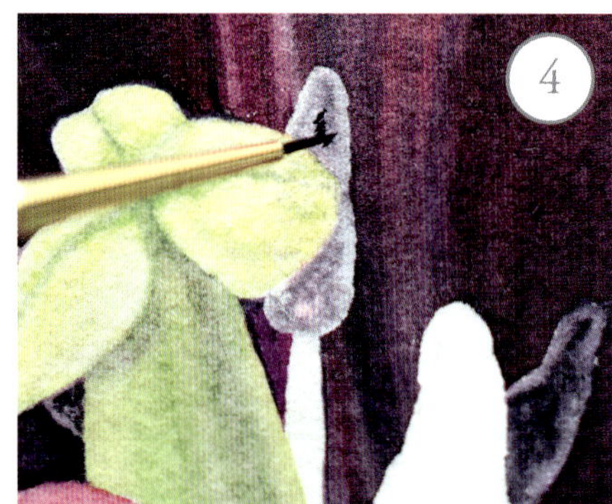

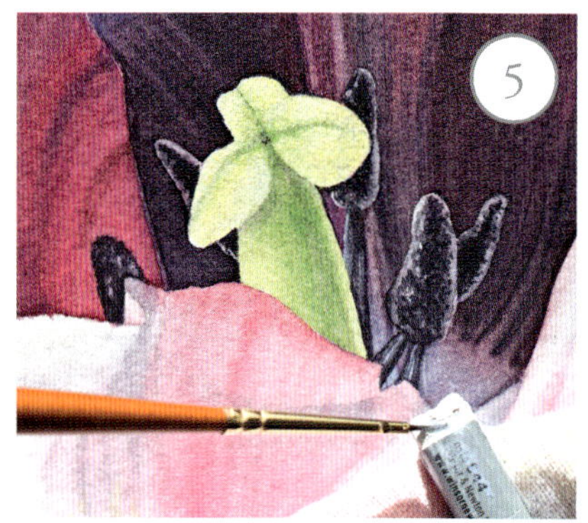

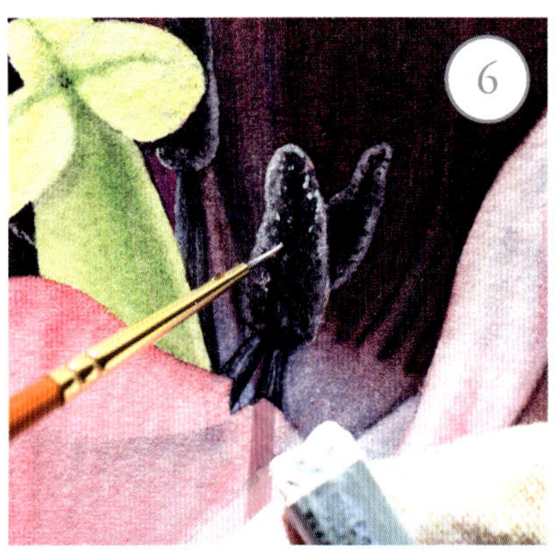

Step 1 Wash in the shadow mix wet-in-wet with a size 2 brush.

Step 2 Tidy up the edges where the masking fluid has left an uneven edge. Use the same colour directly behind any edge that needs help.

Step 3 Paint the pistil with a diluted wash of yellow, dropping in a little bit of green along the style.

Step 4 Start adding some black to the stamen, using the undiluted shadow mix. Add a touch of Magenta to the anthers and a bit of blue to the filaments.

Step 5 Rub a 3/0 brush on the white pigment stick.

Step 6 Stipple some white onto the black anthers to create the powdery effect of the pollen.

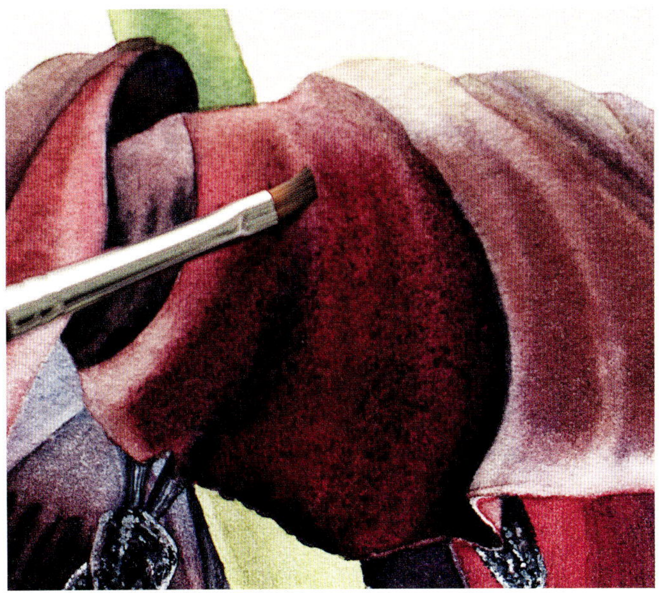

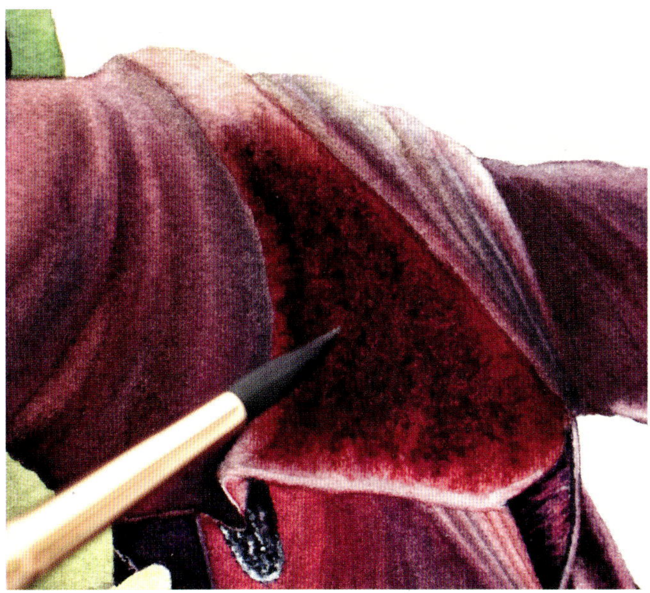

Step 7 The left half of the most central front tepal is darker towards the bottom. To get the darkness while keeping some intensity, wet the paper (including the highlight) then drop in some pure Phthalo Blue in the darkest areas and some Quinacridone Lilac in the lightest. Leave this wash to dry, re-wet the paper and add the purple mix with some extra Perylene Violet added. Make sure you reserve the strong highlights all along.

Step 8 This is the last wet-in-wet wash, so make it count. Drop in a lot of colour to boost up the intensity. Here, I started with the Quinacridone Lilac and dropped in some Perylene Violet while it was still wet.

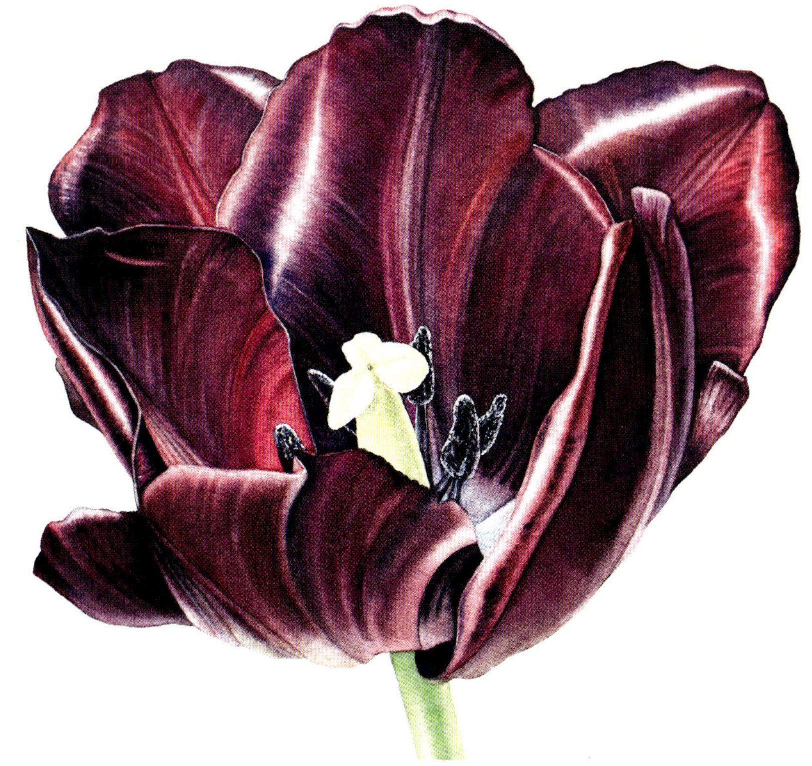

Now all the wet-in-wet washes are done. There is a point where trying to layer more wet-in-wet work will start lifting the previous washes rather than adding more colour, especially with dark subjects, which have potentially thicker washes than pale ones. If adding more water to the paper for the next wet-in-wet wash starts lifting paint, it is time to move on to some dry-brush work.

Last details

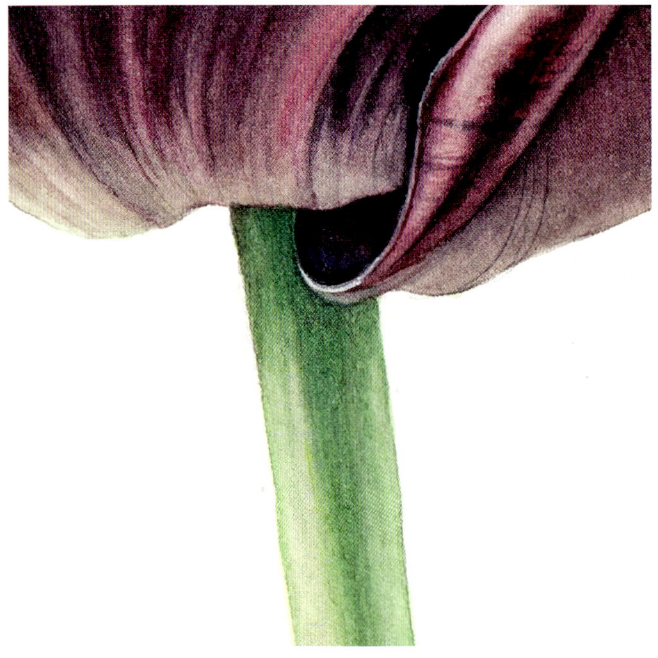

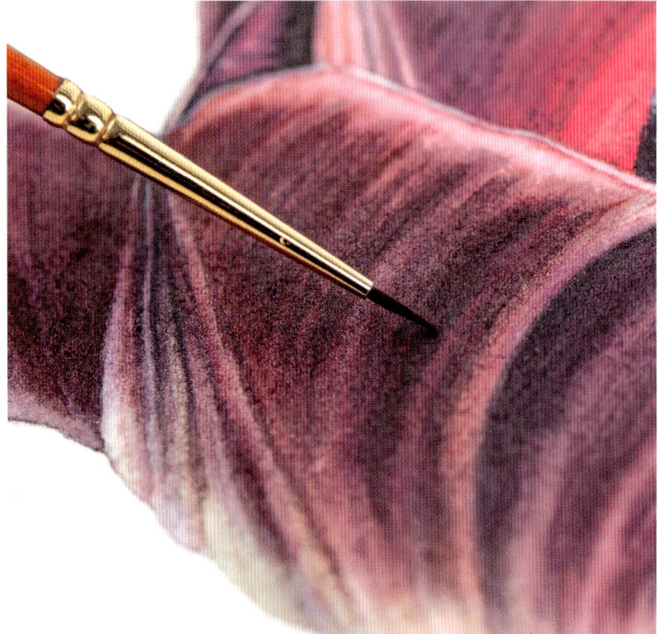

Step 1 Time to add a bit more colour to the stem. Wet the whole stem and drop in some green under the tulip and down along the shadows. The green is mixed from the blue and yellow used in the Harmonic Shadow colour. Reserve a highlight down along the stem to give the rounded shape.

Step 2 Last details such as veins are painted on dry paper, with a 3/0 brush. A larger brush is loaded with clean water. First draw a few veins with the small brush. then, before they dry, brush along with the larger brush gently so that it doesn't lift the paint and doesn't erase the veins. Painting the veins without blending them in results in the veins looking like a series of lines drawn onto the tepal rather than integrated into the texture.

Finishing touches

- Check that the edges on the white paper are neat. You can tidy them up with a tiny brush loaded with a strong mix matching the colour of the area you are touching up.

- Check that the overlapping edges are clear and visible. You can lift the overlapping edges with a flat brush to make them lighter. If they become too wide, it is possible to narrow them down by adding some dry-brush work behind them (on the underneath petal) or up to them (on the front petal).

- Check that the stamens stand out. If they merge too much into the petals, use the white pigment stick to add a few highlights or grains of pollen.

- Is there enough reflected light under the tulip tepals? Unlike direct highlights, reflected light can be lifted so it can still be added at this late stage.

- If you feel brave, you can add a glaze of green on the reflected light. This will illustrate the green stem and foliage below reflecting in the petals.

- If you need to darken areas further, you can add a wet-in-wet wash. You can always add a few veins afterwards with a dry brush.

Opposite, Tulip 'Queen of Night'
Watercolour on paper.

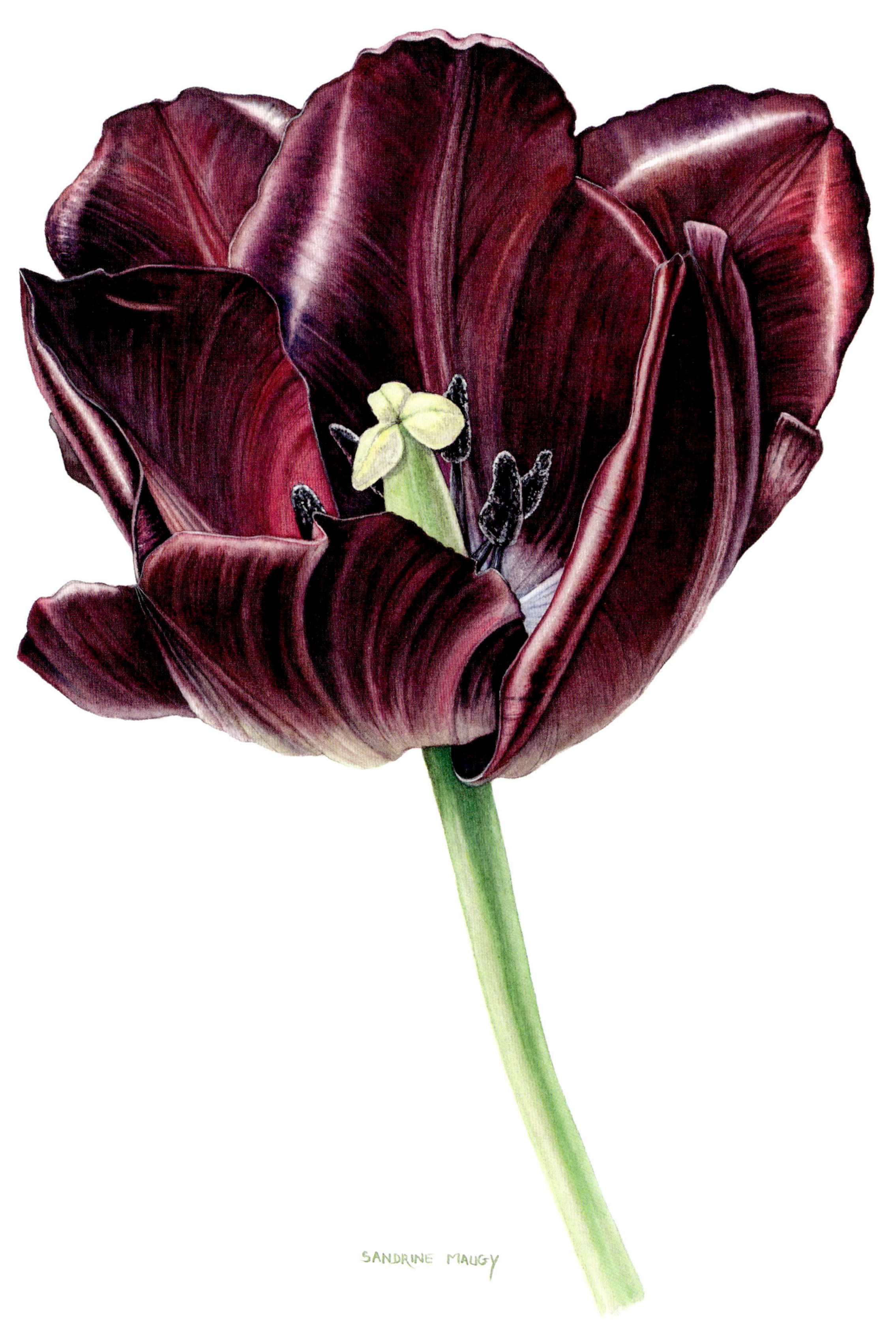

SANDRINE MAUGY

Summer

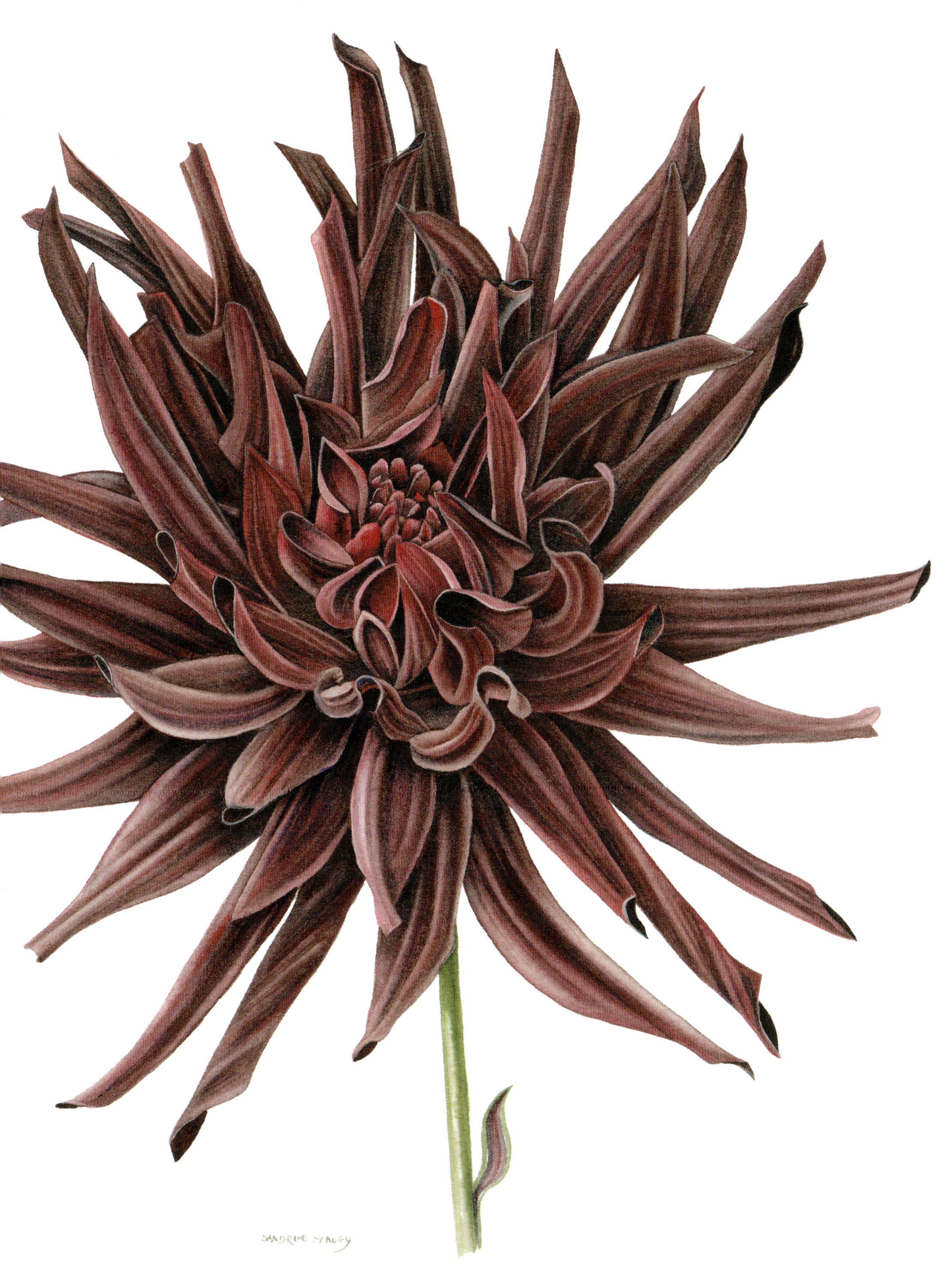

SANDRINE MAUGY

SUMMER SUBJECTS
and their palette

As the days have become longer and warmer, the garden has come to life again and is now in full swing. Between the weeding of the rose borders and the detangling of rampant passionflowers, let's explore the characteristics of the Summer garden.

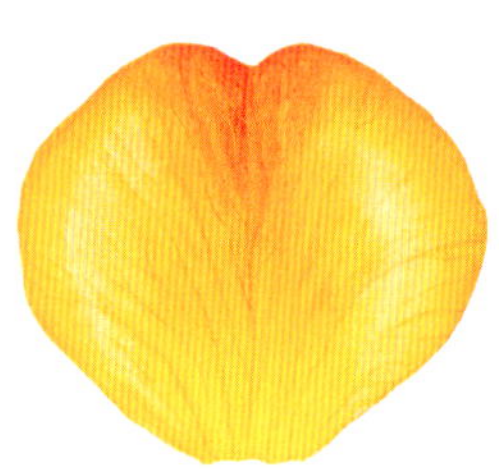

Texture

Frosts are a forgotten memory and plants can now grow in the safety of warmer nights. The thick, waxy texture of the fleshy leaves, striped with parallel veining, gives way to thinner consistencies and lightweight flowers. Petals as delicate as crumpled silk make their appearance. Without the risk of freezing storms to take them down, stems are getting longer as the blooms reach for the nourishing sun.

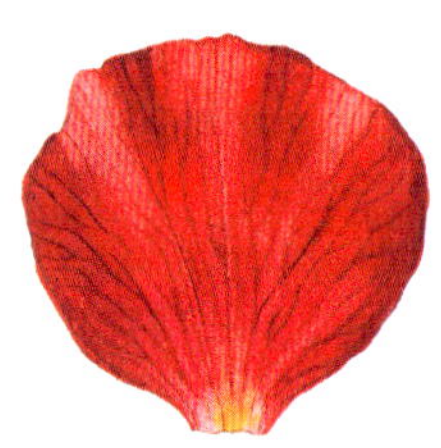

The rose border

Roses are the pride of many a Summer garden. They are easy to grow and, with such an array of varieties, there is a colour for everyone. Their foliage is usually thick and glossy, with an anastomosing veining pattern, which means that the veins loop back at the top to join the next vein up the leaf. This is a specific pattern that is seen in a lot of foliage in the Summer garden.

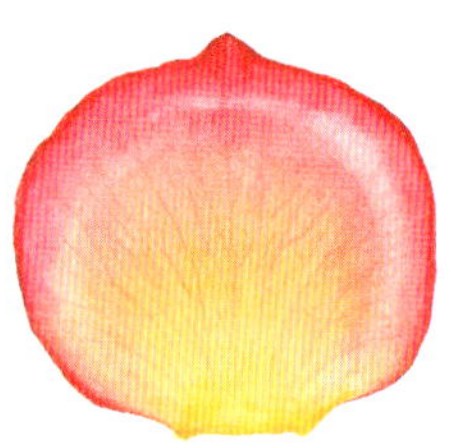

Heat protection

A mechanism developed by some plants to withstand the heat is to use their petals or leaves to store water, thus displaying a leathery appearance. Calla lilies or the wild arum have a spathe made of a single bract that retains moisture. Hollyhocks have a similar texture and can flaunt their huge flowers in a south-exposed border without flinching. Pelargoniums use their leaves to the same effect.

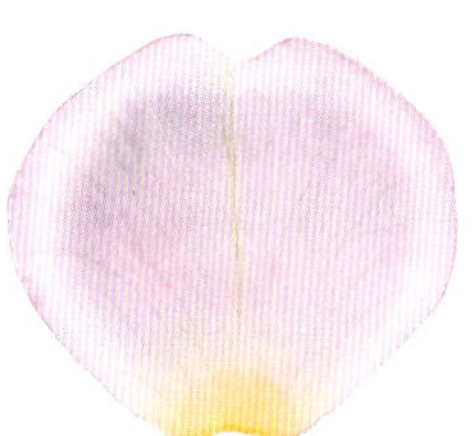

Stillness in the Summer garden

It is rare to find stillness in our busy lives. Sunday afternoon on a sizzling day in the Summer garden is one of those moments when we can revel in it. Crushed by the weight of the hot air in an almost comfortable deckchair, everything seems immobile. Even the butterflies have given up their erratic flight and rest on a sunny leaf, marooned by the lack of lifting currents. The sky is a deep blue, light hurts the eyes, nothing happens. If we are blessed and it lasts long enough, we can even afford the rare luxury of getting bored... a moment to treasure in the Summer garden.

Palette

Other colours appear in the three tutorials, but if you would like a basic palette from which to mix all your colours, the list below is a good starting point for Summer subjects.

Hansa Yellow Light   Green-bias yellow – a luminous yellow for glowing petals and fresh greens.
Subjects: Sunflowers and pale yellow roses.

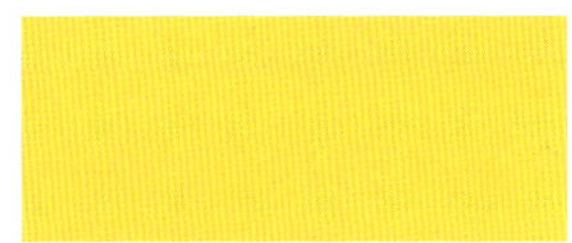

Quinophthalone Yellow   Mid-yellow – deeper yellow for mixing saturated orange hues as well as natural-looking greens.
Subjects: Sunflowers and juicy buttercups.

Pyrrol Red   Mid-red – for the strongest red petals.
Subjects: Velvety roses and delicate poppies.

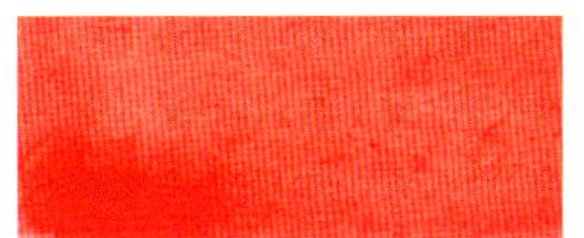

Quinacridone Coral   Coral pink – anything from pale peach to deep coral.
Subjects: Sweet peas, roses, pelargoniums and *Impatiens*.

Quinacridone Pink   True pink – anything from pale pink to cerise.
Subjects: Cheeky roses, fuchsia and heart-warming hydrangeas.

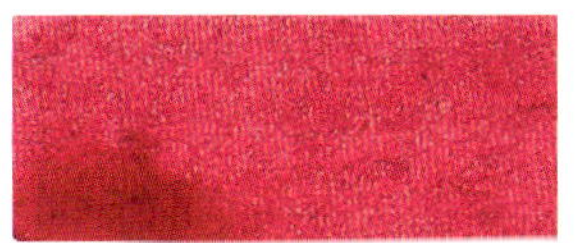

Quinacridone Lilac   Violet-bias red – when pink goes blue and turns into violet.
Subjects: Geranium, lavender, lupins, scabious and purple hydrangeas.

Perylene Violet   Maroon dark violet – for deep purples and maroon shades.
Subjects: Dahlias, mysterious roses and maroon sunflowers.

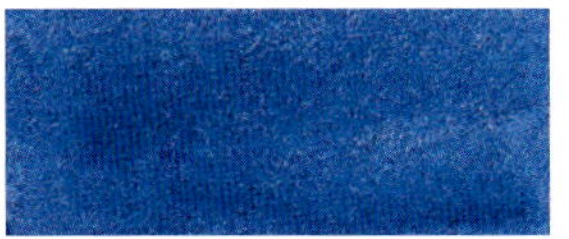

Phthalo Blue Red Shade   Mid-to-violet-bias blue – for delicate blue flowers and some bluer foliage.
Subjects: Delphinium, lavender, *Salvia* and passionflowers.

Phthalo Green Yellow Shade   Bright pure green – to be used as a base for fresh greenery.
Subjects: Any foliage.

Anatomy of a
SWEET PEA

Common name Sweet pea	**Flowering** Summer	**Hardiness** Hardy annual
Botanical name *Lathyrus odoratus*	**Sowing time** Autumn or Spring	**Propagation** Seed
Family Fabaceae	**Aspect** Full sun	**Native** Sicily and southern Italy

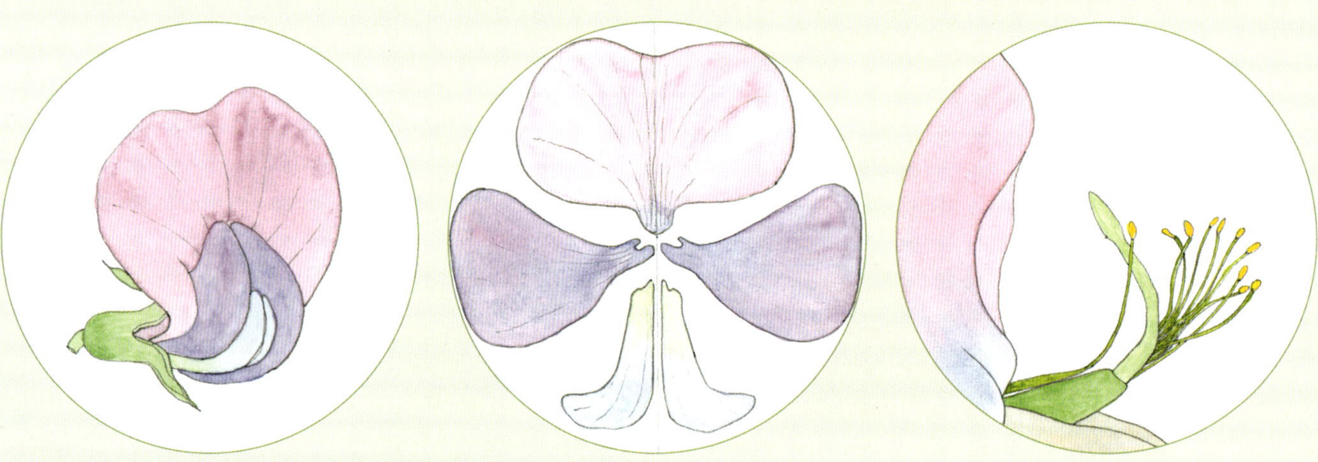

Botanically speaking…

- The sweet pea is a climbing plant and needs a support structure to grow well.

- It is an annual plant, meaning that it will only flower for one year and then die.

- Seeds can be gathered and planted for next year's crops.

- The flower is zygomatic, meaning that it is symmetrical along a vertical line.

- There are five petals – one top petal called 'standard', 'banner' or 'vexillum', two side petals called 'wings' (or 'ala') and two bottom petals called 'keels' (or 'carinae').

- The base of the petals can be a different colour from the rest: for example, ivory on a pink petal or greeny white on a purple one. If the base is paler than the rest, it is wise to paint it first so that it doesn't get lost in the deeper colour.

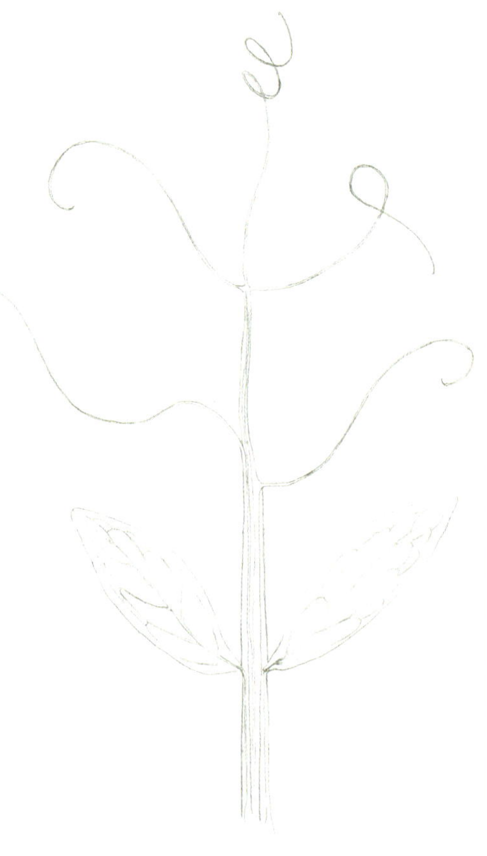

Sweet pea studies
Graphite, monochrome watercolour
and full-colour watercolour.

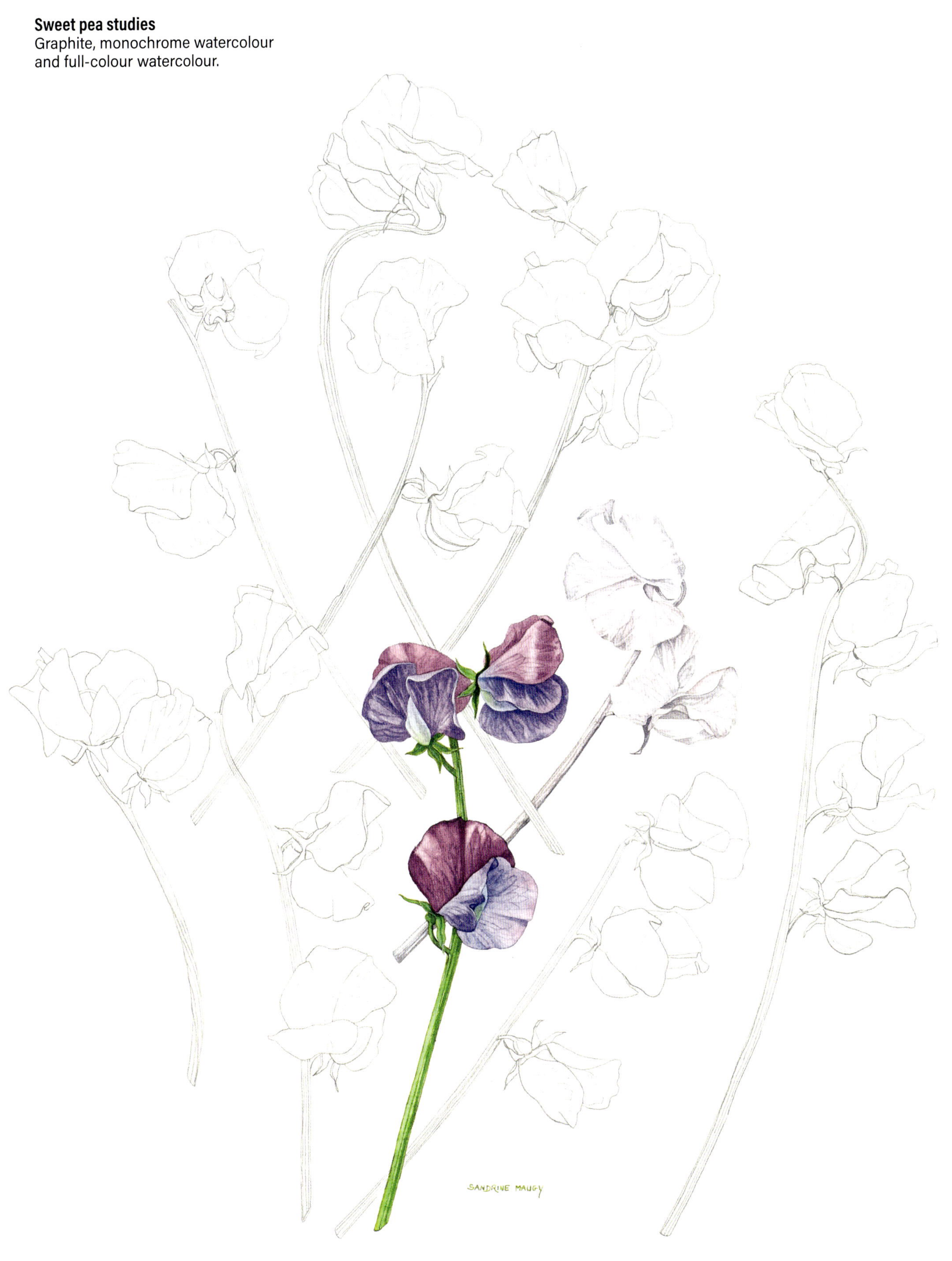

SANDRINE MAUGY

Level 1

SWEET PEAS
Drawing

Sweet peas are some of the most fragrant, delicate, pretty, sweet flowers of Summer. They are also, supposedly, easy to grow. I've never had much luck with them. When young, they get pecked by birds and the survivors get a bit yellow in the leaf, or they get mildew. My crop is never spectacular. Fortunately, I have friends who know how to talk to their sweet peas and I always manage to scrounge a few for a painting.

Step 1 Some flowers are easy to draw but difficult to paint, and vice versa. Sweet peas can be tricky to draw, especially the frilly kind. Once the drawing is right, the painting is not as difficult. This means that the drawing is crucial to get a good painting. The flowers need to be distinguished from the start. With this subject, I started by drawing some rough outlines, trying to see the overall shapes and ignoring the details. Once I had the outlines, I went back in with a harder pencil and filled in the details, folds and frills.

Step 2 When you have multiple flowers on the same stem, the likelihood of all of them being in the optimal position for a good composition is close to non-existent. At this stage I decided how many stems I wished to draw and roughly how many blooms. I sketched about twice this amount, drawing them exactly as they were rather than as I would have liked them to be. This would give me more options later.

Step 3 I now had many flowers to choose from, so I could start working on the composition. I thought that the top of the stems looked better, because they had more movement compared to the stiffer lower parts. I therefore focused on the tops.

To start the composition, I drew the stems, which would become the backbone of the painting. Then I could place the blooms, spreading them harmoniously and always checking the negative spaces. For future reference, I numbered the blooms I picked from the initial sketch. 9R means bloom number nine reversed.

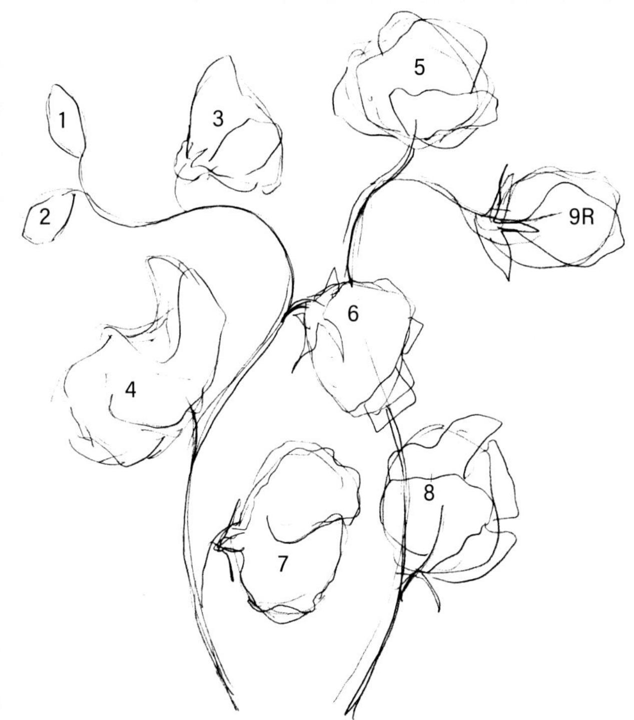

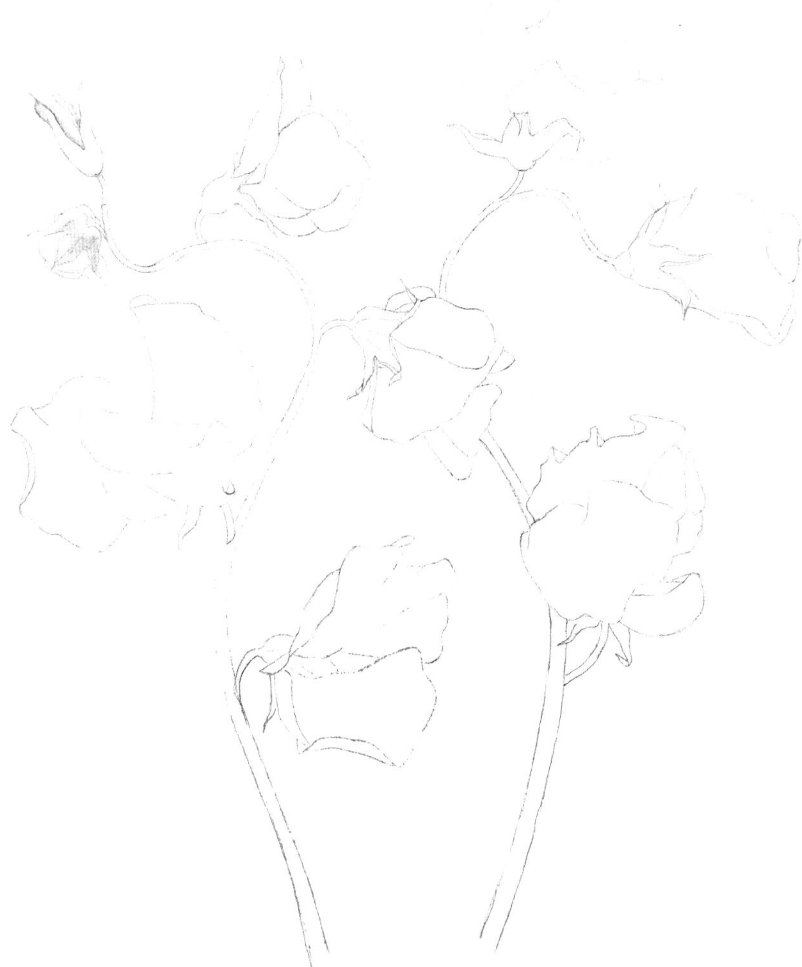

Step 4 Once I had selected the nine winning flowers, I traced them individually and placed them along the two stems, nudging the heads to the left or right, or tilting them if necessary. This was possible because the flowers could be facing any direction. Moving them up and down the stems is not as flexible, as the distance between each stalk must be respected.

With the tracings and some transfer paper, the drawing is transferred to the watercolour paper.

Palette and shadows

I had two different varieties of sweet peas to draw my inspiration from and I couldn't choose between the two, so I decided to include one of each colour in my composition. The lighter one is called 'Rosy Frills' and is a soft pink with a hint of coral, the petals' edges being lined with darker hues. The darker sweet pea is called 'Parfum Coral', and is a stronger pink with a more saturated coral deepening the colour.

Palette

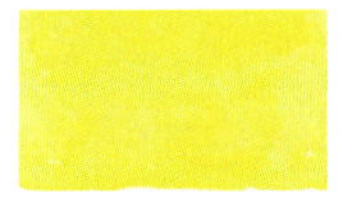

Hansa Yellow Light   Green-bias yellow that fades to ivory when highly diluted. If your brand stays too yellow, add a touch of Quinacridone Lilac to tone it down.

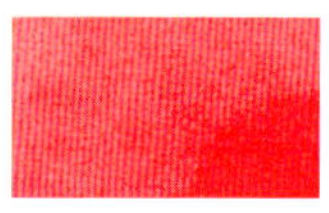

Quinacridone Pink   This pink is the base colour for both varieties and is included in the first colour wash.

Quinacridone Coral   This coral pink is the colour that links the two varieties.

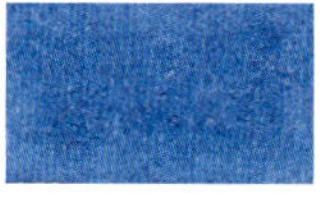

Phthalo Blue Red Shade   A violet-bias blue that doesn't granulate. It darkens the greens and is also used in the Harmonic Shadow mix.

Quinacridone Lilac   Magenta pink, for the darkest sweet pea.

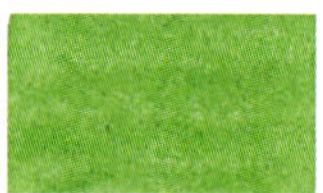

Phthalo Green Yellow Shade   The base colour for the green parts.

Sweet pea mixes

Soft pink mix: Quinacridone Pink + Phthalo Green Yellow Shade   This mix is softer than pure Quinacridone Pink and is perfect for the paler sweet pea.

Dark green mix: Phthalo Green Yellow Shade + Phthalo Blue Red Shade.

Harmonic Shadow mix: Phthalo Blue Red Shade + Quinacridone Pink + Hansa Yellow Light.

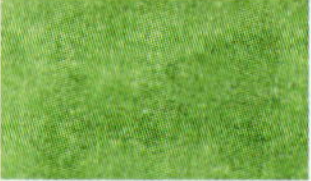

Sweet pea shadow mix

Hansa Yellow Light, Quinacridone Pink and **Phthalo Blue Red Shade** are mixed together to make the grey shadow colour, at three different dilutions, creating three different strengths.

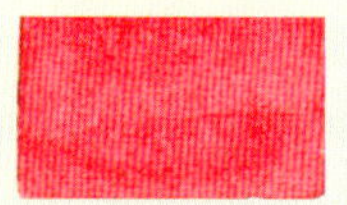

As the flowers change from bud to open bloom and then from young bloom to fading flower, the colours change quite dramatically. This means that each flower along the stems will be painted with slightly different mixes of various colours. As much as possible, I am trying to use the same pigments for both varieties, to make sure that the arrangement looks harmonious.

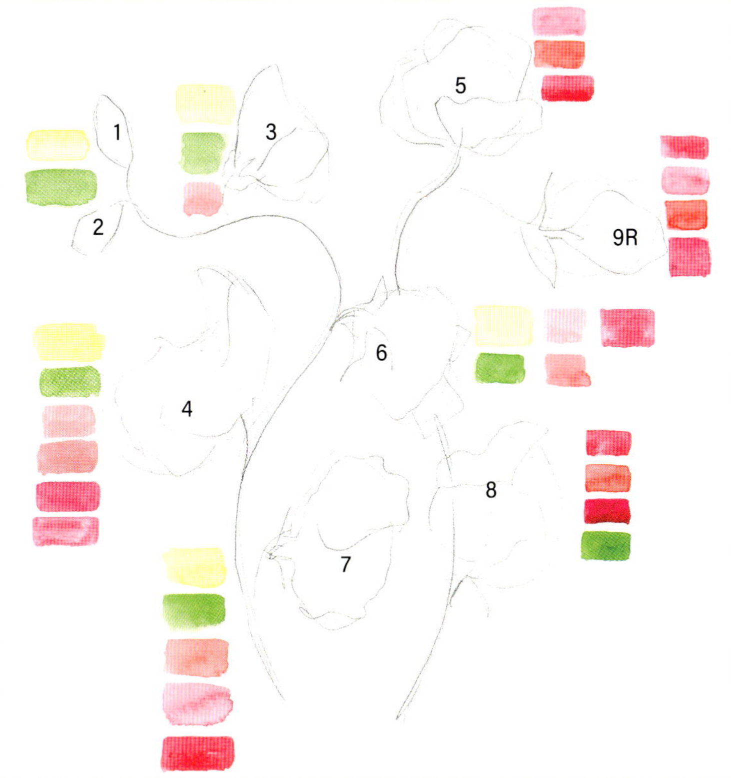

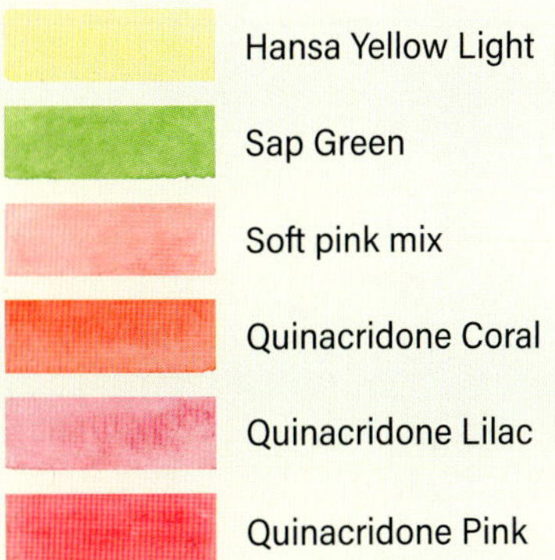

Tone

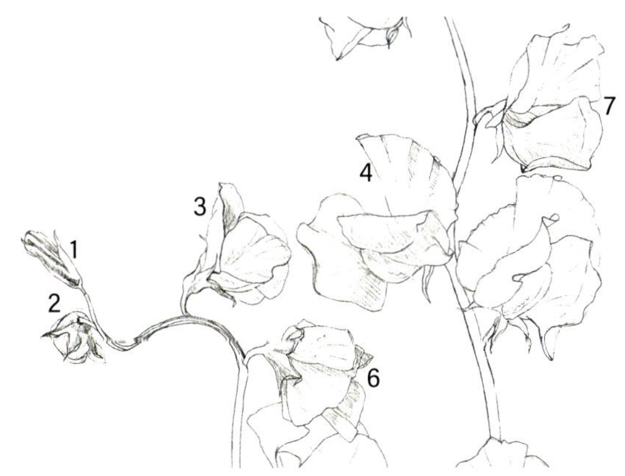

Step 1 The next step was to do a quick tone study on the flowers that I selected for the final composition. The light source is from the top left, with emphasis on the sweet peas' characteristic folds.

Step 2 It is now time to move to the watercolour paper. After transferring the drawing to a piece of Fabriano Artistico HP Extra White, 640gsm (300lb), I used the Harmonic Shadow mix to paint the shadows in, following the tone study I drew on the cartridge paper.

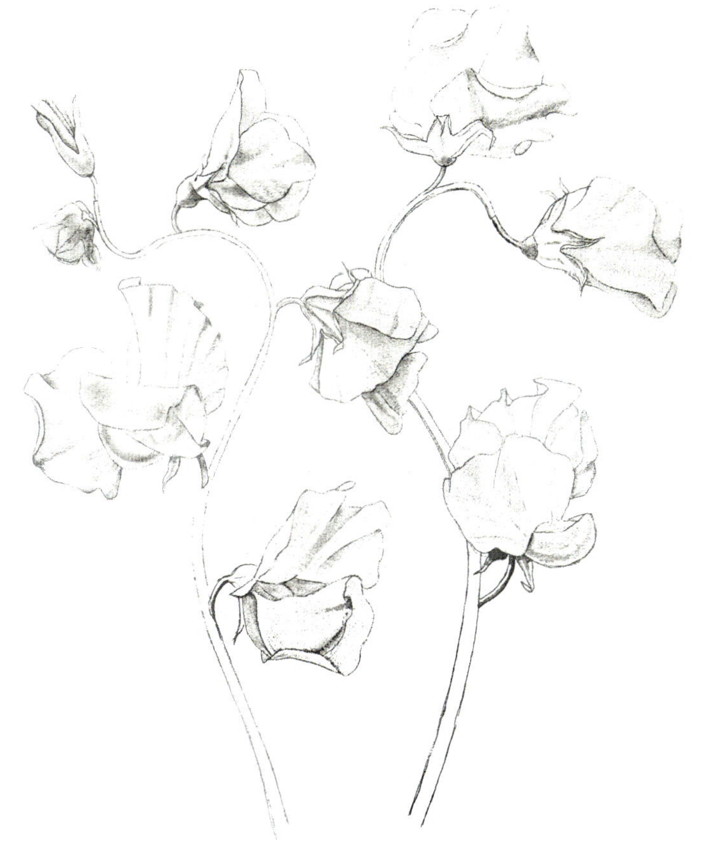

Soft pink

As the buds on the soft-pink stem were less open, painting them had to be the priority. I knew I didn't have much time before they would unfold and change colour. Therefore, I started with the top three blooms of the soft-pink stem.

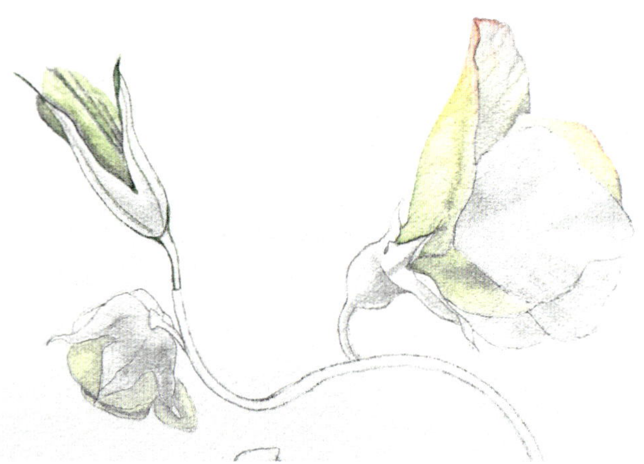

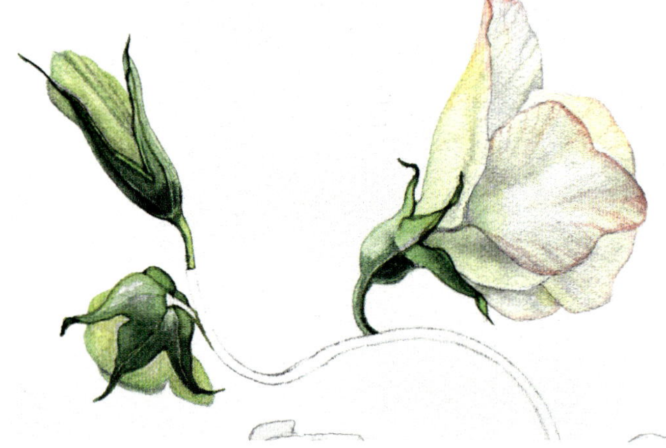

Step 1 The unopened buds are a yellowy shade of ivory, getting greener towards the base of the petals and appearing greener over the shadows too. The unfurling petals are the same ivory colour, for which I used a pale wash of Hansa Yellow Light. The green is more localized at the very base of the petals. The outer edges are painted wet-in-wet, running a 3/0 brush loaded with the soft-pink mix on the edge, letting it bleed into the pale yellow. This creates a crisp line on the outside while being soft on the inside.

Step 2 The sepals and receptacles are painted using two different greens: in the light, I used a watery wash of Phthalo Green Yellow Shade; in the mid-tones, the same Phthalo Green Yellow Shade, less watery; in the shadows, I used the dark green mix, which is the same Phthalo Green Yellow Shade mixed with Phthalo Blue Red Shade.

I continued to paint the petals on flower number 3, with the pale Hansa Yellow Light and soft-pink mix.

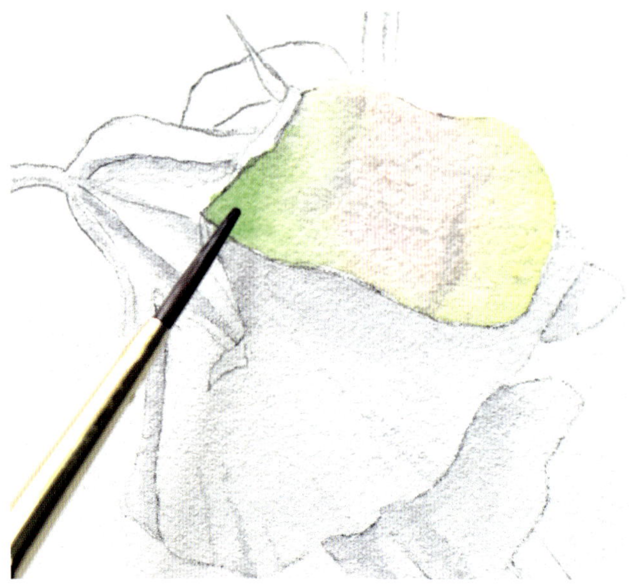

Dropping several colours into the same wet-in-wet wash ensures a seamless transition of colours. After thoroughly wetting the paper, I dropped in some ivory at the top, some of the soft-pink mix in the middle and base and finally I added some pure Phthalo Green Yellow Shade under the sepals.

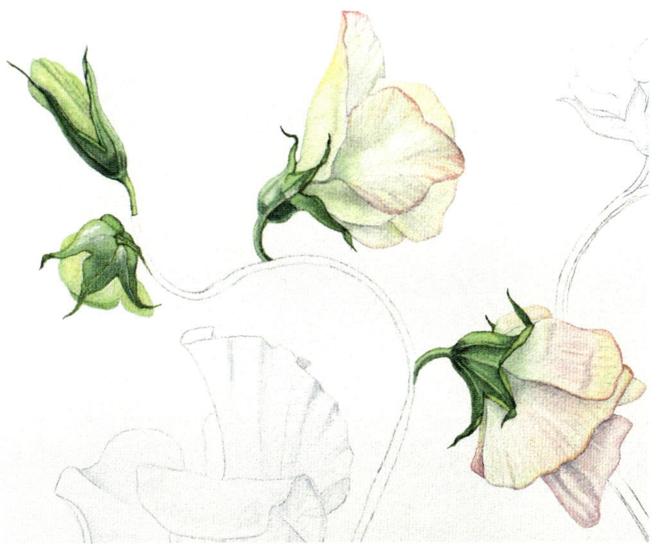

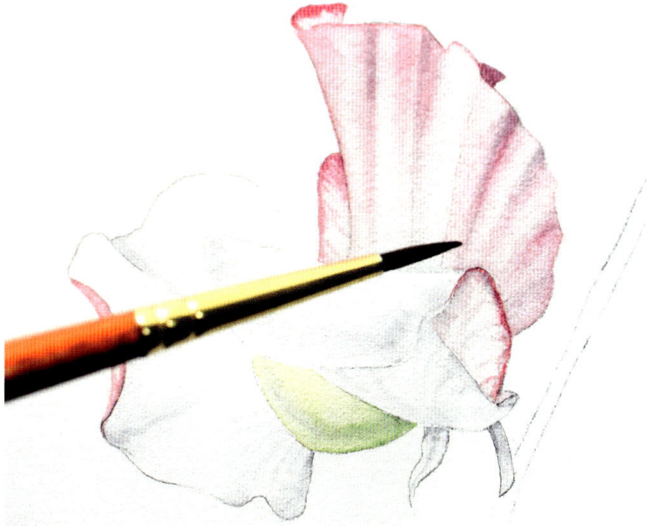

Step 3 I continued going round the petals of my top pale flowers, making sure the petals I was working on were not touching any other petals that wouldn't have had the chance to dry. As I worked down the stem, the flowers started to have stronger pink edges. I first used the soft-pink mix and added paint to the edges while each petal was still wet. If this wasn't strong enough, I went back with a dry brush loaded with Quinacridone Pink, blending the inner edge of the line into the petal with a damp brush.

Step 4 The folds are already clearly defined by the shadows. The colour layer is only reinforcing what is already there. After wetting the petal, I dropped in some of the soft-pink mix towards the edge, bringing in the colour towards the base, following the veining direction. In order to show some light as well as some shadows, I was careful to reserve my highlights, not adding any pink to the high parts of the folds. I also added a touch of ivory towards the base.

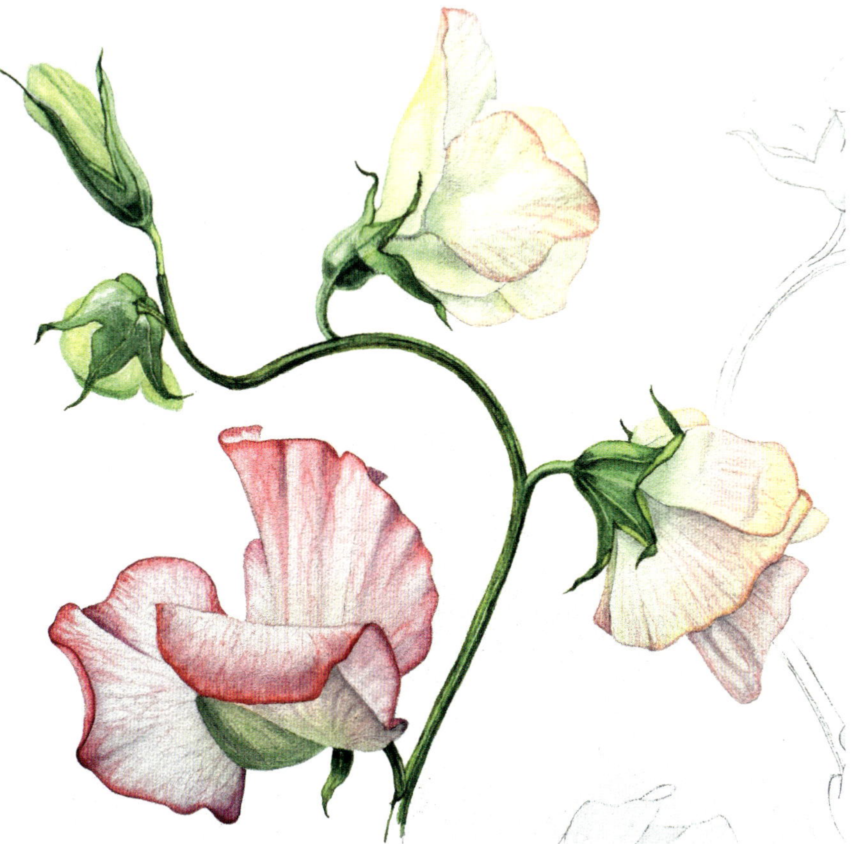

Step 5 The stems, stalks and receptacles are worked with three different green colours: the paler colour is pure diluted Phthalo Green Yellow Shade, the dark colour is the dark mix of Phthalo Green Yellow Shade + Phthalo Blue Red Shade, and the very dark colour is the dark green mix with a tiny bit of shadow mix added.

Between the finished two buds and three flowers and the colour notes I took earlier, I had enough information on the light stem to finish it later, even if the subject died.

It is time to move on to the darker coral stem before the shade and the colour changes too much. We come back to finish the light stem later.

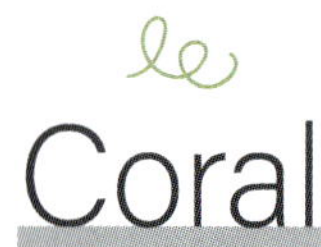

Coral

Painting this darker shade of pink requires a different approach. Whereas the paler sweet peas called for different colours to be blended into the same wet-in-wet wash, this darker colour is more suitable for the layered technique. The colour needs to be applied more heavily, and each transparent layer can modify and enhance the colour of the previous washes.

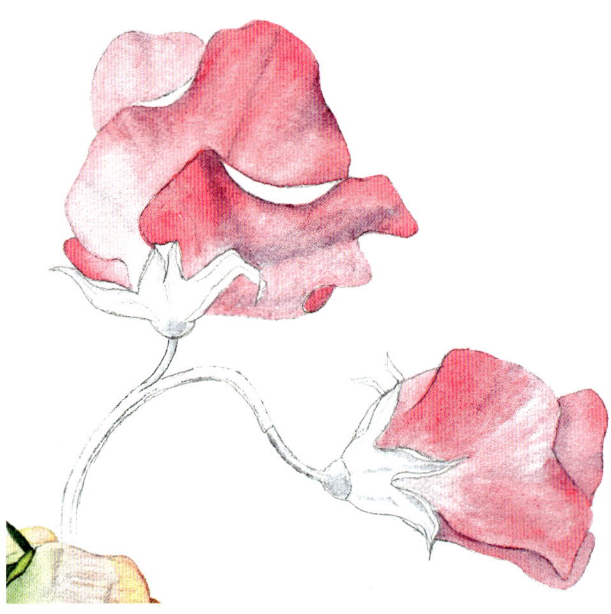

Step 1 The first wet-in-wet wash is pure Quinacridone Pink. This is done one petal at a time, reserving highlights and adding more pigment over the shadows.

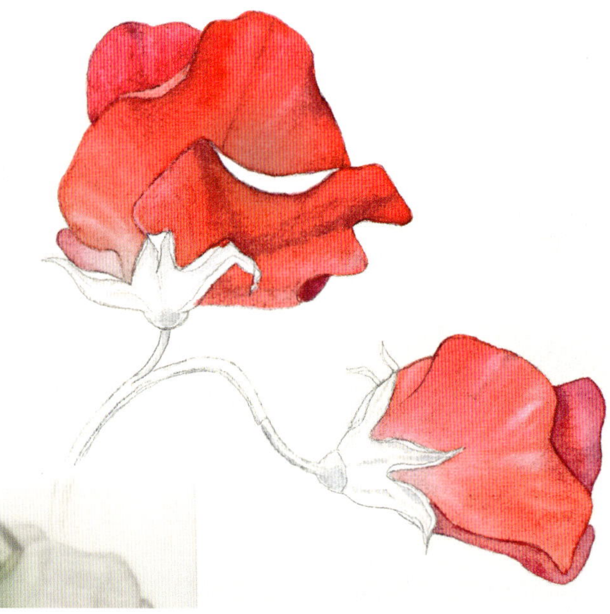

Step 2 The second wet-in-wet wash is pure Quinacridone Coral. This is a strong colour and also a peculiar pigment that behaves in a unique way: applied thinly and highly diluted, it has a definite pink-bias but applied more thickly with less water, the bias shifts towards orange, turning the pink a coral hue. This is a very useful quality for this sweet pea.

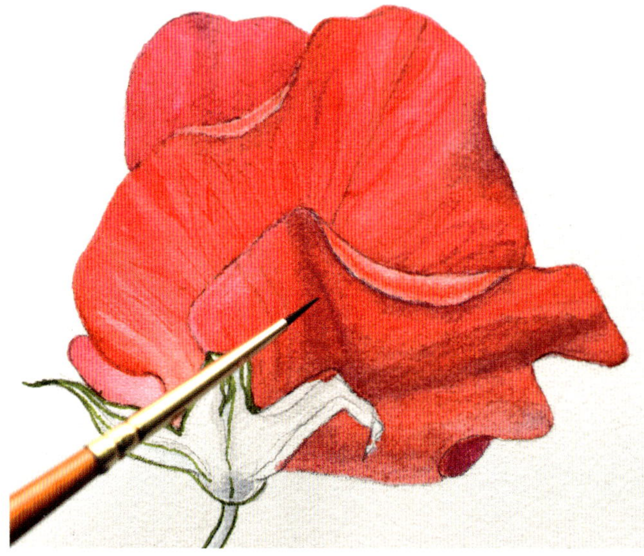

Step 3 While some of the veins are hinted at as part of the initial wet-in-wet washes, the more distinct ones are painted with a tiny, dry brush. Here I used a size 3/0 synthetic brush loaded with Quinacridone Lilac. As soon as a vein was painted, I used a damp size 2 brush to blend it into the petal texture.

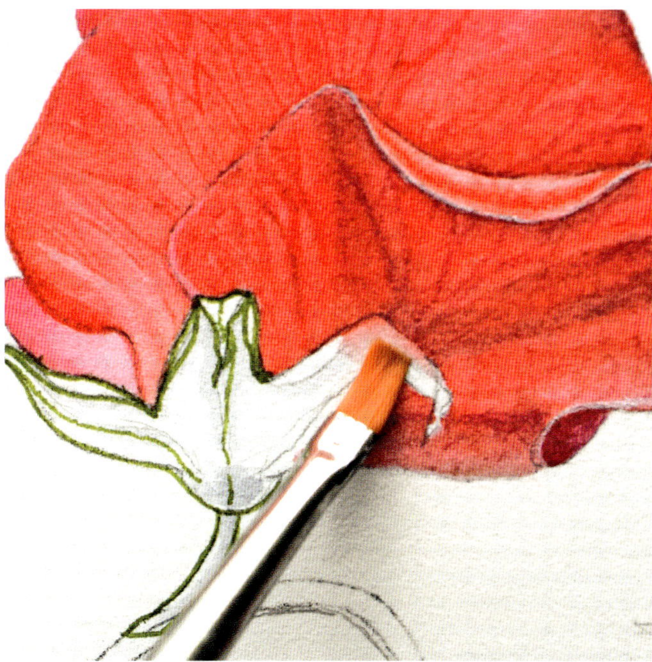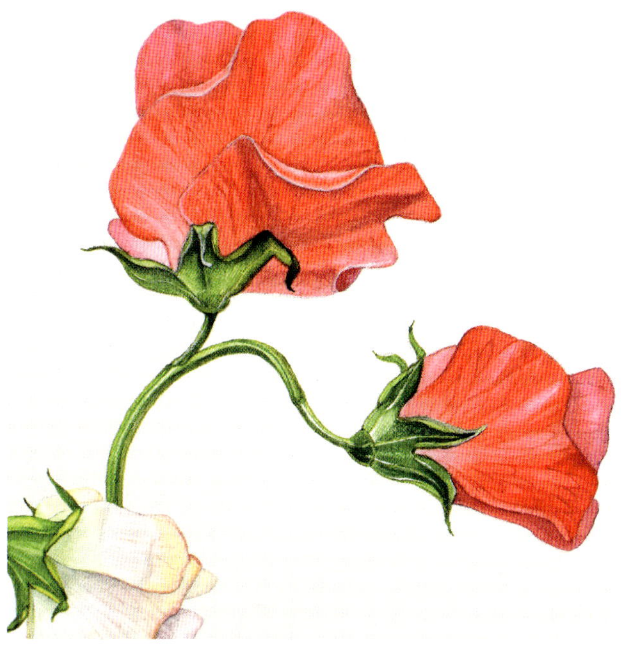

Step 4 Once the petals have enough colour, paint the receptacle and sepals. I started with an outline, to make sure I knew where I was going. If I found a bit where I went over the line with the coral, I performed an emergency stop and cleared it up before I continued. For this, I used a small flat brush on its side, moving it in a motion parallel to the line I needed to tidy up.

Step 5 Then I let it dry and continue with the green, alternating washes of pure Phthalo Green Yellow Shade over the highlights and mid-tones and the dark green mix over the shadows. The stems are heavily ridged. This makes them easier to paint because it is possible to paint them in sections separated by the ridges, avoiding the difficult task of painting a narrow stem wet-in-wet.

Stamens

Because the stamens are so thin, I opted for overpainting with the white watercolour stick rather than masking or painting around them. Waiting for the petals to be thoroughly dry, I applied the white with a size 3/0 brush, let it dry, then covered it with pale green for the filaments and yellow for the anthers.

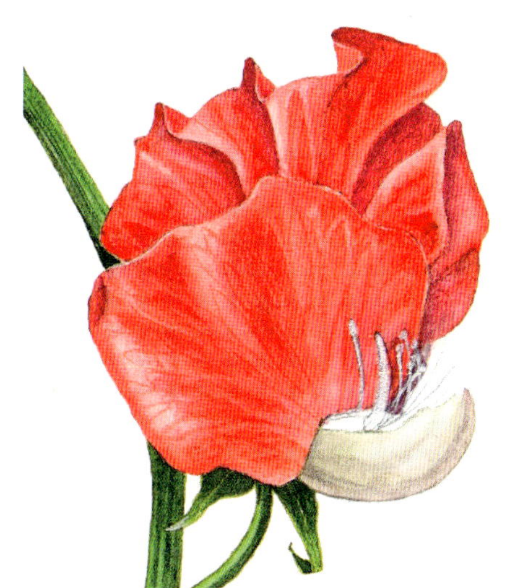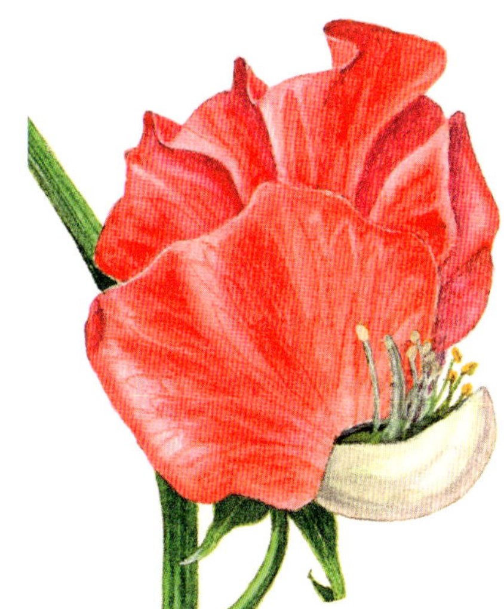

Finishing touches

It is now time for painting the remaining sweet peas and adding the final touches with dry-brush work. Unless there is an unlimited supply of sweet peas in the garden, the original subjects might be faded by now, either unusable or with their colours changed beyond recognition.

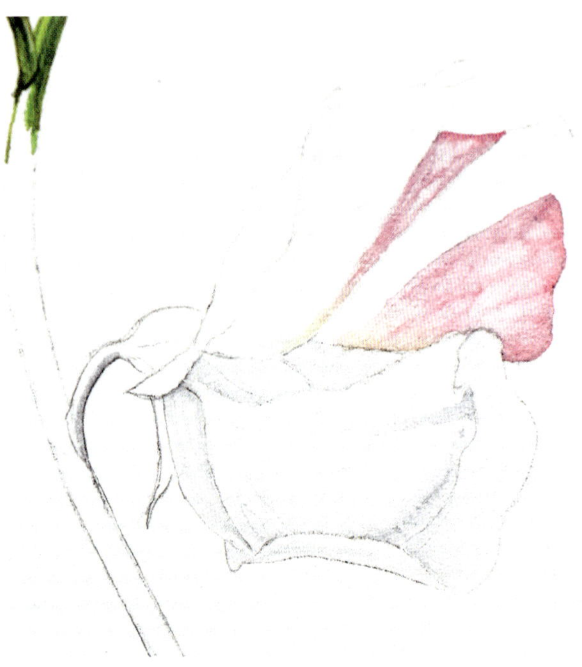

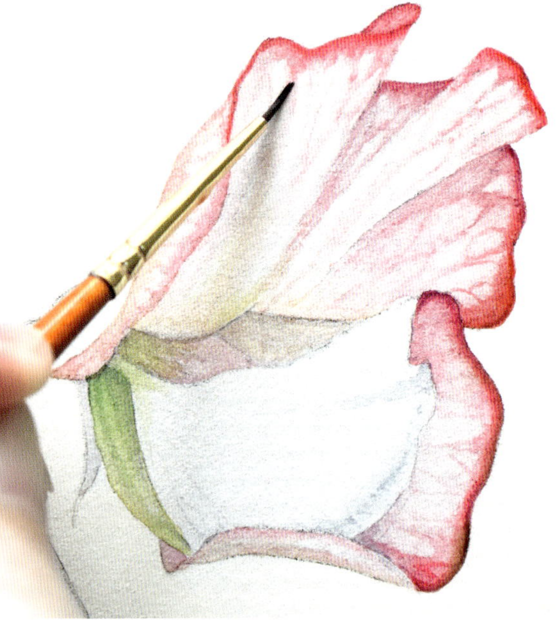

Step 1 With the amount of information gathered in the drawings, colour swatches, studies and the flowers higher on the stems that are already painted, it is now possible to continue with the lower flowers even without the subjects being at their most useful.

Step 2 The veins and the strongly coloured borders on the rosy frills can be strengthened with dry-brush work, as long as they are blended straight away with a clean, damp brush.

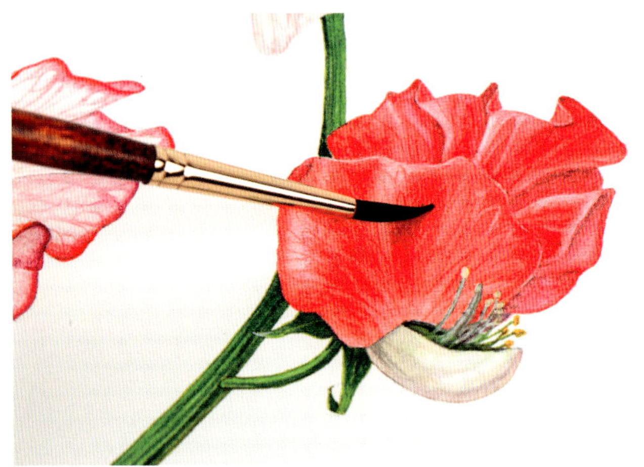

Step 3 The sweet pea 'Parfum Coral' boasts saturated, bright colours. Again, the dry-brush technique is useful to strengthen the wet-in-wet washes, using them as a map to follow, indicating where the colour needs more intensity, which is mainly in the mid-tones.

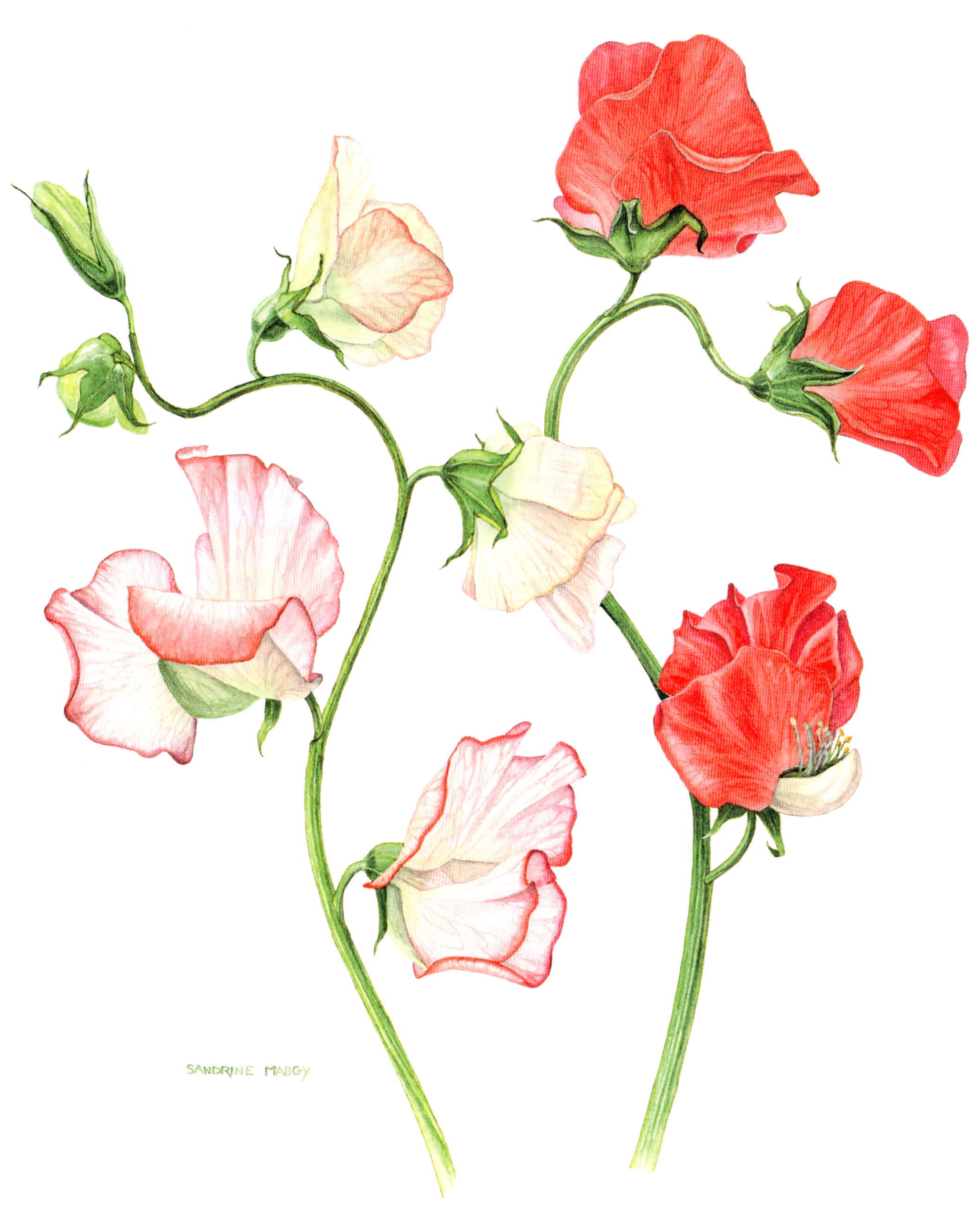

Sweet peas: *Lathyrus odoratus* 'Rosy Frills' and 'Parfum Coral'
Watercolour on paper.

Anatomy of a

ROSE

Common name Rose	**Flowering** Spring to Autumn	**Hardiness** Fully hardy
Botanical name *Rosa*	**Planting time** Autumn to Winter	**Propagation** Cuttings or division
Family Rosaceae	**Aspect** Full sun	**Native** Asia, Europe and North America

Rose section

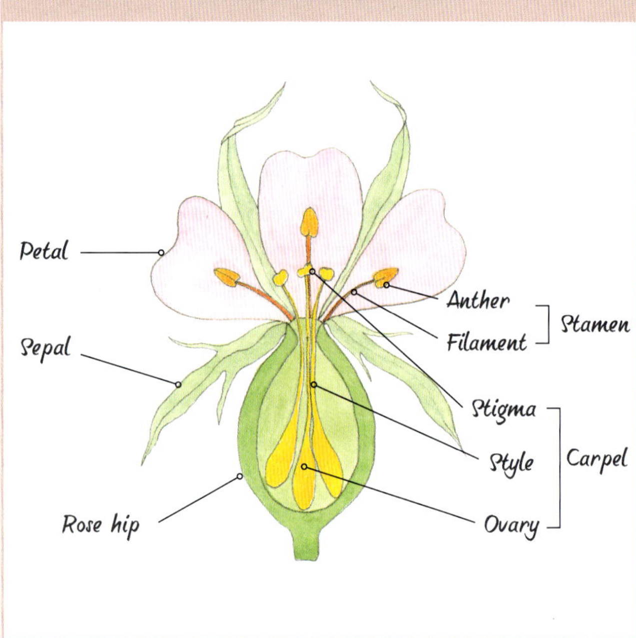

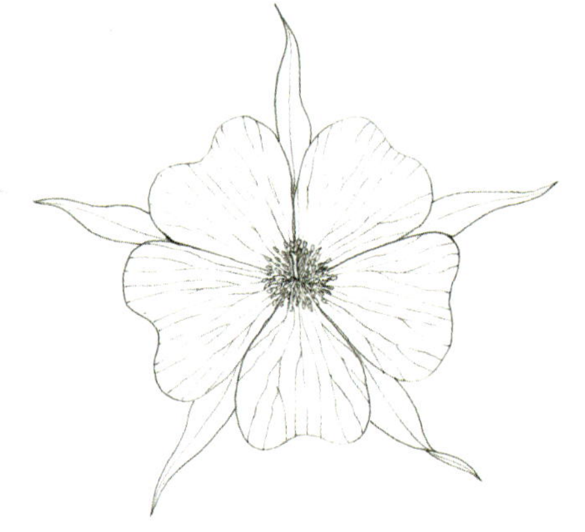

Botanically speaking…

- The original varieties have five petals and five sepals but there are hundreds of hybrids with many more petals. Up to a dozen petals require a precise drawing but with several dozens of petals embedded within each other, the exact number becomes lost.

- When there are five petals, they alternate with five sepals. The petals are on the inside and the sepals on the outside, protecting the flower as a shield. When looking at the flower from above, the sepals can be seen between the petals.

- Some roses have only one flower per stem but most garden varieties branch out to carry several flower heads from each main stem. Spray roses can have many small flowers coming from a single stem.

- The base of the petals is usually a different colour from the rest: for example, yellow on a red rose or white on a purple one. If the base is paler than the rest, it is wise to paint it first so that it doesn't get lost in the deeper colour.

- The veining pattern on the petals is fan-shaped: one central vein running from base to tip, then a few veins coming off this central vein toward the edges, then side veins starting from the base and curving towards the edges.

- The stigma, style and ovary form the carpel, which is the true fruit. Each carpel contains one seed. A rose hip is a false fruit containing a number of fertilized true fruit.

- Each rose has multiple stamens and multiple carpels, the number of which varies depending on the variety.

Rose shapes

Depending on which international horticultural or gardening organization is used as a reference,
roses come into seven or eight identifiable shapes. Flowers can show several characteristics, such
as 'cupped rosette'. They can also change shape as they mature, for example starting as globular
opening to a cupped shape.
The Royal Horticultural Society uses the following classification:

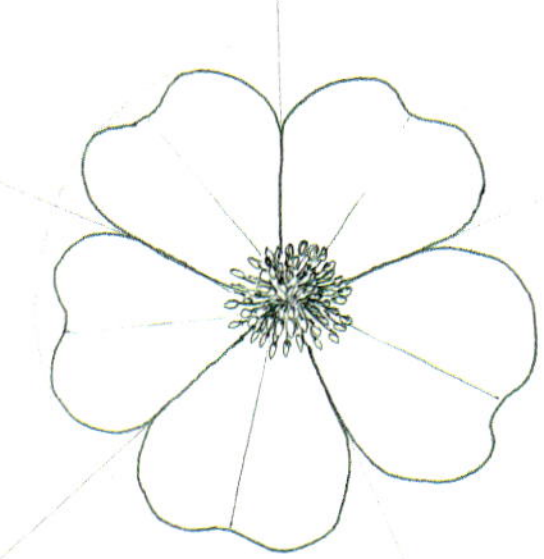

Flat   Open rose with visible stamens. Can be single or double.

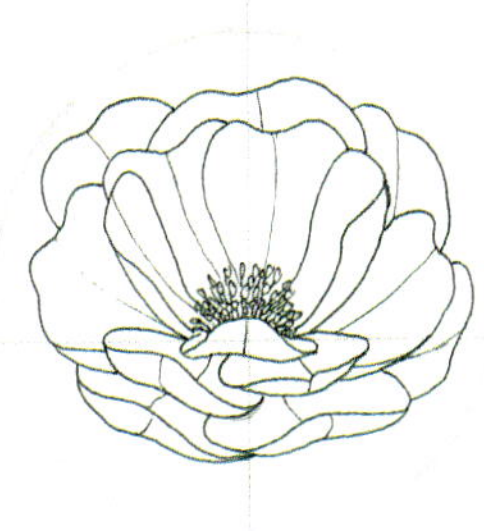

Cupped   Open rose with petals curving towards the centre.

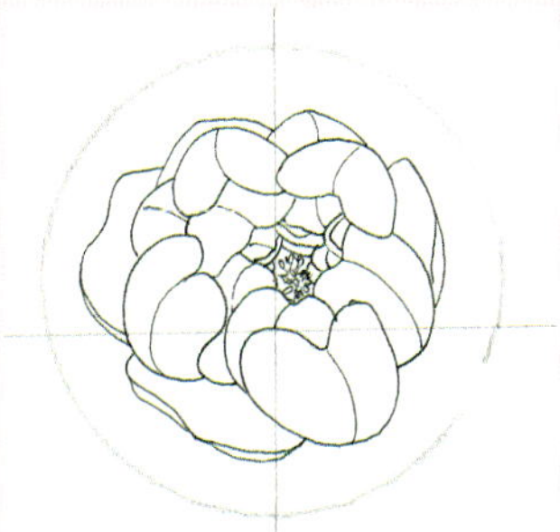

Rounded or globular Round rose with strongly curved petals.

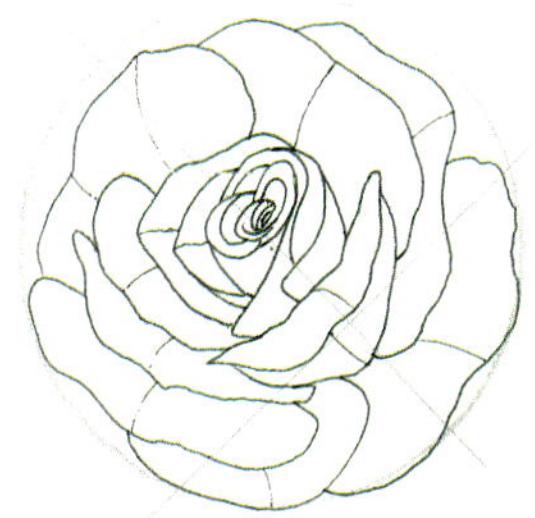

Urn-shaped   High petals with a flat top and outside petals curving outwards.

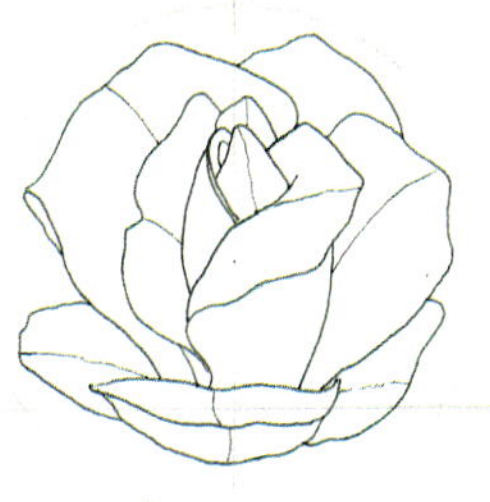

Pointed or high-centred Closed blooms with high petals in the centre forming a peak.

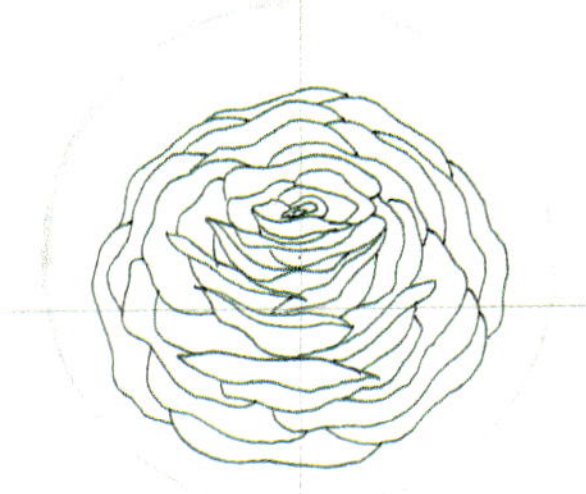

Rosette   Semi-double to fully double layered petals.

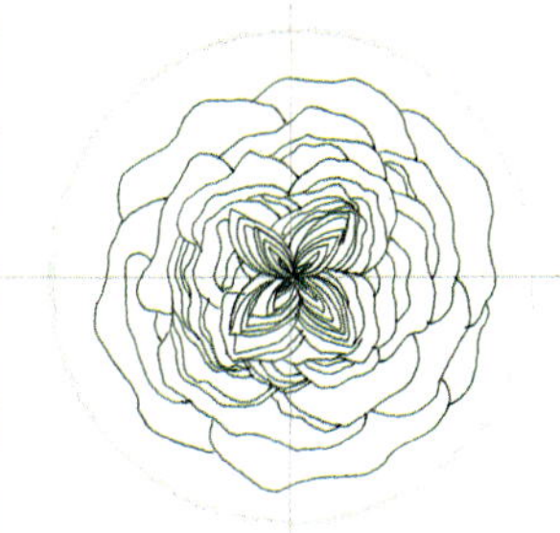

Quartered   Confused and different sized multiple petals arranged in quarters.

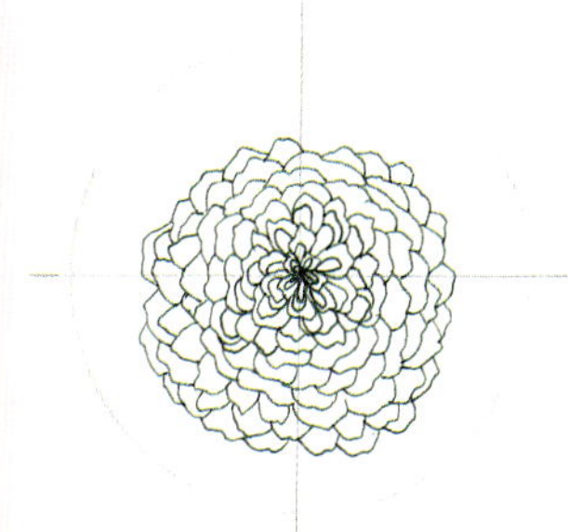

Pompon   Small, fully double flower heads that often grow in sprays.

Foliage

- Rose leaves are usually serrated. The shapes vary from round to oblong, depending on the variety.

- Roses have compound leaves, usually in groups of three or five.

- The veining pattern on the leaves is called 'anastomosing'. It is advised to pay particular attention to this, as most people miss it and paint an inaccurate veining pattern as a result. The central vein goes from base to tip and the secondary veins run from this central vein towards the margins. However, before they reach the margins, the veins loop back and join the next secondary vein.

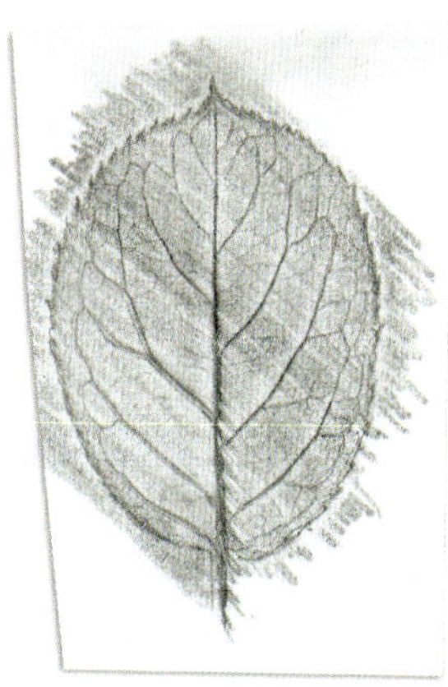
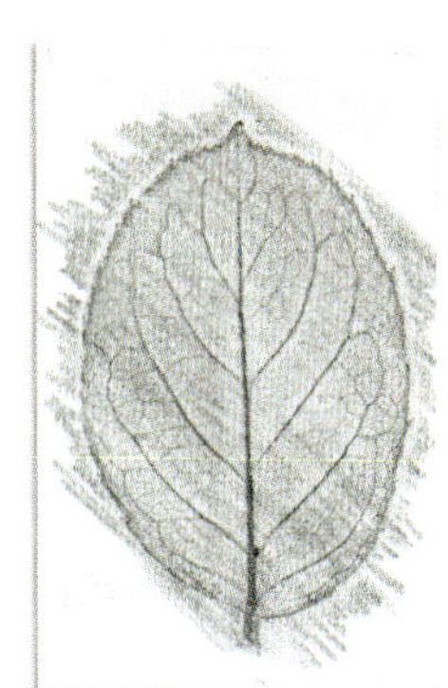

Rubbings of rose leaves

Drawing a rose

Drawing a rose can be intimidating, especially when attempting to portray the fully double varieties. I find it helpful to start with a geometrical outline that will fit the overall shape of the bloom within its borders. It can be a circle or an oblong shape. With flat roses drawn from the side, the shape is an ellipse. Here are a few examples of steps for different types of roses drawn from different viewpoints.

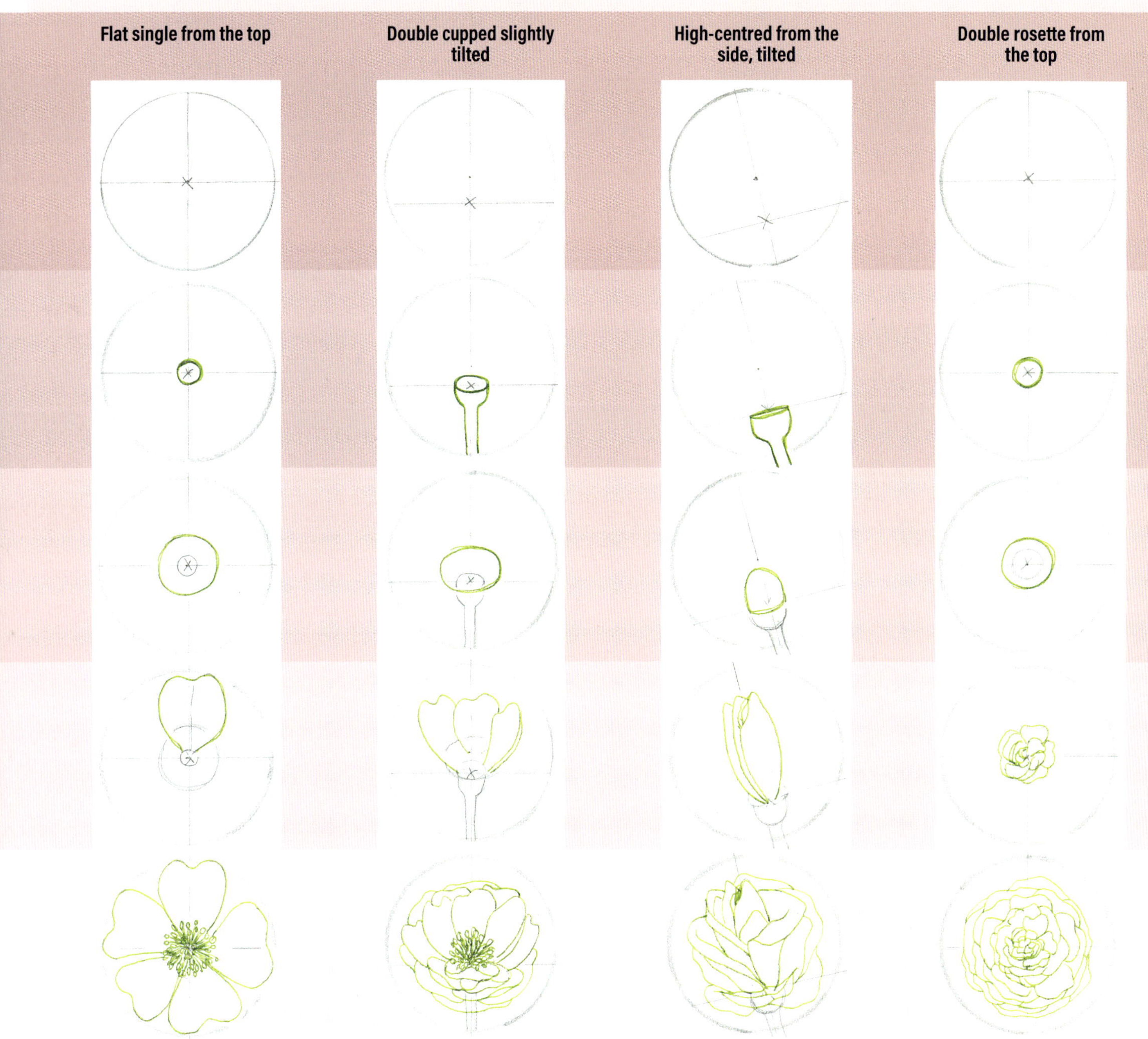

Step 1 Draw an overall shape that will encompass the whole bloom. Draw a vertical (or tilted) line that will cut down the rose centrally in line with the stem, then a perpendicular line that cuts through the top of the receptacle. At the intersection of these two lines is the anchor point.

Step 2 Draw the stem and the receptacle (top of the stem and base of the gynoecium), even if it is hidden behind the petals.

Step 3 Circle the stamen area as another reference point, even if it is hidden.

Step 4 Draw the first petals – in the centre for a top view or closest to the front for a side view.

Step 5 Build up the petals around and in front of the previous ones, always going back to the anchor point for reference. Add the stamens if visible.

While the rose is still a bud, the sepals cover the petals and gynoecium for protection. Some of the coloured petals become visible in between the sepals as the bud starts to open. The sepals will open up and eventually peel back towards the stem to let the flower bloom.

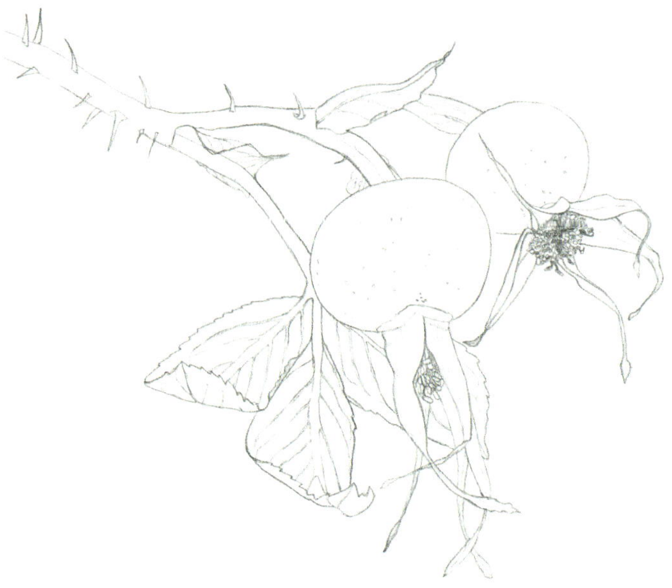

Rose hips are a false fruit. The real fruit are formed by the carpels and are contained within the hip. Each hip contains several fruit and each fruit contains one seed. The five sepals start to shrivel and form some interesting shapes to paint along with the rose hips.

ROSE

Painting roses is such a joy every year, as they invade the garden in a rainbow of colours, from the most delicate hues to the deepest shades.
Here are a few mixes that are useful to paint such a large range of rose colours.

Palette: Rose mixes

Ivory: **Hansa Yellow Light + Perylene Violet**   This pale neutral colour can be tricky to mix. Use plenty of water.

Pale yellow: **Hansa Yellow Light** can be deepened with **Hansa Yellow Medium** in stronger parts.

Strong yellow: **Hansa Yellow Deep**.

Golden yellow: **Nickel Azo Yellow**.

Orange: **Permanent Orange** for yellow-bias oranges to **Pyrrol Orange** for red-bias ones.

Pale peach: **Hansa Yellow Light + Quinacridone Coral** The two colours can be layered separately or mixed on the palette.

Bright coral: **Quinacridone Coral + Nickel Azo Yellow**.

Scarlet: **Pyrrol Scarlet**.

True red: **Pyrrol Red**.

Crimson: **Carmine**.

Almost black (very deep red): **Carmine + Perylene Violet + French Ultramarine**.

Pale pink: **Permanent Rose + Viridian**   the typical pale rose of a garden climber.

True pink: **Permanent Rose** or **Quinacridone Rose**.

Magenta: **Quinacridone Lilac**.

Purple: **Quinacridone Lilac + French Ultramarine**   in different proportions, depending on the rose.

Maroon: **Perylene Maroon** Dirty red.

Green: **Sap Green**   Often seen on ivory roses or as markings on pink ones.

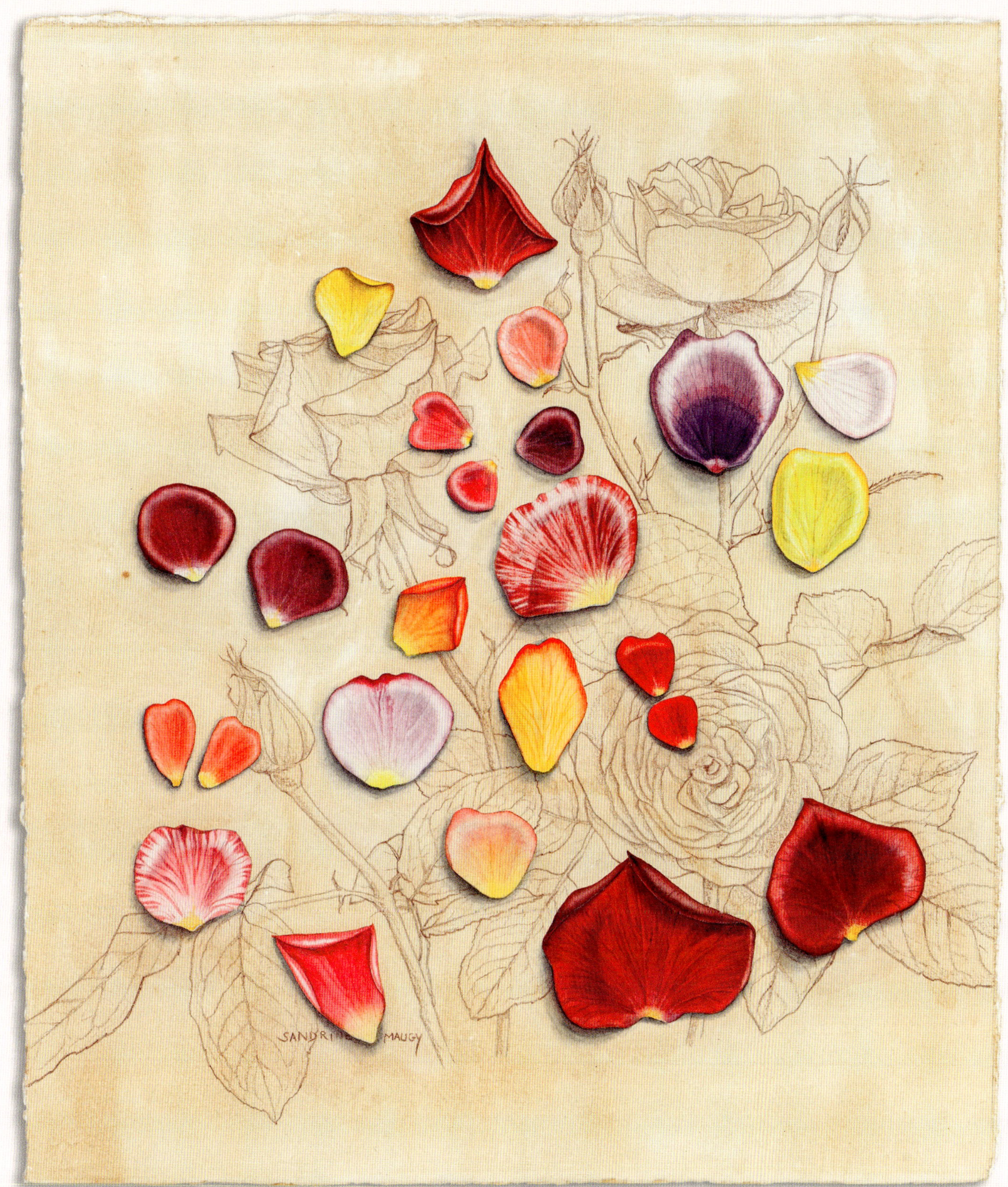

Scattered Rose Petals on Old Drawing
Watercolour, pencil and tea on torn paper.
Roses come in a vast array of colours: pure white, ivory, pale to strong yellow, orange, pale
peach to bright coral, scarlet, true red, crimson, an almost black deep red, all hues of pink,
magenta, purple, maroon, green and patterned with stripes and splodges. The only missing
colours are true blue and true black.

Level 2

ROSA 'ODYSSEY'
Drawing and palette

Rosa 'Odyssey' is a pale lilac beauty who displays her delicate, large, open flowers on slender stems. When tiny songbirds land on her branches to pick at invisible grubs, they arch down to the ground and I always worry that the fragile twigs are going to snap. But the birds fly away and the stems bounce back. The buds are a strong fuchsia pink that borders on magenta, and when the flowers open to reveal their lilac hues, some pink remnants linger in rare and random flashes. The stamens are a deep red crowned by orange anthers. 'Odyssey' is a spectacular rose in the garden and an exciting subject on the easel.

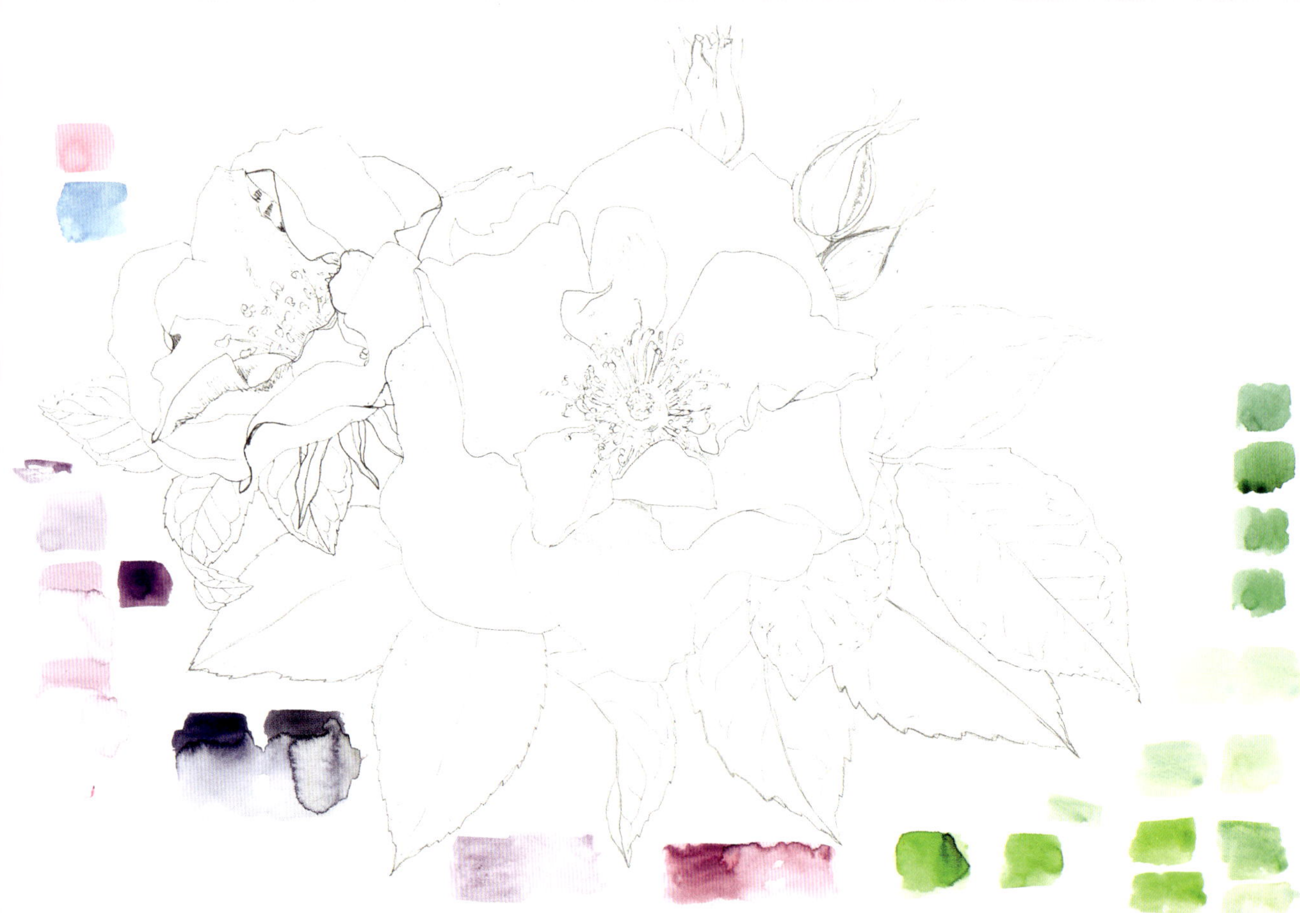

The drawing is a patchwork of several flowers and different bits of foliage. The main flower is the focus. I found a semi-opened flower that I drew from the side and tucked behind my main subject. The buds were in a similar position on yet another flower. When working a composition from several subjects, the trick is to position the assembled parts in places where they would naturally fit. This keeps the composition natural-looking.

88

Materials list

PAPERS

Cartridge paper or sketchbook
Tracing paper
Transfer paper
Watercolour paper: Fabriano Artistico
HP Extra White, 640gsm (300lb)

DRAWING

Pencils: 0.5mm B pencil; thicker pencil
for tone study
Eraser and putty eraser

PAINTING

Brushes: Pro Arte Prolene Plus Series
007 in sizes 3/0, 2, 4 and 8
Masking fluid + any old small brush

Palette

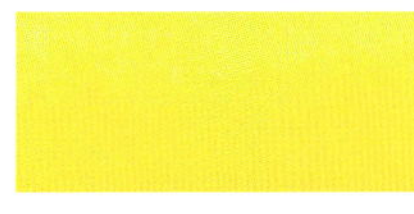

Hansa Yellow Light   A pure, bright, pale and transparent yellow, delicate enough for this fragile rose. Used for the stamens and for lightening the green.

Pyrrol Red   A mid-red, saturated and strong. Mixed with the yellow, it makes a slightly muted orange that can be used on the stamens.

Carmine   A violet-bias red for the filaments.

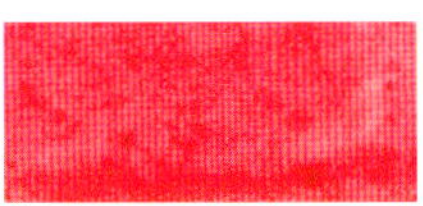

Quinacridone Pink   Can be used for a thin glaze if the violet gets too blue or if the petals need brightening up in some parts.

Quinacridone Lilac   The main colour for the whole painting. It is used for the buds, for the markings on the petals, for the violet mix and for muting the green.

Perylene Violet   For darkening the filaments without making them too grey.

Phthalo Blue Red Shade   Mixed with the **Quinacridone Lilac** for the petal colour and also used to darken the green.

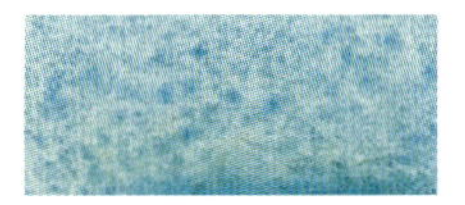

Cerulean Blue   Used in the green mix for the underside of the leaves.

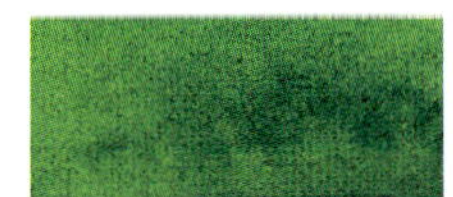

Sap Green   The base colour for the foliage.

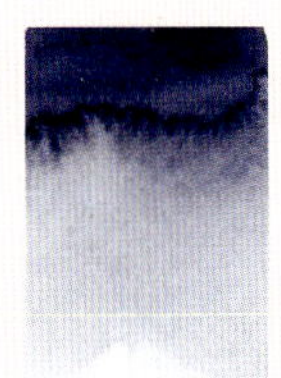
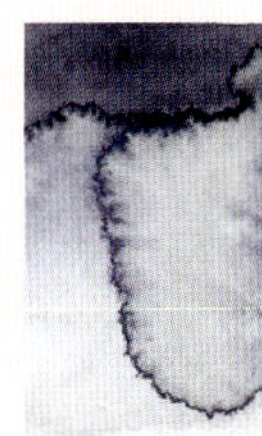

Harmonic Shadows

The three primary colours for the Harmonic Shadow mix are chosen as follows: the only yellow on the palette is **Hansa Yellow Light**. The blue is **Phthalo Blue Red Shade**. As **Quinacridone Lilac** is the main colour and is used in all the parts, it is the obvious choice for the red.

Shadows and masking fluid

There are several ways to paint stamens on an open flower: you can draw them first and paint around them; you can ignore them, paint the petals and add the stamens on top after the surrounding areas are done; or you can use masking fluid to protect them, paint the petals, unmask and paint the stamens last of all.

In this case, option one seemed too fiddly. There are too many stamens to allow for broad wet-in-wet washes to happen without accidents. Option two wouldn't work because the anthers are too bright. An underlayer of shadows and purple washes would not allow the yellow to stand out enough. This leaves option three: using masking fluid.

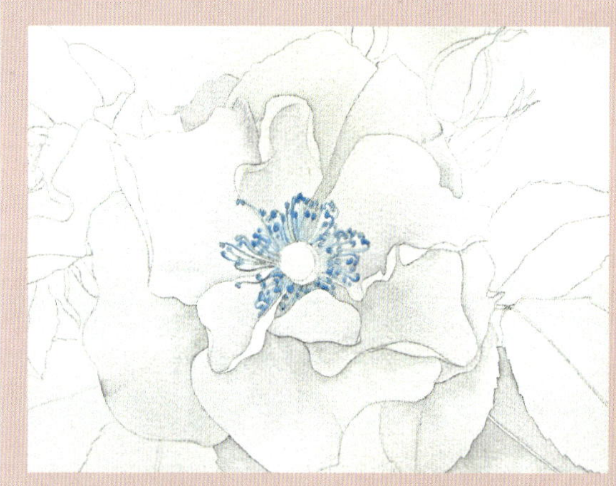

Applying masking fluid

When applying masking fluid, follow these simple rules:

- Make sure the paper is dry;
- Use a small, old brush to get the details right;
- Wait until the fluid is thoroughly dry before starting to paint around and over it.

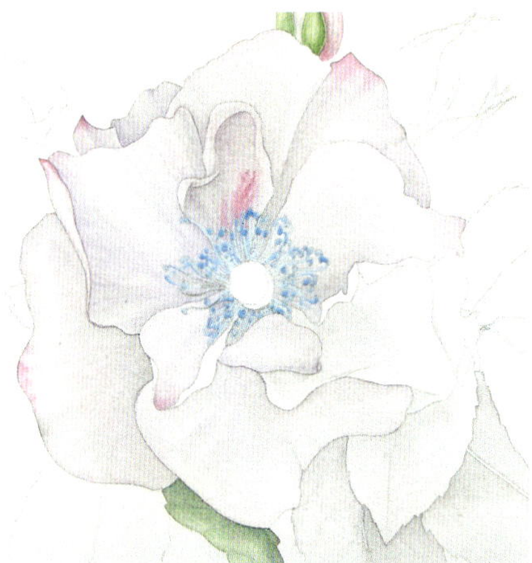

Step 1 Once the fluid is dry, paint a layer of Harmonic Shadows on the petals of the first rose. Normally I would paint shadows over the whole composition before starting on the colour, but because the fluid needs to be on the paper for as short a time as possible, it is better to focus on the flower head, with just a hint of the foliage to introduce a bit of green and keep the colours balanced.

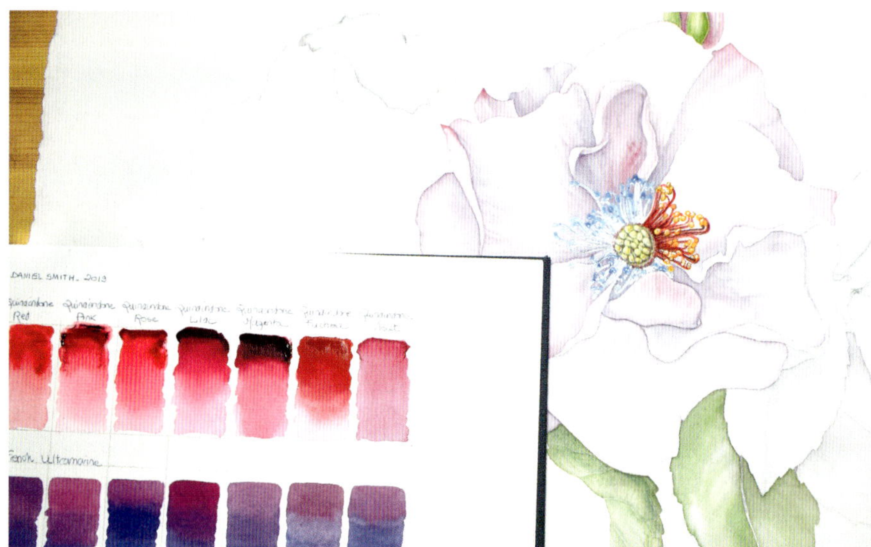

Step 2 After all the wet-in-wet washes on the surrounding petals are done and completely dry, it is time to remove the masking fluid, one section at a time, to avoid getting lost in the multiple lines. This has to be done using a putty eraser very carefully to make sure the paper doesn't get damaged. The painting of the stamens can then start. Keep your colour trials at hand for reference.

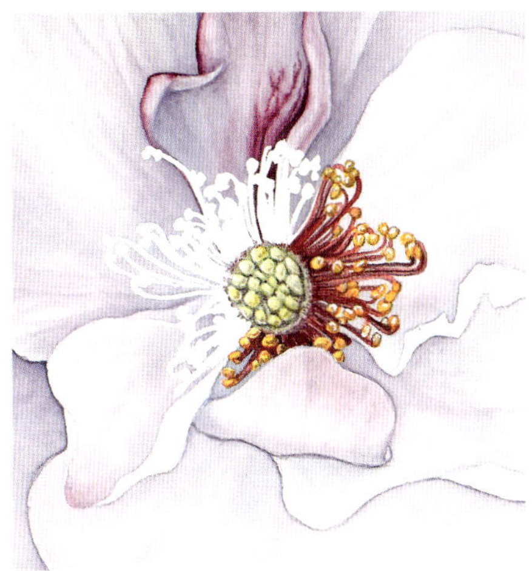

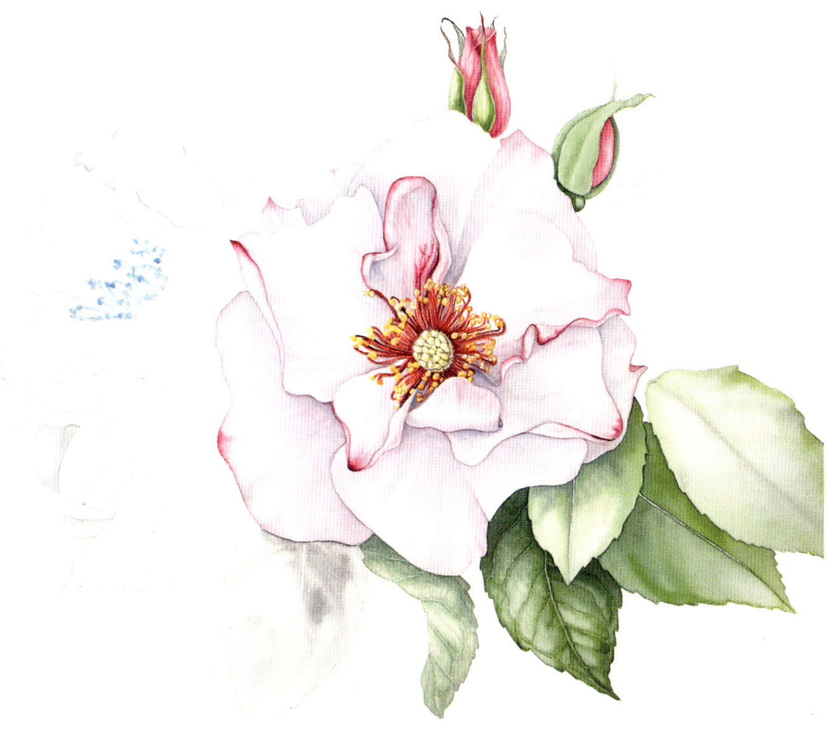

Step 3 Work your way around the stamens of the first flower, painting them with a size 3/0 brush loaded with paint not wet enough that the colour runs but not too dry, so that the mark stays smooth and fluid. The stamens are first painted using Carmine and Pyrrol Red, with a touch of Perylene Violet on the ones underneath. The anthers are painted with Hansa Yellow Light, to which a touch of Pyrrol Red can be added in the more orange parts. The very centre is a juxtaposition of very watered-down Sap Green and Hansa Yellow Light, not forgetting the shadow mix in between.

Step 4 Before starting on the second rose, paint a few washes on the leaves to keep the purple and green balanced. The main purple will look different against the white paper than it will with some green around it. The main green mix is Sap Green with Quinacridone Lilac to mute it down a little. Over the shadows, a touch of Phthalo Blue Red Shade is added to the mix to darken it. The buds are painted wet-in-wet, their strong magenta-pink hue adding depth and contrast, helping to keep all the colours together. Once satisfied that enough colour information is added, it is time to mask the stamens on the second rose, to bring it up to the same level as the first one.

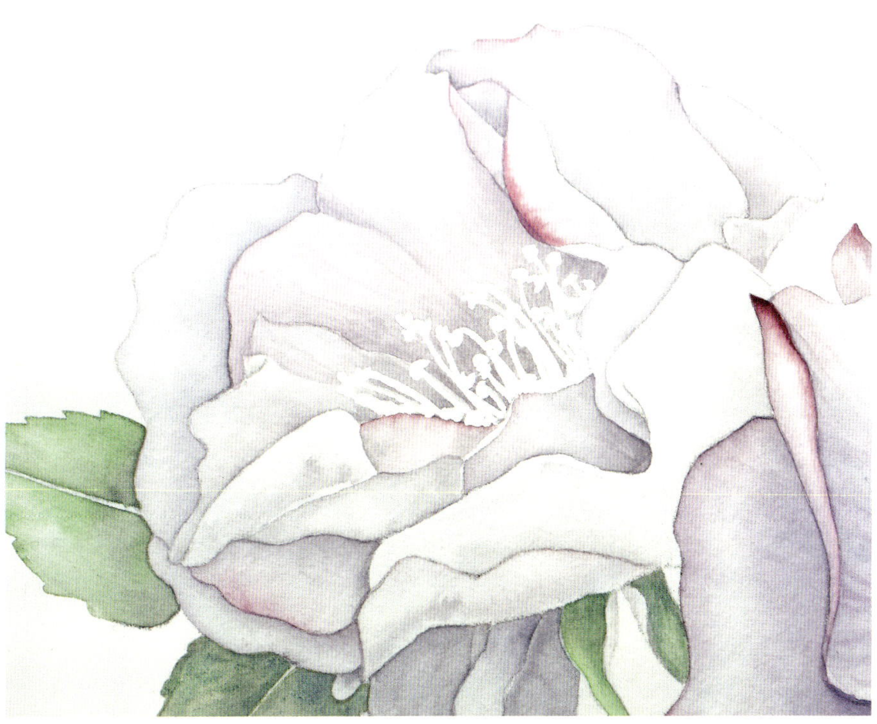

Step 5 While the stamens are masked, a wet-in-wet wash of shadows is painted on the whole rose of the second rose, then some colour added to the petals directly in contact with the masking fluid. After these washes have dried, the masking fluid can be removed.

Second rose, and painting stamens

Now that the stamens are unmasked, the plan is to work from
the back of the rose towards the front – starting on the petals at
the very back, then the next layer and so on, working towards
the stamens.

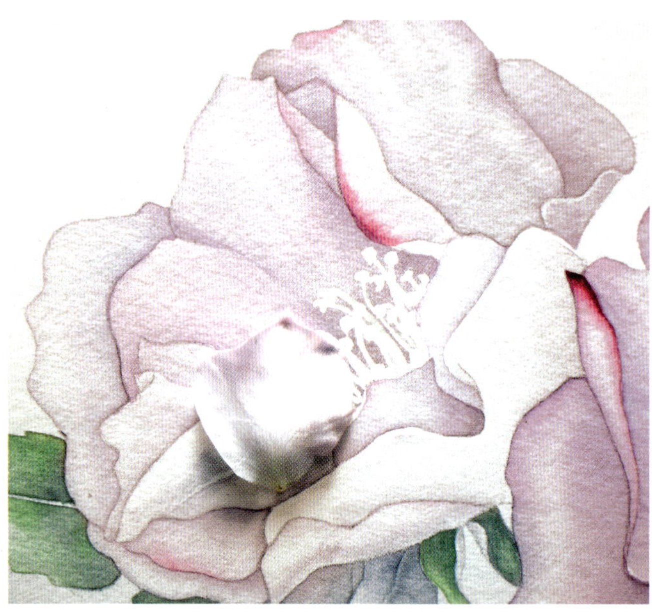

Step 1 Observe the petals of your rose individually.
You will find that the colour may vary between a young
bloom barely open and a more mature rose, or between
the back and front of the petals. Here, I have placed
a petal directly onto the painting for comparison.

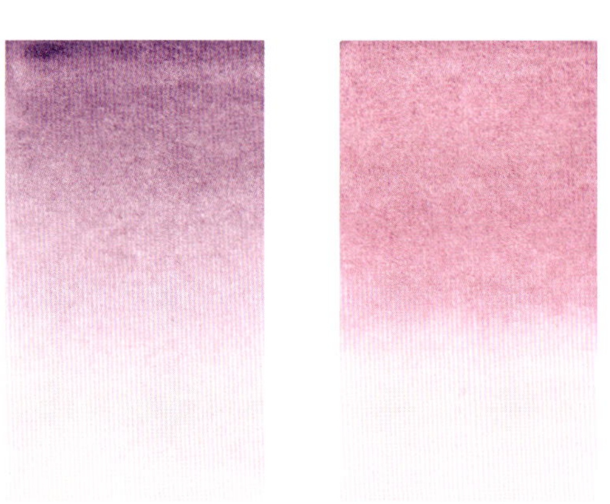

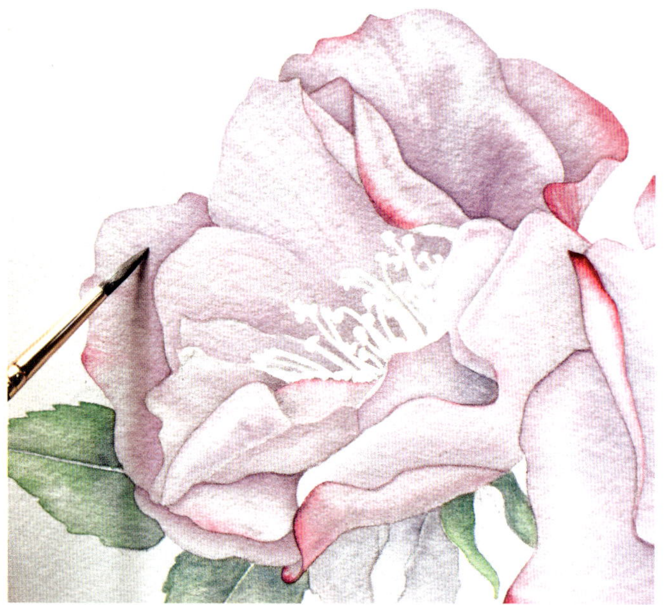

Step 2 For 'Odyssey', work with two main colours mixed from the
same two pigments: Phthalo Blue Red Shade + Quinacridone Lilac
in different proportions.

Step 3 Build up washes on the back petals, varying intensity
and colour, playing with your two colours. Tidy up the edges with
a little more colour, if needed. At this stage, you can also add pure
Quinacridone Lilac accents on the edges.

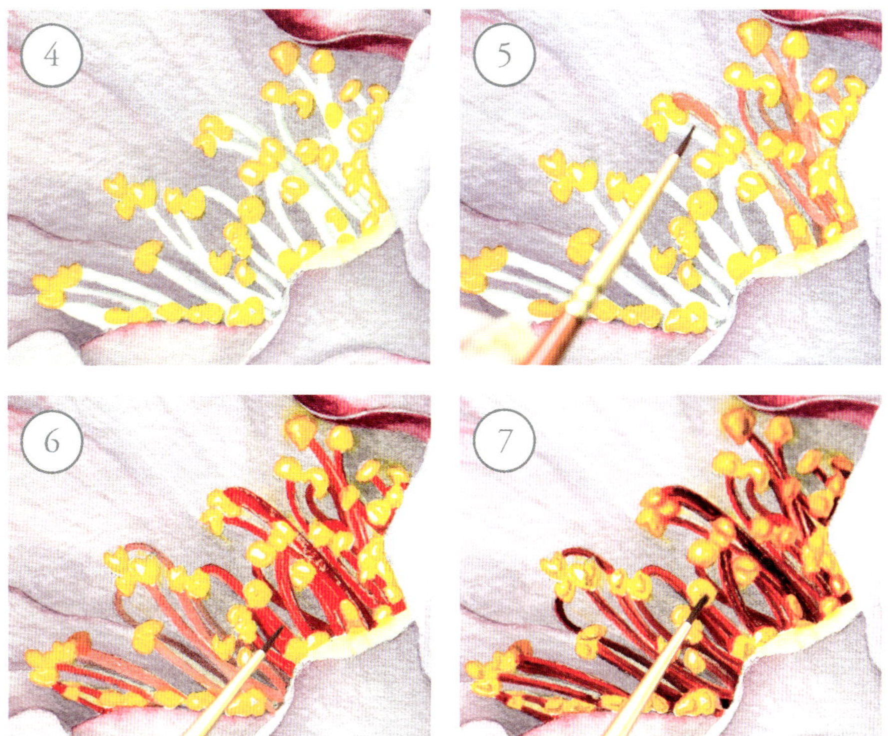

Step 4 Use a tiny brush, which will not only allow for small marks but will also help by not carrying too much pigment. As the anthers are more likely to be in front of the filaments, it is better to paint them first. As their colour is less strong, it is also safer to do so. A filament can always be added going across an anther, but painting an anther in front of a red filament would be trickier. Check the colour of the anthers carefully. They can be any colour but are usually yellow. 'Odyssey's anthers are orange-bias, turning to green-bias Hansa Yellow Light in the highlights. The orange-bias yellow is obtained from adding a touch of Pyrrol Red to Hansa Yellow Light.

Step 5 When painting the filaments, start with a watery wash. This allows for mapping them in without committing too much. Once they are all in, have a look at the overall effect and decide if they look balanced and are in the right places. Make alterations if necessary. Here I used a watered-down Carmine.

Step 6 Once you are happy with the dispersion, you can start strengthening the colour. Again I used Carmine, or Pyrrol Red for the brightest ones, but this time less diluted. Add some depth with a darker, duller colour, such as Perylene Violet, painted on the side opposite to the light source and where filaments and anthers are overlapping.

Step 7 Some of the anthers had a slight orange hue to them, which I portrayed with Hansa Yellow Light with a bit more Pyrrol Red mixed in.

Now the stamens are finished, the petals in front of them can be completed.

Foliage and buds

The flowers are finished and it is now time to concentrate on the foliage and buds.
I added a few green washes along the way in order to offset the various shades of violet
and keep the balance. The green base colour is Sap Green, altered with a touch of
Quinacridone Lilac where it needs muting down, Phthalo Blue Red Shade where it
needs darkening, or Hansa Yellow Light where it needs lightening.

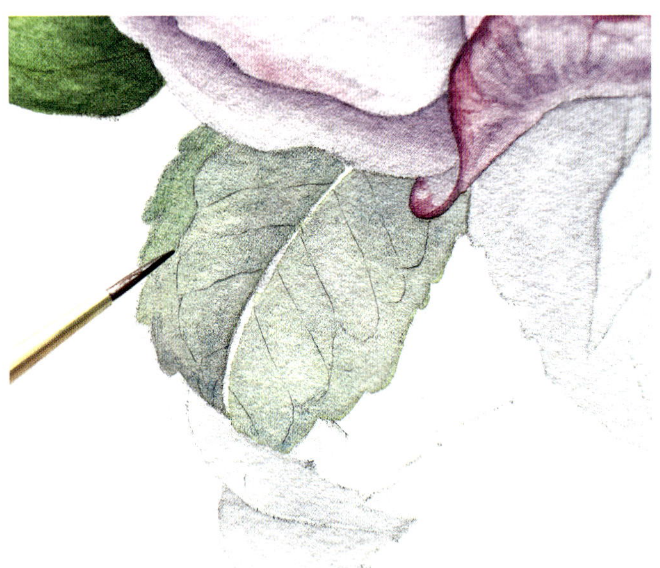

Step 1 The colour of the leaves' undersides is different from the colour on the topsides. They have a milky texture and an almost turquoise hue. A good colour for this type of blue-green is Cerulean Blue. It is an opaque and granulating colour with a chalky finish, perfect for the kind of texture we are looking for. The green mix is Sap Green + a touch of Quinacridone Lilac + Cerulean Blue. After the shadow wash and a first underwash of this mix, the veins are re-drawn and the Cerulean green mix added around the veins.

Processes for painting the leaves

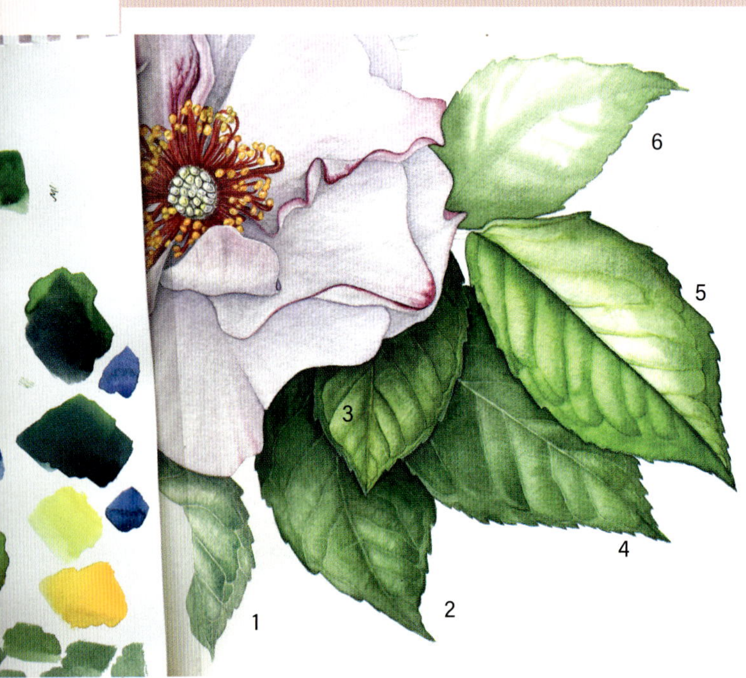

Leaf 1: Painted with the Cerulean mix.

Leaf 2: One layer of shadows followed by green mixes containing more blue to make it darker and Quinacridone Lilac to make it duller.

Leaf 3: One layer of shadows followed by four green washes, containing more blue under the flower overhang and more yellow towards the tip. This leaf is finished.

Leaf 4: One layer of shadows followed by washes containing more blue, as this leaf is receding under the top ones.

Leaf 5: One layer of shadows followed by green-mix layers containing more yellow as more light is hitting this top leaf. The left side has one more wash than the right side.

Leaf 6: One layer of shadows followed by a single green wash so far.

All of these washes are painted wet-in-wet, always reserving the highlights, starting with whole-leaf washes, then half-leaf washes, then between-the-veins washes.

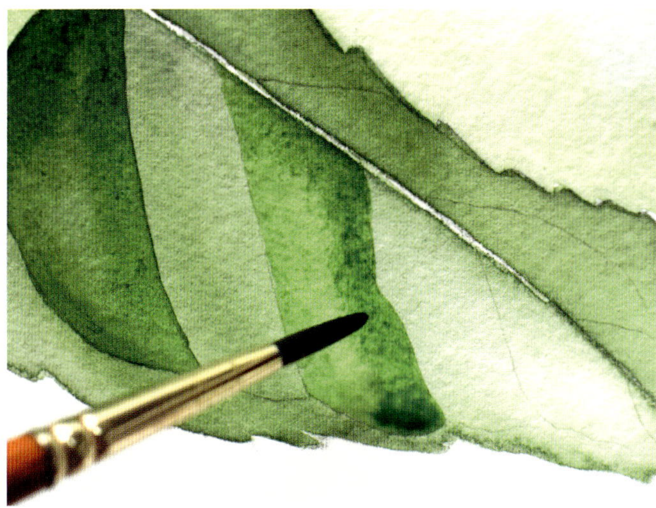 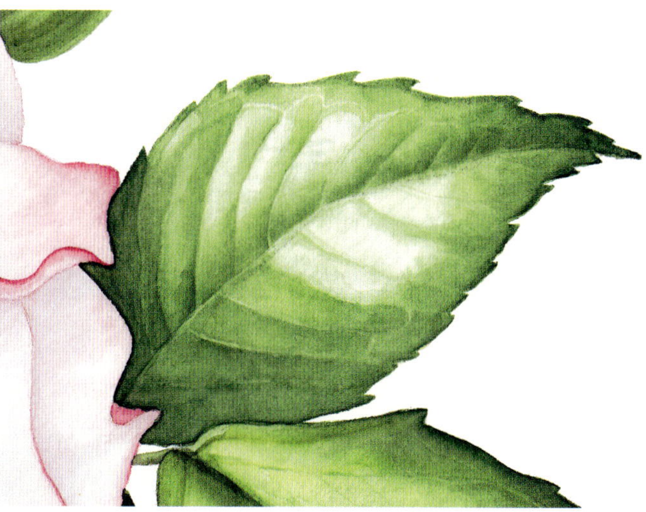

Step 2 Once the under washes have provided a soft base, start to divide the leaves into smaller sections, using the veins as borders. The wet-in-wet washes can then continue in these smaller sections.

Step 3 Leaf number 6 is the one that shows the most light so even more care has to be taken to reserve the highlights. There are shadows under the rose and mid-tones towards the tip as the leaf flattens away, but the core of the leaf is in the light.

The petals peaking out of the buds are pure Quinacridone Lilac, toned down by the grey mix where the shadow layer shows through. The green is Sap Green + Phthalo Blue Red Shade on the shadow sides and Sap Green + Hansa Yellow Light on the light side. The sepals are edged in Quinacridone Lilac, darkened with Perylene Violet at their tips.

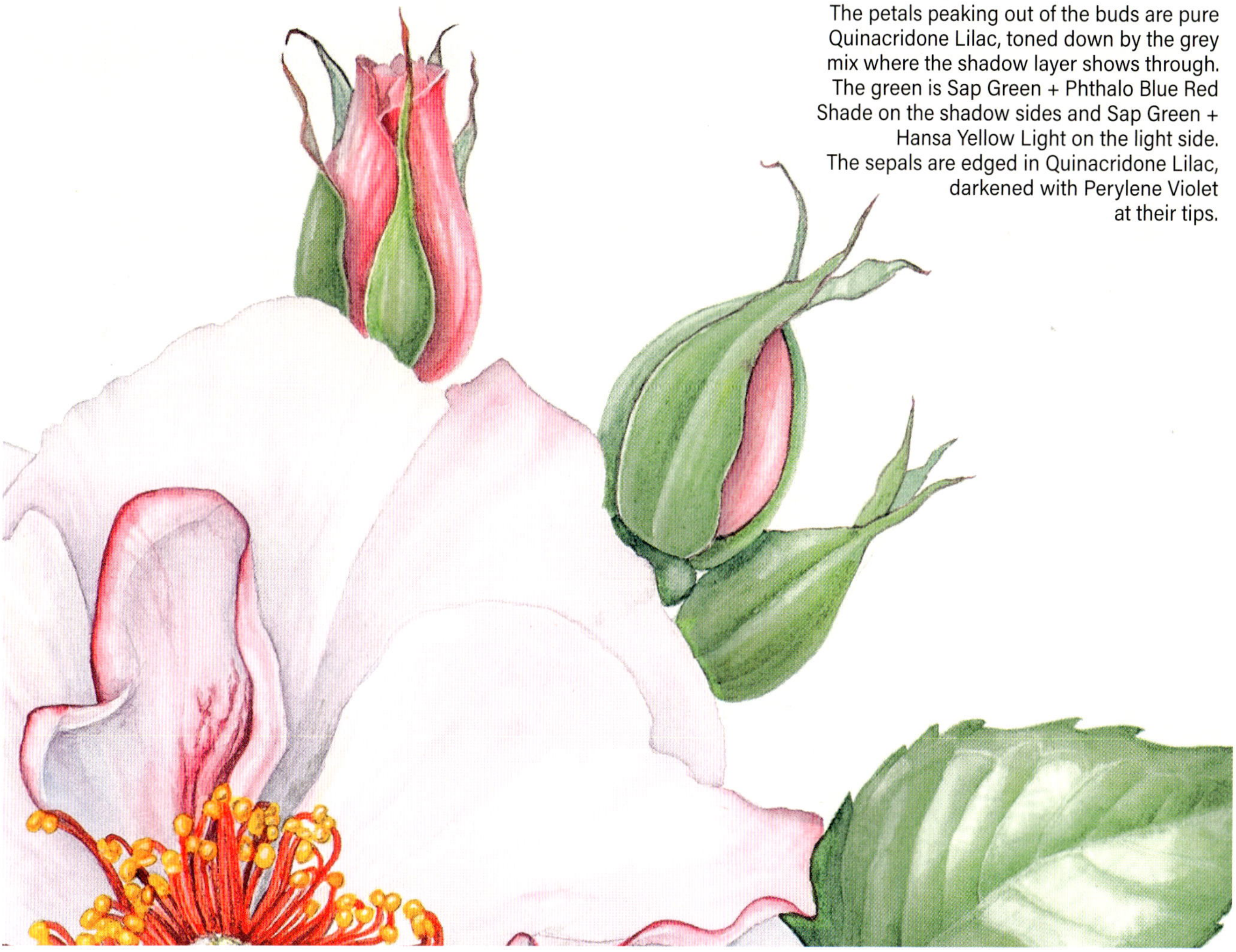

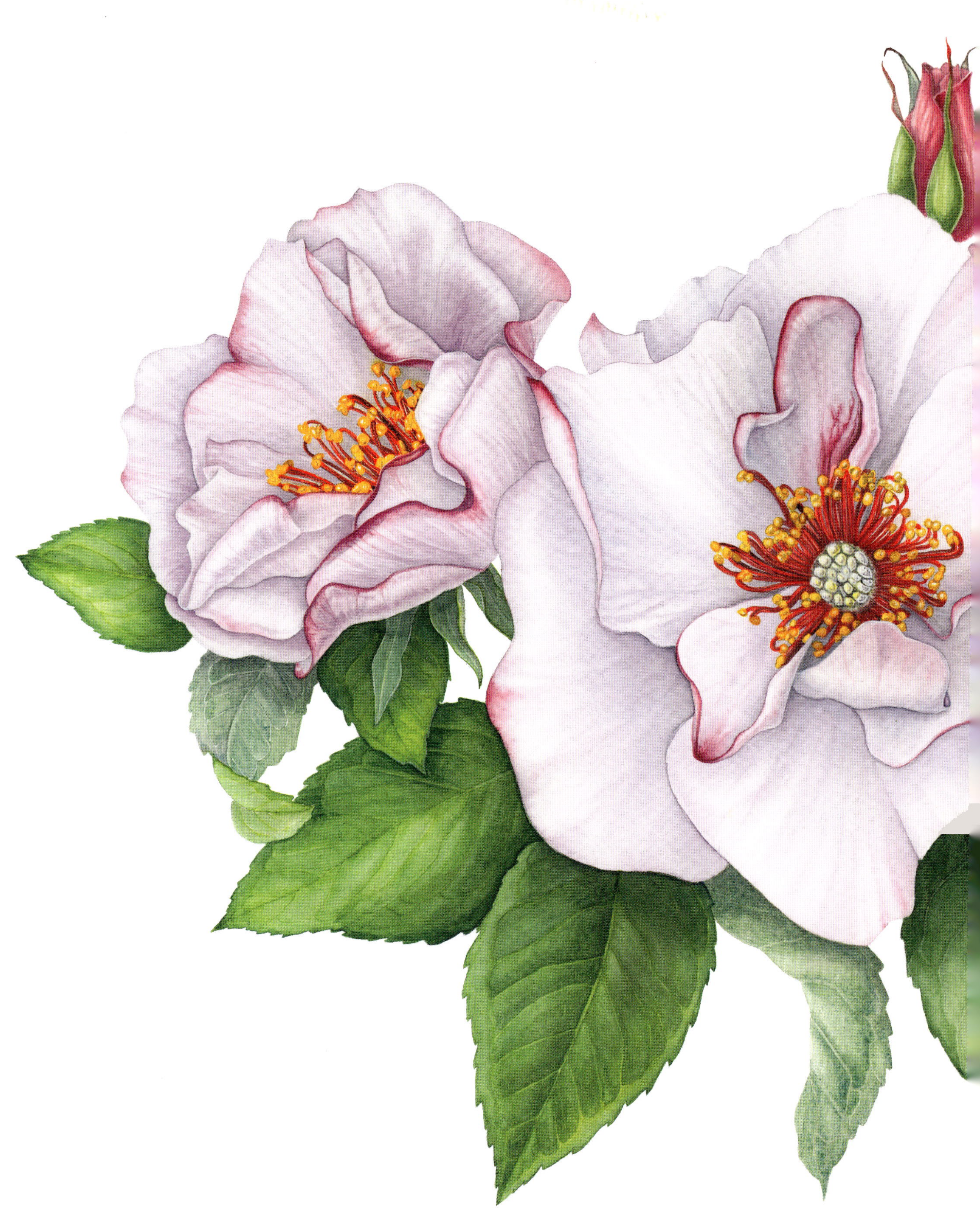

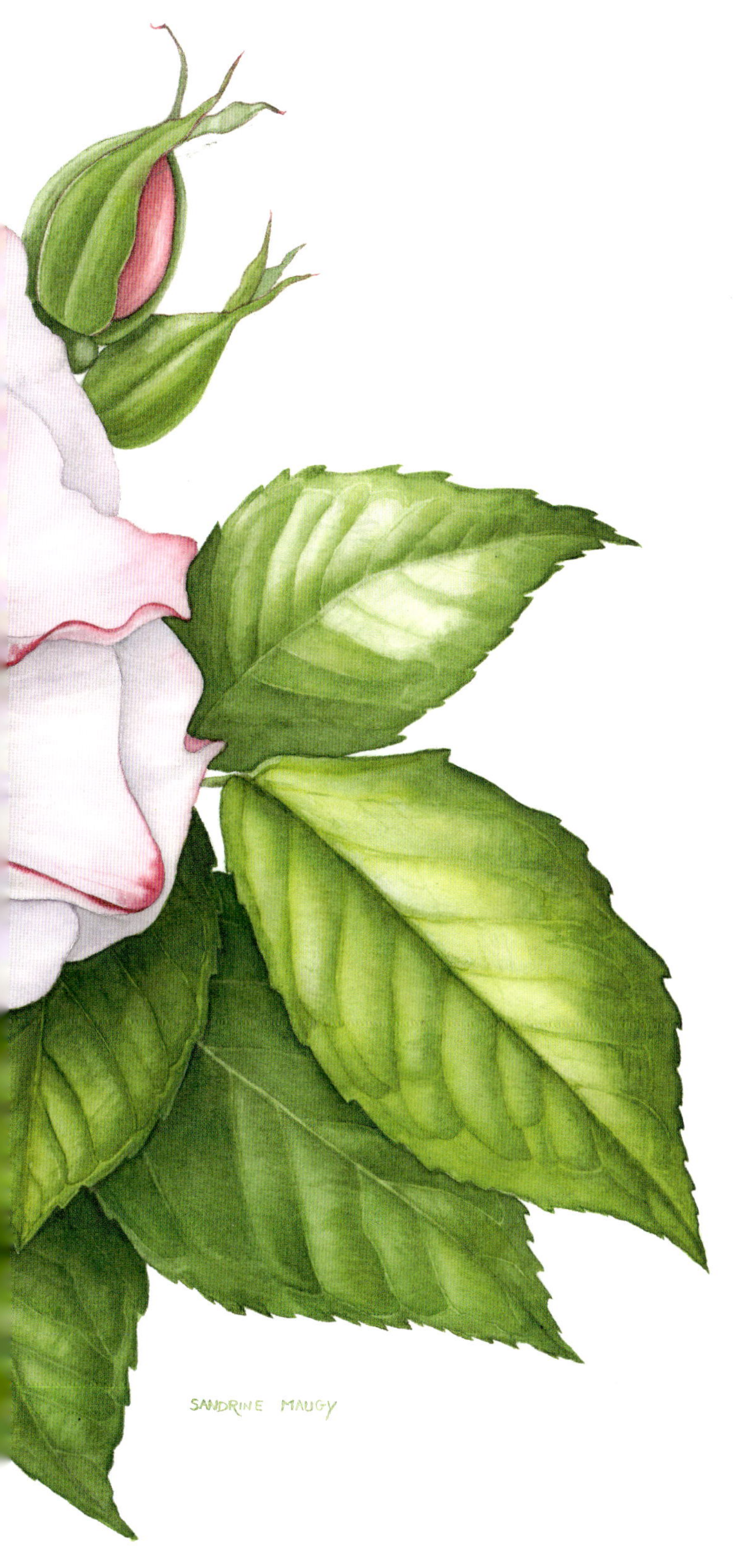

Rosa 'Odyssey'
Watercolour on paper.

Anatomy of a
SUNFLOWER

Common name Sunflower	**Flowering** Summer into Autumn	**Hardiness** Dies at first frosts
Botanical name *Helianthus annuus*	**Sowing time** April to May	**Propagation** Seeds
Family Asteraceae	**Aspect** Full sun	**Native** North America

Sunflower section

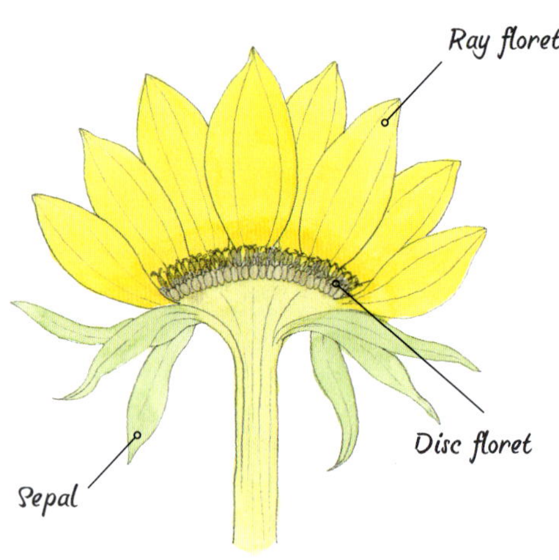

Disc floret

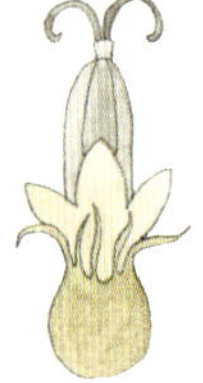

Botanically speaking…

- The flowering system of sunflowers is complex: the flower head is made of numerous tiny five-petalled flowers called disc florets. The outer flowers, which resemble petals, are called ray florets and are sterile.

- Each disc floret produces a seed.

- Some hybrid versions grown for flower arrangements do not produce seeds.

- The disc florets are arranged in spirals, one running clockwise and the other anticlockwise. When you count how many spirals there are in each direction, you will probably get two consecutive numbers from the famous Fibonacci sequence. Typically, there are 34 spirals in one direction and 55 in the other; however, in a very large sunflower head there could be 89 in one direction and 144 in the other. This pattern produces the most efficient packing of seeds mathematically possible within the flower head.

- The disc florets can be green, yellow, orange, brown or maroon to almost black.

- The ray florets are usually yellow, with a deeper colour (going towards orange) at the base. New varieties can be maroon or dark red.

- Sunflowers are both cross-pollinating (by bees, butterflies, moths or beetles) and self-pollinating.

- The strong stems are thick, ridged and hairy.

- Currently the record for the tallest sunflower is 9m 17cm (30ft).

- Sunflowers can be used to extract toxic ingredients from soil, such as lead, arsenic or uranium.

- They can also be used to clean water and were planted around ponds in Chernobyl and Fukushima after the nuclear disasters.

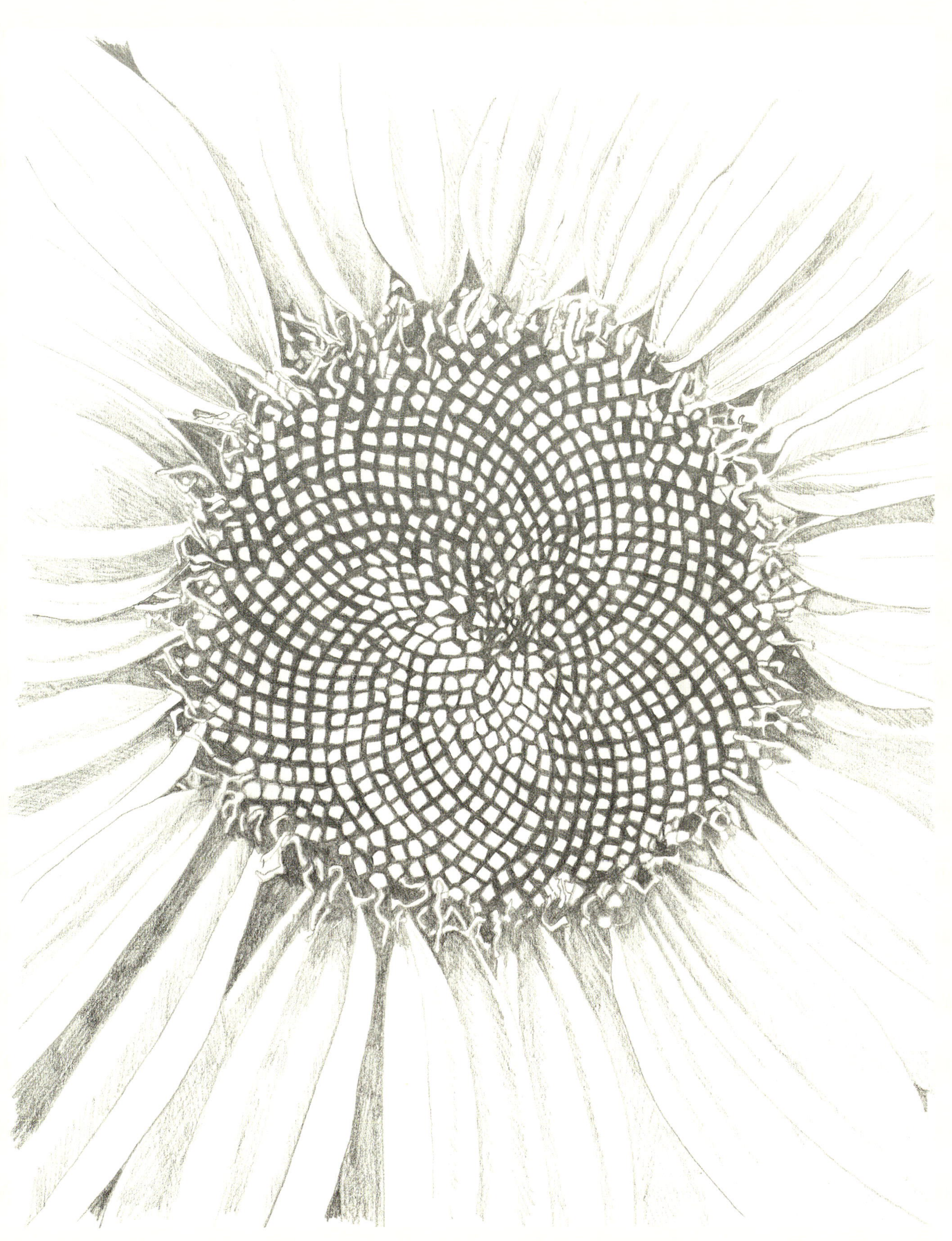

The spirals in the centre of a sunflower inflorescence, showing all
the small disc florets.

<h1 style="text-align:center">Level 3</h1>

<h1 style="text-align:center">SUNFLOWER
Drawing and tone study</h1>

Sunflowers are such a glorious sight when they come into full bloom in the middle of Summer. Although they are not the easiest of subjects to paint, the results are highly rewarding when you capture the cheerful yellow colour and the wild rhythm of the many sepals.

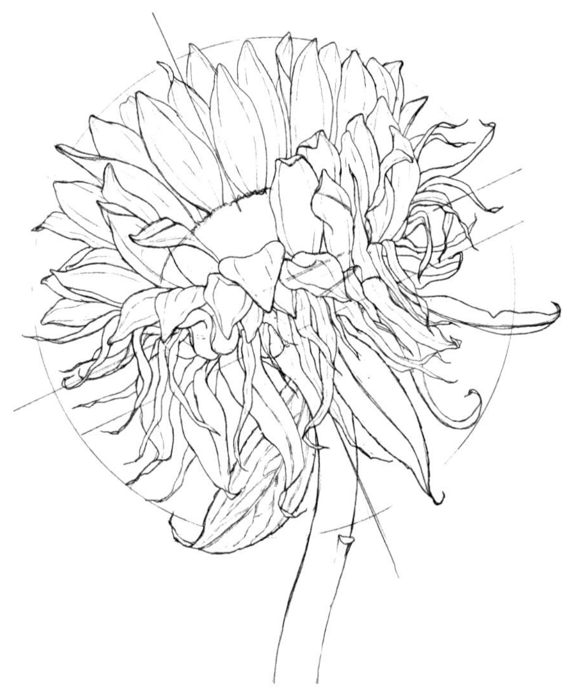

Drawing

Step 1 Drawing a sunflower is not a simple task. As we've seen on pages 98–99, the centre with all the small florets is intricate and the sepals are curling and turning in a wonderful pattern of swirls. In order to make the most of the flower's design, I would suggest choosing a flower head with some foreshortened petals at the front, revealing some of the dark centre. This creates a gorgeous contrast between the bright yellow and the dark maroon, as well as being representative of the sunflower everyone knows and loves.

I start my drawing with some guiding lines, which will help me stay balanced with all the small parts that form the flower head, the sepals and some leaves that are close to the flower:

- A large circle englobes the whole composition, apart from the stem coming out at the bottom of the circle.
- The anchor point is at the top of the stem, in the middle of the ring of sepals, underneath the exact centre of the group of florets. It is hidden from view but marking it helps keep everything balanced and more or less symmetrical.
- A straight line splits the circle in two vertically (although this shows as a diagonal on the drawing, as the flower head is at an angle), evenly dividing the crown of petals at the back, going through the centre, dividing the petals and sepals at the front, and finally running through the middle of the stem, through the anchor point.

- A horizontal line (again at an angle because of the position of the flower) crosses the vertical line at 90 degrees, forming a square cross and dividing the circle into four equal parts.
- The flower head occupies the two top sections while the sepals and top leaves occupy the two bottom sections.
- There should be roughly the same number of petals in the left section as there is in the right one. Following the same principle, there should be roughly the same number of sepals in the bottom-left section as there is in the right one.
- The foliage does not require to be as equally balanced. Use your subject for guidance but never forget you have artistic licence to create the painting you want.

Materials list

PAPERS

Cartridge paper or sketchbook

Tracing paper

Transfer paper

Watercolour paper: Fabriano Artistico
HP Extra White, 640gsm (300lb)

DRAWING

Pencils: 0.5mm B pencil; thicker pencil for
tone study

Eraser and putty eraser

PAINTING

Brushes: Pro Arte Prolene Plus Series 007
in sizes 3/0, 2, 4 and 8

Daniel Smith Moonglow for tone study

Tone study

Step 2 Preparing a tone study for a subject like this one is even more important than usual. When painting time comes, there will be much to think about in the intricate design without having to observe tonal variations at the same time. The tone study will provide all the information needed while the flower sits ignored in a cool dark place, ready to come out later when it is needed for painting the colour and details.

For the tone study I placed my flower in the window with the light coming from the top left. I used Moonglow, a ready-made grey by Daniel Smith. It allows for quick, delicate washes that can be applied swiftly before the flower decides to move or open up more of its petals.

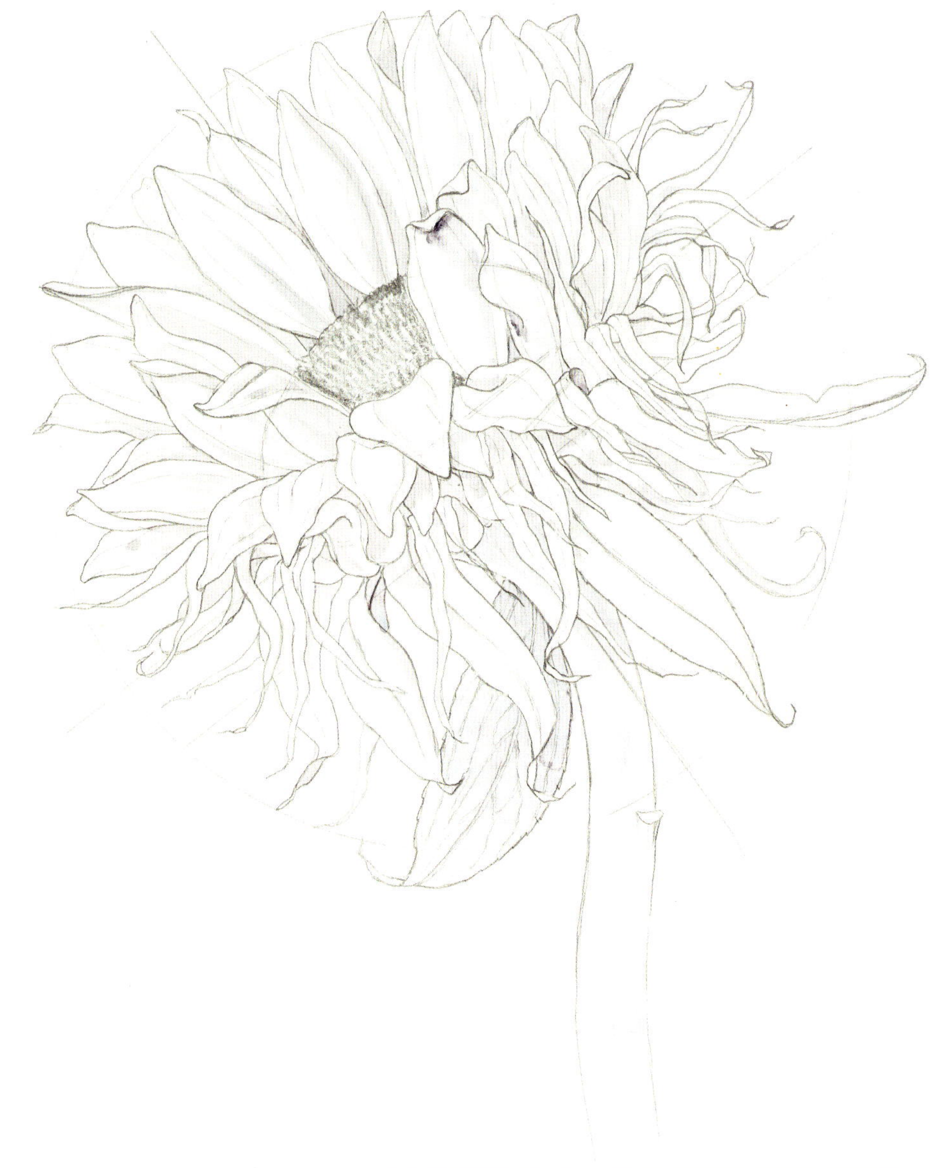

Palette and Harmonic Shadows

When a subject has a dominant colour, I like to use several versions of that colour to stop the painting from looking flat. Even if it looks like the petals are the exact same yellow as one of the yellows in your palette, the colour on any plant is never uniform. There are many factors that affect it and these natural variations look too stunning to be ignored.

For this sunflower I used four different yellows. The underlayer is **Hansa Yellow Light**. This is a very luminous yellow that makes a lovely base layer to build on.
For the top side of the petals, I also used **Quinophthalone Yellow**, a bright mid-yellow that will add saturation and give the sunflower a very sunny disposition.
The base of the petals is **Hansa Yellow Deep**, an orange-bias yellow, giving a more orange hue to the yellow without turning it true orange.
For the underside of the petals, I used **Mayan Yellow**, a slightly orange-bias yellow with a matte and chalky finish.

Palette

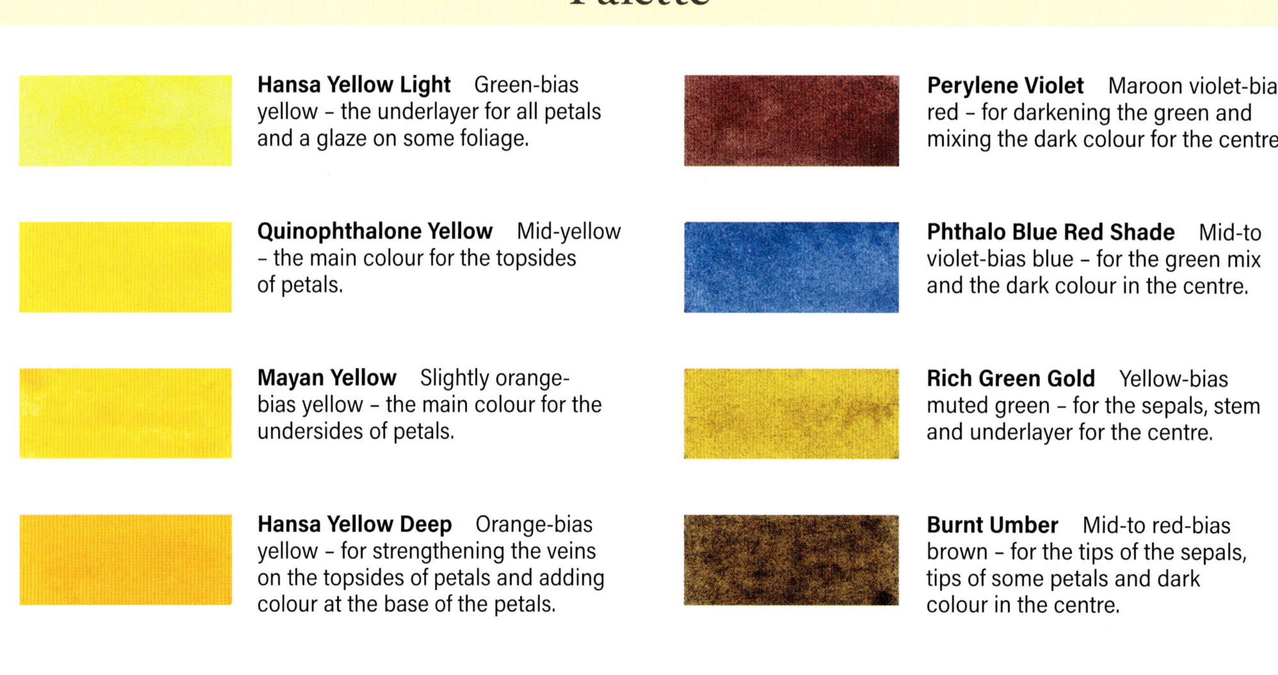

Hansa Yellow Light   Green-bias yellow – the underlayer for all petals and a glaze on some foliage.

Perylene Violet   Maroon violet-bias red – for darkening the green and mixing the dark colour for the centre.

Quinophthalone Yellow   Mid-yellow – the main colour for the topsides of petals.

Phthalo Blue Red Shade   Mid-to violet-bias blue – for the green mix and the dark colour in the centre.

Mayan Yellow   Slightly orange-bias yellow – the main colour for the undersides of petals.

Rich Green Gold   Yellow-bias muted green – for the sepals, stem and underlayer for the centre.

Hansa Yellow Deep   Orange-bias yellow – for strengthening the veins on the topsides of petals and adding colour at the base of the petals.

Burnt Umber   Mid-to red-bias brown – for the tips of the sepals, tips of some petals and dark colour in the centre.

Green mixes

The **light green mix** is **Hansa Yellow Light + Phthalo Blue Red Shade**.

Medium green mix: Quinophthalone Yellow + Phthalo Blue Red Shade.

Golden-green mix for the stem: **Rich Green Gold**. Add the medium green mix as a glaze in the darker parts.

To mix a **darker green**, add more **Phthalo Blue Red Shade**.

To mix a **lighter green**, add more **Hansa Yellow Light**.

To mix a more **muted green**, add **Perylene Violet**.

To mix a **bluer green** for the underside of the foliage, add more **Phthalo Blue Red Shade**.

Glazes can be added after the initial washes: **Hansa Yellow Light** to brighten up, **Rich Green Gold** to add a golden glow, diluted **Phthalo Blue Red Shade** to darken.

Harmonic Shadows

Phthalo Blue Red Shade + Perylene Violet + Hansa Yellow Light.

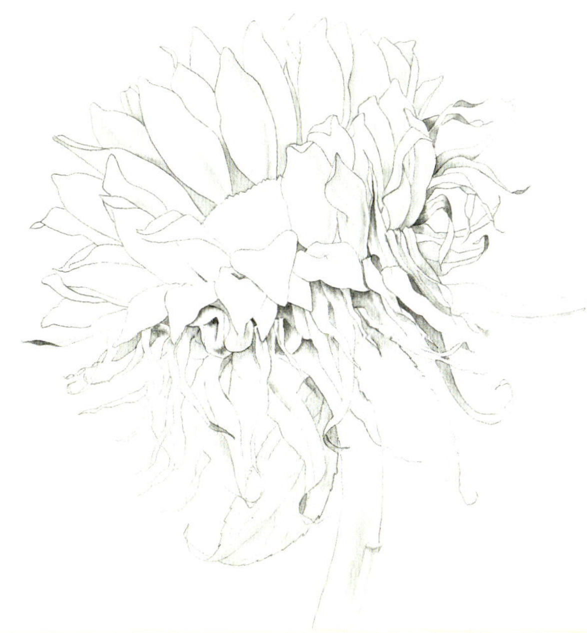

Step 1 The Harmonic Shadows are painted first, following the tone study. The same shadow mix is used for all the elements of the painting. It is more diluted on the petals, in order to keep the yellows bright and vibrant. It is less diluted for the foliage, so that it shows through the darker greens. The centre is left unpainted until later.

Washes

When painting wet-in-wet washes, I usually paint one first wash over all parts of the painting and then move on to the second wash. Adding the same number of washes to all elements ensures that the painting stays balanced throughout. However, I also think that rules are there to be broken sometimes. The creative process should not be impeded by a rigid routine. There should always be room for artistic licence and improvisation. This sunflower is a good example: I felt that with the complexity of the sketch, it would make more sense to tackle small areas to a higher degree before moving on to another small part.

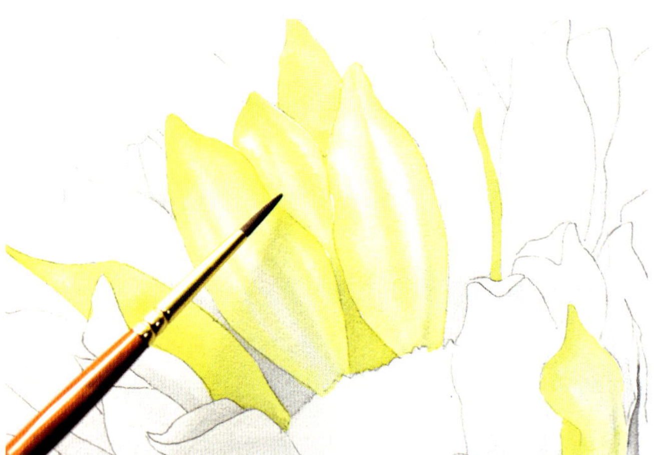

Step 1 The first wash on all petals, top side or underside, is Hansa Yellow Light. This is painted wet-in-wet, reserving the highlights. Sunflower petals are not glossy, so the highlights are not reserved completely white, only a paler yellow.

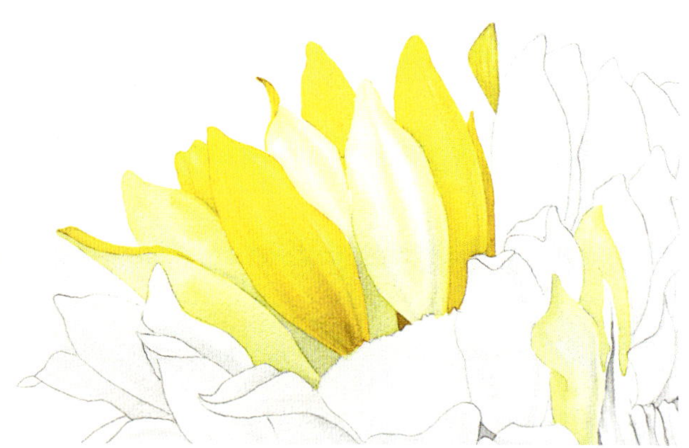

Step 2 The second wash, also wet-in-wet, is Quinophthalone Yellow. This colour is painted along the veins to add depth. Before the wash dries, drop in a touch of Hansa Yellow Deep at the base of the petals, to make it merge softly with the other yellows.

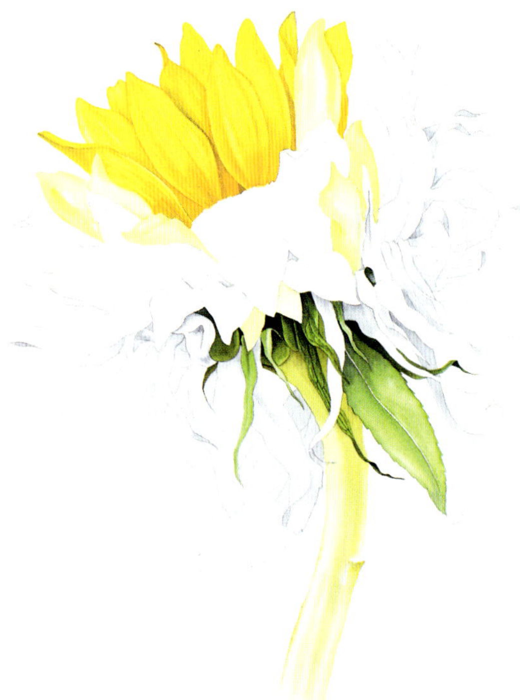

Step 3 After working on that section at the back of the inflorescence, I moved on to the greenery. Using the medium green mix as a base, I added more blue to the back of the sepals. I started with the sepals (and the stem) situated towards the back before moving to the front.

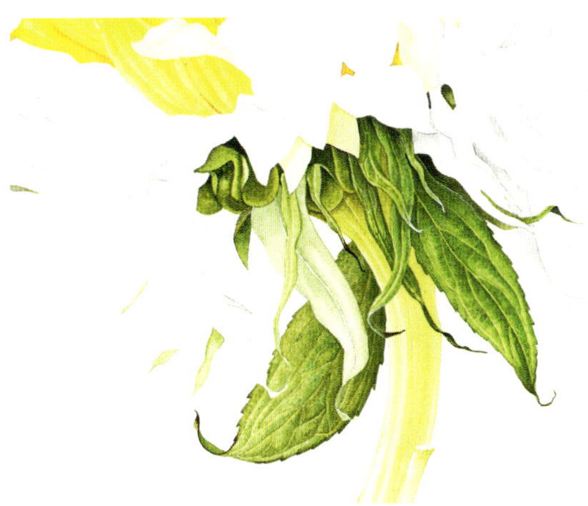

Step 4 I continued working my way around the crown of sepals, working from back to front and varying the greens: more blue when the back was showing, more yellow on the top side. The veins are quite thick so it is possible to work in between them, leaving them unpainted to start with and then painting a line of Rich Green Gold over them.

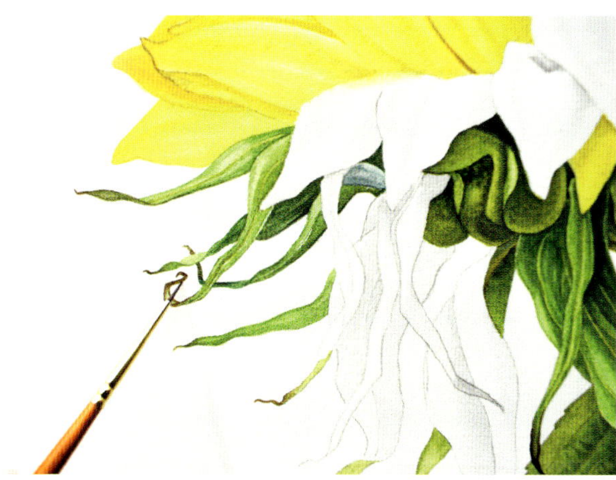

Step 5 The smaller, thinner sepals are painted with a 3/0 brush for sharp details. The same green mixes are used, with a touch of Burnt Umber at the very tip where they are a bit dried up or show some damage. Don't be afraid to portray the sepals in disarray. They give a lot of personality to the sunflower.

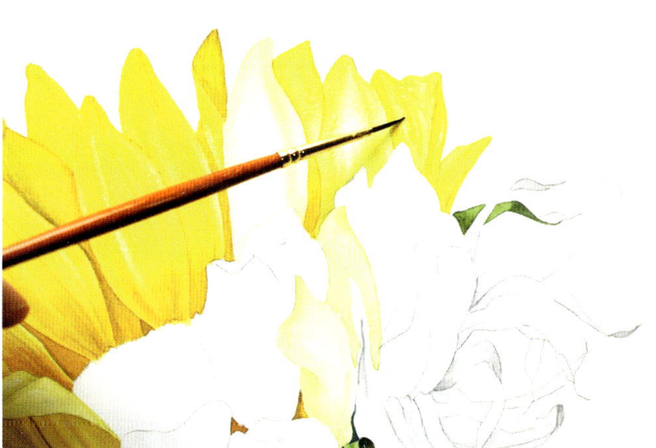

Step 6 Moving back to the petals, it is time to finish all the elements that are behind the almost-black centre. The main colour for the underside of the petals is Mayan Yellow. Some of the petals also show a bit of damage or ageing. Burnt Umber is again used to show this.

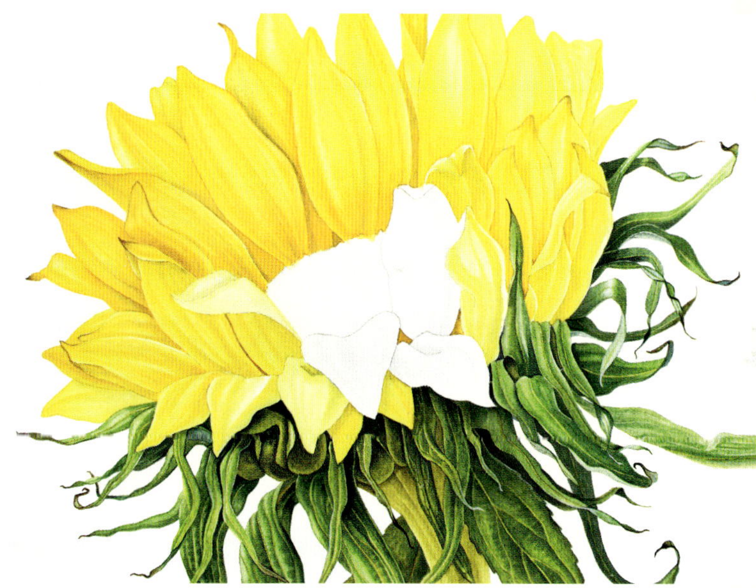

Step 7 The foliage is now finished and all the petals at the back and side completed. A few thin glazes can be added at this stage to modify the colour and bring the different parts to their final hues. A glaze of Hansa Yellow Light will add luminosity while Rich Green Gold will add a golden reflection. It is now time to tackle the centre...

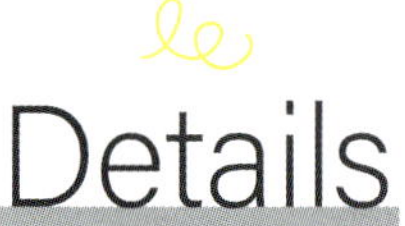

Details

Painting the centre of the sunflower is perhaps the most daunting part.
Being so much darker than the rest, the array of small disc florets are bound to
stand out and make a strong statement. The best way to approach them is to
deal with them as if they are a drawing, albeit a drawing with paint, using a 3/0
brush and undiluted paint.

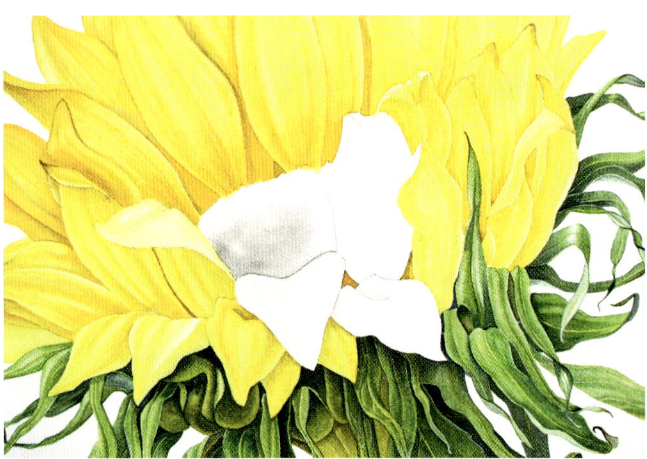

Step 1 The first step in painting the centre is to introduce
shadows. They will not show through the very dark florets, but they
will make the background darker to peep between the florets. This is
enough to create the illusion.

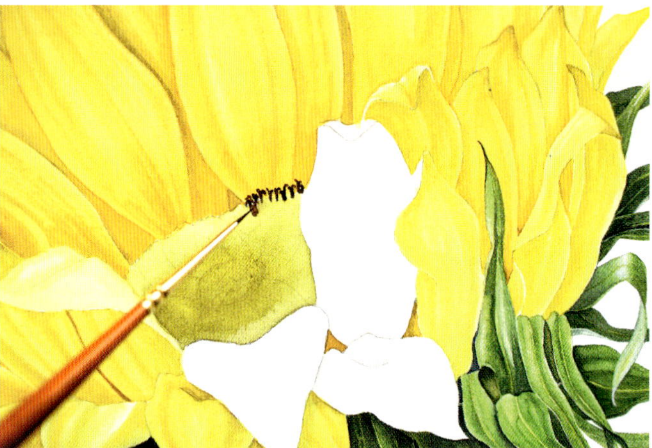

Step 2 The next step is to paint the background colour. This is
a simple flat wash of Rich Green Gold. After this has dried, the first
florets can go in, painted with a tiny brush and a mix of Perylene
Violet + original Harmonic Shadow mix. Depending on the colour of
your subject, some Burnt Umber may be added to the mix.

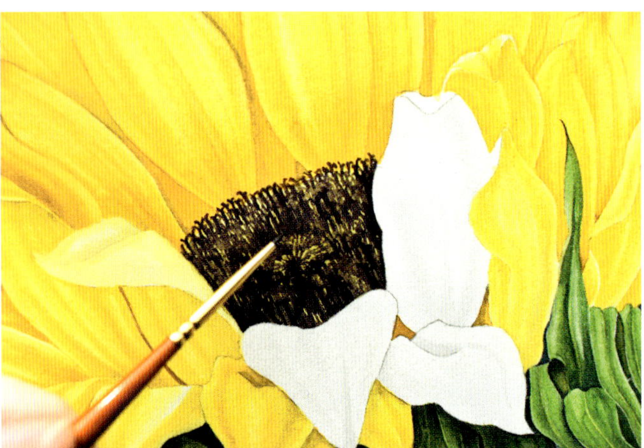

Step 3 Continue to paint the florets, one by one, following the
spiral pattern. Some florets in the centre might still be flattened
against the background, facing the centre.

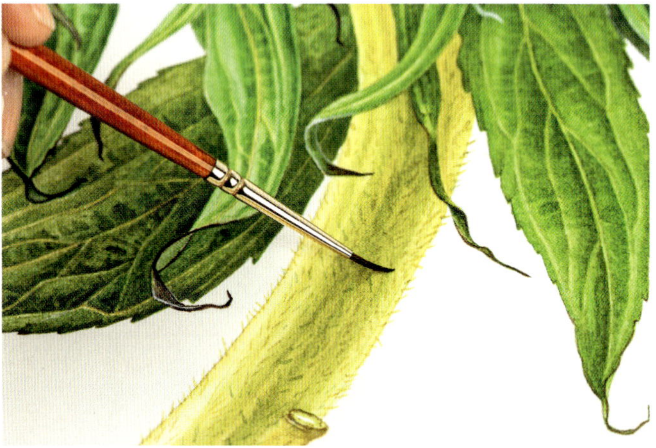

Step 4 The finishing touch is painting the hairs on the stem,
using all the greens mixed together. Make sure you vary the angles
and give an air of randomness.

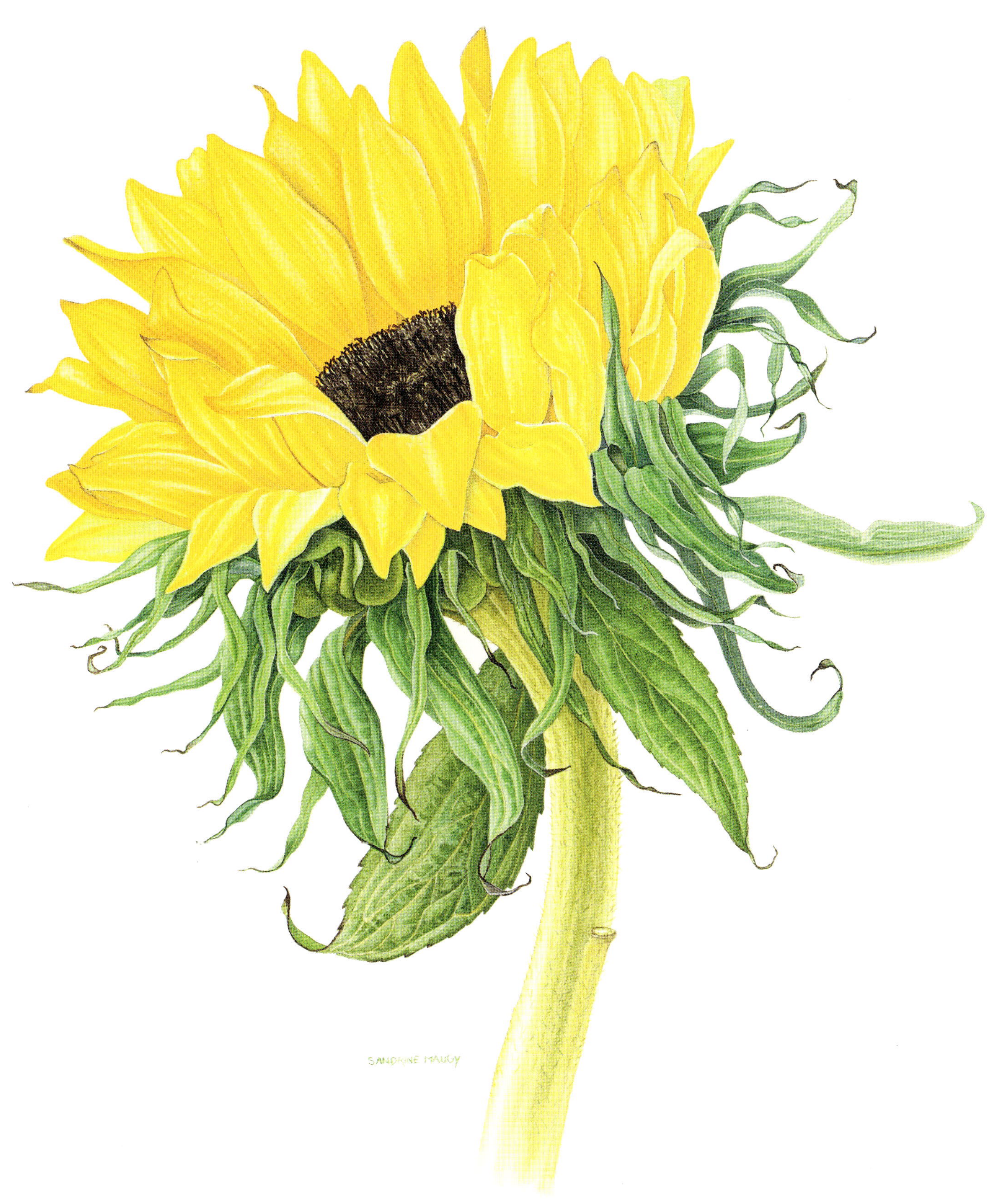

Sunflower
Watercolour on paper.

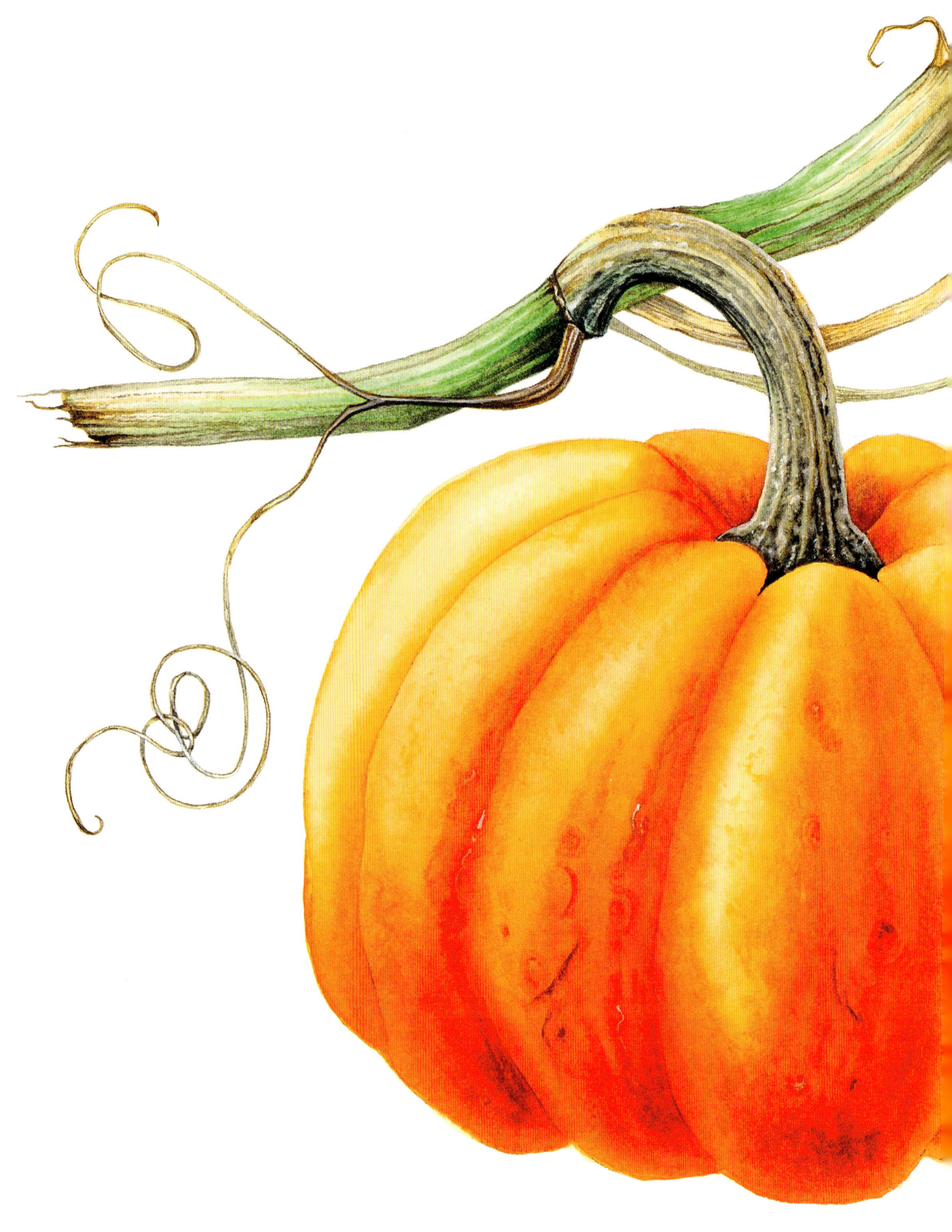

Autumn

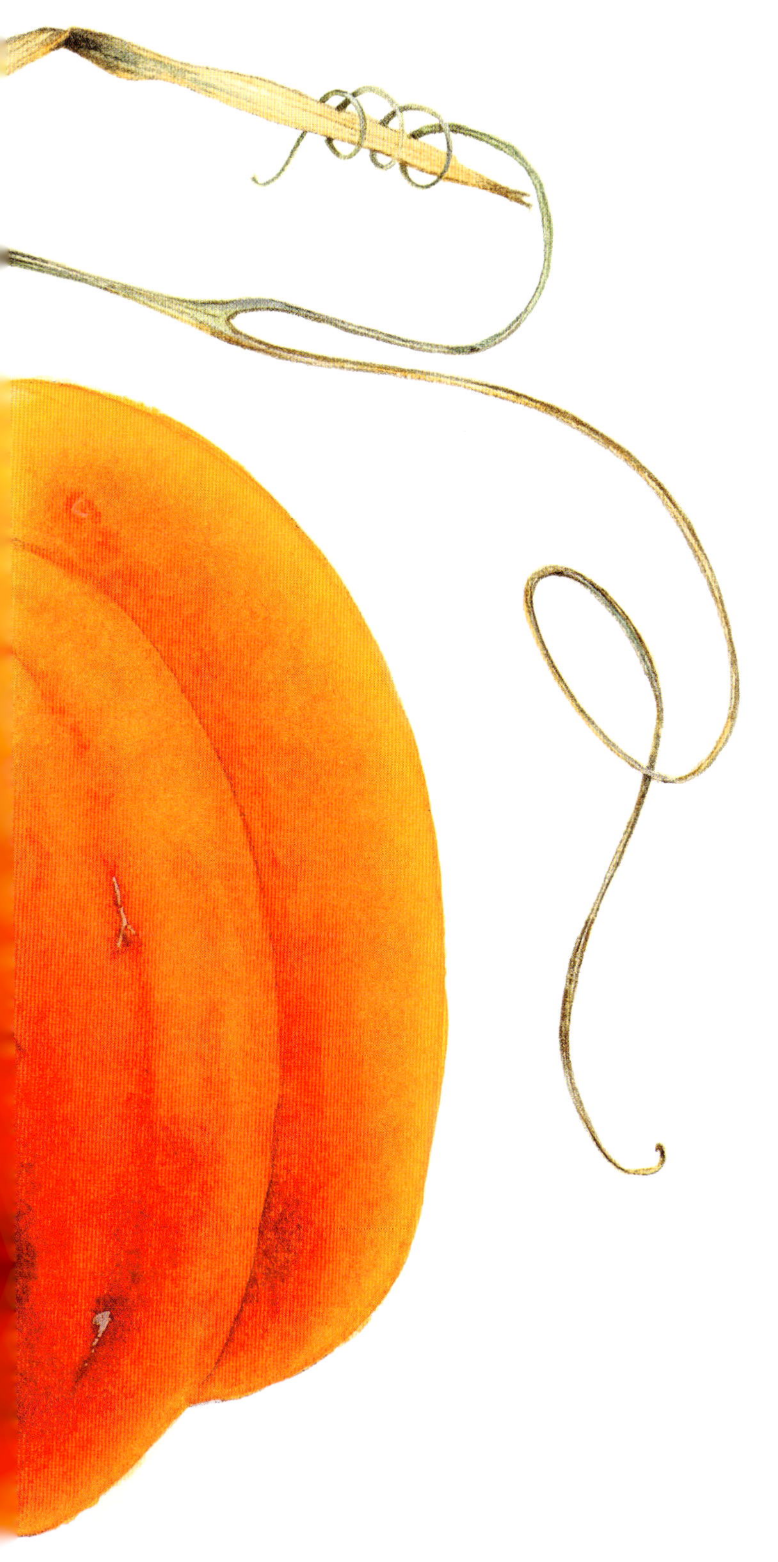

AUTUMN SUBJECTS
and their palette

Trying to cling onto the idea of long warm days, we regard the Autumn as
a transition between Summer and the cold damp Winter that lies ahead. However,
Autumn is a beautiful season in its own right, full of dramatic subjects waiting to
be painted as the chlorophyll in the leaves begins to break down, allowing
the bright reds and golds to give a last show before they fall.

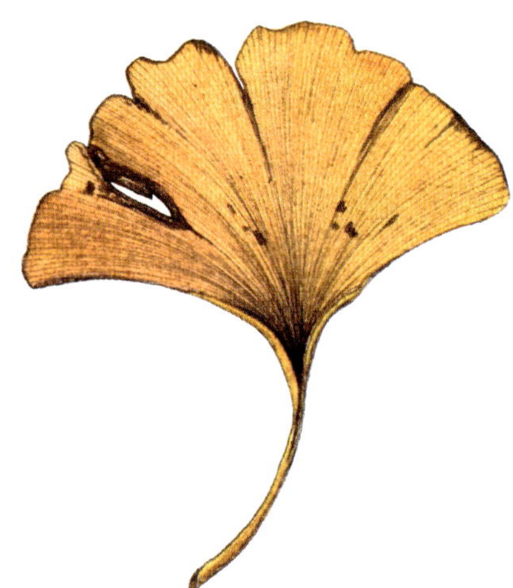

Autumn palette

The bright blues and vivid purples of Summer have disappeared, replaced by more
muted hues. Even the greens become dirtier before turning to gold and red. Carmine
shifts its duty from flowers to foliage. Perylene Violet, a rich velvety maroon, is ideal for
that dark dahlia that will last until the first hard frosts.

Fruit picking

From September I am on the scrounge, visiting all my friends' gardens and looking
for fruit to pick, preferably with a bit of branch and a few leaves. I love to paint the
roundness of fruit, the plumpness of their flesh, the tantalizing smell and the promise of
the flavour. However, I never eat my subjects. Notwithstanding the fact that as I paint
quite slowly they are usually past their edible stage by the time I am finished with
them, after spending hours looking at them and sometimes even talking to them, I lack
the courage to eat them. I also find it hard to throw them away. It seems insulting and
ungrateful. To their delight, the resident blackbirds usually get them, making the most of
this unexpected inheritance and sharing them with their ever-increasing families.

Rich Green Gold is useful for pears and Perylene Violet for the dark plums. The blush
on pears and apples can be painted with light washes of Carmine.

Last moments in the Autumn garden

The pink and white Japanese anemones are bravely standing the first frosts; the
hydrangeas are drying up their petals of dark reds and greeny-blues, keeping the flower
heads in order to protect the emerging leaf buds during the Winter months; the trees
are starting to let go of the bright leaves that gave us such a good show for a few weeks.
Amongst the golden hues and the remaining passionflowers, under a timid pale-blue
sky and a weakening sun, we can enjoy our last warm moments of the year in the
Autumn garden.

Palette

Other colours appear in the three tutorials, but if you would like a basic palette from which to mix all your colours, the list below is a good starting point for Autumn subjects.

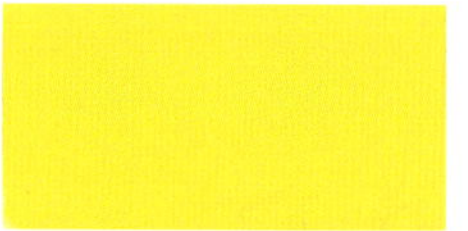

Hansa Yellow Light   Green-bias yellow – luminous yellow for the first wash on leaves and fruit as well as top glazes.
Subjects: Pears and yellow foliage.

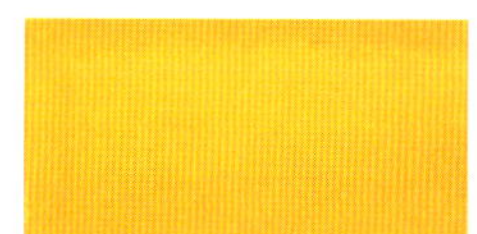

Hansa Yellow Deep   Orange-bias yellow – golden yellow for foliage and orange mixes.
Subjects: Autumn leaves and rose hips.

Carmine   Violet-bias red – a deep red that mixes well with yellows for peachy tones.
Subjects: Autumn leaves, from *Liquidambar* to Acers.

Perylene Violet   Maroon dark violet – for deep purples and maroon shades.
Subjects: Dahlias, branches and dark foliage.

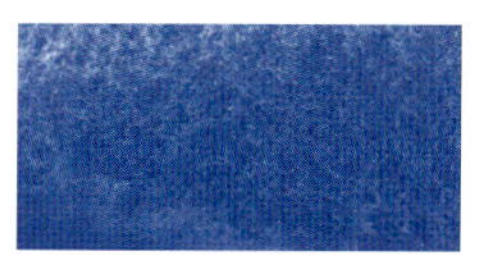

French Ultramarine   Violet-bias blue – a granulating blue to add texture to shadows mixes.
Subjects: Velvety pansies and chunky fruit.

Cerulean Blue   Green-bias blue – milky granulating blue for texture and the underside of leaves.
Subjects: Any foliage (underside) and washed out, fading flowers.

Sap Green   Slightly muted mid green.
Subjects: The last of the green foliage and fruit.

Rich Green Gold   Bronze green with a yellow bias.
Subjects: Fruit and golden leaves.

Burnt Umber   Reddish brown.
Subjects: Dying or dried-up leaves, branches and blemishes.

GINKGO BILOBA

Common name Maidenhair Tree	**Foliage** Deciduous	**Hardiness** Fully hardy
Botanical name *Ginkgo biloba*	**Planting time** October to November	**Propagation** Seed
Flowering Spring	**Aspect** Full sun	**Native** China

Botanically speaking…

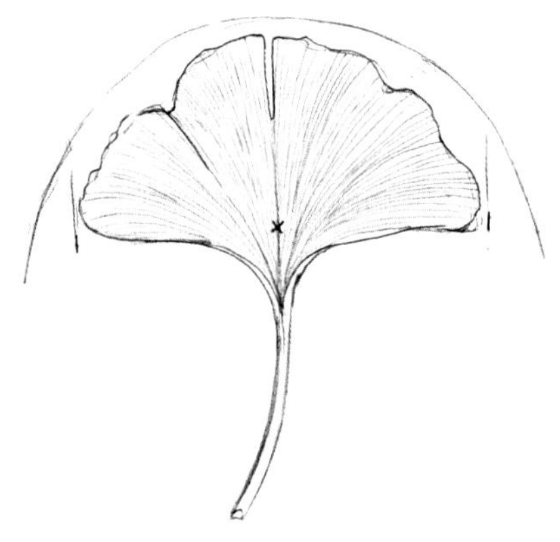

- Ginkgo trees grow up to 35m (114ft) tall, some specimens reaching over 50m (164ft).

- They are generally pest-free, disease-free and low maintenance. As a consequence, they are long-lived; some specimens are over 2,500 years old!

- From the order *Ginkgoales*, *Ginkgo biloba* is a living fossil, as fossils from the early Permian era (over 290 million years ago) have been identified as related to the modern ginkgo.

- The modern *Ginkgo biloba* is the oldest tree in the world, going back to the mid-Jurassic period, 170 million years ago. Trees living in the Jurassic period were contemporary with dinosaurs such as the *Diplodocus* and the *Stegosaurus*.

- The genus name *Ginkgo* is regarded as a misspelling of the Japanese *ginkyō*, which means 'silver apricot'.

- The leaves are bilobed, giving the tree its second name. They are unique among seed plants, being fan-shaped with veins radiating out into the leaf blade, sometimes bifurcating (splitting). Two veins enter the leaf blade at the base and fork repeatedly in two; this is known as dichotomous venation.

- The leaves are green in Spring and Summer, turning an amazing golden yellow in the Autumn. Even when emerging they are fully formed, a tiny version of the future larger leaf.

- The fruit is round, pale orange, with an exceedingly unpleasant smell.

- *Ginkgo biloba* is an extremely resilient tree: six trees survived the Hiroshima atom bomb in 1945 as close as 1km (⅝mile) to the explosion site. Although charred, they survived, were soon healthy again and are still alive to this day.

Opposite page
Ginkgo biloba
Walnut ink on paper.

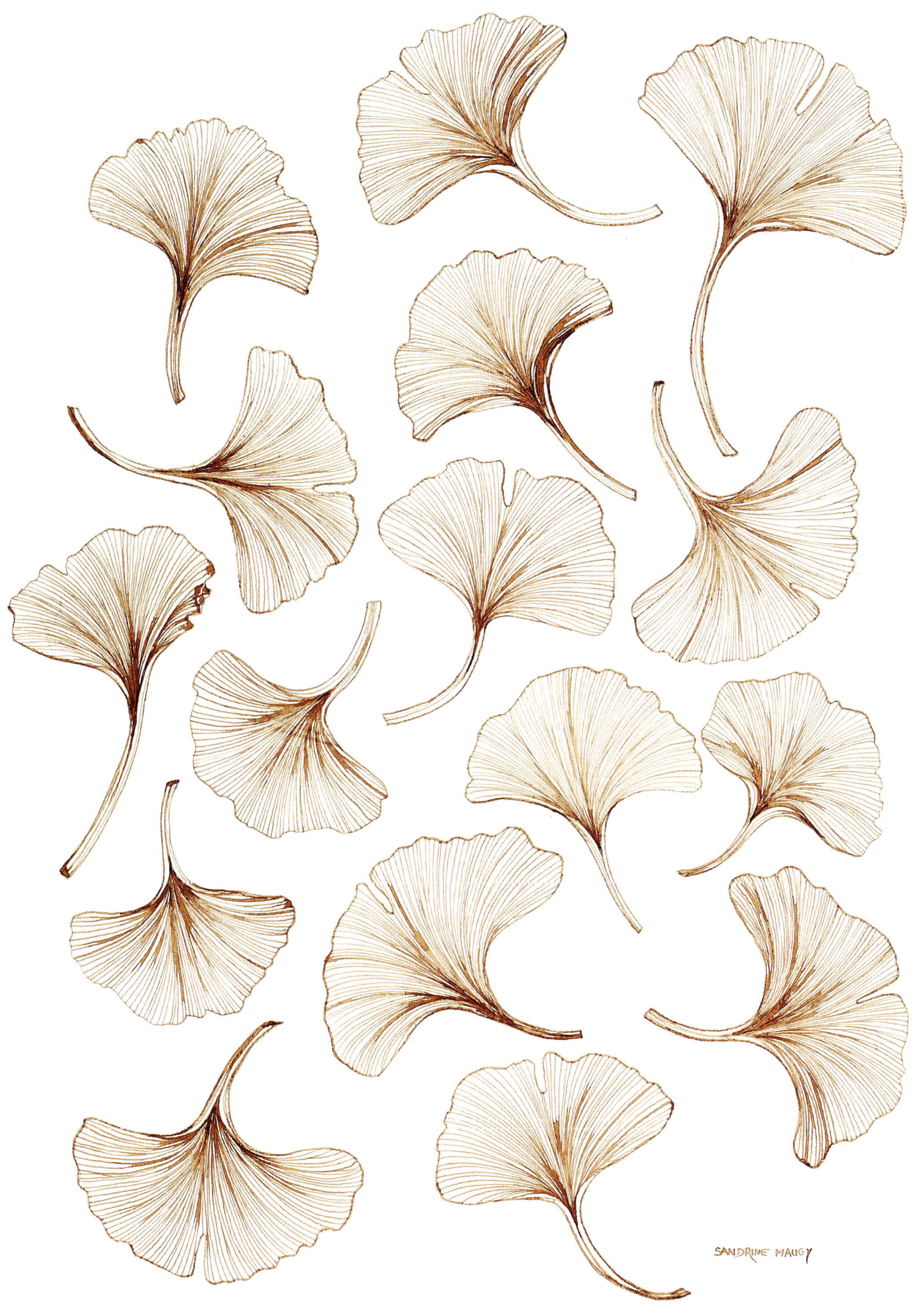

SANDRINE MAUGY

GINKGO BILOBA
Sketches and palette

Ginkgo biloba is a prehistoric tree that was around at the time of the dinosaurs. To me that makes it the coolest tree on the planet. Added to that, the beautiful fan-shaped leaves, which create some very strong shapes design-wise, the gorgeous colours especially in Autumn, the architectural structure of the tree itself… But really, it had me at 'dinosaur'.

Colour trials

The brown hues of the decaying leaves go from a rich maroon to a pale, much cooler brown with some beige accents as the leaves start to dry and get brittle. Rather than introducing a ready-made brown, I wanted to use a range of yellows that would already be part of the palette. I had a feeling that, when mixed with Perylene Violet, different yellows would produce the range of rich to pale browns I needed. One by one, I mixed all the yellows in my palette with Perylene Violet, starting with pure yellow at the beginning of the line, adding more and more Perylene as I moved along to the right. I then placed the real leaves on the multicoloured squares and chose the closest matches.

Perylene Violet and yellow mixes

Hansa Yellow Light

Quinophthalone Yellow

Hansa Yellow Deep

Permanent Orange

Quinacridone Gold

Rich Green Gold

Nickel Azo Yellow

Drawing

Materials list

PAPERS
Cartridge paper or sketchbook
Tracing paper
Transfer paper
Watercolour paper: Fabriano Artistico
HP Extra White, 640gsm (300lb)

DRAWING
Pencils: 6B clutch pencil; a finer pencil
for details

PAINTING
Brushes: Pro Arte Prolene Plus Series 007
in sizes 3/0, 2, 4 and 6; Princeton Neptune
synthetic squirrel round brush series in
size 6 (for wetting the paper and for
light-touch glazes)

While they are on the tree, *Ginkgo* leaves are usually flat, with perhaps a rare curved edge here and there. This makes them an easy subject when it comes to tone, as there isn't much going on when it comes to shadows. When the leaves fall off the tree in Autumn and they start going brown, their edges curl at the same time as the blemishes increase, making the details more interesting.

In this composition, I wanted to have a selection of leaves at different stages of health and decay. The top ones are still green with only a few blemishes caused by insect damage while the others, fallen from the tree, are getting yellow then brown, with some russeting appearing and bits starting to break off.

The sketchbook studies are done one leaf at a time, without much thought about composition yet. Then the leaves deemed best suited to the final painting are traced onto separate pieces of tracing paper, allowing for trying different arrangements until a satisfactory composition is found.

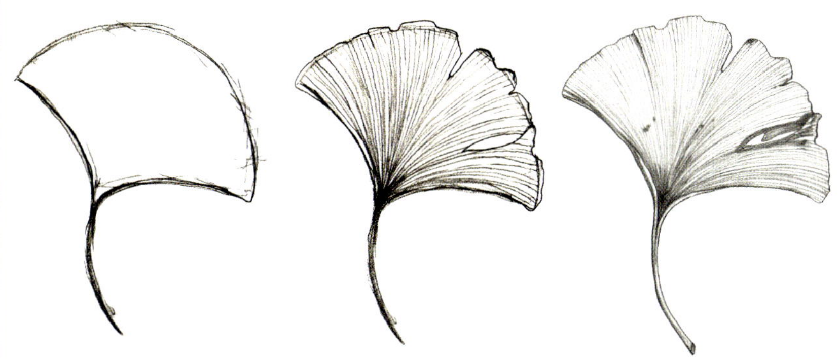

Palette

My favourite stage of the *Ginkgo* leaf cycle is the bright yellow of Autumn. Therefore I decided to make yellow the base colour and work the other colours around it. I selected three yellows from the colour trials opposite:

Hansa Yellow Light   Green-bias yellow – the underlayer for all the leaves and for the palest, beige Perylene mixes.

Quinophthalone Yellow   Mid-yellow, the brightest in my palette – for the strongest colour of the yellowest leaves, catching the glory of the Autumn sun. Also used for the richest brown Perylene mixes.

Hansa Yellow Deep   Orange-bias yellow for the most golden tones and the medium Perylene mixes where the brown has some almost pink hints to it.

French Ultramarine   Violet-bias blue   The granulation will come in useful to gives some texture to the damaged leaves.

Perylene Violet   Muted maroon violet – there is no red in the Autumn *Ginkgo* leaf but some of the brown markings have a slightly violet tinge to them and, when mixed with a range of yellows, Perylene will provide all the required browns.

Raw Umber   A dull green brown – for the dark blemishes.

Harmonic Shadows: French Ultramarine + Perylene Violet + Hansa Yellow Light.

Washes

In a composition made of a large number of small elements, it is
important to keep the whole painting well balanced. One way
to achieve this is to paint the same number of washes on all the
leaves, reaching the same degree of intensity, range of tone and
details. Therefore, I painted a first and second wash on all the leaves,
finishing all the wet-in-wet work before adding the dry details.

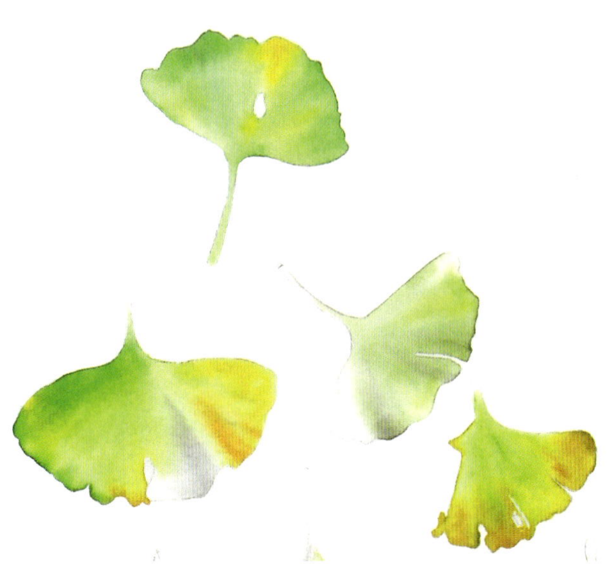

Step 1 With the light source in the top-left, the shadows are
straightforward and bear no surprises. They are painted wet-in-
wet, keeping to the deepest shadows and the cast shadows of the
curls, without venturing too far into the mid-tones, thus allowing
clean mid-tone areas that will reveal the bright yellows and rich
browns. Each leaf is painted in one wash, wetting the whole leaf
and dropping in the shadow mix. In order to keep the yellows
clean while allowing the grey to show through the browns, the
shadow mix is more diluted when painted under yellow and more
concentrated when darker colours will sit on top. The order in which
the leaves are painted is not important. Here, I worked my way
down from the top.

Step 2 The top four leaves are still mainly green. I mixed a range
of greens from French Ultramarine, adding the different yellows
to create variations: Hansa Yellow Light for the freshest, brightest
green; Quinophthalone Yellow for the medium green; Hansa Yellow
Deep for the dullest green.

While the green was still wet, I dropped in some other colours,
letting them mix directly on the paper, letting them meld into each
other and create natural variations, while following the patterns on
my live subjects.

Here, again, the different yellows reflect the different stages of the
lives of the leaves: Hansa Yellow Light for the leaf at the top, moving
down to Quinophthalone, then to Hansa Yellow Deep when the
yellow starts to turn almost orange.

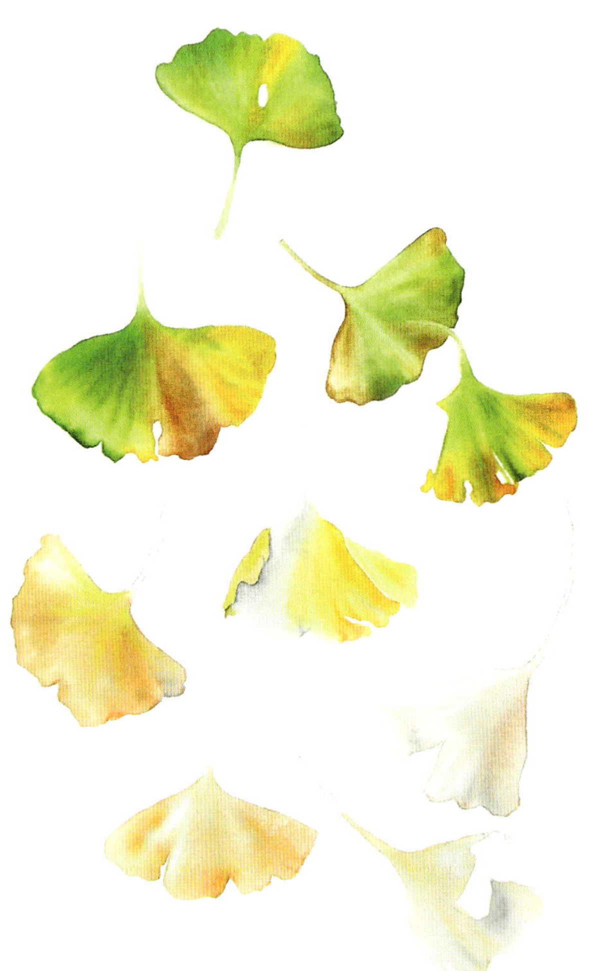 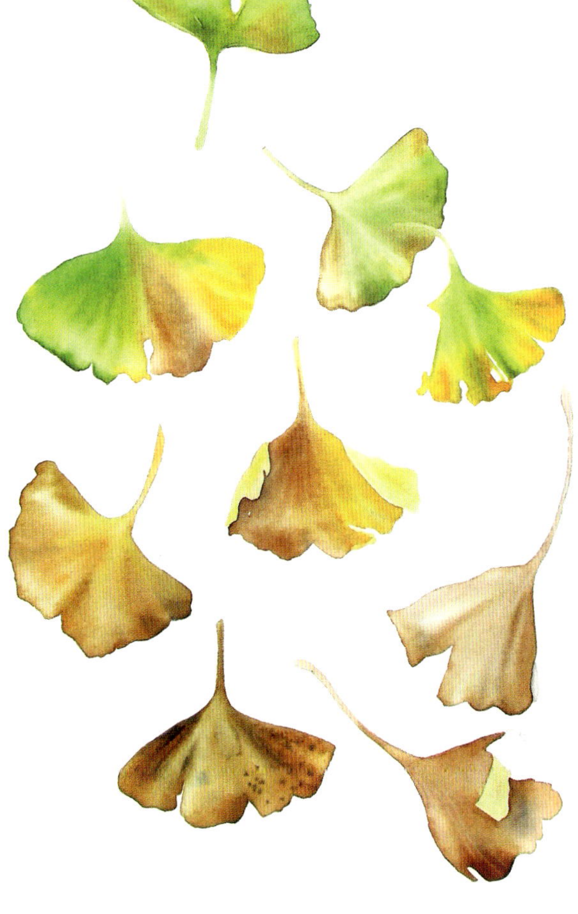

Step 3
As I work my way down the painting with wet-in-wet washes, there is less and less green and more and more brown. Perylene Violet is omnipresent in the painting, but it never appears as a colour on its own. As a consequence, all the Perylene + yellow mixes are prepared on the palette and painted onto the wet paper as a ready-mixed colour. This is a different method compared to the way I paint the yellows, which are dropped in as pure colours and mix as they will directly on the paper.

Step 4
Once there is a first wash on all the leaves, they are ready for a second wet-in-wet wash. This wash is a repeat of the first one, deepening the colours and accentuating the hues and effects created with the first wash.

Because the composition is a representation of leaves falling from the tree and being airborne, I don't want to paint too many washes at the risk of getting too heavy with the paint. I need a light, windblown feel. Therefore, I am stopping at two wet-in-wet washes and paint the rest with a dry brush, adding veins and details with a small brush.

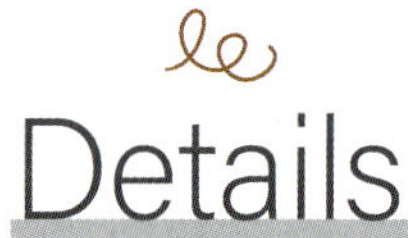

Details

The dry-brush details are going to bring everything together,
sharpening the painting and accentuating the differences between the
almost intact leaves and the ones that are decaying, drying or dying as
they reach the ground.

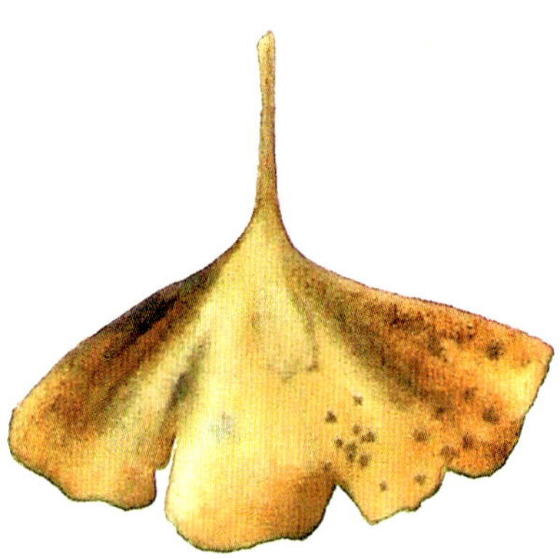

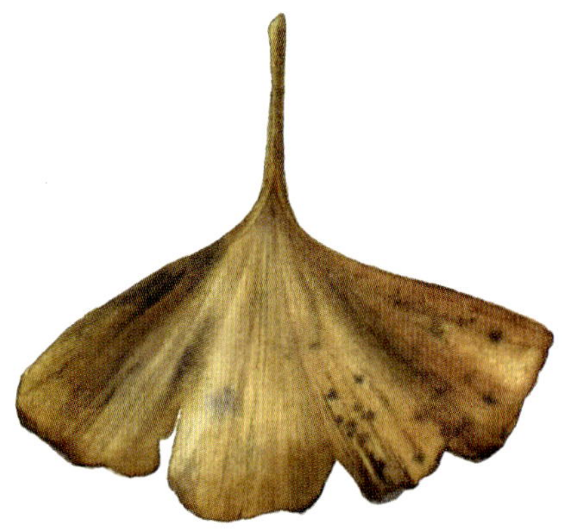

Some of the details are hinted at while painting wet-in-wet. Some of
the leaves are showing mould dots that look blurry rather than sharp.
These are better painted wet to keep them soft. They can be refined
with a little dry-brush work later if needed.

Following the principle that it is always easier to dull down a saturated
colour than brighten up a dull one, the wet washes are painted
brighter than their intended final colour. The details are then painted
with a dry brush and concentrated paint, then blended straight away
with a damp brush into the surrounding colour. This does two things:
it blends the details into the texture of the leaf and it adds more colour
to it, modifying the hues created by the wet washes.

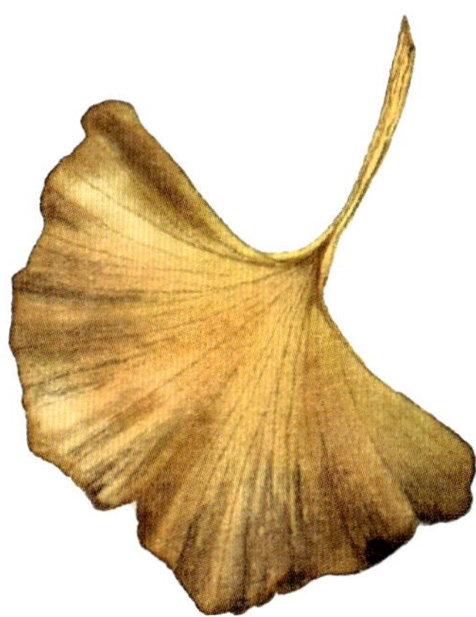

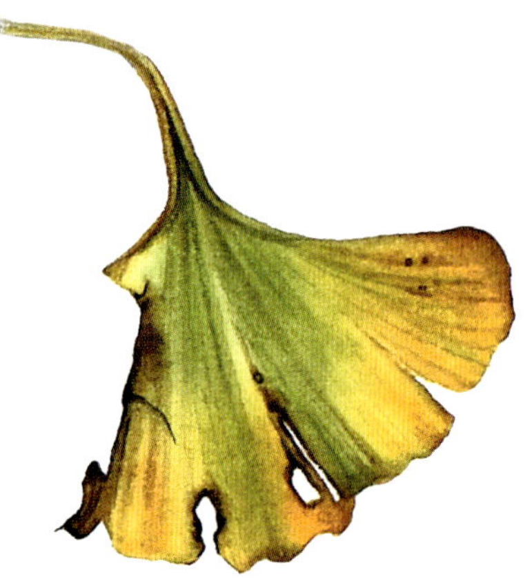

The veins are painted in the same way as the details: using a 3/0
brush and concentrated Raw Umber or the dull green mix, draw two
or three veins on dry paper. Blend straight away with a size 4 brush,
damp but not soaking wet, to avoid erasing the vein altogether.
Some veins will disappear, some will blend and some will stay
quite visible. This is exactly the serendipitous effect you are trying
to achieve.

The darkest blemishes are painted with Raw Umber, which can be
made less flat by using a touch of Perylene Violet and/or some of
the Perylene and yellow mixes. The strongest blemishes are left
sharp on the outer edges of the leaves and are slightly softened with
a damp brush on their inner border.

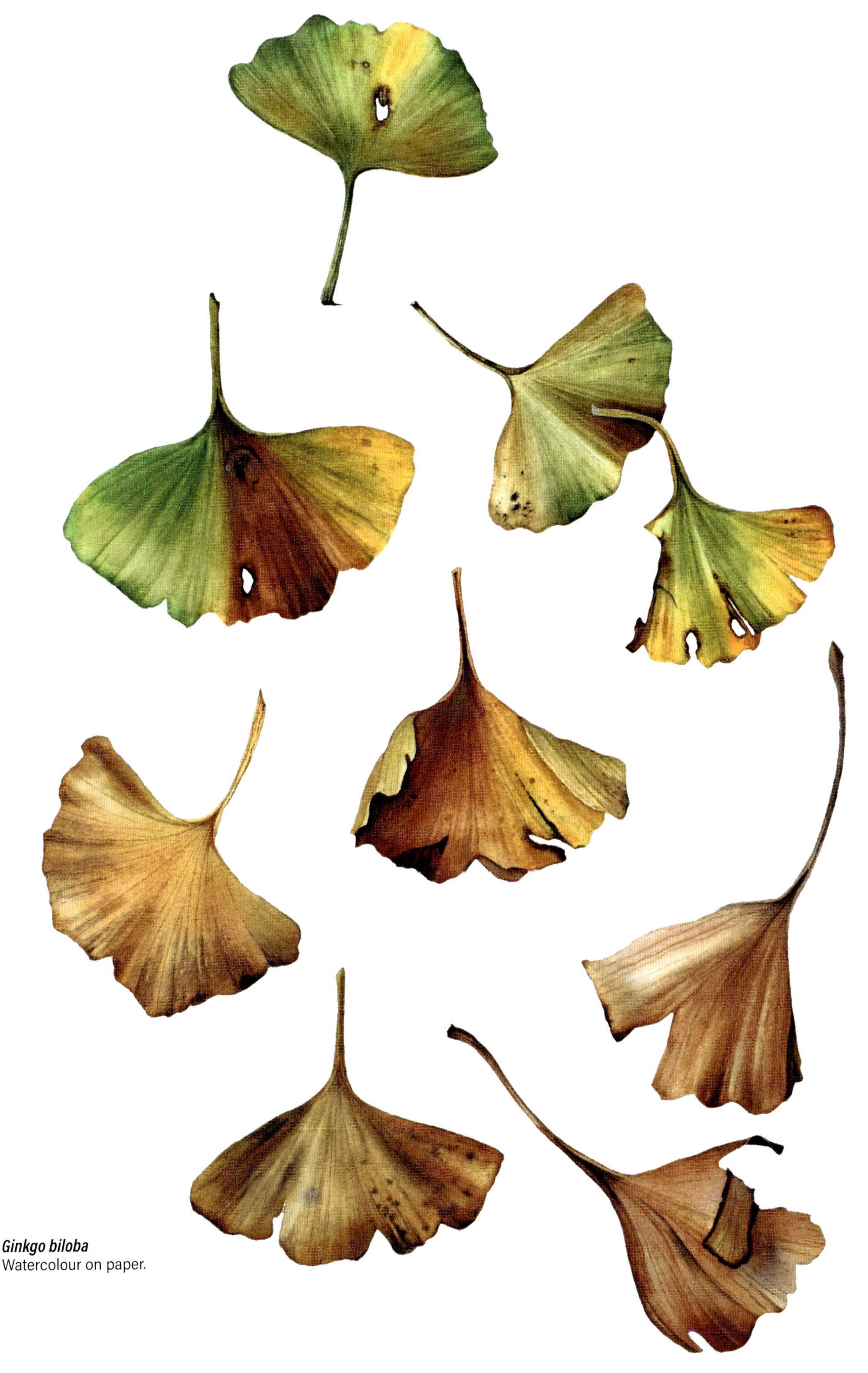

Ginkgo biloba
Watercolour on paper.

PEAR

Common name   European/
Common Pear
Botanical name   *Pyrus communis*
Family   Rosaceae

Flowering   Spring
Planting time   October to March
Aspect   Sunny or sheltered
Hardiness   Fully hardy

Propagation   Graft or seed
Native   Central and Eastern Europe
and Southwest Asia

Botanically speaking…

- Pear trees are deciduous and belong to the rose family.

- They grow to about 12m (39ft), though some can reach up to 20m (65½ft).

- Pear trees can live up to 250 years old.

- There are over 3,000 varieties of pears but fewer than 25 are grown commercially (in any significant amount).

- Pear trees are available to buy already grafted on a variety of rootstocks, which will determine the size of the mature tree. They can also be trained to grow in different shapes, including *espalier,* against a wall.

- Even the self-fertile varieties will fruit better when paired with a compatible tree.

- The leaves are tooth-edged and long-stalked.

- They are mid-green in the Spring, dark green in the Summer, turn gold in the Autumn then brown and finally black in the Winter.

- The blossom is white and grows in clusters. The flowers have five petals.

- The fruit is usually oblong and tear-shaped. Different varieties come in different shapes, though all variations of the original tear shape.

- The base colour of a pear is usually yellow, from a very pale lemon yellow to more golden hues. The top colours range from acid green to bright pink to deep maroon.

- The inside is fleshy and grainy and contains the pips in the bottom half of the fruit.

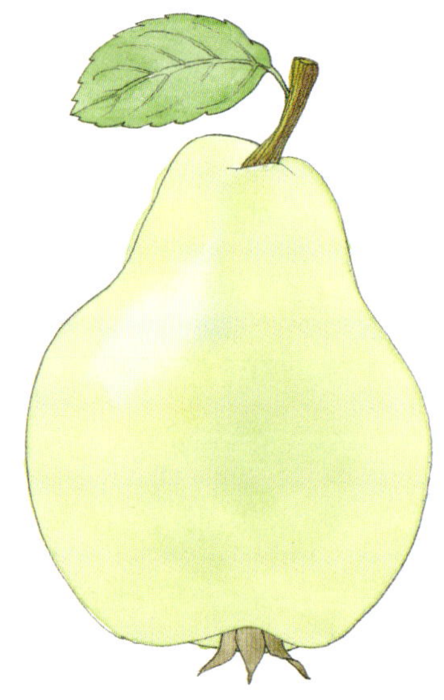

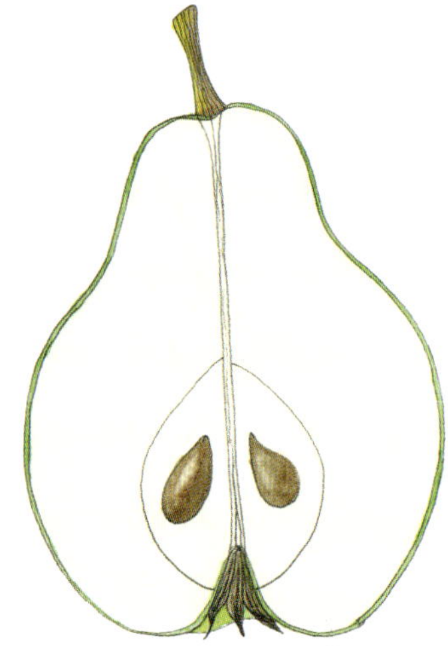

A selection of pear varieties

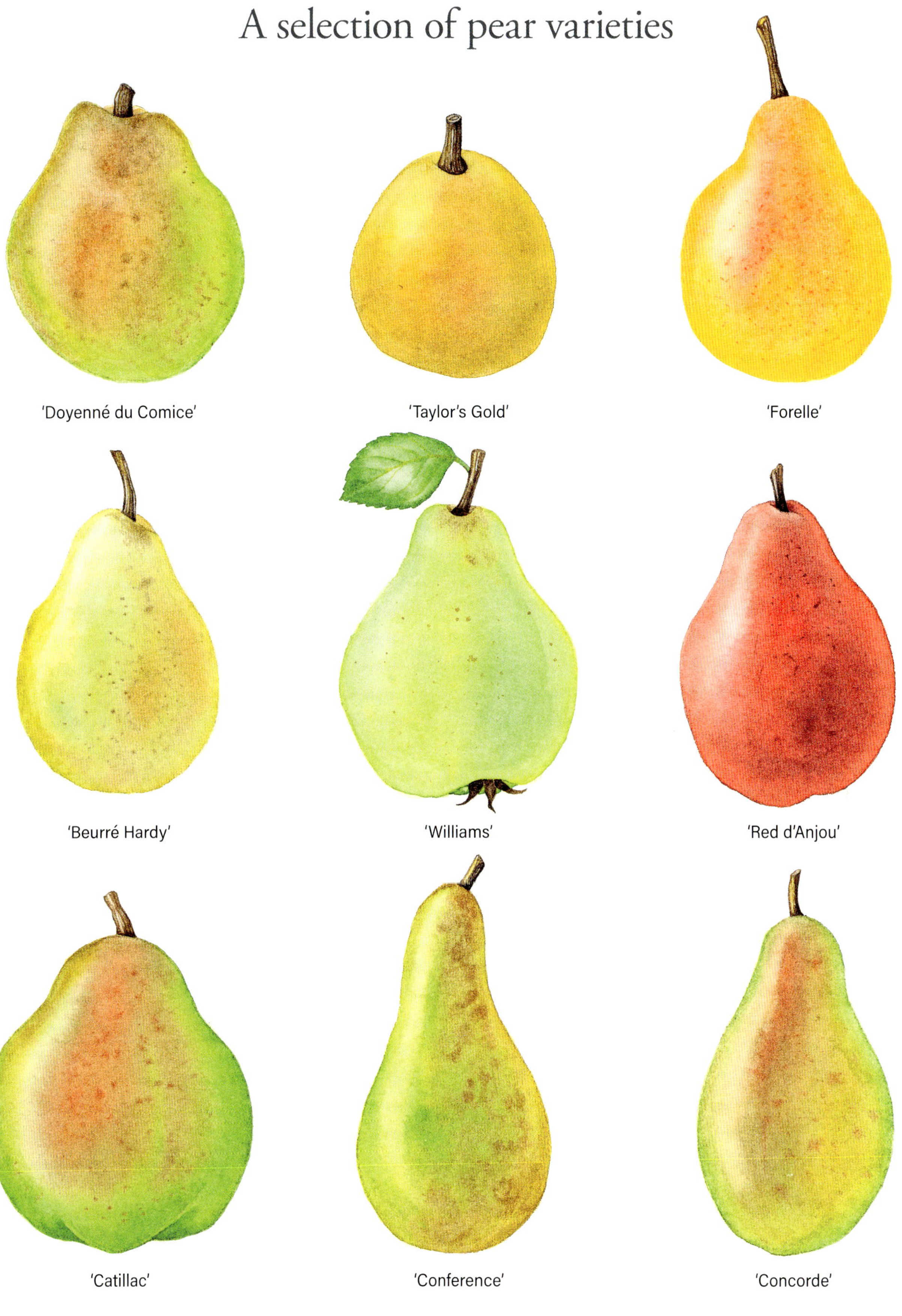

'Doyenné du Comice'

'Taylor's Gold'

'Forelle'

'Beurré Hardy'

'Williams'

'Red d'Anjou'

'Catillac'

'Conference'

'Concorde'

'CATILLAC' PEAR
Sketch

The orchards of West Dean Gardens in West Sussex, UK are the home of
45 pear varieties. *Pyrus communis* 'Catillac' is one of my favourites and
I have painted it several times over the years. I even planted one tree in my
own garden but it has yet to bear fruit. It is a triploid variety, meaning it
needs two pollinators in order to fruit. Dating from the mid-seventeenth
century, this old French variety produces cooking pears that can be kept
until the following Spring. It also has the largest and heaviest fruit I have
ever seen on a pear tree, being almost as large as a coconut, and just as hard.

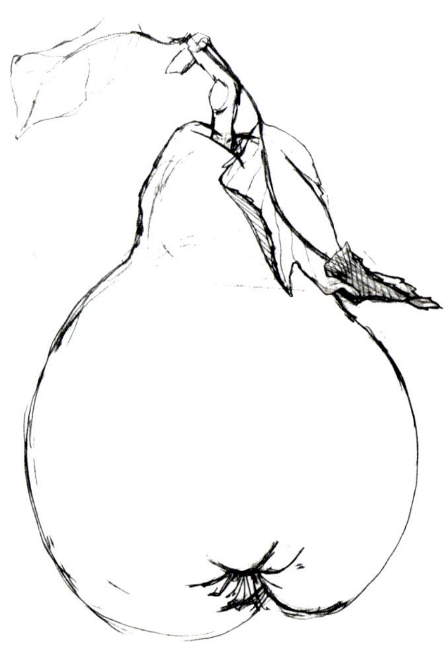

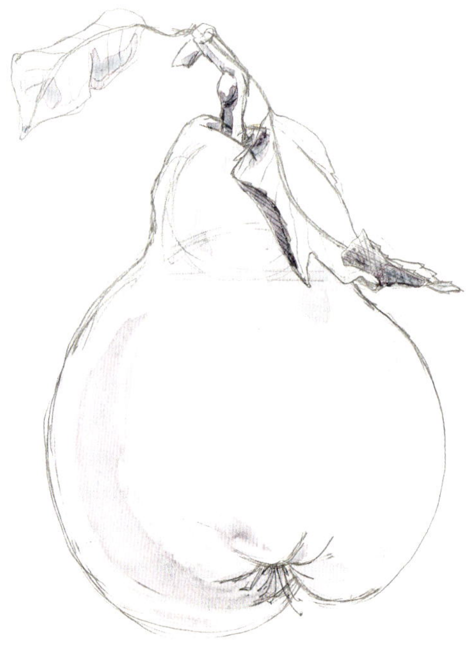

The initial sketch is made using two circles on top of each other.
For the 'Catillac', the bottom circle is much bigger than the top one
and the shape stays round, without any elongation. By the time
I started drawing the pear, the two leaves had broken down and
turned brown. For the composition, I had the option of going back
to the orchard and picking some fresh leaves, swapping old for new
and painting a pear with brand-new foliage. However, I thought that
the tired leaves looked beautiful and created a nice contrast with the
plump and juicy pear. I also liked the fact that the fading had turned
the leaves some interesting shades of brownish turquoise instead of
the more common mid-green.

Once happy with the drawing, trace it and transfer it to a piece of
watercolour paper as shown on page 14. It is now time for a tone
study in purple-grey, using Daniel Smith Moonglow.

Materials list

PAPERS

Cartridge paper or sketchbook
Tracing paper
Transfer paper
Watercolour paper: Fabriano Artistico
HP Extra White, 640gsm (300lb)

DRAWING

Pencils: 6B clutch pencil; finer pencil
for details

PAINTING

Brushes: Pro Arte Prolene Plus Series
007 in sizes 2, 4 and 6; Princeton
Neptune synthetic squirrel round brush
series in size 12 (for wetting the paper
and for light-touch glazes)
Daniel Smith Moonglow for tone study
Titanium White pigment stick

Choosing the colours

The first three colours to choose are the three primaries that make up the
Harmonic Shadows:

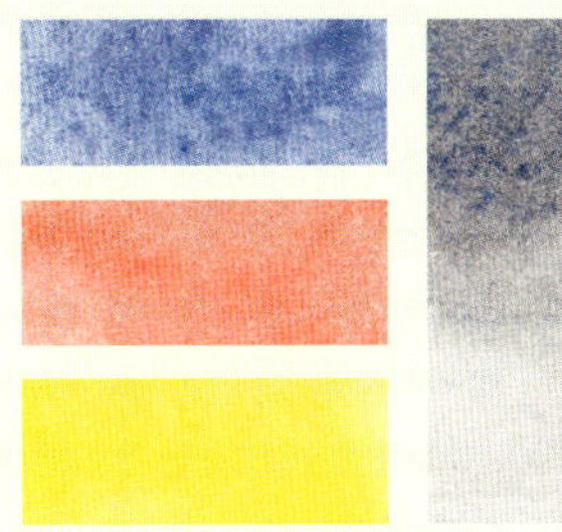

Yellow: a light yellow is preferable for the
undertone of the pear. Most of the pear
is green so the yellow also needs to mix
a clean green. **Hansa Yellow Light** has
these qualities.

Red: the red patch on the pear is a muted
red, almost maroon. **Perylene Red** is just the
right colour.

Blue: the pear has a slightly rough skin.
French Ultramarine is granulating, giving
some texture to the washes.

Other colours

Rich Green Gold: a muted golden green that adds a glow to the mid-tones.
Sap Green: the main colour of the pear and the base for the foliage mixes.
Raw Umber: mixed with **Cerulean Blue** and **Rich Green Gold** for the topside of the leaves
and mixed with **Burnt Sienna** for the underside.
Burnt Sienna: mixed with **Raw Umber** for the russeting.
Cerulean Blue: for the granulation and chalky texture of the underside of the leaves.

Palette

	Hansa Yellow Light		French Ultramarine
	Rich Green Gold		Perylene Red
	Sap Green		Burnt Sienna
	Cerulean Blue		Raw Umber

Wet-in-wet washes

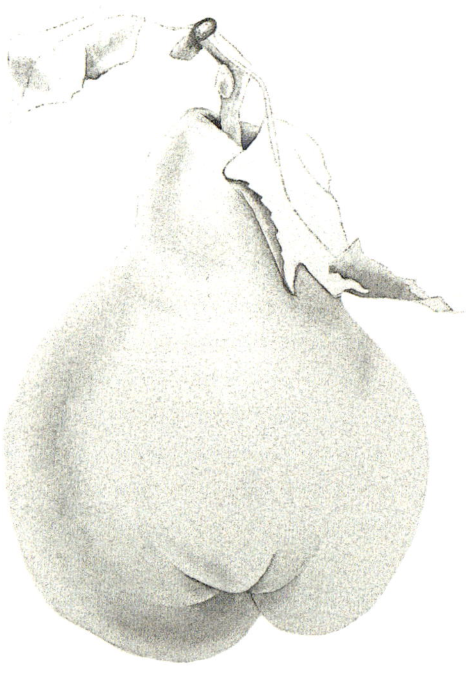

Shadows

The shadows are painted wet-in-wet, using the Harmonic Shadow mix of French Ultramarine + Perylene Red + Hansa Yellow Light. The deepest shadows are around the bottom of the pear and around the stem. As my light source is on the right, there is also a cast shadow under the right leaf.

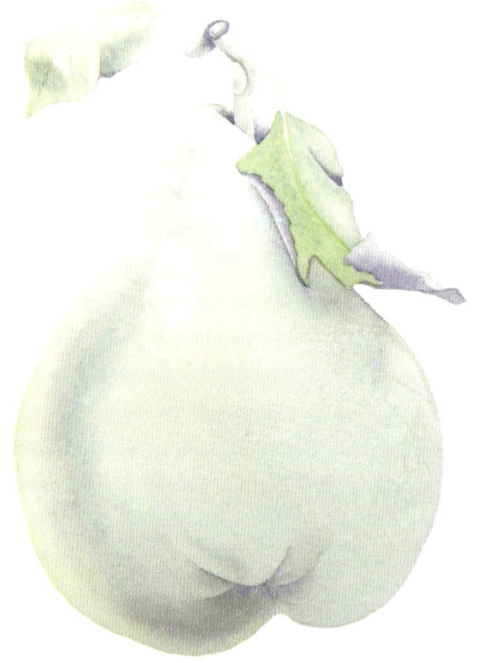

First colour wash

Covering the pear with clean water doesn't lift the shadow wash as long as it has been painted thinly enough to sink into the paper. The body of the pear is large, meaning that the paper will buckle if the paper weight is not substantial enough. This first wash is the undertone of Hansa Yellow Light on the pear, with some Cerulean Blue dropped in, wet-in-wet, into the yellow on the right leaf.

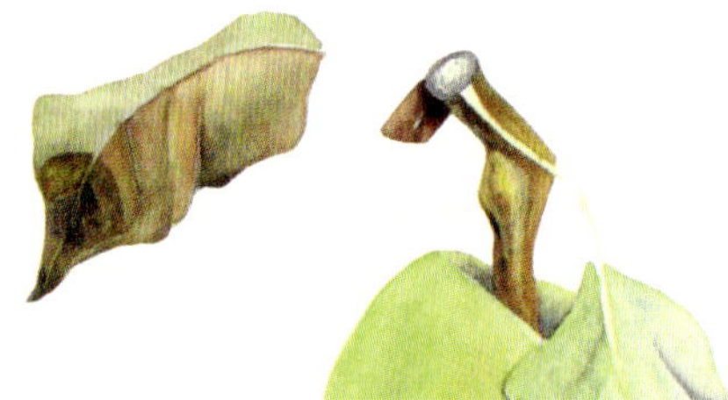

Top leaf: stage 1

Working on damp paper between veins, add some washes of Raw Umber, Burnt Sienna and Sap Green, respecting the areas set out for highlights. Start adding some washes to the stalk, first in Hansa Yellow Light then Burnt Sienna.

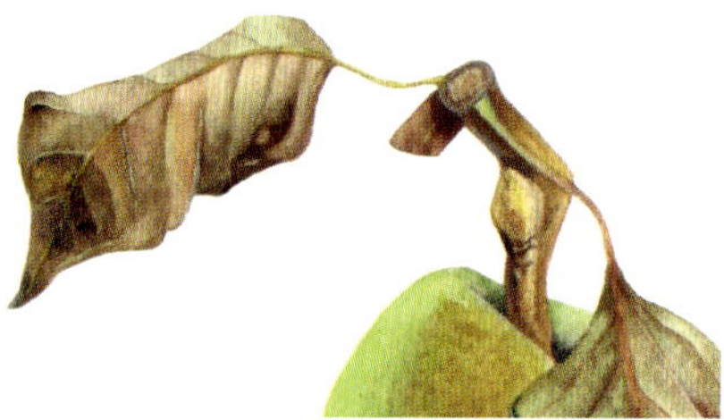

Top leaf: stage 2

Continue to build the damp washes and start introducing some blemishes. These are worked with a small dry brush after the washes have dried, using Raw Umber and Burnt Sienna. Darken and sharpen parts of the stalk with dry-brush work of Raw Umber.

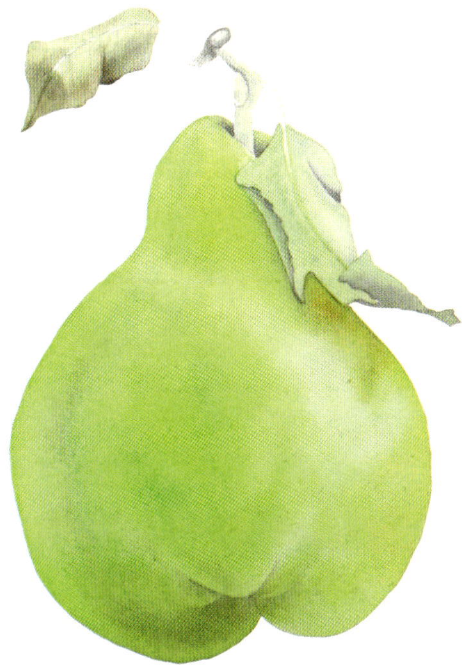

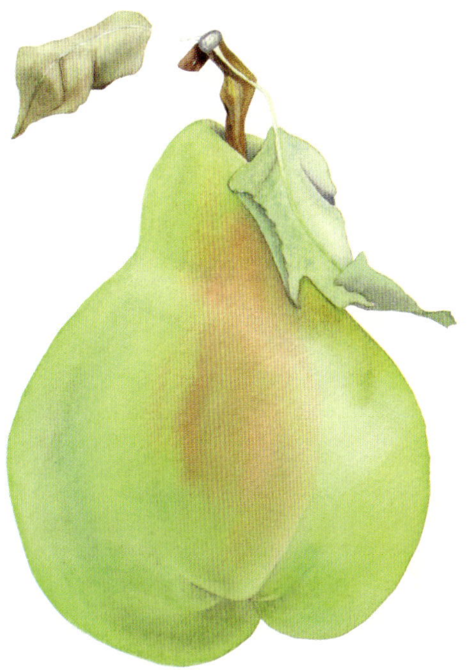

Second colour wash

On the pear, start a wet-in-wet wash of Hansa Yellow Light, then drop in some Sap Green while the yellow is still wet, being careful to reserve the highlights. A pear is not a glossy subject, so you can allow some colour to wander into the light, but not too much so that you still get the tonal variations.

Start introducing some Raw Umber on the topmost leaf and some Sap Green on the side leaf.

First blush

For the next wash, wet the pear again with pure water, then add some more green all over, reserving the highlights in order to avoid a build-up of colour where you want some light. While the green is still wet, add the Perylene Red where the blush is, using a vertical brush stroke to reflect the texture of the pear.

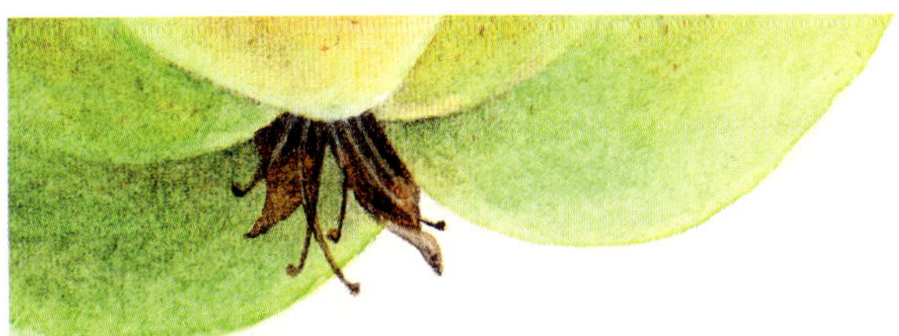

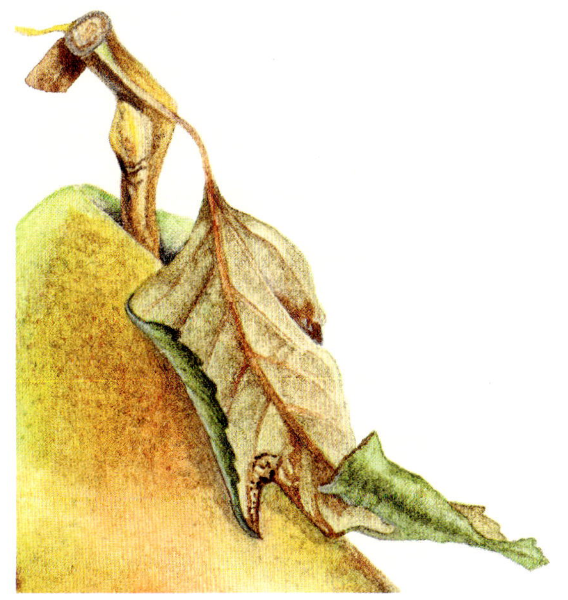

Sepals and side leaf (right)

The sepals and remnants of the stamens are worked very dark to balance the stem and add depth and weight to the painting. Use a combination of Raw Umber and Burnt Sienna. Where the stamens are in front of the sepals, use Titanium White to draw them with a very fine brush. This will make them stand out. Work on the side leaf the same way as for the top leaf.

Wet-in-wet washes and dry-brush details

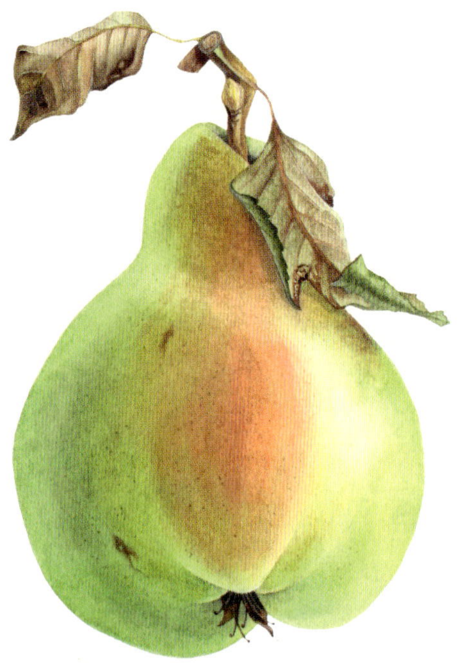

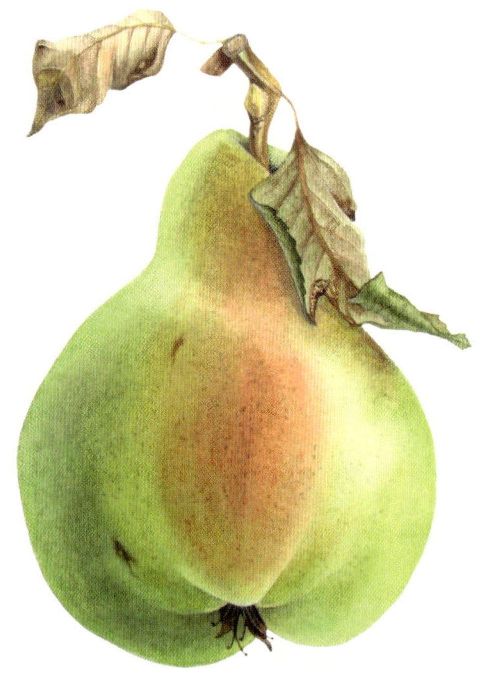

More blush

Wetting the whole pear again, drop in more green on the bottom and sides and some Rich Green Gold in the mid-tones, with more Perylene Red over the blush. All these are added in the same wet-in-wet wash so that they mix directly on the paper and merge naturally.

More shadows

Now is the time to strengthen the shadows, if needed. Another shadow layer can be added wet-in-wet, but try always to finish with a layer of bright colours, else the painting might be too dull. This additional layer of shadows is sandwiched in between two layers of saturated colours.

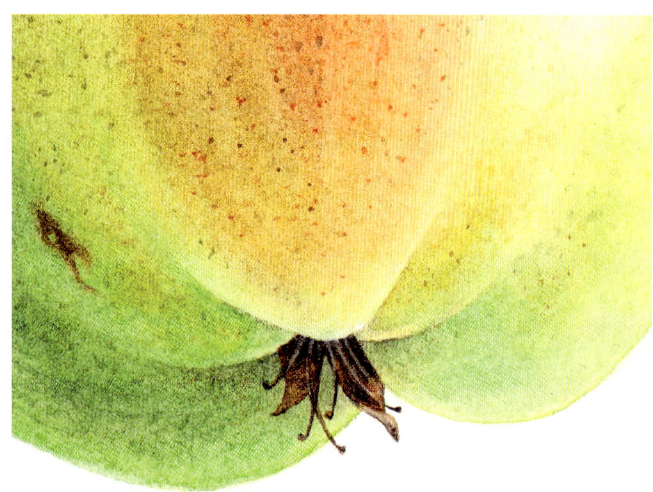

Dry-brush details

You can add a few blemishes with a small dry brush, using Raw Umber and Burnt Sienna. Add them very dry and blend them in straight away with a larger soft brush so that they don't stand out too much. The same applies to the small dots covering the pear: paint them dry with a small brush and after they have dried thoroughly, add a wash of pure water over the whole pear. The russeting around the stem is painted with a ruffled old brush and dry Raw Umber and Burnt Sienna (see page 124).

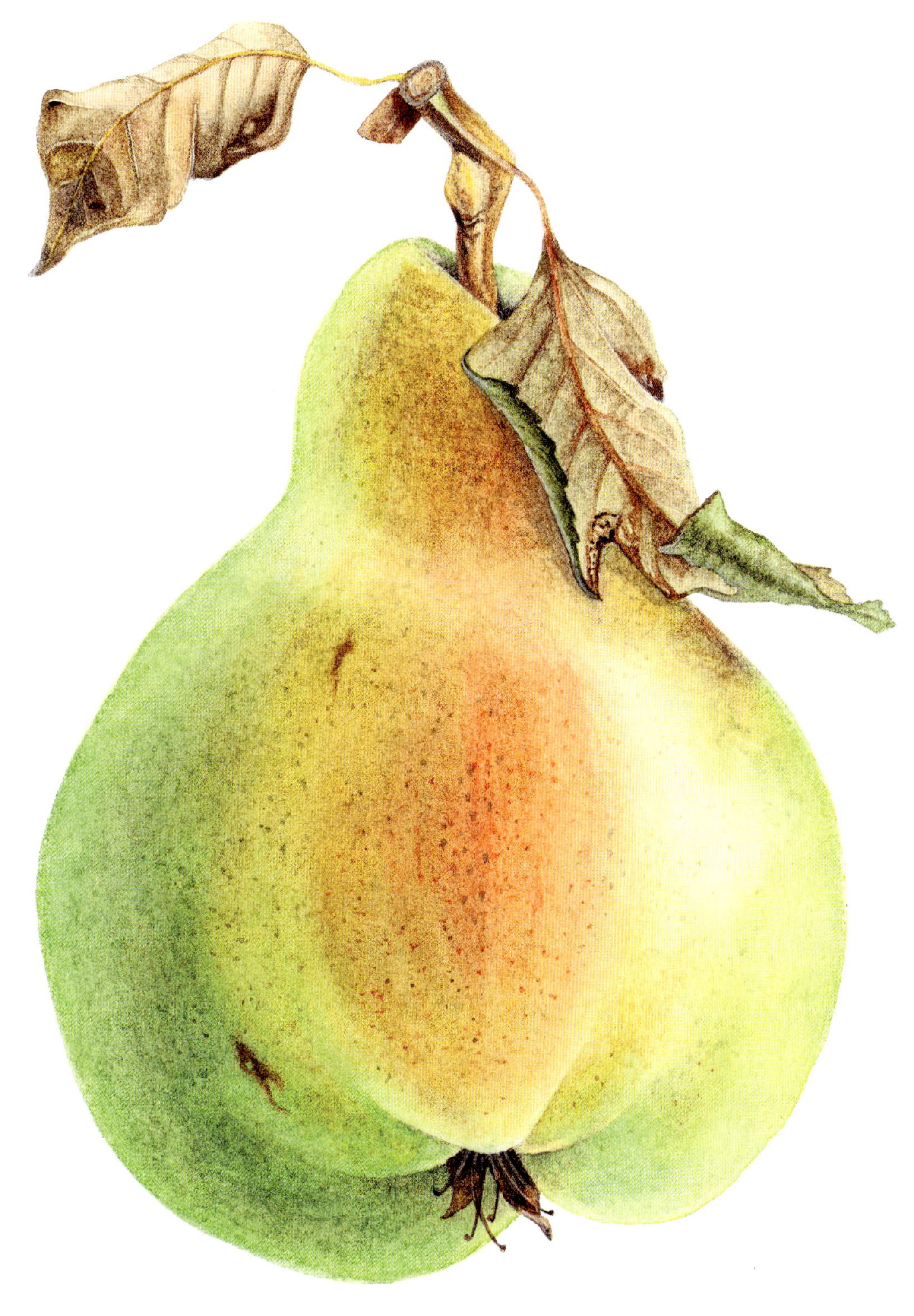

'Catillac' pear
Watercolour on paper.

Anatomy of a

HYDRANGEA

Common name Hydrangea, Hortensia	**Flowering** Spring to Autumn	**Hardiness** Fully hardy
Botanical name *Hydrangea*	**Planting time** October to March	**Propagation** Graft or seed
Family Hydrangeaceae	**Aspect** Sunny or sheltered	**Native** Asia and Americas

Botanically speaking…

- Hydrangea's earlier name, Hortensia, is a Latinized version of the name Hortense, in honour of the French astronomer and mathematician Nicole-Reine Hortense Lepaute (1723—1788).

- Depending on the variety, hydrangea flowers are produced from early Spring to late Autumn.

- A hydrangea flower head is, in fact, an inflorescence, a group of sepals growing around a centre of tiny fertile flowers.

- The sepals are the part of the plant that carry its colour. Typically wild varieties have more of the tiny flowers and fewer showy sepals, while cultivated varieties have been bred to have more colourful large sepals.

- 'Mophead' varieties have a round, pompom-like inflorescence while 'lacecaps' have a flatter inflorescence with the small middle flowers surrounded by a ring of large-sepalled flowers.

- Hydrangeas dehydrate easily but the sepals can also absorb water: immersing flowers in room-temperature water will rehydrate them.

- Hydrangeas are botanically unique in that instead of their colour being the result of different pigments for different coloured varieties, they contain only one type of pigment called anthocyanin. The colours of different varieties depend on the concentration of the pigment in the sepals and the type of soil the plant grows in. More concentration means more intense colours while soil acidity affects the hue. In this way, the sepals act as litmus paper, indicating the acidity in the soil.

- Adding organic materials such as coffee grounds or citrus peel to the soil will increase its acidity and turn some hydrangea flowers blue.

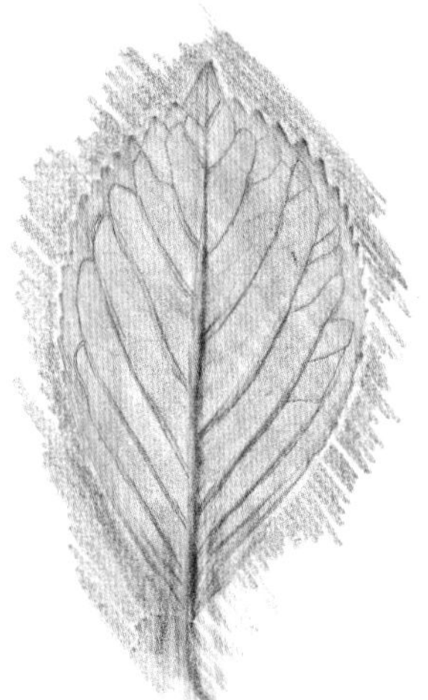

Hydrangea-leaf rubbing.

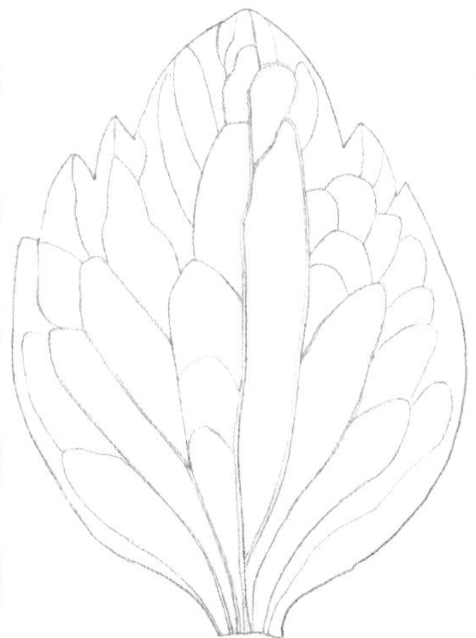

Venation pattern on a hydrangea sepal.

Hydrangea botanical plate

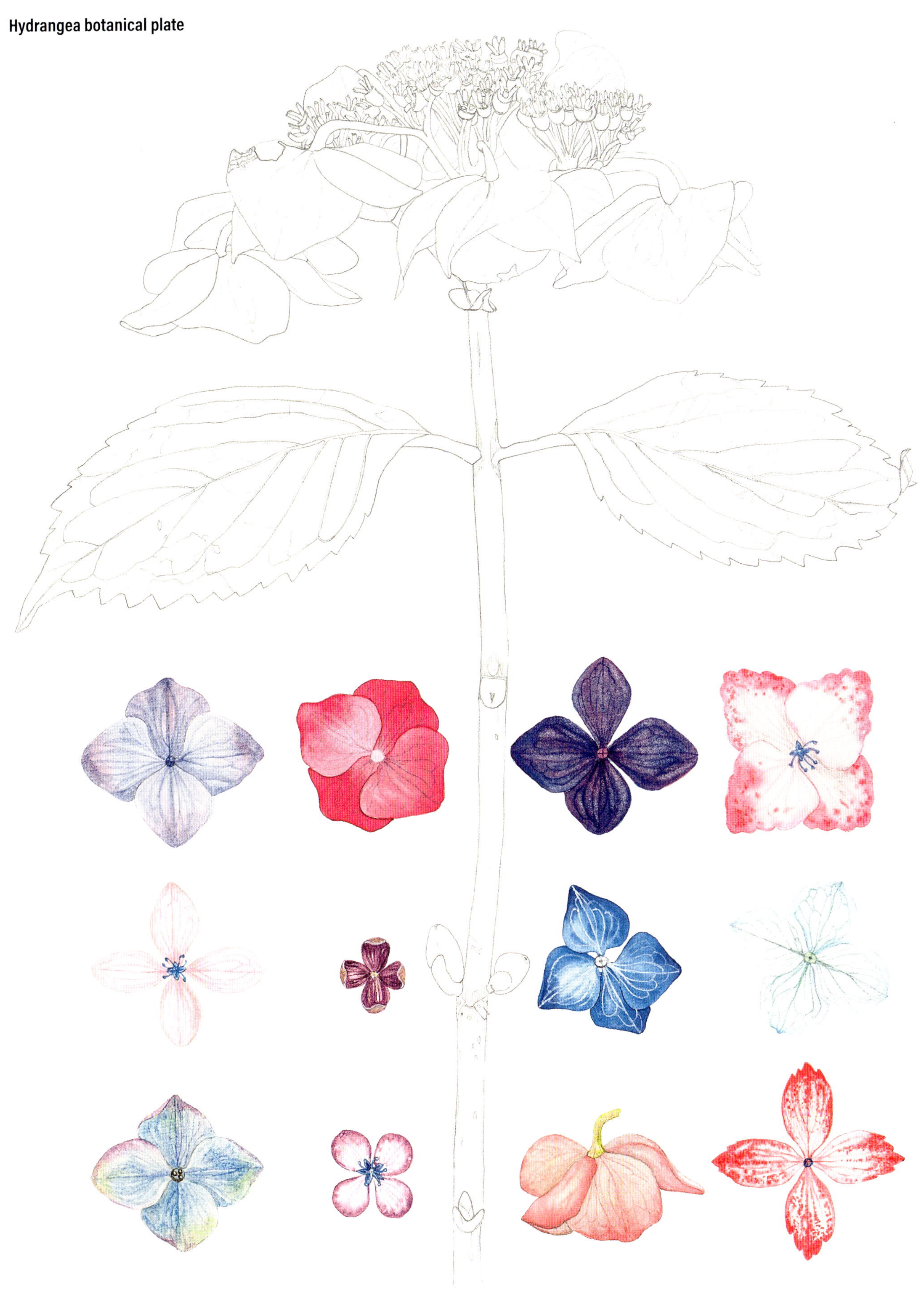

Level 3

HYDRANGEA
Sketch

I have many hydrangeas in my garden. I love their colours, their long flowering time and their low-maintenance attitude. I enjoy them all Summer but I also appreciate their Autumn colours, between the fresh blooms and the desiccated state.

I have been admiring a certain hydrangea in a nearby churchyard for many years. When I decided to paint a hydrangea for this tutorial, I knew it had to be that one. I don't know the variety: it spends the Summer in the deepest blue robe but come October the colour shifts. It becomes pale grey-blue with underlying greeny yellow on the petals that are dropping away from the light, while the parts of the petals exposed to the mild Autumn sun turn a deep muted purple. It is a fascinating combination and I knew I would have to create a mix I had never used before. Irresistible!

Step 1 I picked several heads from the tall bush, knowing that none of them would possess all the features I wanted in my painting. Most of them were too tired-looking and the fresher ones didn't necessarily have the right colours in the right places. For the sketch, I chose a head with an attractive shape, ignoring the colours for the time being.

Unusually, I started my sketch in the centre rather than towards the top of the stem. The full flower in the centre left seemed a good anchor point: I worked my way outwards and around the inflorescence, then down the stem. Hydrangea leaves grow in opposite pairs: the leaf on the right did belong to this particular head but the one on the left I borrowed from another stem.

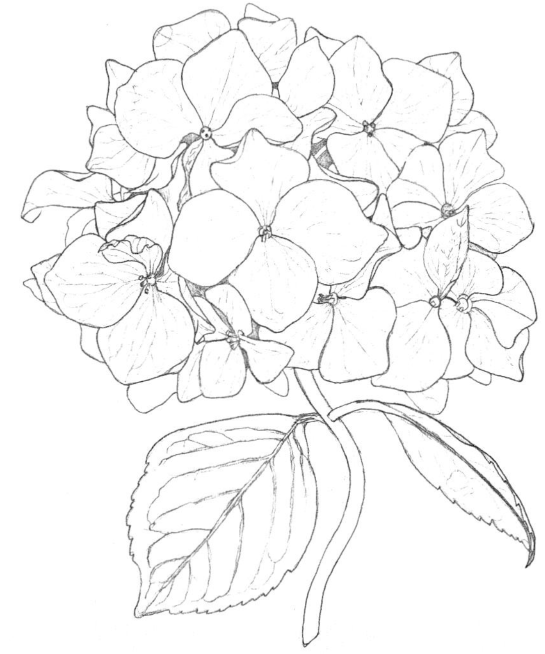

Step 2 Next, I traced the line drawing, omitting the small details such as veins and concentrating on the main outlines. I then transferred the tracing to watercolour paper using transfer paper. It is better to do this before the tone study, while the outlines are still clear of any tonal pencil work.

With the drawing safely transferred, I came back to the sketch and added the tone, using a thicker pencil – a 6B clutch pencil. On such a complex drawing, the tonal values are less logical and less obvious than on a simple shape. There are a lot of cast shadows, reflected lights and colours and lights bouncing off each other. On top of this, the slightly withered texture of the old petals is matte, which means that the highlights are not as bright and white as they would be on a shinier surface.

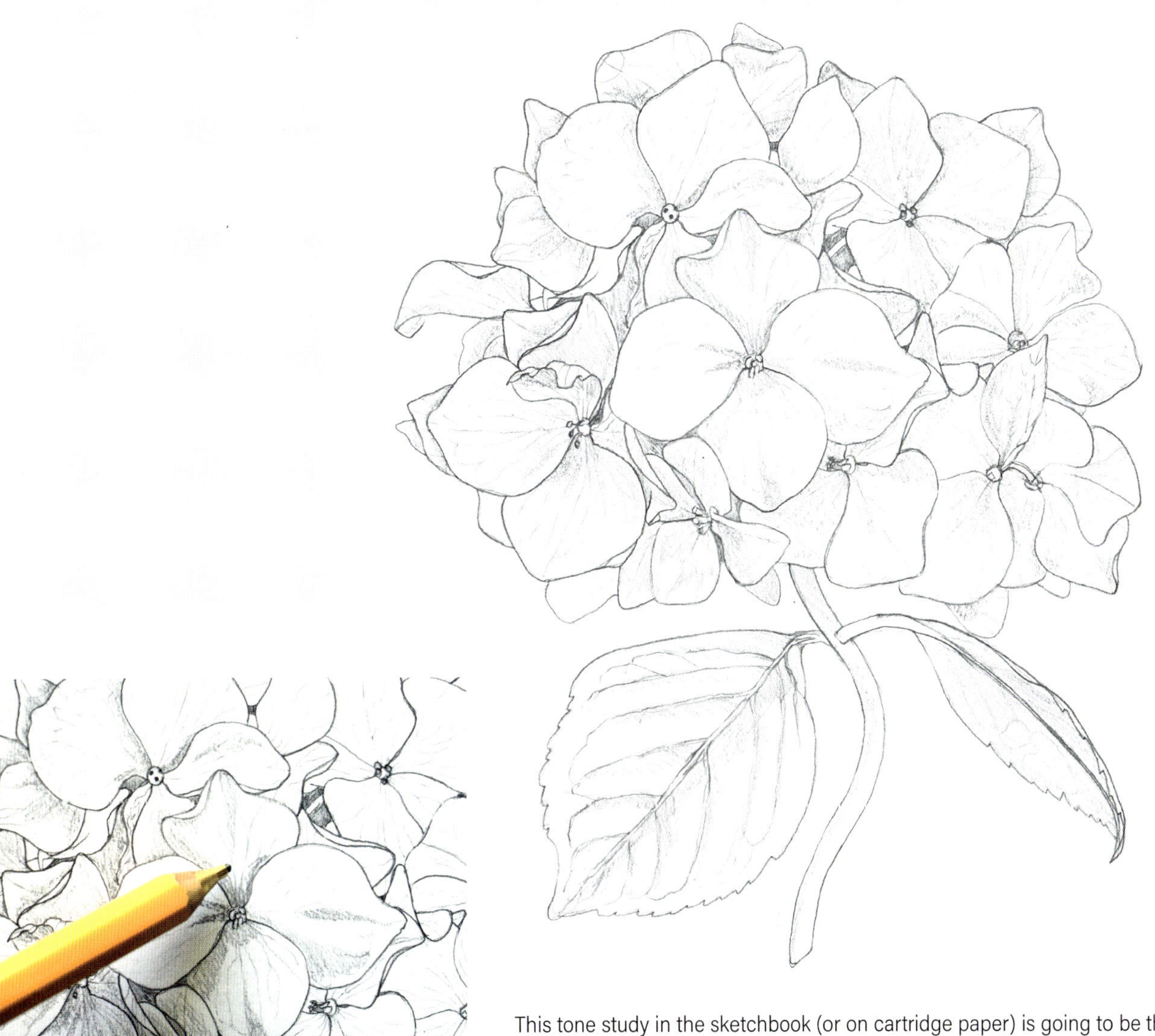

This tone study in the sketchbook (or on cartridge paper) is going to be the tonal map that you will follow at the next stage, which is painting the Harmonic Shadows in watercolour on the heavy watercolour paper.

ℓℓ

Palette and shadows

My drawing was a hybrid of two hydrangea stems. For the colours,
I am using at least four different hydrangea heads, finding individual
inflorescences I want to include in my painting. What attracted me to
this hydrangea in the first place was the mix of yellow, sky-blue and
Ultramarine, all thrown in together with some purples.

Palette

Rich Green Gold

Quinacridone Lilac

Perylene Violet

French Ultramarine

Cerulean Blue

Sap Green

Burnt Sienna

Raw Umber

Blue

The main colour is **Cerulean Blue**, a paint I don't often use. It tends to be
gummy (the pigment is separating from the gum Arabic, making the paint
tricky to handle), more opaque than my other colours and heavily granulating.
However, its milky appearance, grainy texture and sky-blue colour make it
perfect for this subject.

Some of the petals also show a deeper blue, for which I am using
French Ultramarine.

Purple

To make the purple colour, I am mixing **Quinacridone Lilac**, a bright magenta,
with **French Ultramarine**. **Perylene Violet** can be added when the mix needs
darkening. This mix will be used in different proportions on different parts of
most petals.

Yellow

The yellowish undercolour in some petals has a definite green tinge to it.
Rich Green Gold is perfect for this and is also a very good layering colour that
will shine through the Cerulean effortlessly.

Green

The Rich Green Gold is not green enough for the foliage, so **Sap Green** is still
required for the stem and leaves.

Brown

The blemishes on both petals and foliage are a mixture of the russet
Burnt Sienna and the greeny brown **Raw Umber**.

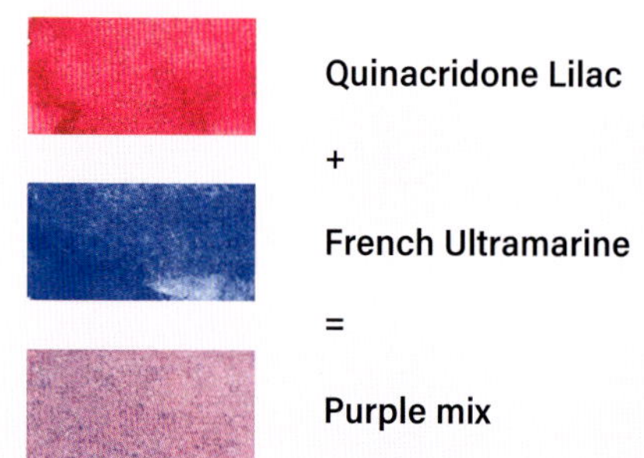

Quinacridone Lilac

+

French Ultramarine

=

Purple mix

132

ℓℓ

Harmonic Shadows

Out of all these colours, the three primaries
I am selecting for the Harmonic Shadow mix are
French Ultramarine for the blue (Cerulean is a
little too unmanageable for unobtrusive shadows) +
Quinacridone Lilac for the red + **Rich Green Gold** for
the yellow. This is not technically a yellow, but there
is no proper yellow needed in the painting and Rich
Green Gold is yellow enough to neutralize the purple.

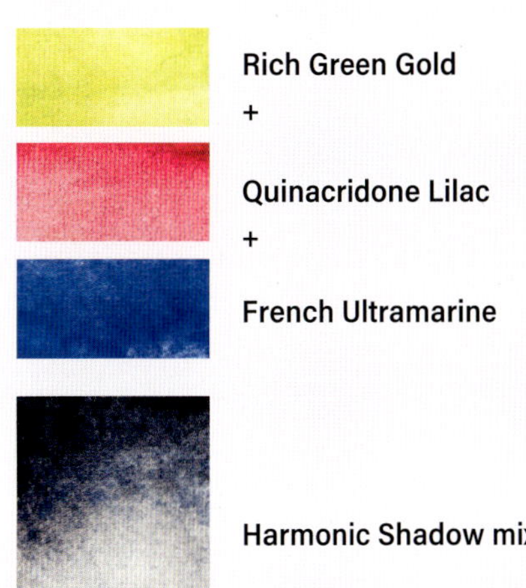

Rich Green Gold
+

Quinacridone Lilac
+

French Ultramarine

Harmonic Shadow mix

The first step on the watercolour paper
is to paint all the shadows, working wet-
in-wet. Sometimes on a complex subject
I paint the shadows in sections rather than
all of them at once, but for this hydrangea
I thought it would be better to paint them
all before tackling the colours. The mixes of
yellow, blues and purples are going to be
the real challenge in this painting. Having
the canvas of shadows ready for the colours
seems essential.

Painting the shadows wet-in-wet ensures
that they stay soft and do not overpower
the pale colours that will follow. Wet a
petal and drop in the shadow mix of
French Ultramarine + Quinacridone Lilac +
Rich Green Gold. Work your way around the
inflorescence, one petal at a time.

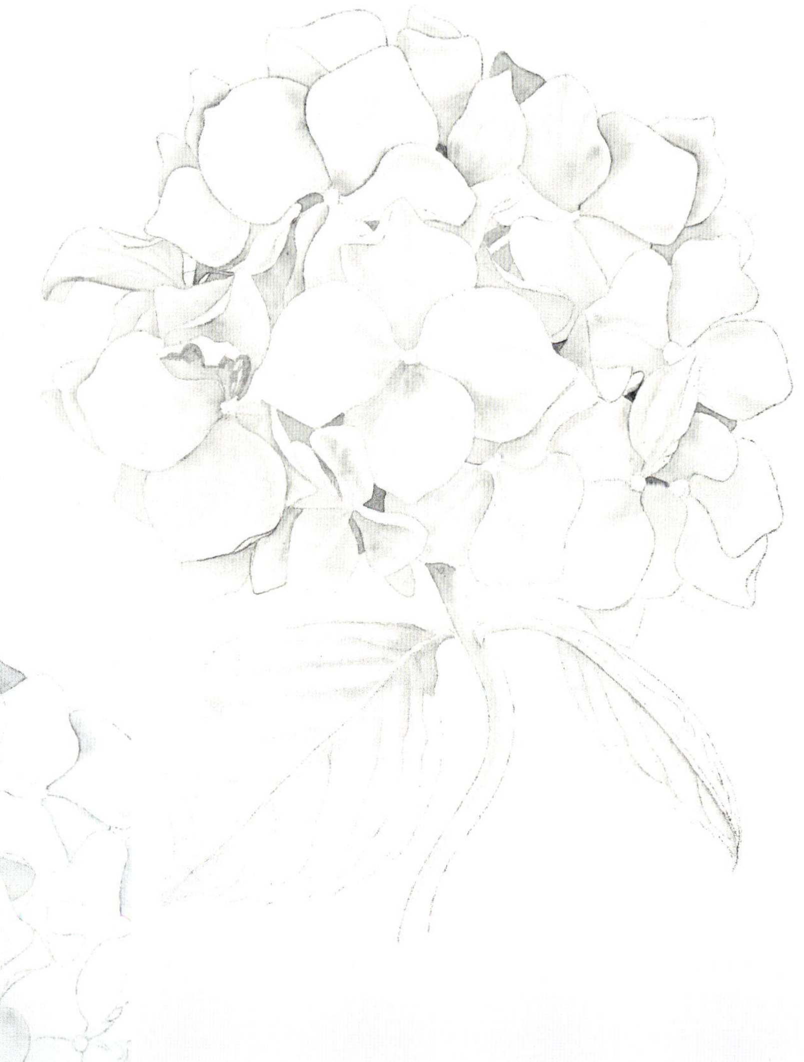

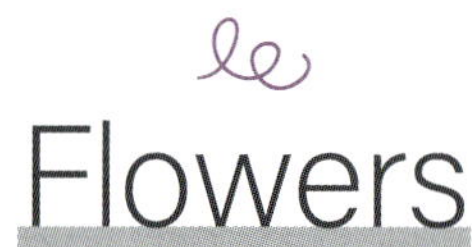

Flowers

All the shadows are done, which gives me an even *grisaille* painting on which to apply
my colours. This time, instead of applying washes evenly throughout the painting,
I will concentrate on one flower at a time, finishing each before starting on the next.

Painting a flower from the front

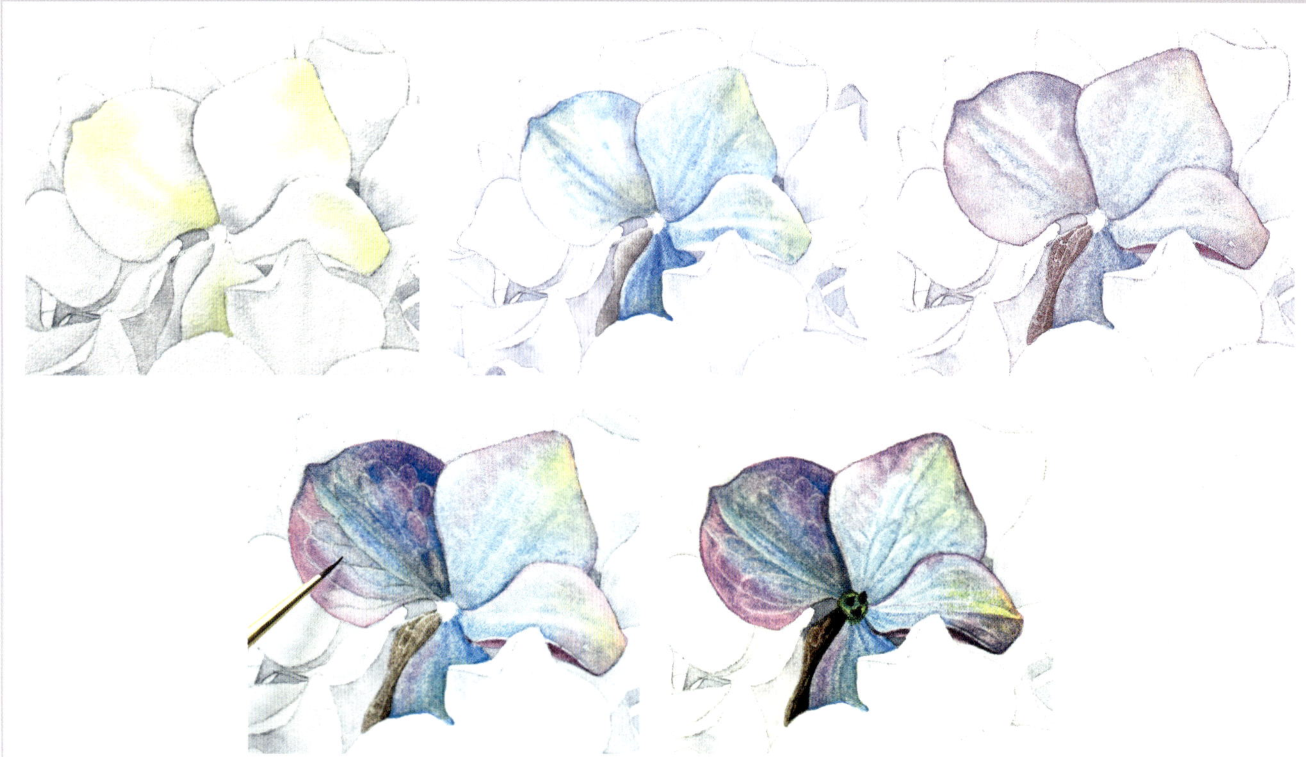

All the colours present in the inflorescence are represented in
this particular flower, so it is a good one to start with and explore
the layering and mixes.

First layer: wet-in-wet Rich Green Gold. Wetting all the
petals, drop in some Rich Green Gold in the areas where the
greeny yellow is showing through the blue.

Second layer: wet-in-wet Cerulean Blue. Wetting one petal
at a time, paint in the Cerulean, roughly following the pattern of
the veins. One withered petal is painted with Raw Umber.

Third layer: wet-in-wet purple mix. Again one petal at
a time, add some purple mix of Quinacridone Lilac + French

Ultramarine towards the edges or anywhere it appears on the
flower. The colours mix and blend by being layered on top of
each other.

Fourth layer: with a dry brush, add the veins to one petals,
then add more colour between these veins. Proceed in the same
manner with all the petals.

Centre: painted with a dry brush loaded first with Cerulean
Blue then Rich Green Gold. The tiny stumps in the centre are a
mix of Raw Umber strengthened with some shadow colour, which
is almost black.

Painting a flower from the back

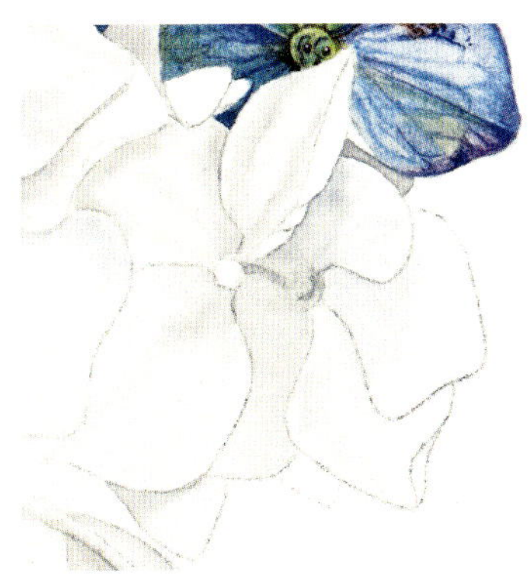 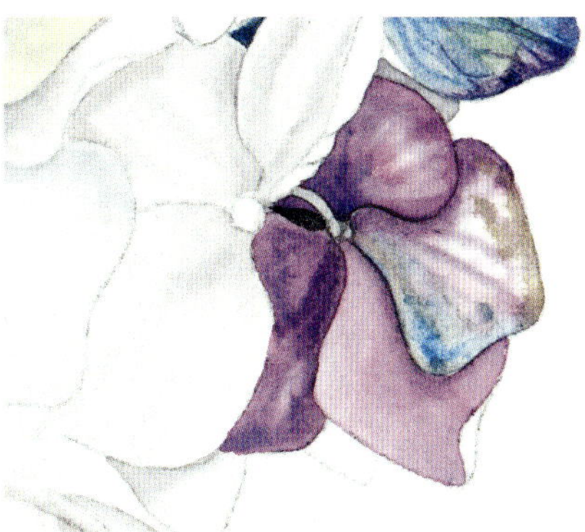 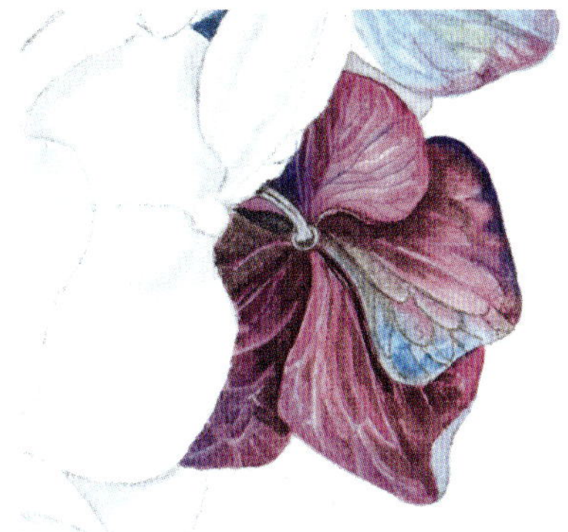

The underside of the petals are mainly purple, ranging from magenta to a deep-blue violet.

First layer: wet-in-wet, same mix of Quinacridone Lilac + French Ultramarine. Some of the Cerulean Blue is showing too. Painting it in the same wet layer allows the colours to blend seamlessly.

Second and third layers: the colour is reinforced and painted between the veins, using the two colours above + Perylene Violet where it gets very dark.

Continue working around the inflorescence, keeping the subject in front of you at all times to follow the colours and patterns. The beauty of a dry subject is that it will not move around and change quickly as a lively fresh flower would.

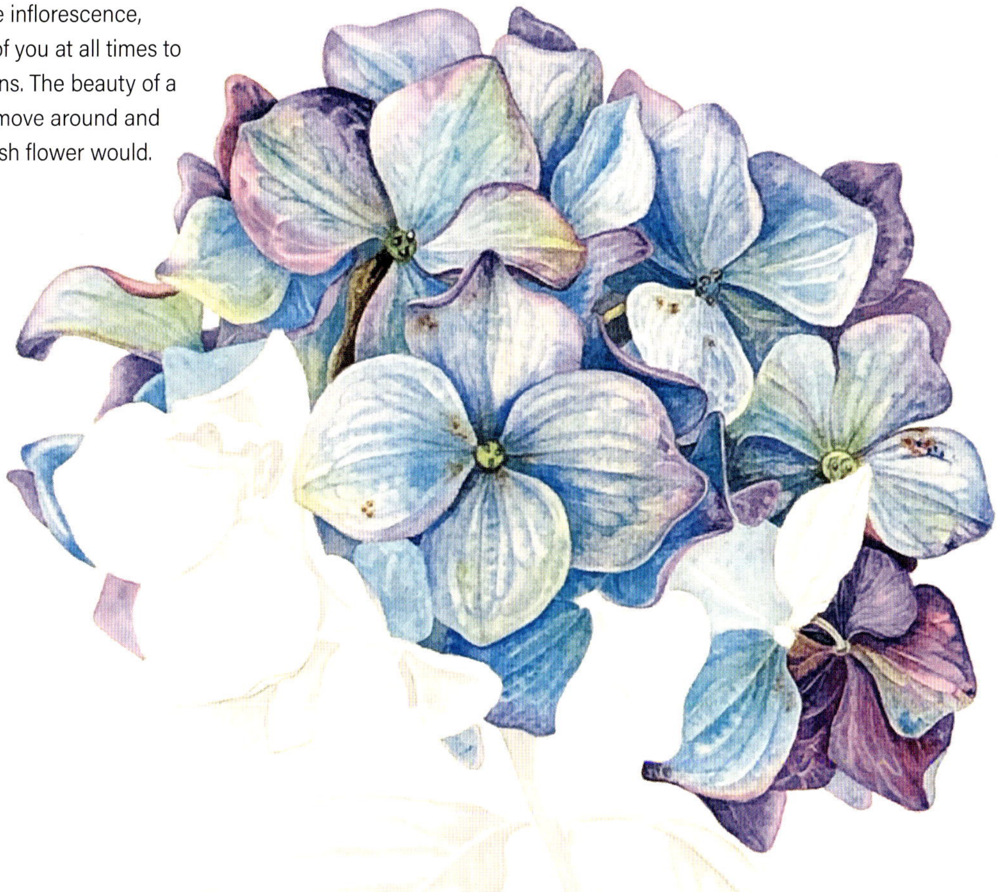

Leaves

In October, the hydrangea leaves are still mainly green but they are starting to show some serious signs of a 'Winter is coming' feeling. The base colour is Sap Green. This is modified with other colours: French Ultramarine to darken, Quinacridone Lilac to mute, Rich Green Gold to lighten and Rich Green Gold + Cerulean Blue to mix the cloudy green of the right side leaf's underside.

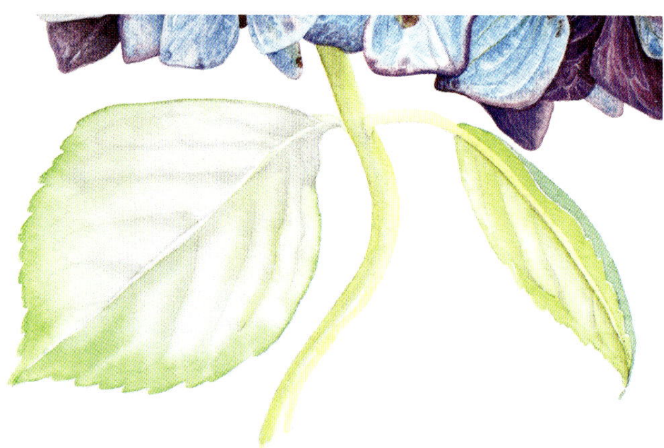

Step 1 After the shadows, the first wash is a watered-down basic green painted wet-in-wet, not forgetting to integrate the serrations. They have to be painted in the same wash as the body of the leaf, or they will stand out, with a hard line separating them from the leaf. You can turn your painting upside down to face the serrations, which will make them easier to paint with the tip of the brush.

Step 2 A first wet-in-wet wash is painted in all areas of both leaves. The top of the right leaf is a little bluer and brighter, while the underside contains more Rich Green Gold and Cerulean Blue to give a cloudy, muted light green.

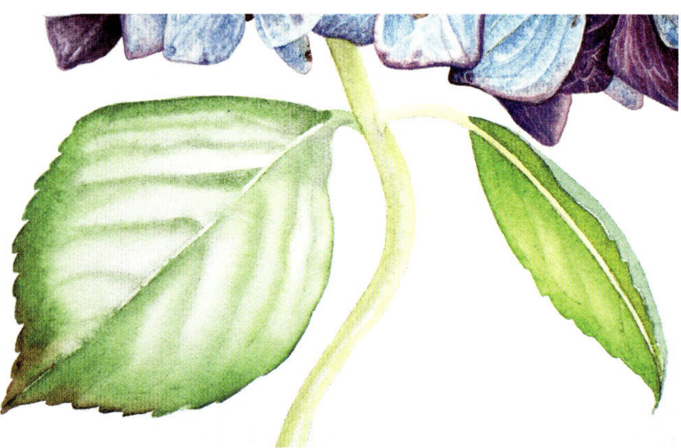

Step 3 The second wash is a repeat of the first, using the same colours, to give more intensity if the first wash was at all shy.

The underside of the leaf has colour added between the veins, varying between the original green mix and some pure Rich Green Gold to avoid the colour looking too flat.

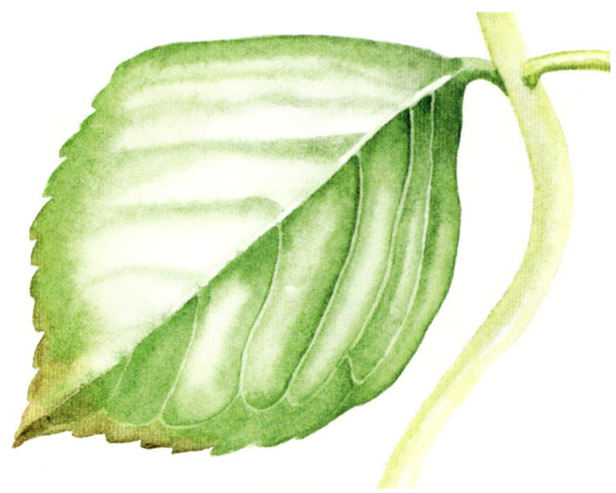

Step 4 Once the overall wet-in-wet base is strong enough, more wet-in-wet colour can be added, this time working in section between leaves, leaving narrow unpainted gaps for the veins.

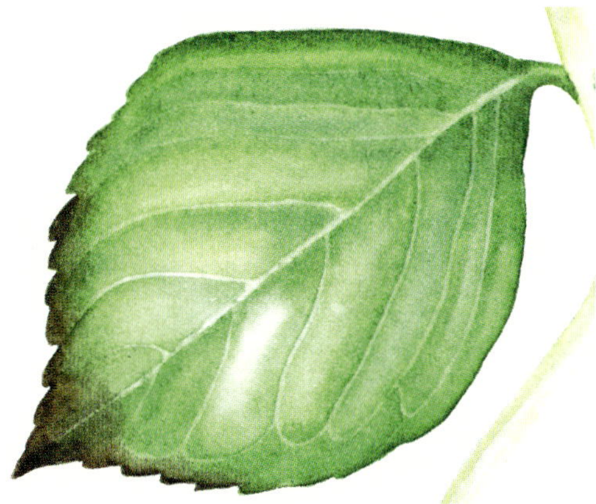

Step 5 All this working between veins has left a lot of hard lines that need to be softened. One last wet-in-wet wash will soften everything up, this time over the whole leaf at once, using green for most of it and Raw Umber towards the tip in the same wash, allowing the colours to blend with each other.

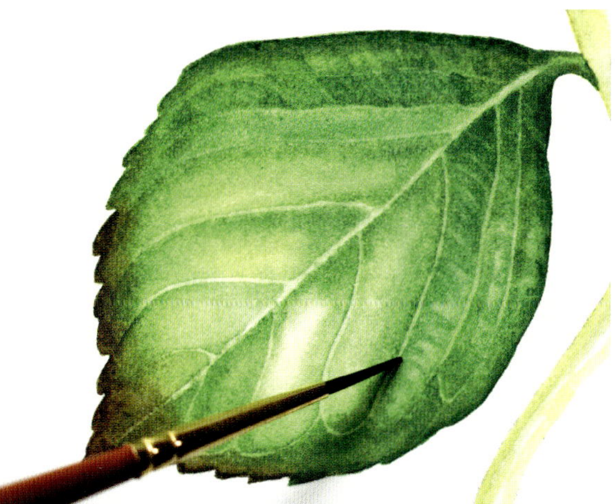

Step 6 Then it's back to working between the veins, adding texture and colour at the same time by painting small areas of damp paint on dry paper, leaving thin unpainted lines to portray the secondary veins.

   At this stage, the stem has only one wet-in-wet wash of Rich Green Gold on top of the shadows.

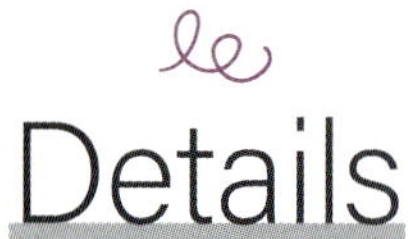

Details

Almost there… The stem needs finishing to bring all the other parts together and some dry-brush work will also tidy up any leftovers and help you to finish off the tiniest details.

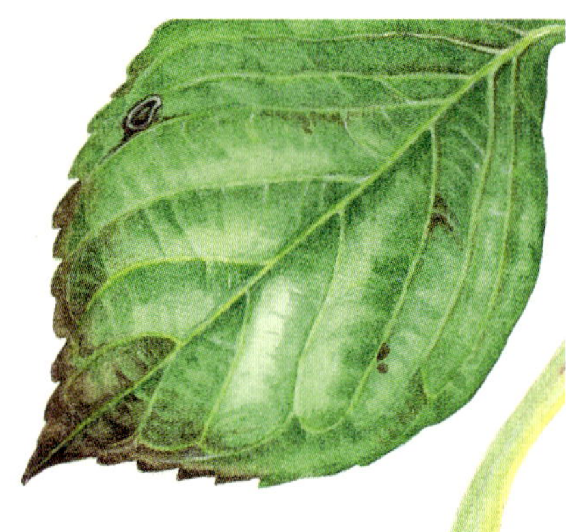

Step 1 To finish the leaf, add some blemishes with Raw Umber and Burnt Sienna. If some blemishes are starting to look a little mouldy, you can also add a tiny touch of Titanium White to refresh them.

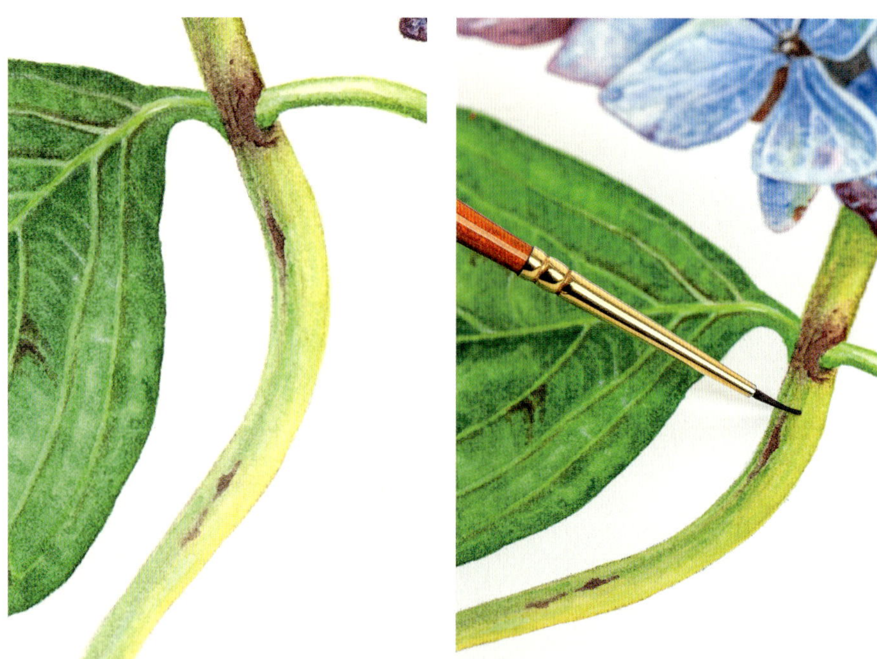

Step 2 The stem is layered wet-in-wet with more Rich Green Gold and some Sap Green. The markings and blemishes are a mix of Perylene Violet painted wet-in-wet, strengthened with some Raw Umber painted dry.

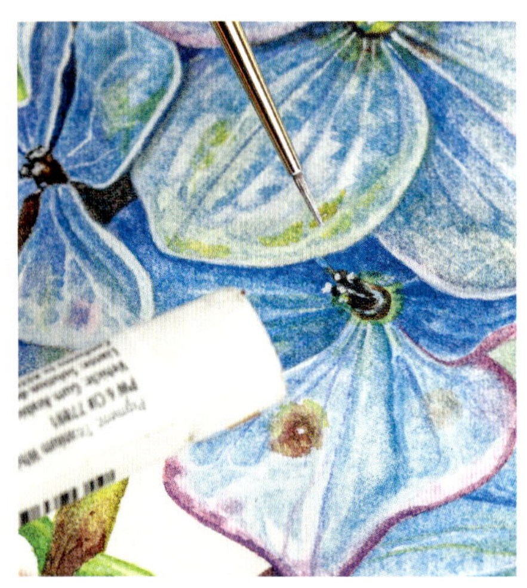

Step 3 On the rare occasions when I use white, I never mix it on the palette with other colours. I prefer to use a Titanium White stick, which allows for more concentration. Here, I used it for the tips of the tiny stamens and also to accentuate the thin veins on the dried-up brown petals.

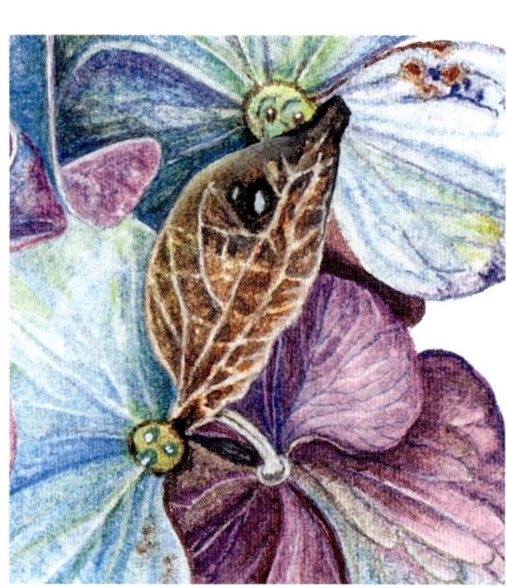

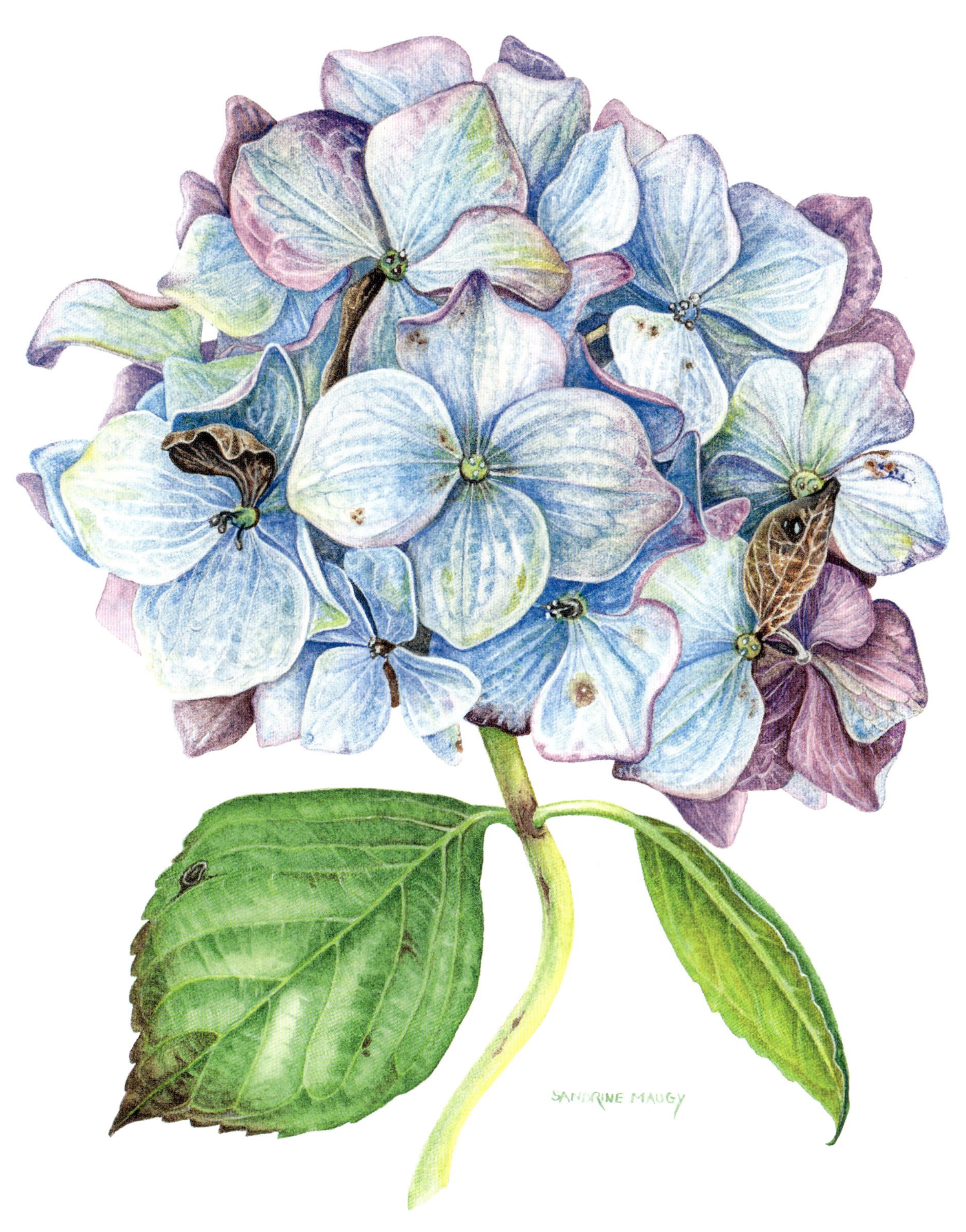

Hydrangea
Watercolour on paper.

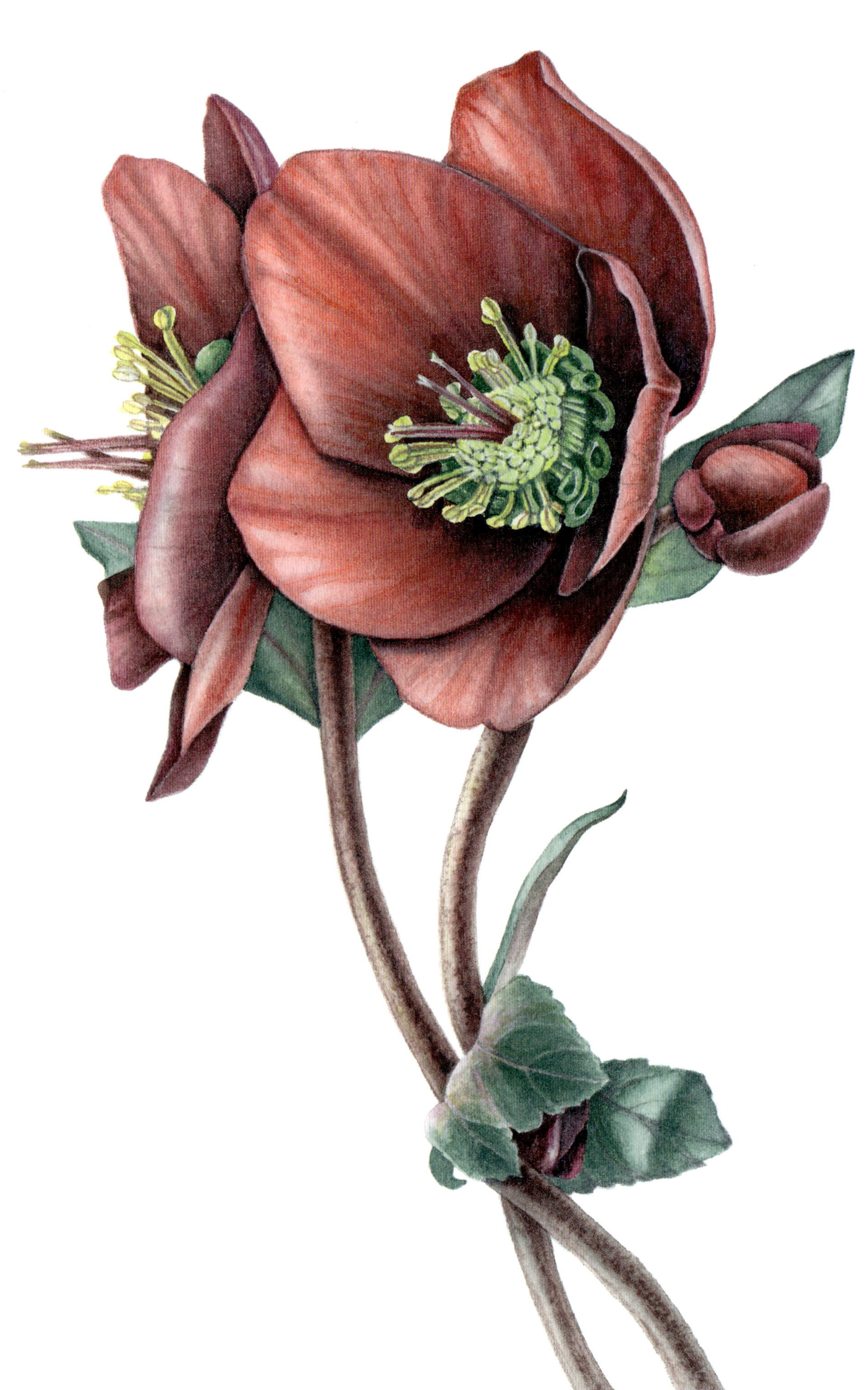

Winter

WINTER SUBJECTS
and their palette

Winter has finally won and the trees have given up their leaves to the relentless winds. Peering out from the protective shells of our houses we watch as water and cold combine to playfully torment our gardens. Cold rain, frost, ice, snow, mist, storms and hoarfrosts assault the dormant flora, while we hope that they will survive the ordeal.

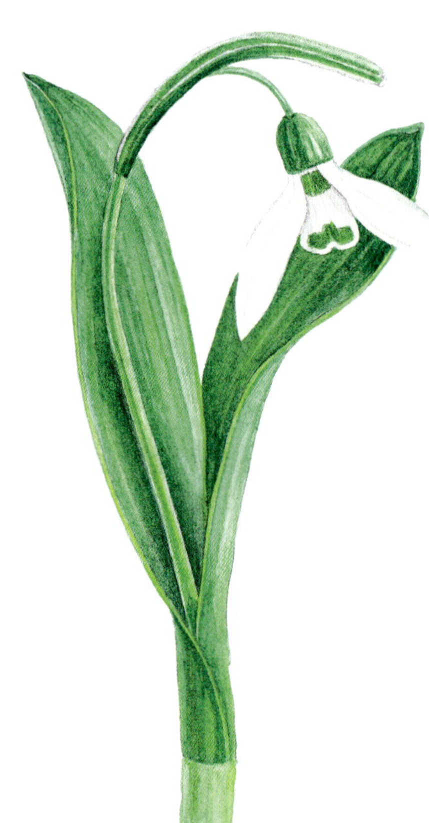

Evergreen foliage

Most evergreen foliage is dark green and glossy, with smooth leaves. This is what nature came up with as the best solution for survival in the harsh Winter weather. The dark colour ensures a large reserve of chlorophyll; the smoothness of the leaves helps the rain and snow to glide off easily, thus avoiding unwanted dampness that would cause decay; the thickness of the leaves makes them more resistant to frost and wind damage. The biggest challenge in painting Winter foliage is the highly glossy surface. The secret is in the contrast: what will portray the shine is the very dark green being adjacent to a very bright highlight.

Bark and berries

Colourful bark, berries and dramatic evergreens all create colour. When denuded of foliage, bark can be an unexpected surprise: it can have a papery or reptilian texture, or a jewel-like sheen, or look freshly painted-on. The snake-bark Acers even leave a greeny bloom on the fingers as if the paint were still wet. My favourite bark has to belong to *Prunus serrula* and is burnished copper. Burnt Sienna and Burnt Umber remain my first choice for browns. No fancy chemical pigment has yet dethroned these ancient earth colours. An array of reds is necessary for a variety of berries: crimson for late rose hips and *Cotoneaster*, Pyrrol Scarlet for pyracanthas, Pyrrol Red for holly and Quinacridone Coral for ash berries.

House plants

If the garden stays resolutely naked in the cold, house plants and florists' tropical flowers offer a good seasonal alternative. I have a small collection of succulents in the most intriguing range of colours and if you are an orchid fan, Winter is a good time to paint them. But still the outdoor plants lure us out…

Sitting for a moment in the cold Winter sun brings a feeling of elation and stolen happiness different from the lethargy of an August heat wave. Painting the Winter garden, even from the indoor studio, is a good way of fully experiencing the season and expressing the feelings it rouses in us. And if it becomes too dark and sad, there are always the seed catalogues to peruse, making us salivate at the idea of future blossoms, vivid blooms and a myriad paintings.

Other colours appear in the three tutorials, but if you would like a basic palette from which to mix all your colours, the list below is a good starting point for Winter subjects.

Hansa Yellow Light   Green-bias yellow – a delicate yellow ideal for Harmonic Shadows on white flowers.
Subjects: Snowdrops and primroses.

Hansa Yellow Deep   Orange-bias yellow – golden yellow for foliage and orange mixes.
Subjects: Autumn leaves and rose hips.

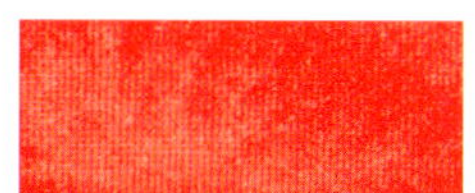

Pyrrol Red   Mid-red – true red for berries and strong red flowers.
Subjects: Holly berries and early red tulips.

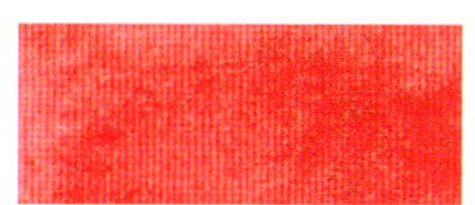

Carmine   Violet-bias red – a deep red for darker blooms and berries.
Subjects: Holly berries, hellebores and some wood.

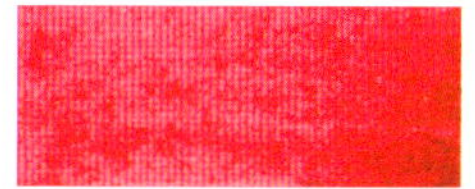

Quinacridone Pink   Violet-bias red – true pink for delicate flowers and for shadows on white subjects.
Subjects: Snowdrops and dragon fruit.

Perylene Violet   Maroon dark violet – for deep purples and maroon shades.
Subjects: Hellebores, orchids and some wood.

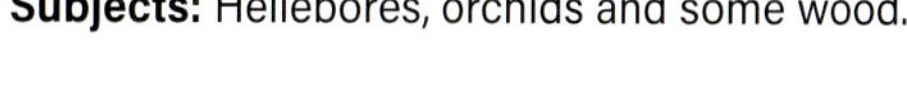

Indanthrone Blue   Green-bias blue – a very dark blue ideal for dark evergreens and shadows on dark flowers.
Subjects: Holly, ivy and hellebores.

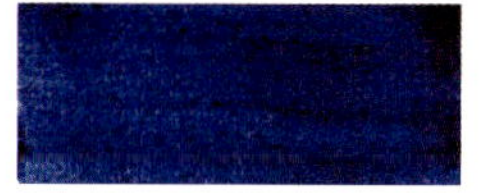

Cerulean Blue   Green-bias blue – milky granulating blue for texture and bloom on fruit and petals.
Subjects: Any foliage (underside) and bloom on succulents or dark hellebores.

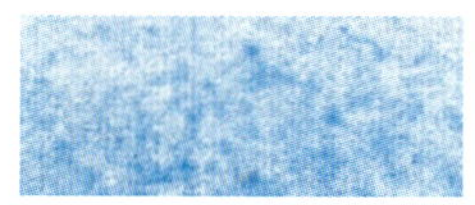

Burnt Umber   Reddish brown.
Subjects: Dying or dried-up leaves, branches and blemishes.

Anatomy of a

PANSY

<table>
<tr><td>Common name Pansy
Botanical name Viola
Family Violaceae</td><td>Flowering Possible all year
Planting time Possible all year
Aspect Full or partial sun</td><td>Hardiness Hardy
Propagation Seeds
Native Europe and Western Asia</td></tr>
</table>

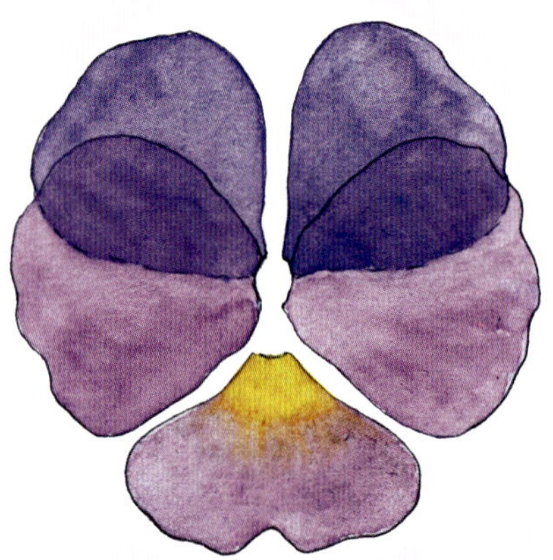

Petal arrangement

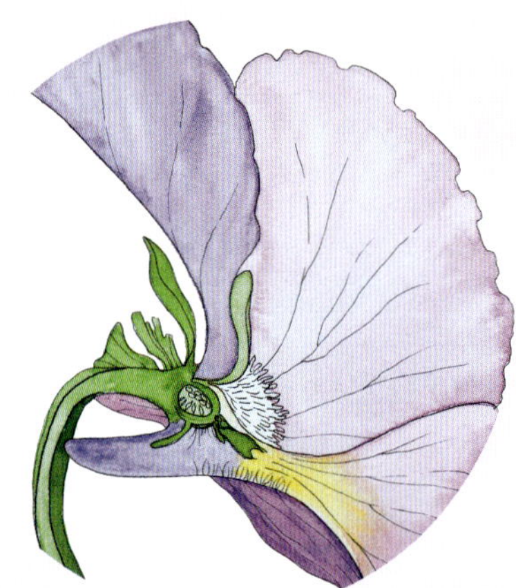

Flower section

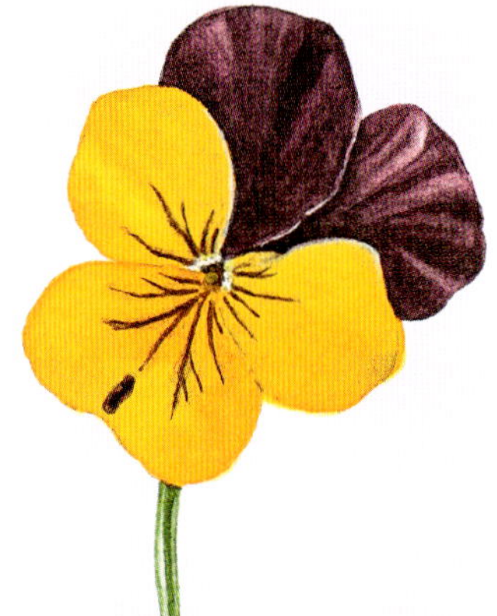

Viola tricolor

Botanically speaking…

- Pansies come from hybridizations of the small wildflower *Viola tricolor*. They have five petals and five sepals. Unlike most flowers, generations of breeding and hybridizations have left the structure mostly unchanged.

- The structure is as follows: there are two back petals pointing upwards, two side petals and a fifth central petal at the bottom, pointing downwards.

- The base of the bottom-central petal usually shows a patch of bright yellow coming from the centre of the flower. If the rest of the petal features strong colours, it is wise to paint the yellow patch first so that it doesn't get lost in the other, deeper colours.

- The bases of the side petals are fringed with hairs that are usually white.

- The dark varieties show a velvety texture.

- Some varieties have 'blotches' on the side petals and the front petal, starting from the centre and expanding toward the middle part of the petals. These are usually darker than the rest of the petals and can be painted last.

- The varieties that do not have blotches still have markings, in the forms of dark lines. These can also be painted last of all.

- The stem is square in section, which can be rendered by painting a hard line down the centre of the stem.

- The leaves have rounded, large-toothed margins and have a satin texture that is not as velvety as those of the petals.

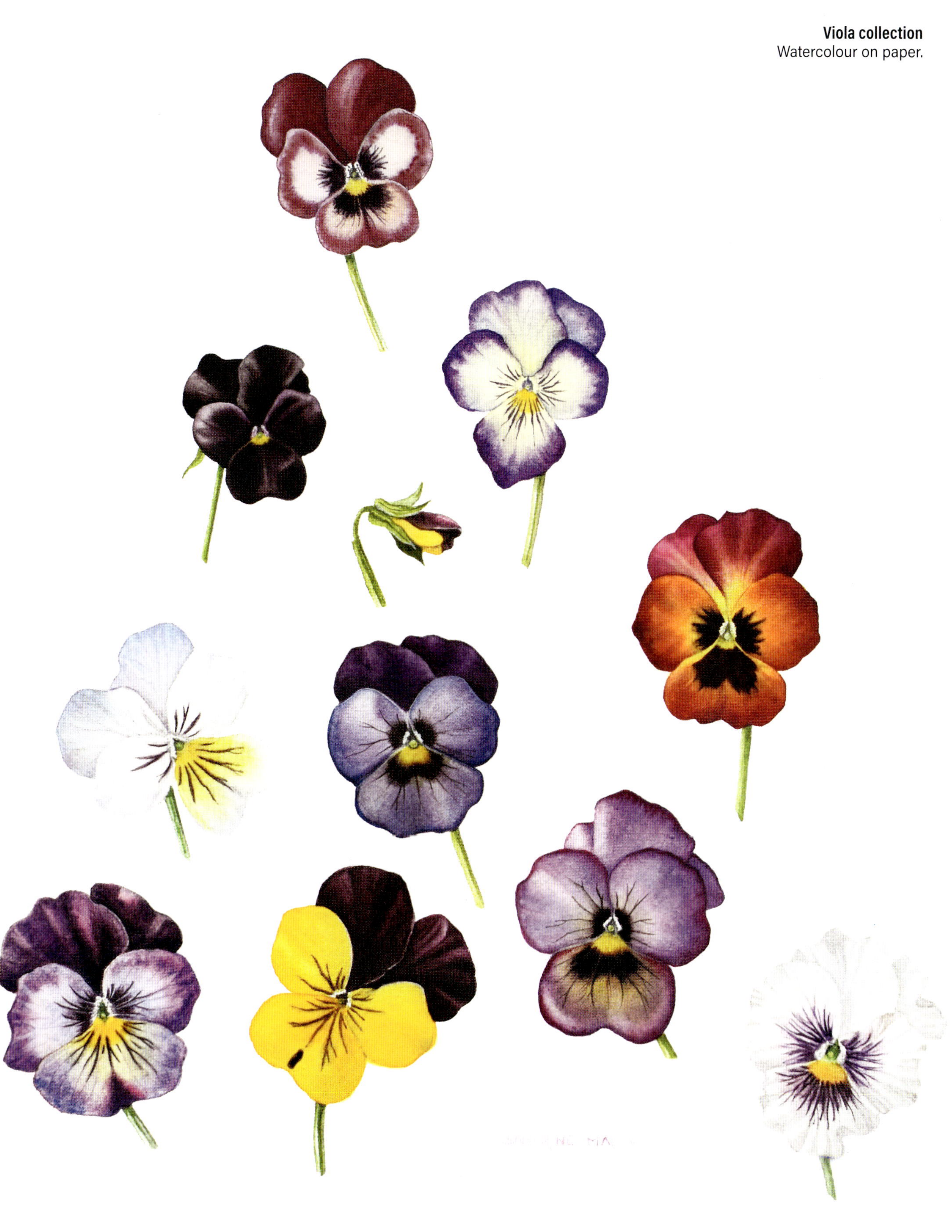

Viola collection
Watercolour on paper.

PANSY 'MIDNIGHT GLOW'
Drawing and palette

Pansies are a wonderful flower to light up the gloomiest Winter day.
'Midnight Glow' is a particularly beautiful variety, with its side petals
looking like butterfly wings in deep blues and purples, accentuated by the
different shades of yellow.

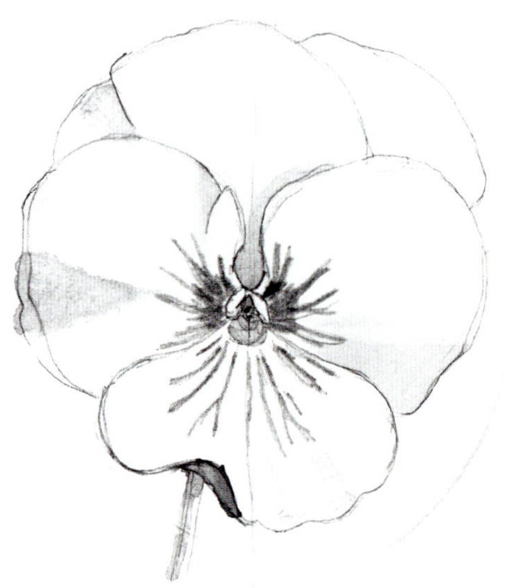

Sketch and tone study

Pansies and violas are a good subject for beginners because they are not difficult to draw. They have only five petals, always in the same positions. The whole flower head can be contained in a circle, with the anchor point at the very centre of the flower, where all the petals meet. You can picture the centre as a little triangle, with the top sides bordered by the small hairy strips and the base as the yellow patch of the bottom petal. While the top petals reach the edge of the circle, the bottom petal is shorter. A vertical line splitting the circle in two equal halves will go through the two overlapping top petals, separate the two side petals and follow the central vein of the bottom petal.

Once you are happy with your drawing, you can trace it, ready to transfer to the watercolour paper. At this stage, only trace the outlines of the petals, the hairy borders at the base of the side petals (to make sure they stay dry and white when you start the wet-in-wet washes), a semi-circle where the yellow patch sits at the base of the bottom petal and the stem. All the other details will be painted on top of the wet-in-wet washes with a dry brush, so they do not need to be transferred yet.

After tracing the line drawing, you can set it aside and start the tone study in the sketchbook.

As the flower head is quite flat, tonal variations are not too problematic either – only a few cast shadows where petals are overlapping and some shadows in a few folds are required.

The quick tone study above, left, was done using Moonglow, a ready-mixed watercolour grey that I love using on simple subjects for convenience. I would not use it on a final piece, but for quick studies in the sketchbook it works well.

Materials list

PAPERS

Cartridge paper or sketchbook
Tracing paper
Transfer paper
Watercolour paper: Fabriano Artistico
HP Extra White, 640gsm (300lb)

DRAWING

Pencils: HB or B
Pair of compasses (optional)

PAINTING

Brushes: Pro Arte Prolene Plus Series
007 in sizes 3/0, 2, 4 and 6; Princeton
Neptune synthetic squirrel round brush
series in size 12 (for wetting the paper
and for light-touch glazes)
Daniel Smith Moonglow for tone study

Palette

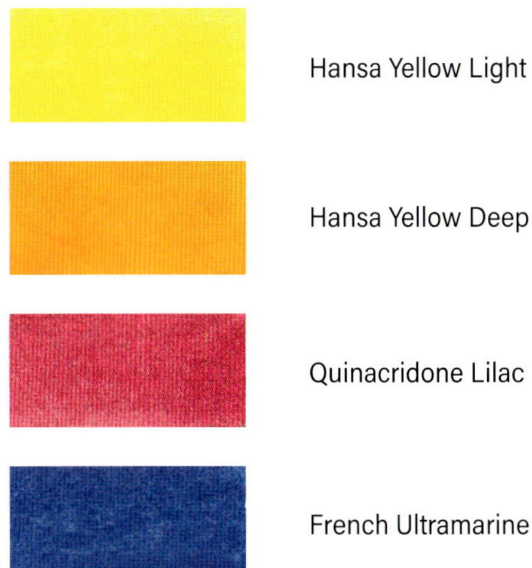

Hansa Yellow Light

Hansa Yellow Deep

Quinacridone Lilac

French Ultramarine

Purple mixes

**Quinacridone Lilac + French Ultramarine in
different proportions:** more Ultramarine for
bluer purples and more Lilac for magenta hues.

Harmonic Shadows

**Hansa Yellow Light
+
French Ultramarine
+
Quinacridone Lilac**

Shadows and colour washes

The preparation work is all done and it is now time to work on the watercolour paper. The drawing has been transferred onto a piece of Fabriano Artistico HP Extra White, 640gsm (300lb). The heavy weight will be able to take a lot of water without buckling, the hot-pressed texture will allow for precise details and the extra-white background will make the blues more luminous.

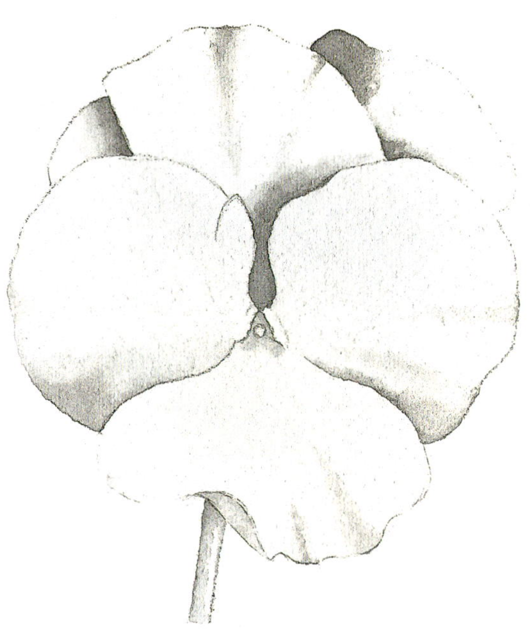

Step 1 Although I am using the same Harmonic Shadow mix, I have separated the paint into two wells in my palette: one highly diluted and one more concentrated. The paler version is for the shadows on the three front petals, where the yellow will be. The darker shadow mix is for the two petals at the back, where it needs to be strong enough to make a difference to the dark purple colour.

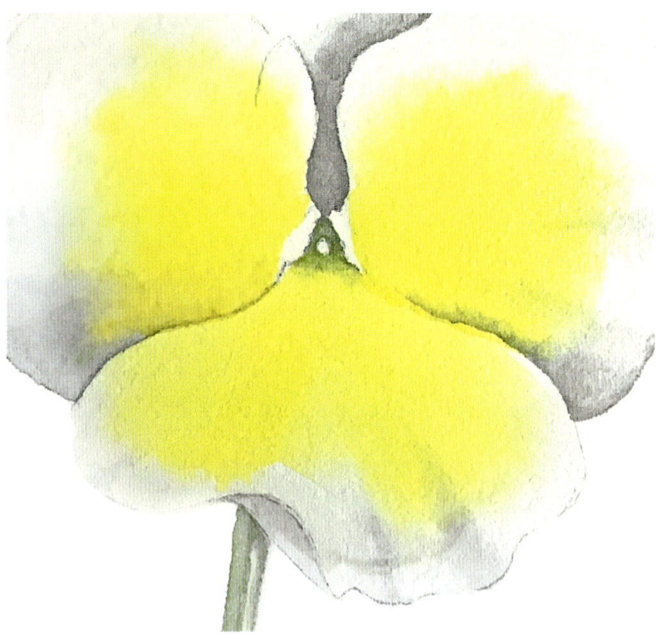

Step 2 The first colour to go in is the yellow. Yellow is a delicate colour and if any other paint covers its territory, it will be irretrievable. The yellow would, as a result, look dirty and not glow as it should. By painting it first, we are allowing it to fill its rightful place and hopefully the blues and purples will be kept away. The first wash is Hansa Yellow Light, applied wet-in-wet to all three front petals.

The green mix for painting the stem is a wash of French Ultramarine + Hansa Yellow Light.

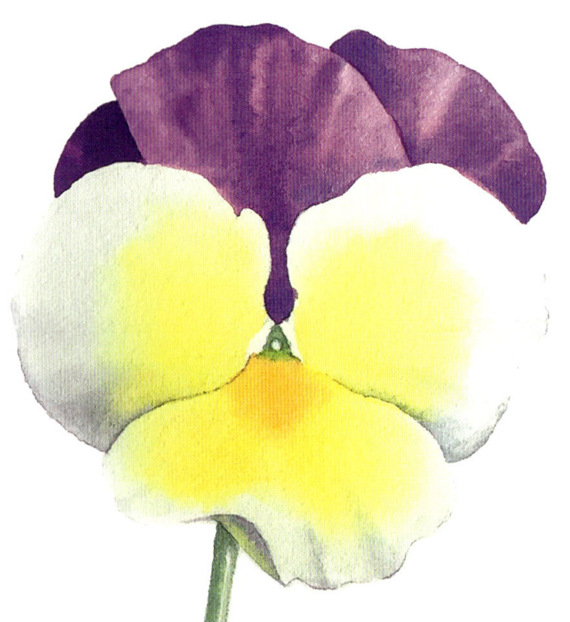

Step 3 When the yellow has dried, the front petal is re-wetted all over and some Hansa Yellow Deep is added towards the centre.

Now that the yellow is established, we can start working from back to front. The two back petals are a very intense, dark mix of French Ultramarine + Quinacridone Lilac. The paint is highly concentrated so that we can paint these petals in only three or four successive washes. The highlights are reserved but not kept completely white. Pansies are velvety, therefore their highlights are not white but a paler version of the local colour. Remember to let the first petal dry before painting the second one, so that they do not merge into each other.

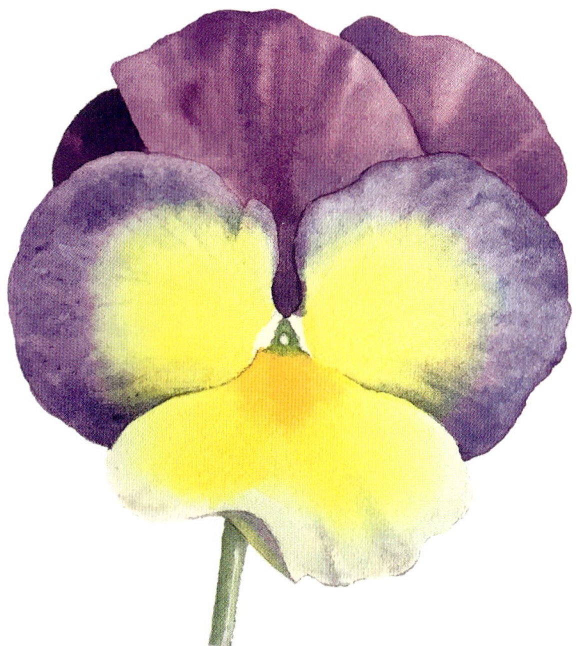

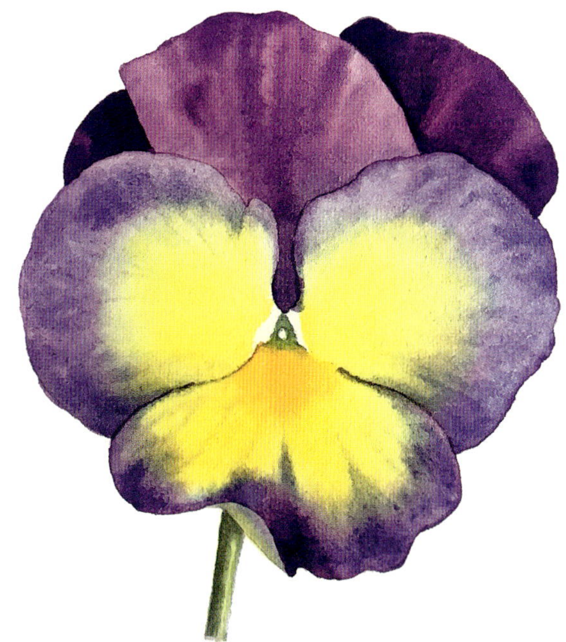

Step 4 Let everything dry thoroughly and re-wet one of the side petals. Although the whole petal is wet, the purple mix of French Ultramarine + Quinacridone Lilac (same mix as for the back petals but in different proportions: more blue and less lilac) is applied to the outer edges. Drag some paint towards the centre of the flower following the veining pattern, but being careful not to cover the yellow. Somewhere in the middle of the petal, the yellow and the purple will be layered as a result, creating a beautiful purple-grey colour. Repeat on the other side.

Step 5 The process in step 4 is repeated on the large front petal, using the same mix. As this front petal is not touching the back petals, it is possible to work on it straight away. Using the same mix as before, add another wash, strengthening the colour and following the structure established in the first colour wash. This will darken the darker parts and the mid-tones while keeping the highlights slightly lighter.

The stem has been given another wash of the same green mix (see page 148, step 2), thinner on the light side, heavier on the shadow side.

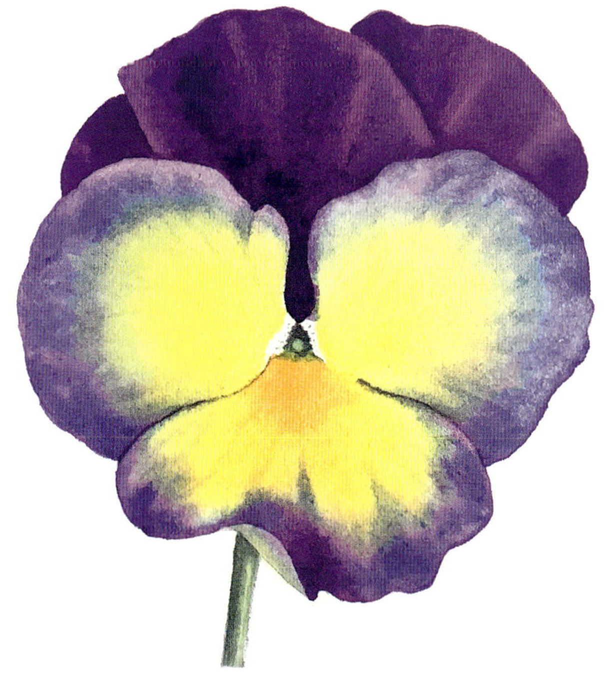

Step 6 Continue adding wet-in-wet washes where they are needed to get the required intensity of colour. Remember to reserve your highlights throughout, and also to keep the two small furry bits at the base of the side petals completely untouched. The inside of the flower has been painted with a green detail in the very middle. You may wish to add more shadow colour right under the two furry areas to add depth to the very centre of the flower.

Painting the centre

The wet-in-wet washes have provided the soft colour and smooth blending required to render the multiple hue variations and the velvety texture. However, the details cannot be painted wet-in-wet, because they need a sharpness that this technique won't be able to provide. It is time, then, for some dry-brush work.

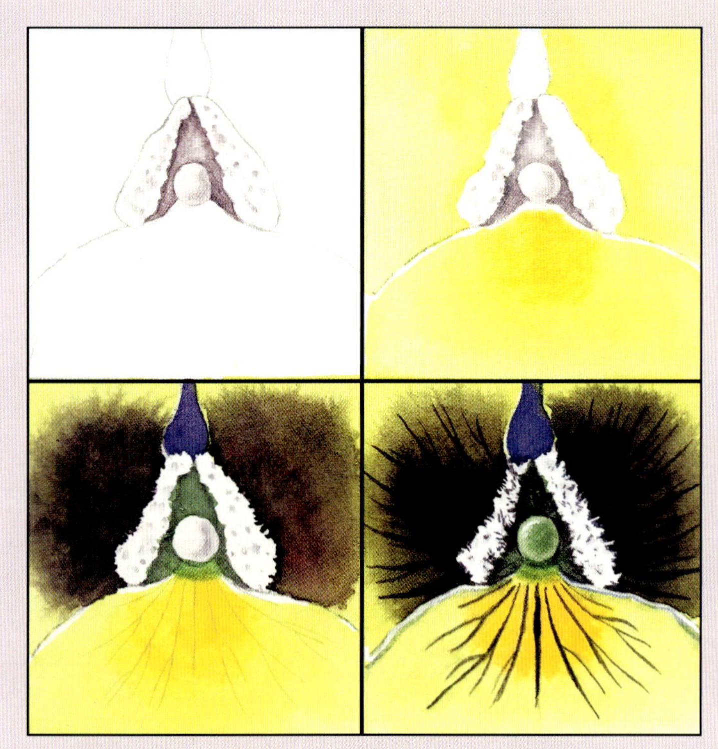

How to paint the centre of a pansy

1 Paint the shadows wet-in-wet, using the Harmonic Shadow mix. Stipple some of the shadow mix over the two small hairy petal bases.

2 Paint the yellow as a first colour, again wet-in-wet. Here, the side petals are Hansa Yellow Light while the bottom petal is Hansa Yellow Light with some Hansa Yellow Deep dropped in at the base. Different varieties will require different yellows.

3 Paint the dark blotches, still wet-in-wet. Wet a petal then drop in some not-too-diluted dark mix at the base, letting it spread outwards. Some varieties have blotches on all three front petals, others only on the side petals and some have none. The centre of the flower is dark green.

4 Draw the lines, first sketched lightly in pencil to place them correctly then with a fine brush on dry paper using a dark purple mix, blending their edges gently with a damp, clean brush to integrate them into the texture of the petals.

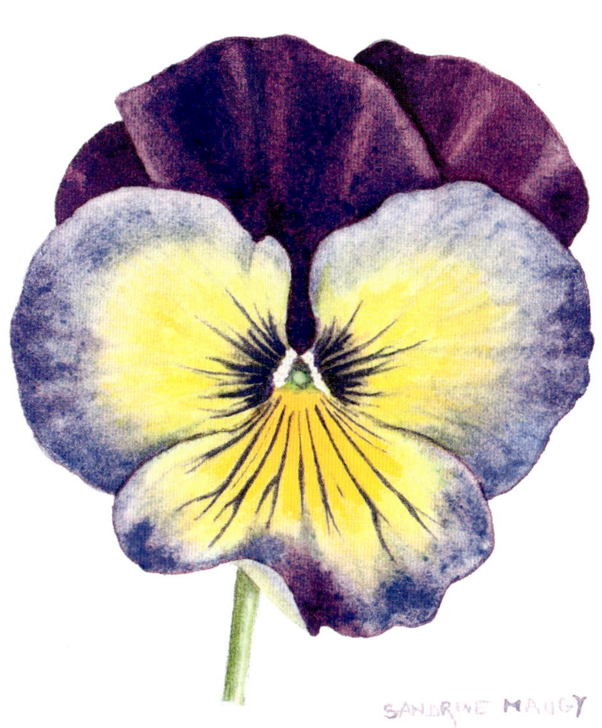

Pansy 'Midnight Glow'
Watercolour on paper.

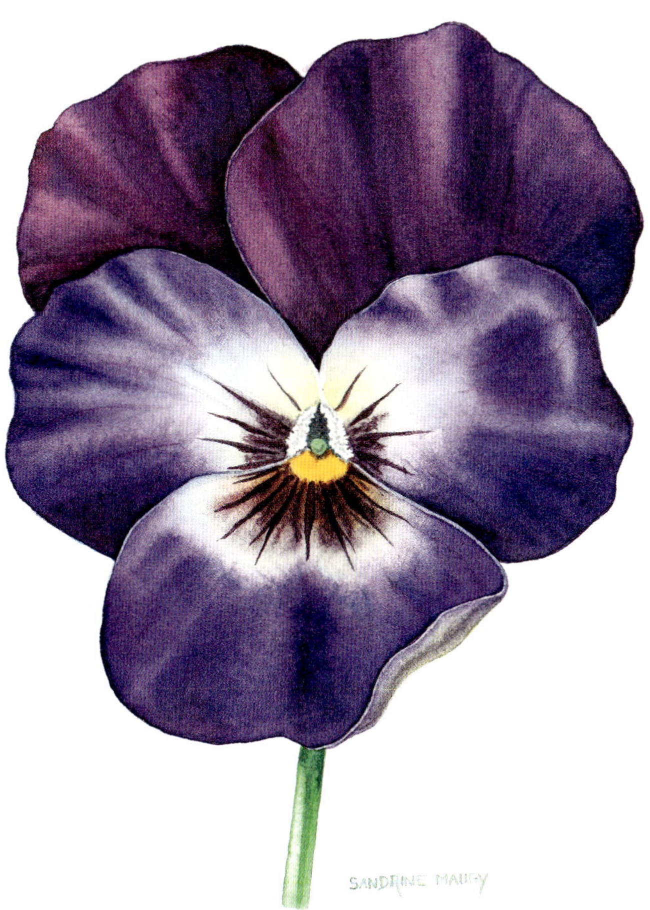

Viola
Watercolour on paper.
This is a viola with a similar structure to the pansy above, but a slightly different colour scheme. Perylene Violet was added into the purple mix to darken it without compromising on the richness of the colour and more layers were painted to obtain the deep violet hue. This viola was painted for a video tutorial I made for Fabriano, which can be found on their YouTube channel.

151

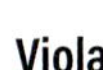

ECHEVERIA

Common name Echeveria	**Planting time** Possible all year	**Propagation** Seeds, leaf cuttings and
Botanical name *Echeveria*	**Aspect** Full or partial sun	offset separation
Family Crassulaceae	**Hardiness** Semi-hardy	**Native** Central and northwestern America
Flowering Possible all year		

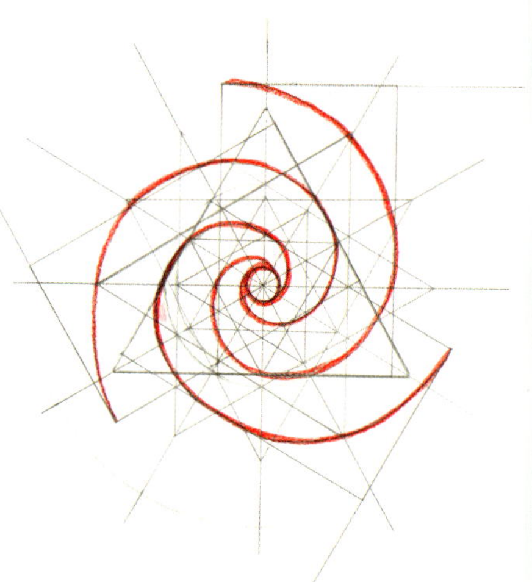

The spiral growing pattern of the leaves.

Botanically speaking…

- Echeveria is named after Atanasio Echeverría y Godoy, an eighteenth-century Mexican botanical illustrator.

- The genus consists of about 150 species. Most species shed their lower leaves in Winter. These need to be cleared or they might decay and cause the whole plant to rot.

- Echeverias can be evergreen or deciduous.

- The offsets are commonly known as 'hens and chicks'.

- Echeverias serve a very important environmental role in their natural habitat, serving as host for several species of butterfly.

- Echeverias are drought-resistant thanks to their desert origins. However, they love a big watering from time to time.

- The flowers (cymes) grow on short stalks, which arise from compact rosettes of succulent fleshy leaves.

- The leaves are fleshy and are coated in a waxy cuticle. They grow in a spiral pattern (see above), similar to the centre of a sunflower. This configuration optimizes the gathering of water and exposure to the sun. If the plant is grown in partial shade, it will lean towards the light and the spiral pattern will become lopsided.

Opposite page: Echeveria pattern and tone studies

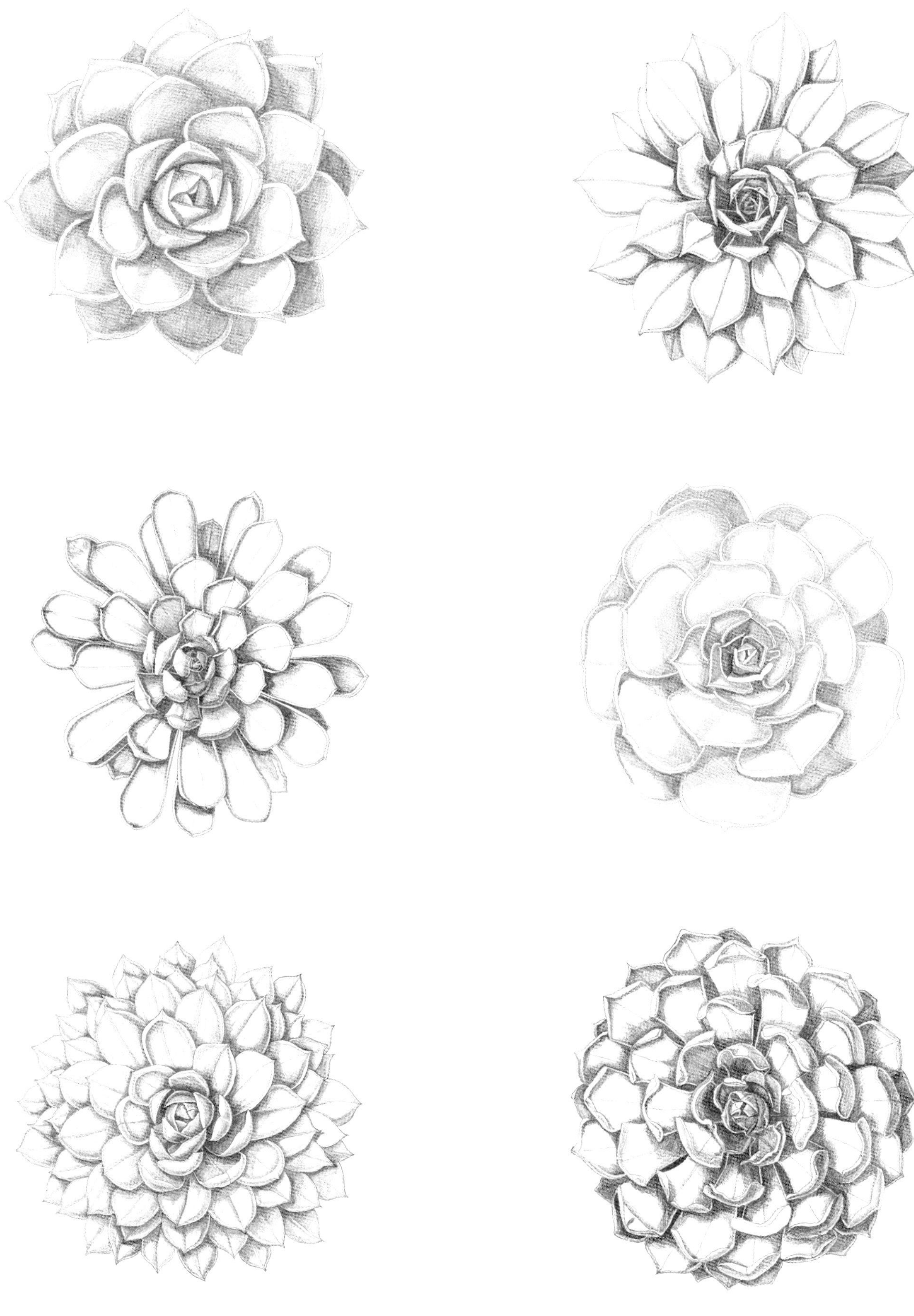

Level 2

ECHEVERIA
Drawing and Viridian palette

I recently started paying attention to succulents. So far, I had largely ignored them. It wasn't love at first sight. It came on gradually and took a long time before I saw the true beauty of the frosty blues, mauve pinks and minty greens. Echeverias are the ones that finally convinced me they were going to be an inspiring subject to paint. Echeverias come in an interesting range of colours that are unique and fascinating to paint. As I was observing my subject and thinking of mixes, one colour came to mind and would not go away. This is a colour I rarely use – indeed it wasn't even in my palette until recently, as I had dismissed it years ago. This mysterious pigment? Viridian…

I was unfamiliar with Viridian and what it could do, while at the same time having a nagging hunch that it was the right colour for the job and that it would allow the painting of three plants of completely different colours with the same base pigment. The first thing to do was to test my theory and paint colour swatches (any excuse for those!).

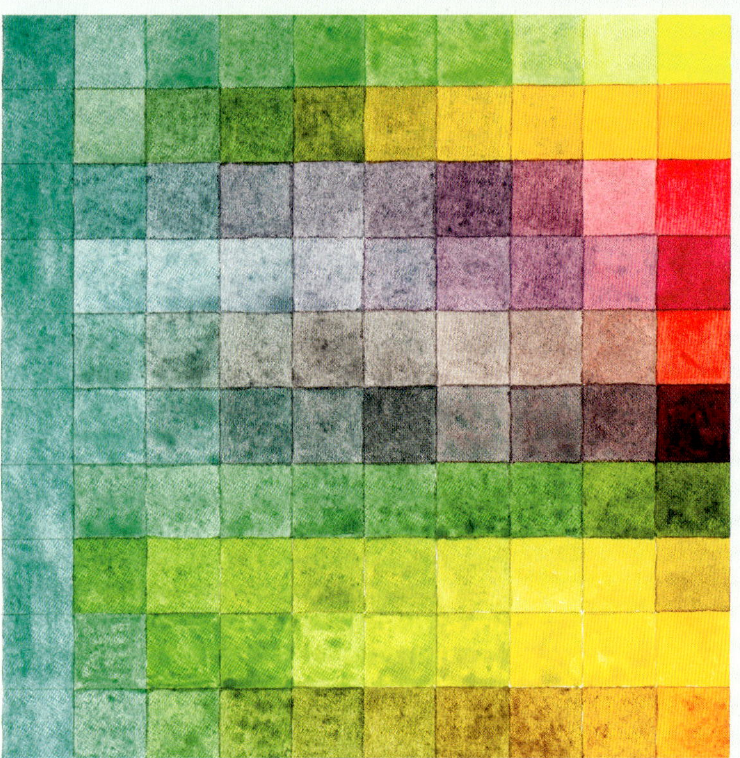

The test was conclusive. Mixed with different yellows and even pinks, Viridian produced the exact colours I needed for the echeverias.

154

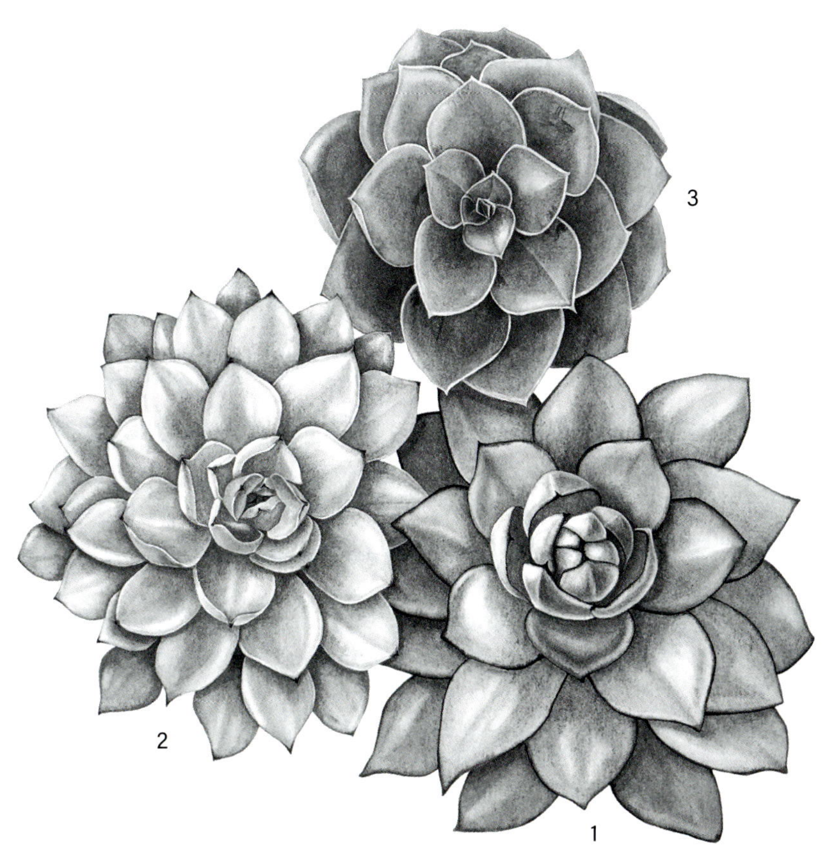

This is a tonal version of the final painting in which I numbered the plants to make it easier to follow the tutorial. For the composition, I placed the larger plants at the bottom and the smaller one at the top, so that the painting wouldn't be top-heavy.

Palette

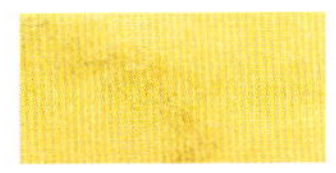 Rich Green Gold

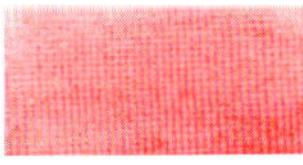 Quinacridone Pink

 Carmine

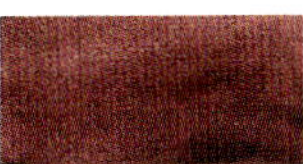 Perylene Violet

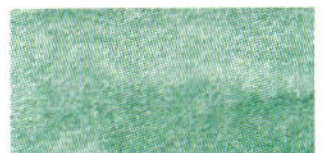 Viridian

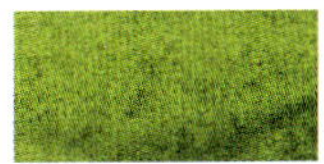 Sap Green

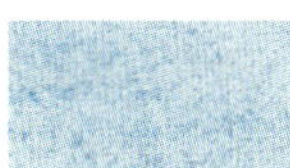 Cerulean Blue

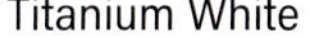 Titanium White

Bloom

For the bloom on some of the petals, I used Cerulean Blue, a milky, granulating opaque blue, which, when used thinly, doesn't cover the previous layers but shows the bloom on top. Where the Cerulean Blue isn't enough, a touch of Titanium White can be mixed with it.

Harmonic Shadow mix

Viridian is the base colour for the painting so I also made it the base colour for the shadows. Mixed with Quinacridone Pink, it makes a gorgeous, clear and transparent grey.

Working on plants 1 and 2

As the three echeverias in the composition show different colours and are
painted with different mixes, I decided to work on one at a time.
As I knew that the small pinkish one at the top would be more
troublesome than the other two, I kept it until last in order to gain some
experience in echeverias before tackling it.

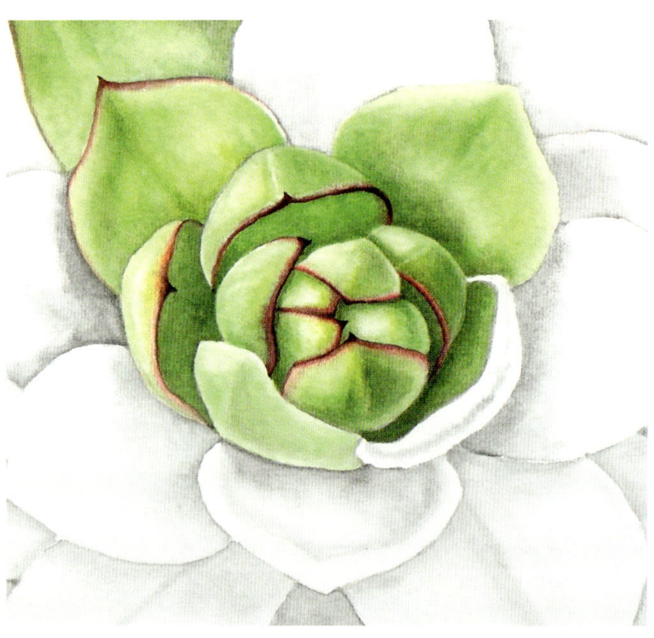

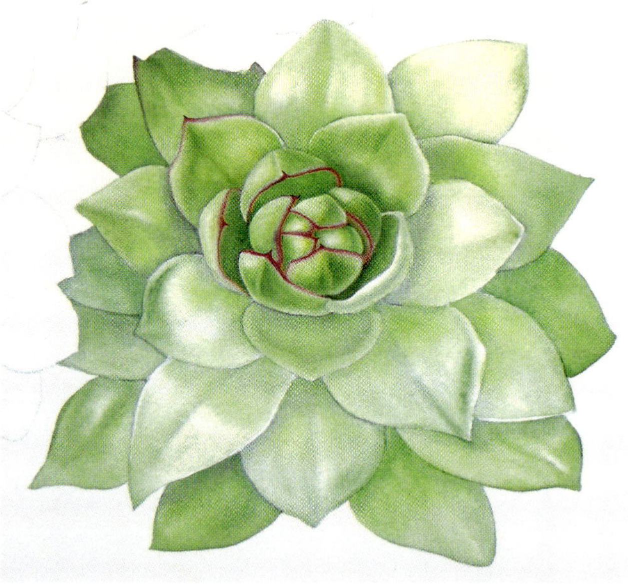

Step 1 The mix for plant number 1 is Viridian + Rich Green Gold.
These two pigments make a very luminous green. As usual, I painted
the shadows first, then painted the green mix wet-in-wet, and then
I tried adding the Carmine border in a separate wash.

Step 2 Once satisfied that the Carmine would work, I finished the
first wet-in-wet wash on the whole plant.

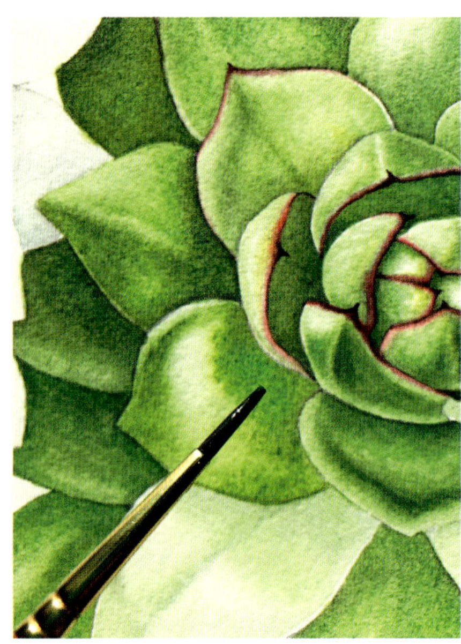

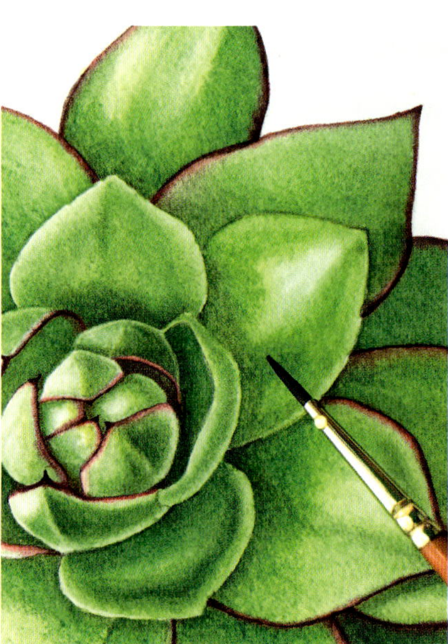

Step 3 I then painted a second and
a third wet-in-wet wash, using the green
mix as a base and dropping in some pure
Viridian in some places (mainly over the
shadows) and some pure Rich Green Gold
in others (mainly over the mid-tones) to keep
the colour lively. All the while, the highlights
are reserved but not completely white, as
the texture of the plant is matte.

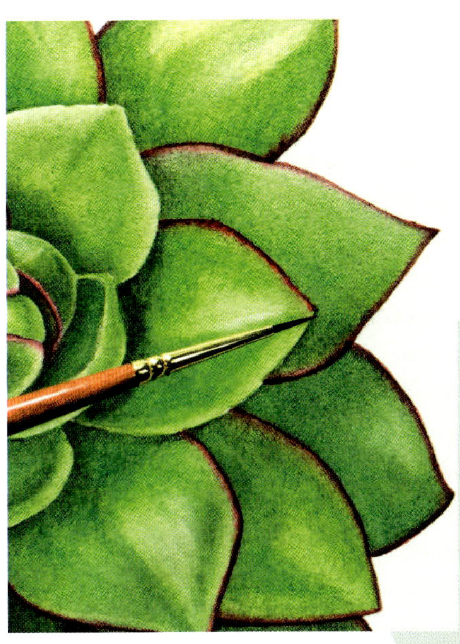

Step 4 To add the red border, wet the whole leaf and paint a thin line of Carmine on the edge, letting it run into the leaf. This creates a hard line on the outer edge, while the inner edge of the line softly blends into the green.

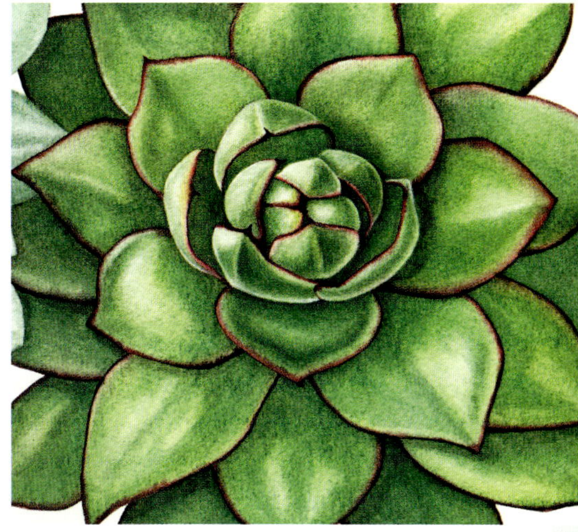

Echeveria number 1 is finished and we can move on to the second one.

Step 5 The first and second wash on plant 2 are both Viridian + a hint of Sap Green, building up some colour first over the shadows, moving into the mid-tones, reserving the highlights.

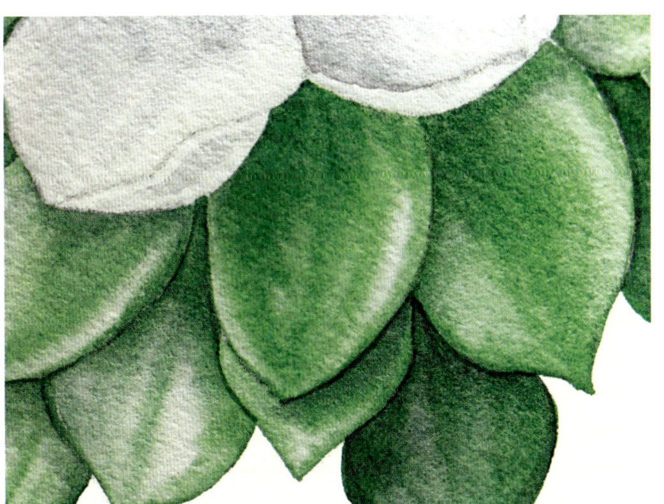

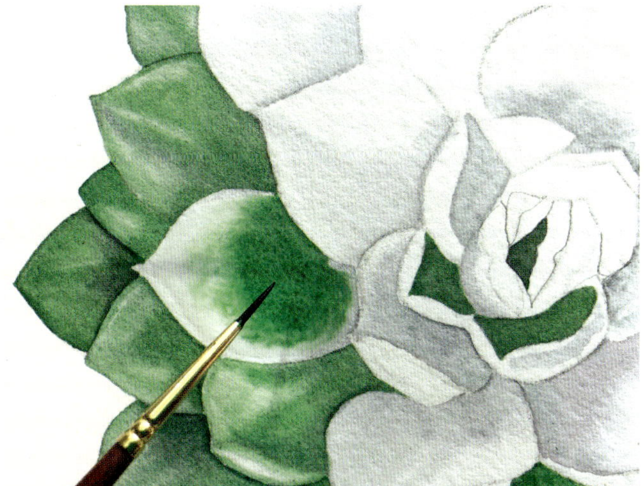

Working on plants 2 and 3

We are still working our way through the painting, one echeveria at a time,
using Viridian as the connecting colour between three very
different-looking plants.

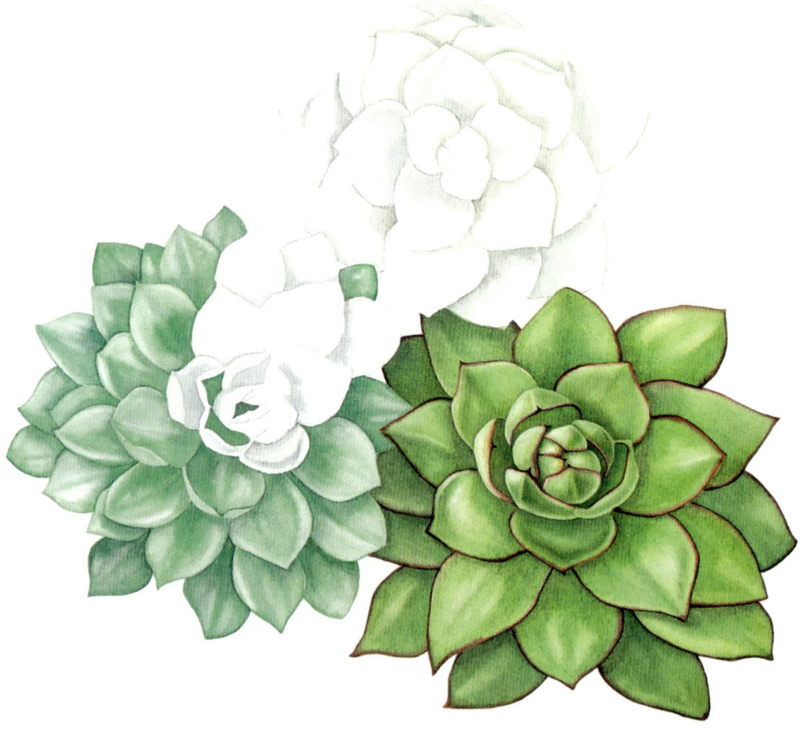

Echeveria 1 is finished, echeveria 2 is half
painted and only the shadows are painted
on echeveria 3.

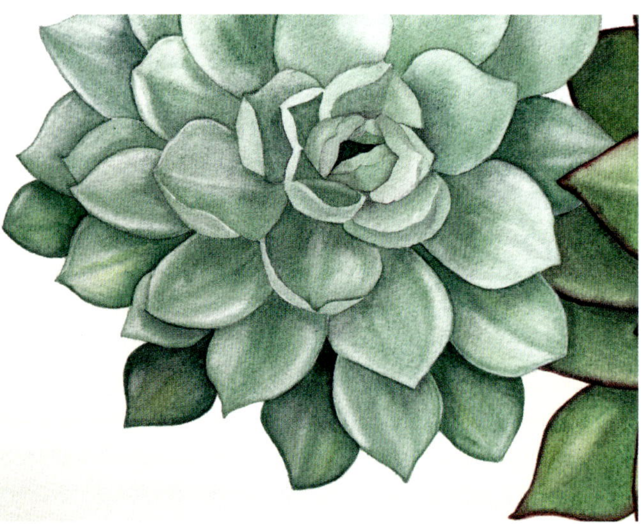

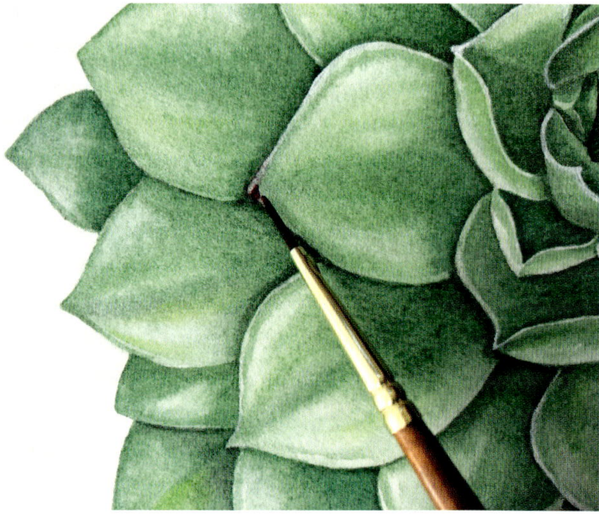

Step 1 The petals at the back of the plant need darkening to give
some depth. The same use of Viridian + Sap Green is used in an
extra wash.

Step 2 If the sharp edges are lost in the wet washes, it is possible
to recover them using Titanium White. It is preferable to wait until
all the wet-in-wet washes are finished before using the dry-brushed
Titanium, or the edges might get lost again.

Echeveria 3 is the trickiest to paint, as it has an odd colour: not quite
pink, not quite blue or grey, slightly golden but not brown. A real
brain-teaser. To tackle these difficult hues, I separated the plant into
three zones: the inner, midway and outer leaves.

Wash 1

Inner leaves: Quinacridone Pink.
Midway leaves: Quinacridone Pink at the base, blending into
Rich Green Gold at the tips, painted in the same wet-in-wet wash to
keep the blending soft and gradual.
Outer leaves: Rich Green Gold.

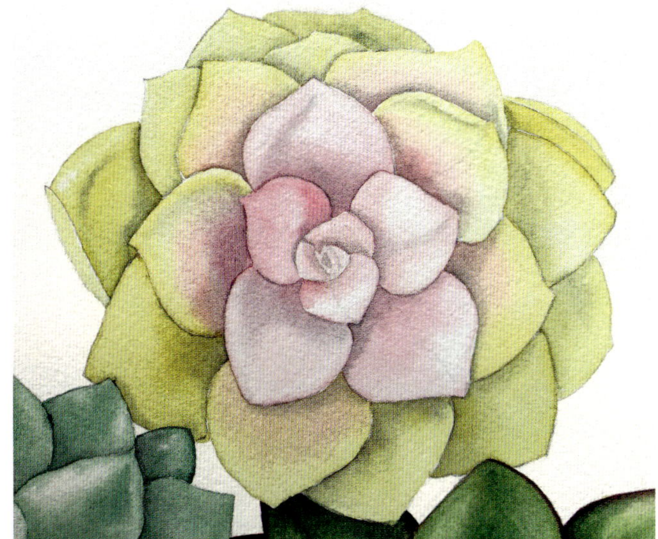

Wash 2

Inner leaves: Viridian.
Midway leaves: Viridian.
Outer leaves: Viridian.

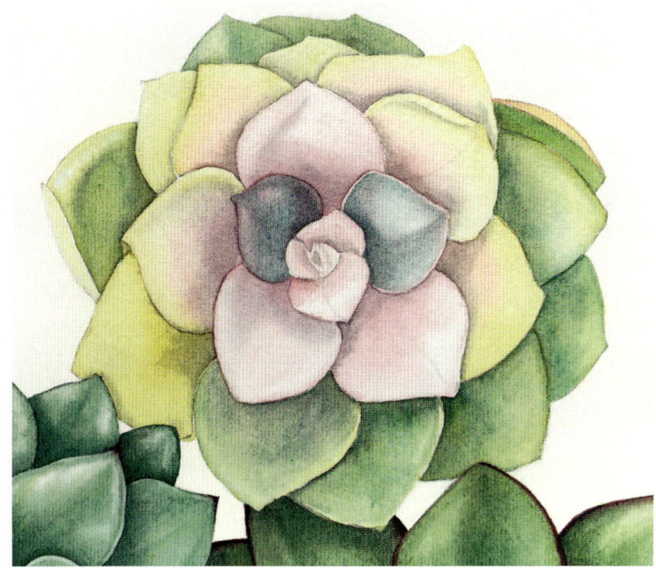

Layering these colours in separate washes means that they make
different colours by optical mixing but the resulting colours are not
flat. For example, if Quinacridone Pink is mixed with Viridian in the
palette, it makes a grey (which was used in the shadows). However,
if Quinacridone Pink and Viridian are applied as pure pigment in
two separate wet-in-wet washes, the resulting colour is green, pink
and grey all at the same time. This effect is perfect for the weird and
confusing colour of this echeveria.

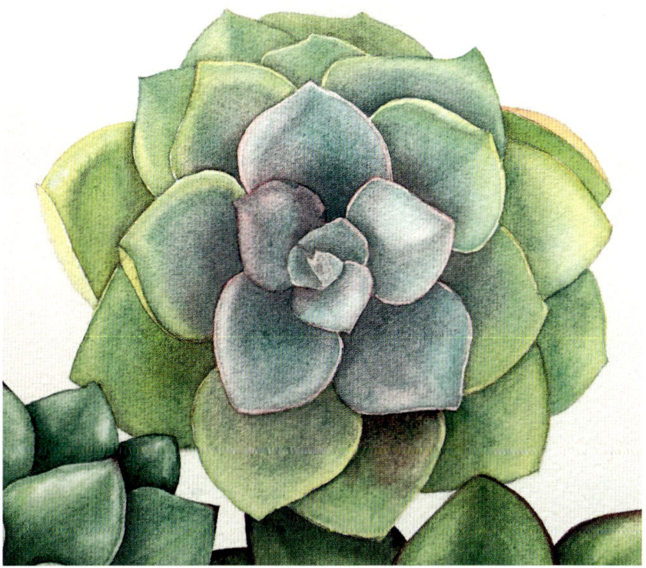

Finishing plant 3

At this halfway stage, the third echeveria is looking a bit confused as to what
colour it should be – but adding the bloom will bring everything together…

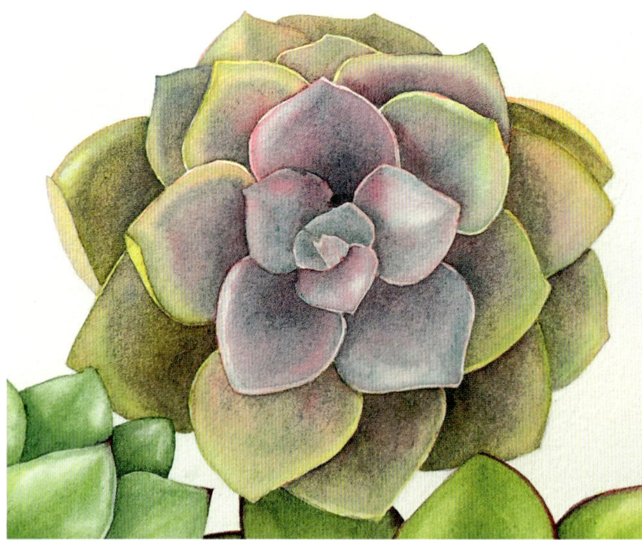

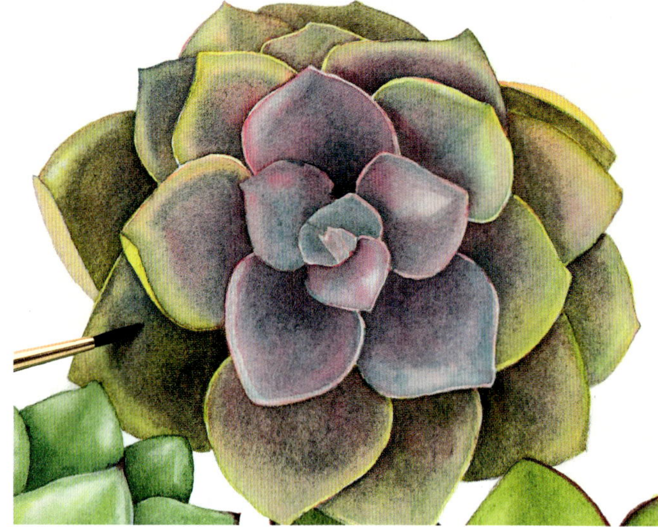

Step 1 The last wet-in-wet wash is Quinacridone Pink over all
the leaves. This will turn the centre leaves pinker, the midway leaves
greyer and the outer leaves golden-grey.

Step 2 Here is the pigment that will bring the varied colours
together and give the leaves their cloudy bloom: Cerulean Blue. This
is added on dry paper, and brushed unevenly where the bloom is
showing the most.

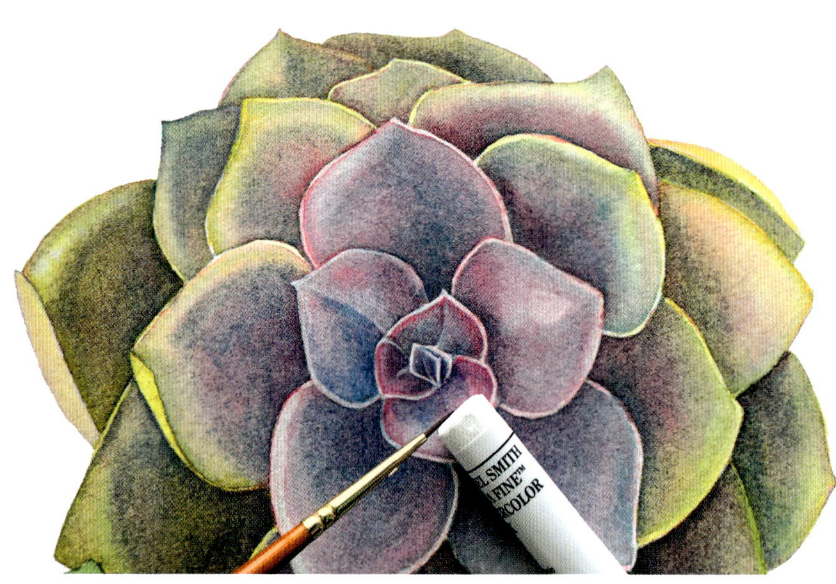

Tip

If Cerulean Blue doesn't
seem enough for your plant,
you can add a touch of
Titanium White to it.

Step 3 The final touch is to outline the
leaves with a Titanium White border, using a
pigment stick, showing the thickness of the
fleshy leaves and adding definition.

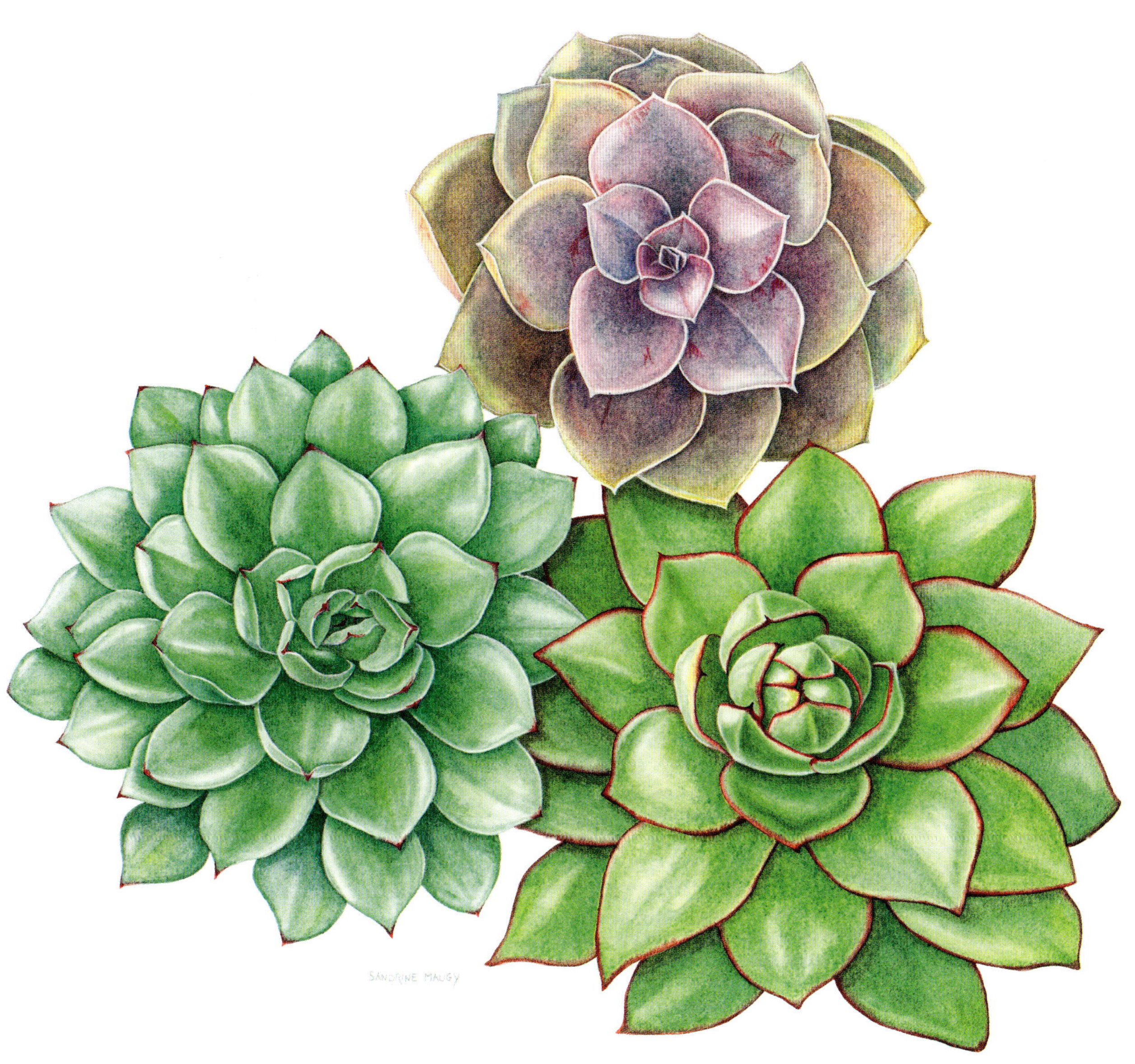

Echeveria hybrids
Watercolour on paper.

Anatomy of

HOLLY

Common name Holly
Botanical name *Ilex*
Family Aquifoliaceae
Flowering Spring

Planting time Possible all year
Aspect Any aspect (full sun preferred)
Hardiness Hardy

Propagation Seeds or cuttings
Native All temperate to subtropical regions

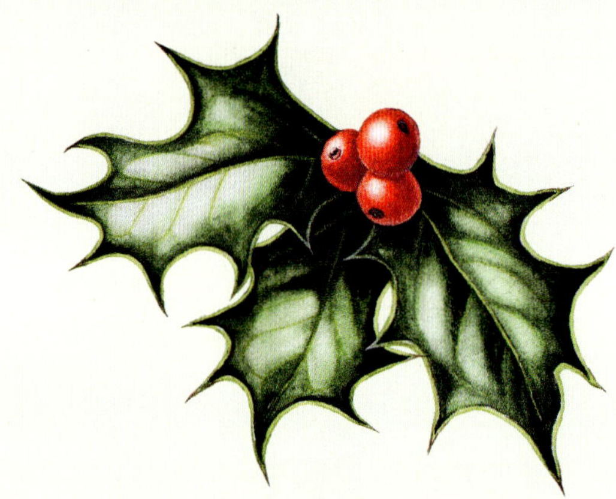

Botanically speaking…

- The genus *Ilex* has over 560 species. The common ancestor of the existing species appeared during the Eocene period, about 50 million years ago.

- The genus was most prosperous during the Paleogene and Neogene periods, when laurel forests (forests of broad-leaved evergreens) covered great parts of the planet, more than 20 million years ago.

- Most of the remaining laurel forests disappeared about 10,000 years ago, at the end of the Pleistocene period. Many of the holly species of that period became extinct because they could not adapt to the new environment.

- Several species are listed as endangered and at least one, *Ilex gardneriana*, is extinct because of the loss of its habitat.

- Holly can be evergreen or deciduous. It is the only non-coniferous evergreen tree in Europe, with leaves staying on the tree for up to three years.

- Many species have wavy margins tipped with spines. The margins usually have a fine border in a lighter green than the leaf colour.

- The spines are extremely sharp and the dense foliage offers sanctuary to small birds and mammals against larger predators such as foxes.

- Young trees have almost exclusively spiny leaves while older trees will have some smoother margins on their foliage.

- The leaves are alternate, smooth and very glossy, dark green on the topside and chalky paler green on the underside.

- Each twig has buds on its sides and one at the tip.

- The tiny greeny-white flowers, sometimes showing a touch of pink, are usually borne in clusters and are unisexual.

- The flowers have four petals and four anthers.

- The female and male flowers are borne on different trees.

- The fruits or berries are called drupes and can be red, yellow or black. The drupes are an important Winter food source for many birds and other animals but are toxic to humans.

- *Ilex aquifolium* is the traditional holly of Christmas decorations and cards.

- A tea-like beverage called *mate* is made from the leaves of the yerba mate (*Ilex paraguariensis*), a species of holly that grows in South America.

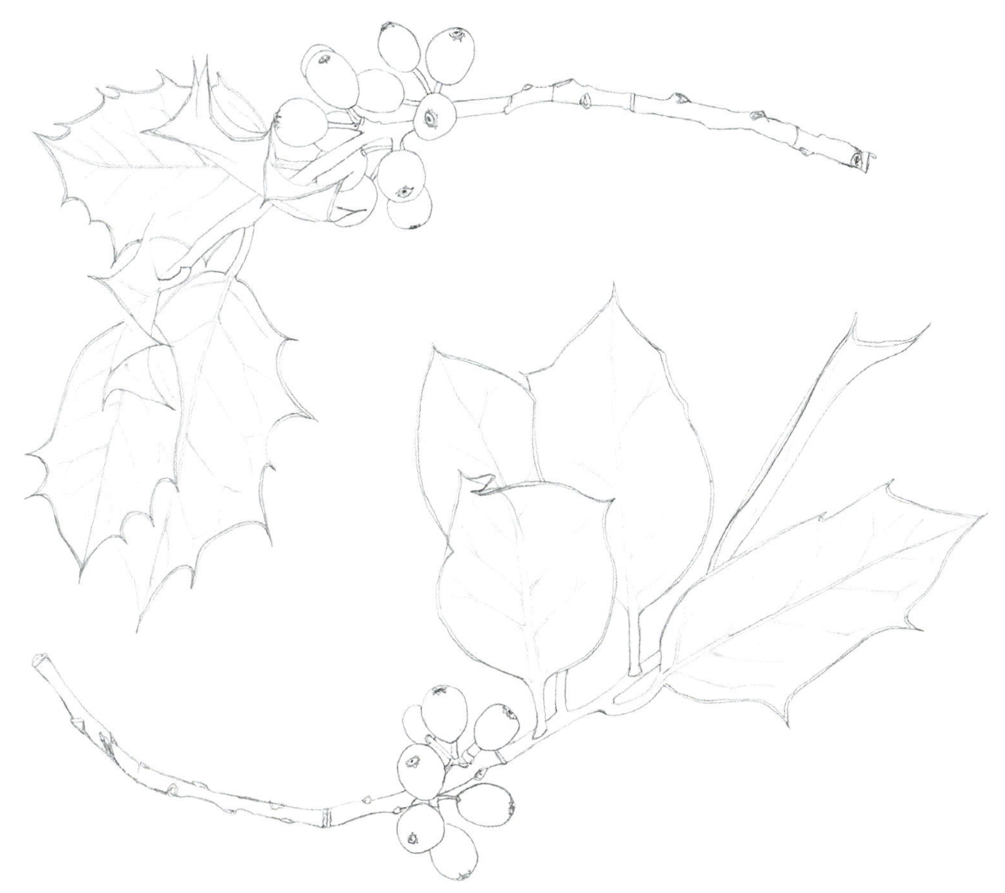

Holly pencil study

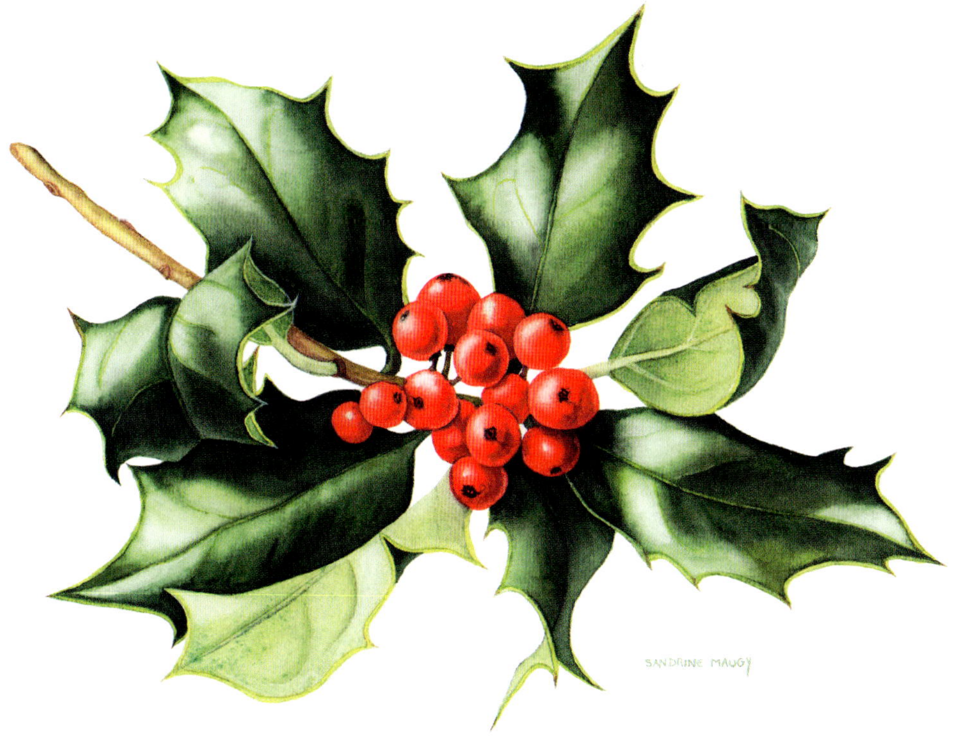

Holly, watercolour

Level 3

HOLLY STAR
Drawing and palette

With its bright red berries and glossy green leaves bringing some colour
into the dormant borders, holly is a feature of the Winter garden.
Although beautiful to look at, it is not easy to paint: getting the very dark
green without ending up with heavy washes can be a challenge. Fortunately,
Indanthrone Blue comes to the rescue…

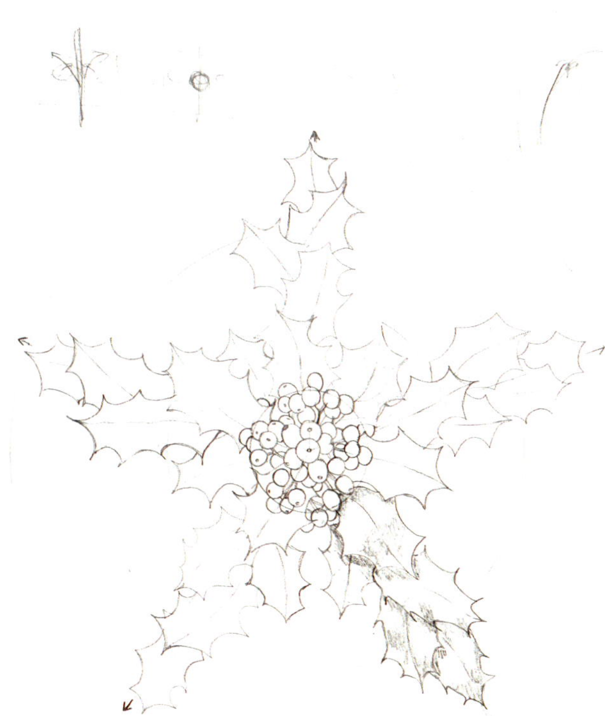

For this holly painting, I wanted to move away from a conventional botanical illustration and venture into the realm of design. I started with studies of holly leaves and berries, drawing them as they would be on the branch. I gradually stylized the studies more and more, keeping them botanically accurate for individual leaves and berries while altering their position to design a star shape.

To make sure that the star was balanced and harmoniously filled with holly, I turned to geometry. Using a pair of compasses, I drew four concentric circles: one in the centre to contain the berries and three larger ones to contain the branches of the leafy star. I then divided the circles with five lines, starting with a vertical one for the top branch and placing the four remaining ones equidistantly around the perimeter, every 72 degrees.

In this sketch, left, you can see the berries gathered in the centre while the leaves are spread along the branches of the star. The top right branch has yet to be drawn and the sketch shows the line going from the centre to the outer circle.

Compared with original botanical sketches, such as the ones on page 163, I took some liberties with my subject:

- There are probably too many berries, even for the most prolific holly tree;

- No leaves are showing their undersides;

- The branch is not showing between the leaves;

- There are no gaps in the foliage;

- The leaves are too regularly overlapped.

Materials list

PAPERS

Cartridge paper or sketchbook
Tracing paper
Transfer paper
Watercolour paper: Fabriano Artistico
HP Extra White, 640gsm (300lb)

DRAWING

Pencils: 6B clutch pencil; finer pencil
for details

PAINTING

Brushes: Pro Arte Prolene Plus Series 007
in sizes 3/0, 2, 4 and 6; Princeton Neptune
synthetic squirrel round brush series in
size 6 (for wetting the paper and for light-
touch glazes); Major Brushes ⅛in (3mm)
flat brush
Titanium White pigment stick

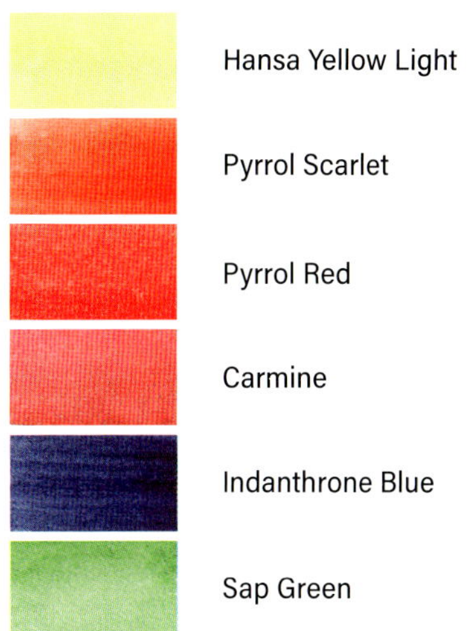

Harmonic Shadows

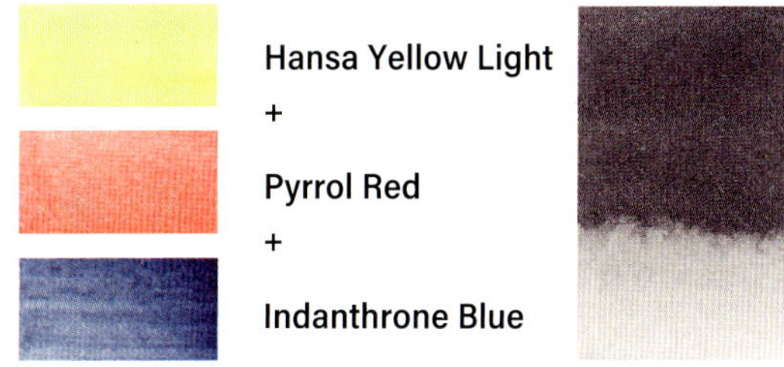

Green mixes

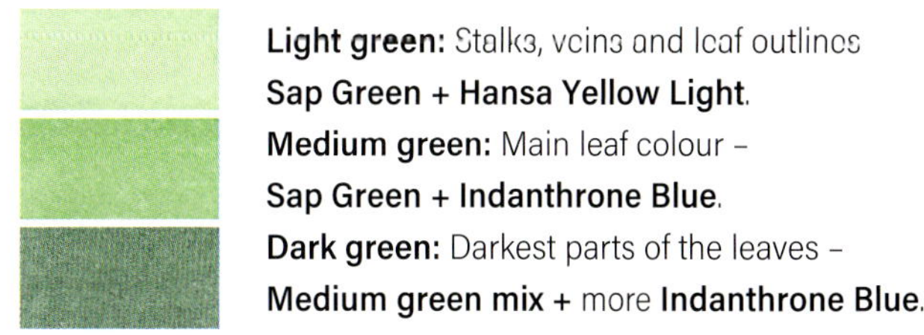

Washes

The first step in painting the Holly Star is to paint the shadows wet-in-wet using the Harmonic Shadow mix, followed by more wet-in-wet washes of colour. This wet base gives a natural and soft look to the painting. I always prefer my work to look like a painting rather than a photograph – as this particular piece is more of a design than a botanical illustration, this is truer than ever.

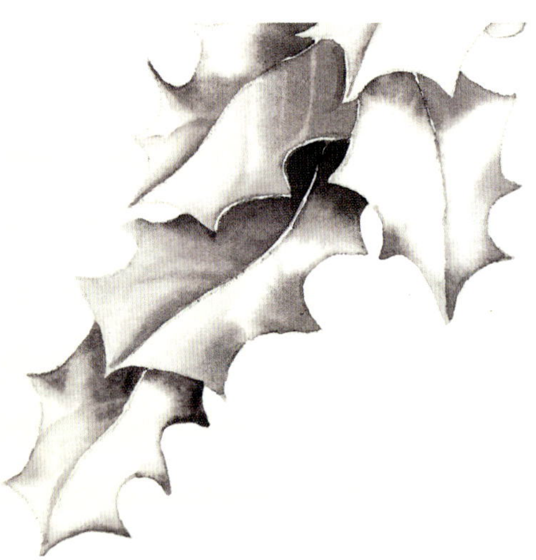

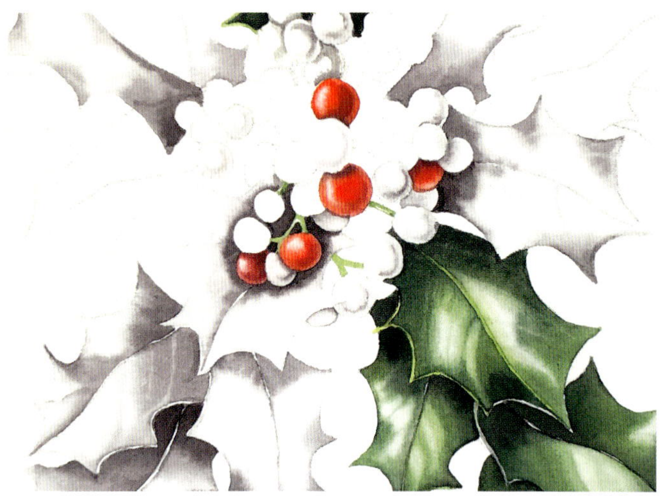

Step 1 The first wash is for the shadows. As the green that covers them will be very dark, it is important to paint the shadows strongly enough to show through the green. The Harmonic Shadow mix contains the dark Indanthrone Blue, which helps to give this dark neutral grey.

Step 2 After the shadows are painted, it is time to play with the colour mixes. At this stage, I didn't follow any particular order but instead painted a little of everything to make sure that the colour scheme worked well.

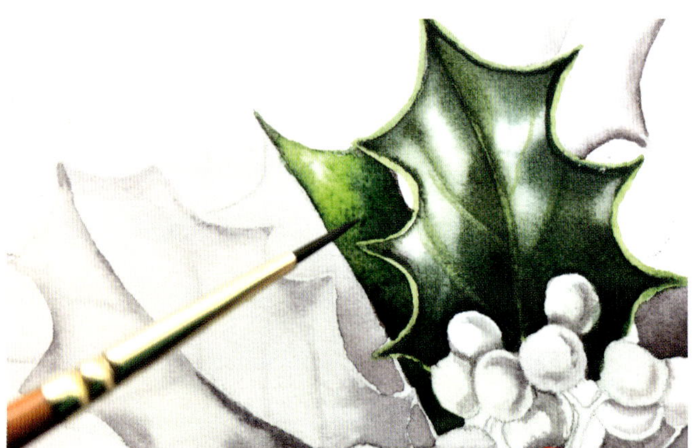

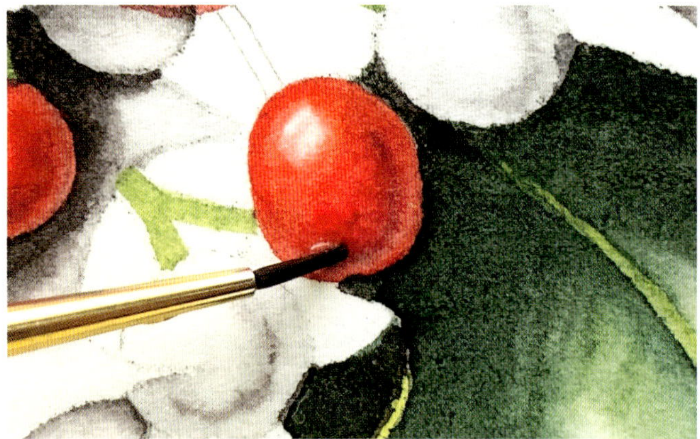

Step 3 The three green mixes are dropped into the wet-in-wet wash at the same time. This allows all the greens to mix together softly rather than creating demarcations between different mixes. Although the paper is still wetted all over the half-leaf, it is crucial to keep the paint from running all over it, so that the highlights stay reserved and completely unpainted. Leaving dry patches over the highlights would result in hard lines.

Step 4 The same is true for the berries: the highlights are reserved but still wet. The three reds are dropped in in the same wash: Pyrrol Red as the main red, Pyrrol Scarlet close to the highlight and Carmine away from the light.

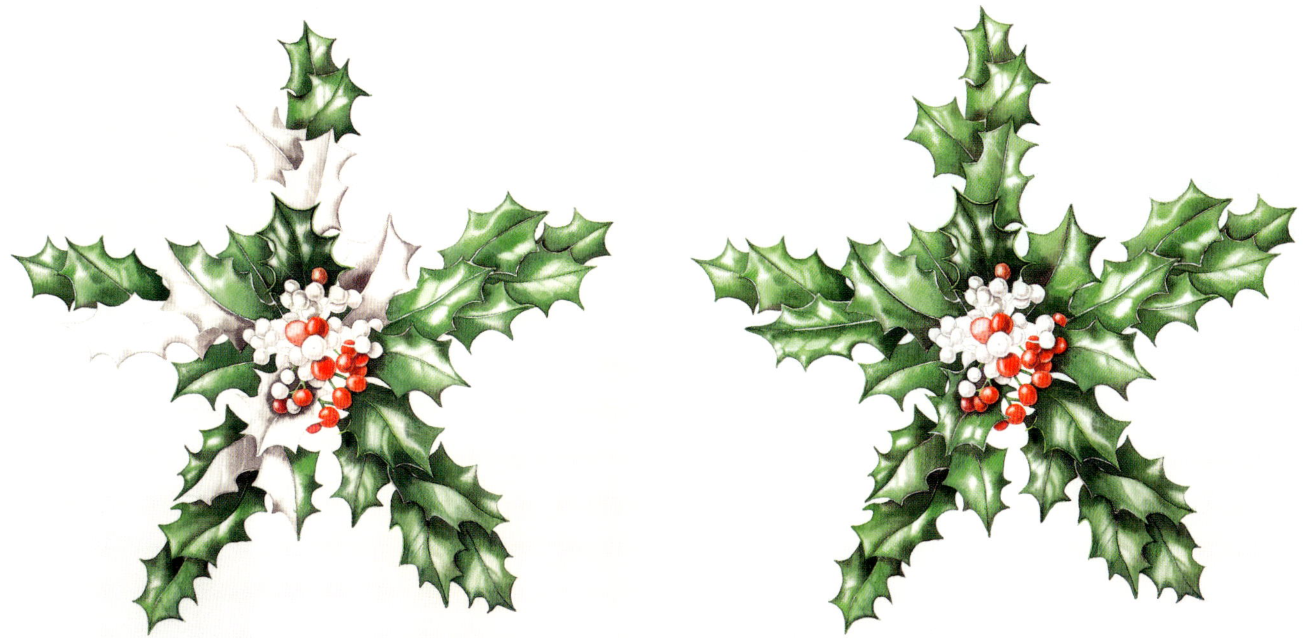

Step 5 Work your way through the painting, adding washes to the leaves and berries, and keeping the painting balanced. The main things to keep in mind at all times are reserving the highlights and leaving an unpainted outline around the holly leaves to show their lighter margins.

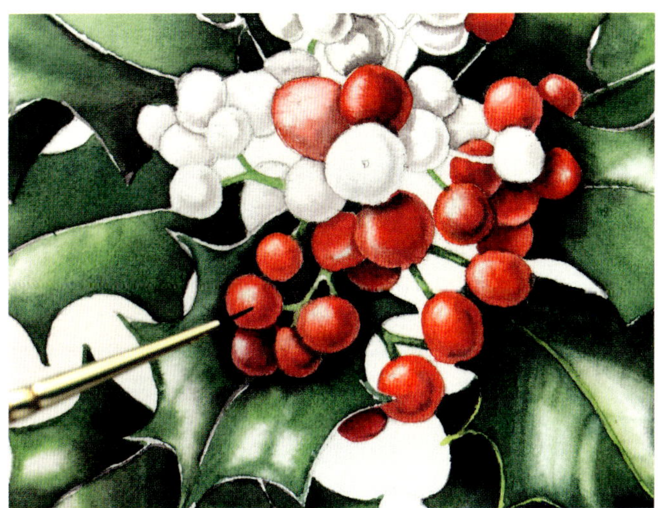

Step 6 Using more Carmine and no Pyrrol Scarlet for the berries at the back will make them recede and create depth. For the highlights on the leaves, stronger, more contrasted highlights will come forward while less contrasted highlights will recede.

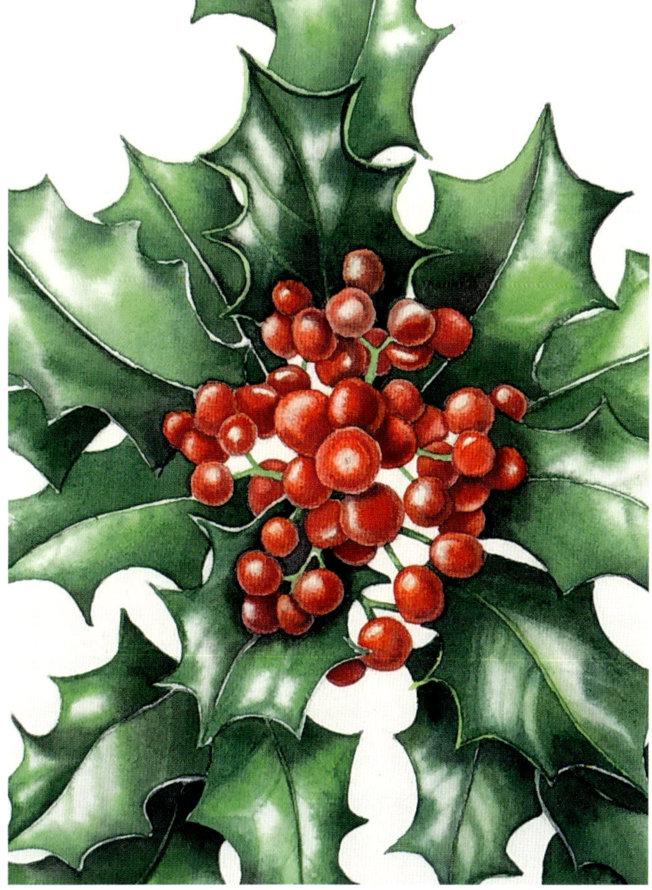

Dry-brush details

Now that all the wet-in-wet washes are done, we can add in some details,
tidying up any light veins or outlines that have been accidentally painted
over and finishing the berries with tiny blobs of dark brown.

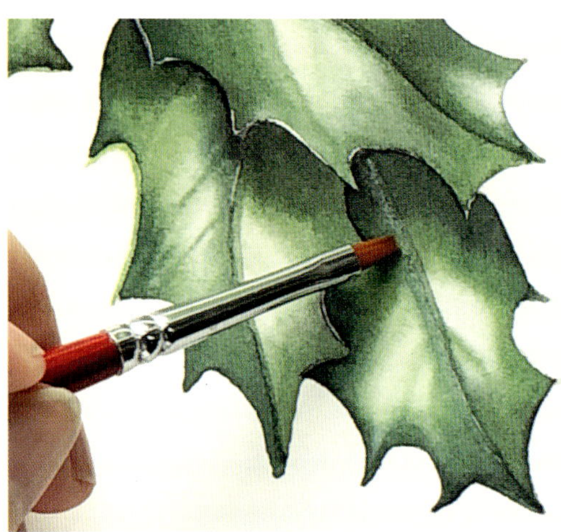

Step 1 Some of the central veins might have partly disappeared
in the enthusiasm of the wet-in-wet work. To recover them, use
a small flat brush on its side, running it along the vein to lift the paint.

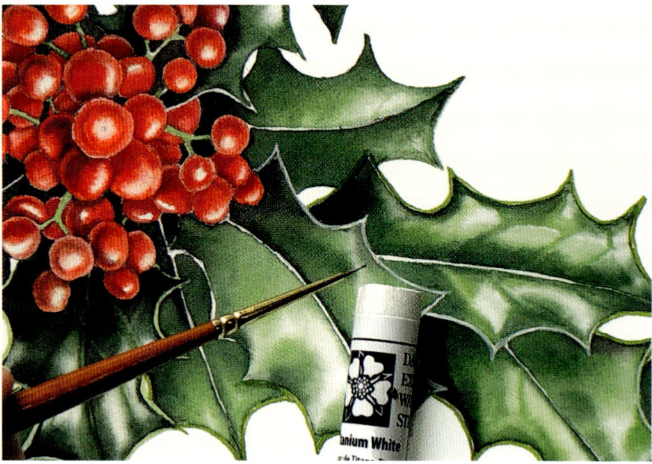

Step 2 If this is not enough, and heavier corrections are required,
use a Titanium White pigment stick. Rub a wet Pro Arte Prolene
Plus 3/0 brush against the pigment and paint along the veins or leaf
edges where required. If the white is too stark, it can be covered
with a glaze of the light green mix.

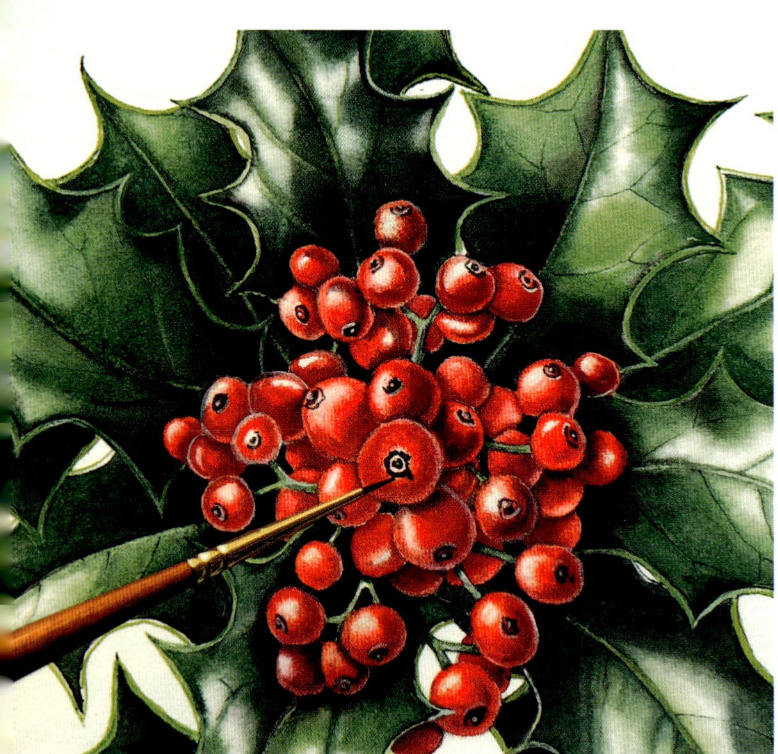

Step 3 To finish off the little knobs on the berries, use a mixture
of the shadow colour with a touch of Pyrrol Red and some
green added to make a very dark brown. These are painted onto
thoroughly dry paper. They can be highlighted with a tiny speck of
Titanium White where the light hits them.

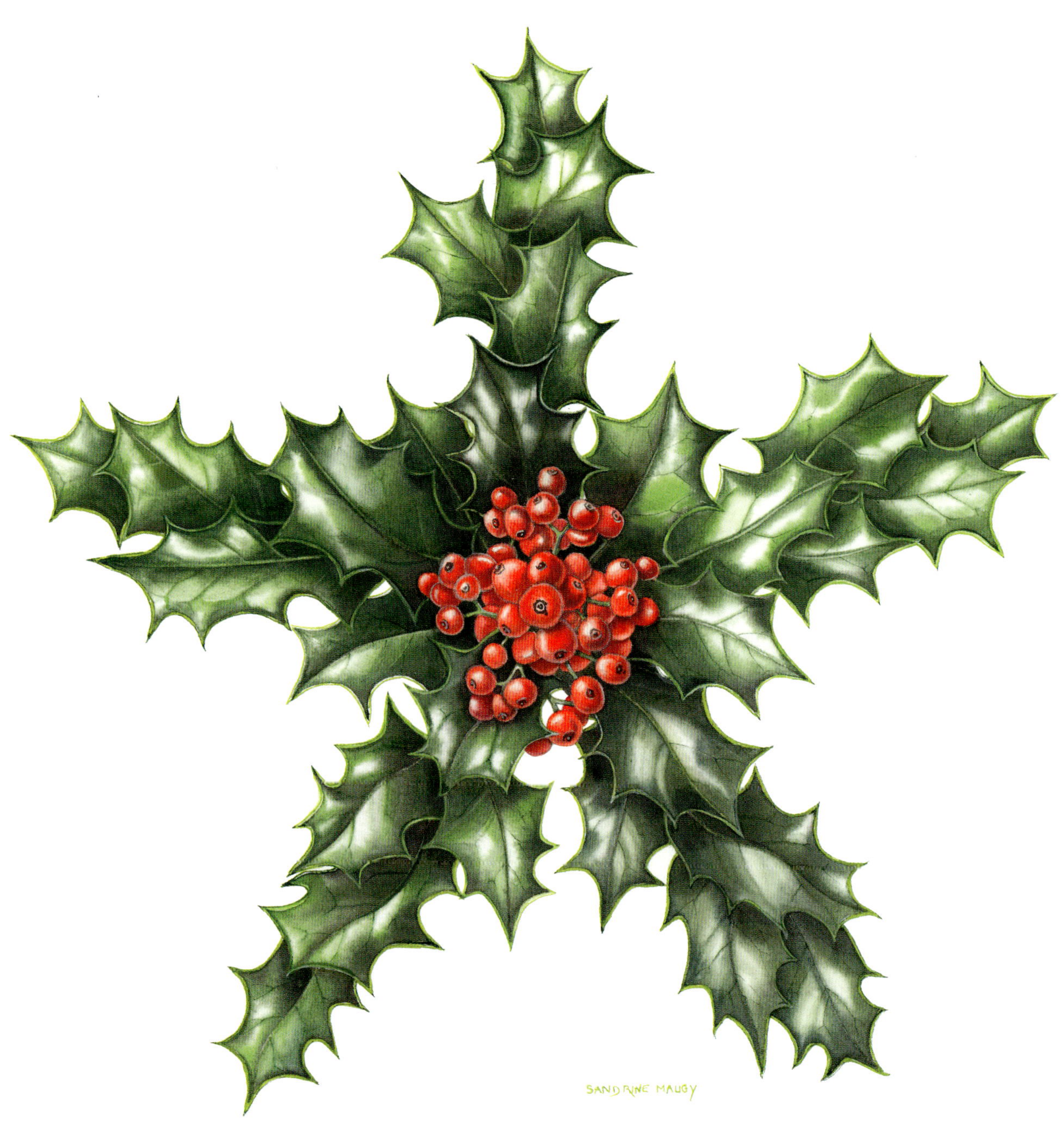

Holly star
Watercolour on paper.

CONCLUSION

In the middle of Winter, under a leaden and cold sky, *Botanical Watercolours through the seasons* is coming to an end.

Together we have explored all the colours on the wheel and built palettes worthy of the boldest, darkest or most subtle subjects, while using pigments that respect the environment and will not harm the very source of our inspiration – nature itself. We have studied tonal ranges and the effect of light on form and colour, giving depth to our subjects with the help of tone studies and found the answer to the mythical botanical grey in fail-safe Harmonic Shadows.

The emerging daffodil promising of longer days, the dark and mysterious 'Queen of Night', the delicate rose, the cheerful sunflower full of warmth, the fading Autumn hydrangea and the shower of falling ginkgo leaves are all part of the cycle of life defined by the passing of the seasons.

Botanical art makes you look at plants and flowers in a different way, appreciating them more fully and adding another dimension to nature. As artists inspired by nature, we are more attuned to its beauty and more aware of its fragility.

Painting flowers is also immensely pleasurable. Whether you respond to a delicate forget-me-not or a chunky quince, whether your heart misses a beat at the sight of a weedy dandelion or a most prized orchid, when you start to look more closely, their shapes, details and colours are always full of surprises.

The pigments used in watercolours today offer unrivalled colours and diverse textures, their names full of poetry. Next time you visit a friend's garden, see a clump of wildflowers by the roadside, find a pear in the supermarket with a leaf still attached or walk by a flowering border, you might get wildly excited and find yourself thinking in terms of Perylene Violet and Quinacridone Rose rather than just seeing a purple or pink tulip.

I hope that you enjoyed this seasonal journey, that my illustrations inspired you and that the tutorials encouraged you to explore colours, while helping you in the development of your own art. If you wish to explore this further in my company, you can find me and my art on my website, YouTube channel and Patreon (see page 4). As your own art continues to develop, we can share new colours and new ideas. I look forward to meeting you and in the meantime, I wish you…

Happy painting!

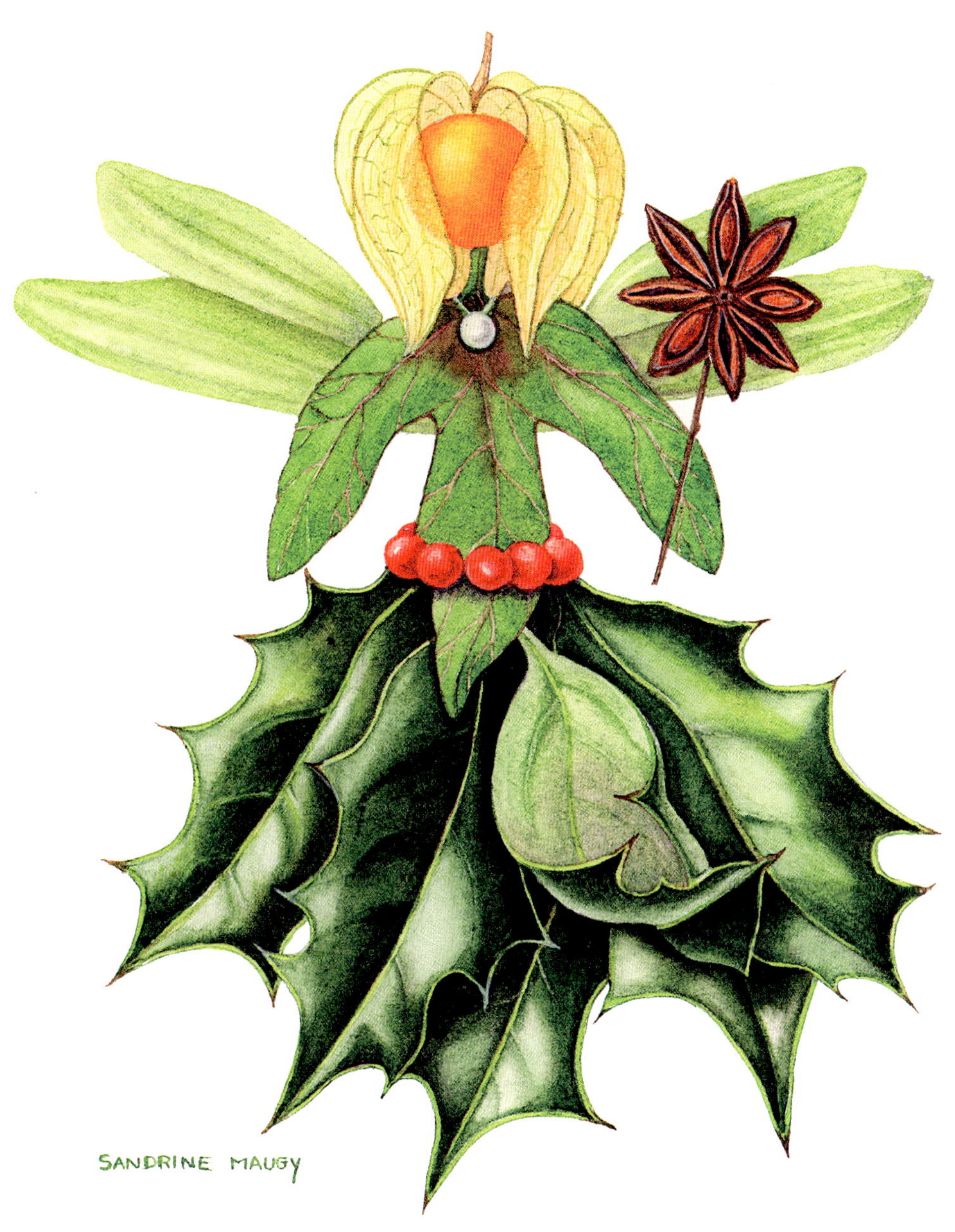

SANDRINE MAUGY

PAINT-CONVERSION TABLE

This table constitutes the full list of paints and pigments I am likely to use in my paintings, with potential substitute paints and mixes.

Daniel Smith pigment name	Pigment code/colour index	Colour	Bias	Transparency	Granulation
Hansa Yellow Light	PY3	Yellow	Green	Transparent	No
Quinophthalone Yellow	PY138	Yellow	Mid	Transparent	No
Mayan Yellow	PY223	Yellow	Mid	Transparent	No
Nickel Azo Yellow	PY150	Yellow	Orange	Transparent	No
Hansa Yellow Deep	PY65	Yellow	Orange	Semi	No
Permanent Orange	PO62	Orange	Yellow	Transparent	No
Pyrrol Orange	PO73	Orange	Red	Semi	No
Pyrrol Scarlet	PR255	Red	Orange	Semi	No
Pyrrol Red	PR254	Red	Mid	Semi	No
Carmine	PR176	Red	Violet	Semi	No
Quinacridone Fuchsia	PR202	Red	Violet	Transparent	No
Quinacridone Coral	PR209	Red	Variable	Transparent	No
Quinacridone Red	PV19	Red	Violet	Transparent	No
Quinacridone Pink	PV42	Pink	Violet	Transparent	No
Quinacridone Rose	PV19	Pink	Violet	Transparent	No
Quinacridone Lilac	PR122	Magenta	Pink	Transparent	No
Quinacridone Violet	PV19	Magenta	Violet	Transparent	No
Perylene Red	PR 178	Red maroon	N/A	Semi	No
Perylene Maroon	PR179	Maroon	N/A	Semi	No
Perylene Violet	PV29	Violet	Red	Transparent	No
French Ultramarine	PB29	Blue	Violet	Transparent	Yes
Phthalo Blue Red Shade	PB15:6	Blue	Mid	Transparent	No
Indanthrone Blue	PB60	Blue	Mid	Transparent	No
Phthalo Blue Green Shade	PB15:3	Blue	Green	Transparent	No
Cerulean Blue	PB35	Blue	Green	Semi	Yes
Sleeping Beauty Turquoise Genuine	N/A	Turquoise	Green	Semi	Yes
Viridian	PG18	Green	Blue	Transparent	Yes
Phthalo Green Yellow Shade	PG36	Green	Mid	Transparent	No
Sap Green	PO 48, PY 150, PG 7	Green	Yellow	Transparent	Yes
Rich Green Gold	PY129	Green	Yellow	Semi	No
Quinacridone Gold	PO49	Gold	N/A	Transparent	No
Quinacridone Burnt Orange	PO48	Russet brown	N/A	Transparent	Yes
Quinacridone Burnt Scarlet	PR206	Reddish brown	N/A	Transparent	No
Burnt Sienna	PBr7	Warm brown	N/A	Semi	Yes
Burnt Umber	PBr7	Mid-brown	N/A	Semi	Yes
Raw Umber	PBr7	Cool brown	N/A	Semi	Yes
Moonglow	PG 18, PB 29, PR 177	Grey	N/A	Transparent	Yes
Buff Titanium	PW 6:1	Cream	N/A	Semi	Yes
Pearlescent Shimmer	PW 20, PW 6	Shimmer	N/A	Transparent	Yes
Titanium White watercolour stick	PW6	White	N/A	Semi	No

Substitute Paint	Substitute Mix
Lemon Yellow (transparent)	Primary colour – N/A
Any transparent mid-yellow	Hansa Yellow Light + Hansa Yellow Deep
Any transparent mid-yellow	Hansa Yellow Light + Hansa Yellow Deep
Transparent/translucent yellow	Hansa Yellow Light + Quinacridone Gold
New Gamboge or Indian Yellow	Primary colour – N/A
Any yellow-bias orange	Hansa Yellow Deep + Pyrrole Scarlet
Any red-bias orange	Hansa Yellow Deep + Pyrrole Scarlet
Scarlet or Vermilion	Pyrrole Red + Hansa Yellow Deep
Any mid-red	Primary colour – N/A
Any Permanent Crimson or Carmine	Primary colour – N/A
Any Permanent Crimson or Carmine	Carmine + Quinacridone Pink
Quinacridone Red in other brands	N/A
Permanent Rose in other brands	Primary colour – N/A
Permanent Rose in other brands	Primary colour – N/A
Permanent Rose in other brands	Primary colour – N/A
Permanent Rose + Magenta	Quinacridone Pink + French Ultramarine
Magenta	Quinacridone Pink + French Ultramarine
Same in any brand	Pyrrole Red + Sap Green
Same in any brand	Pyrrole Red + Perylene Violet
Same in any brand	Carmine + Sap Green
Same in any brand	Primary colour – N/A
Same in any brand	Primary colour – N/A
Indanthrene Blue	Primary colour – N/A
Same in any brand	Primary colour – N/A
Coeruleum blue	Primary colour – N/A
No equivalent	Cerulean Blue + Phthalo Blue Green Shade
Same in any brand	Phthalo Green Yellow Shade + French Ultramarine
Same in any brand	Phthalo Blue Green Shade + any mid-yellow
Same in any brand, but Sap Greens vary a lot	Phthalo Blue Red Shade + any mid-yellow
Green gold	Sap Green + Hansa Yellow Light
Transparent muted golden yellow, Raw Sienna	Nickel Azo Yellow + Permanent Orange
Burnt Sienna	Raw Sienna + Permanent Orange
Burnt Sienna	Raw Sienna + Permanent Orange
Same in any brand	Raw Sienna + Permanent Orange
Same in any brand	Pyrrole Red + Sap Green
Same in any brand	Pyrrole Red + Sap Green + French Ultramarine
No equivalent	Viridian + French Ultramarine + Carmine
No equivalent	Titanium White + Yellow Ochre
No equivalent	No equivalent
Same in any brand	N/A

GLOSSARY

Bias The bias of a colour is the hue towards which the colour is leaning. A green-bias yellow is a yellow leaning towards green, for example. (See pages 20–21.)

Colour Index Name The Colour Index Name is the code by which pigments are identified. For example, Perylene Violet's Colour Index Name is PV29. The letters stands for the colour group and the numbers stand for each particular pigment. PV29 identifies Pigment Violet Number 29.

Complementary colours Colours on opposite sides of the colour wheel – for example, yellow and violet, orange and blue, and red and green. Each pair contains one primary colour and one secondary colour.

Fugitive Temporary/not lightfast. A fugitive paint will fade when exposed to light.

Granulation Some paints wash out smoothly while others separate on the palette and on the paper. They make small clumps of visible grain, creating texture. This is described as granulation. Two smooth paints, when mixed, can react and granulate.

Hot-pressed, Not and Rough Paper is defined by weight, but also by texture. Hot-pressed is very smooth, Not (meaning not hot-pressed) has a medium texture and Rough has a rough texture.

Hue Another word for colour. When used in the name of a colour (e.g. Vermilion Hue), it means that the paint, whilst being the same colour as Vermilion, is not made of the genuine Vermilion pigment. Sometimes it means that the paint is made with an inferior, cheaper pigment. However, hue is not necessarily employed in a negative sense. For example, Alizarin Crimson Hue is likely to be a better paint than the genuine Alizarin Crimson, as the genuine pigment is fugitive.

Lightfast Resistant to exposure to light. A lightfast pigment is permanent, a non-lightfast pigment is fugitive.

Neutral colours Colours obtained when mixing complementary colours. Neutral colours are browns, greys, dull/muted greens, dull/muted oranges and dull/muted violets. While the primary and secondary colours are situated on the outer ring of the colour wheel, the neutral colours are in the centre. (See page 21.)

Opaque Opaque paints are those that do not allow light to pass through them. An opaque paint is the opposite of a transparent paint. Between these two extremes are the semi-transparent and semi-opaque paints. (See page 18.)

Permanent Lightfast. A permanent paint is resistant to fading when exposed to light.

Pigment The element that gives the colour to a paint. Pigments can be organic or inorganic. vegetable, animal, mineral or chemical. They are ground into powder before being added to a binder.

Primary colours Yellow, red and blue. (See page 20.)

Secondary colours Orange, violet and green. (See page 20.)

Transparent A paint is transparent when the light can go through the painted layer to reflect off the paper, and bounce back up through the paint layer. In watercolours the level of transparency depends on the pigment. (See page 18.)

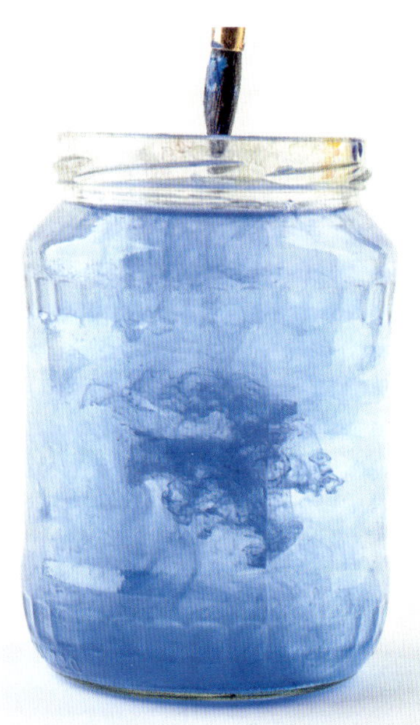

CREDITS

Acknowledgements

My parents, who supported me in whatever I chose to do, even if at the time they couldn't really see where it was going.

My husband, for the patience, love and support, always.

Penelope, the Studio Rabbit, who took great delight in the successive lockdowns when I was confined to the studio, painting and writing.

To my Patreon subscribers for their support: sorry I sometimes ran behind when deadlines were looming.

Justin Sullivan, Kim Richey, Trent Reznor, Francis Cabrel, Gavin Rossdale, Robert Smith, Ligabue and Christian Kane, for singing while I paint.

Caleb Marshall and Britney Spears, who kept me dancing during lockdown.

Everyone I worked with at Search Press, especially Beth: it has been such a pleasure.

The Association of Illustrators and the Society of Authors, who gave me a grant so I could keep working on this book during lockdown.

And finally to the Goddess Flora, for all the beauty and colours of nature.

Books of note

The Cambridge Illustrated Glossary of Botanical Terms, by Michael Hickey and Clive King
Understanding the Flowering Plants: A Practical Guide for Botanical Illustrators, by Anne Bebbington

These two books sit by my painting table. I find them invaluable to help me understand what I am looking at when faced with a new and less than straightforward subject. In addition, Anne is always only an email away when I stumble over a set of stamens – thank you, Anne.

Websites of note

www.microscopy-uk.org.uk A great site for seeing flowers in close-up.

www.rose.org The website of the American Rose Society, which features a lot of information about roses.

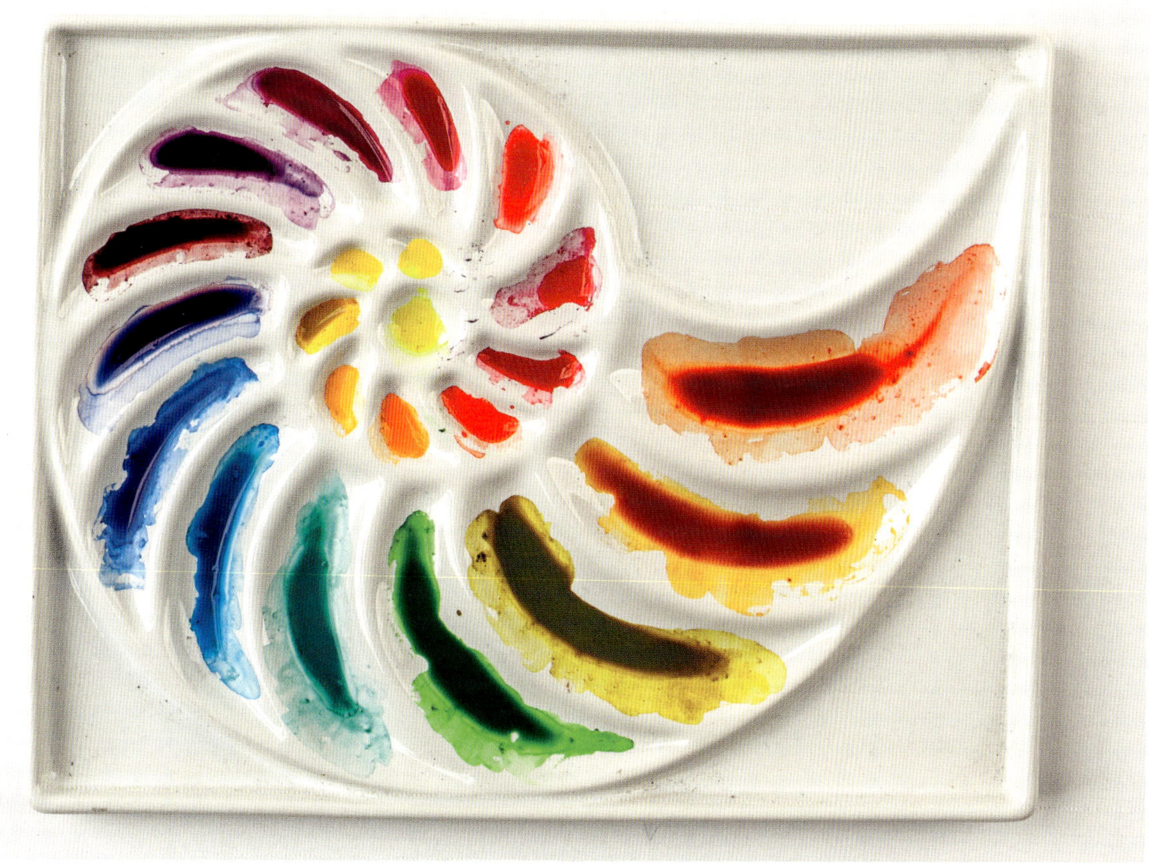

INDEX

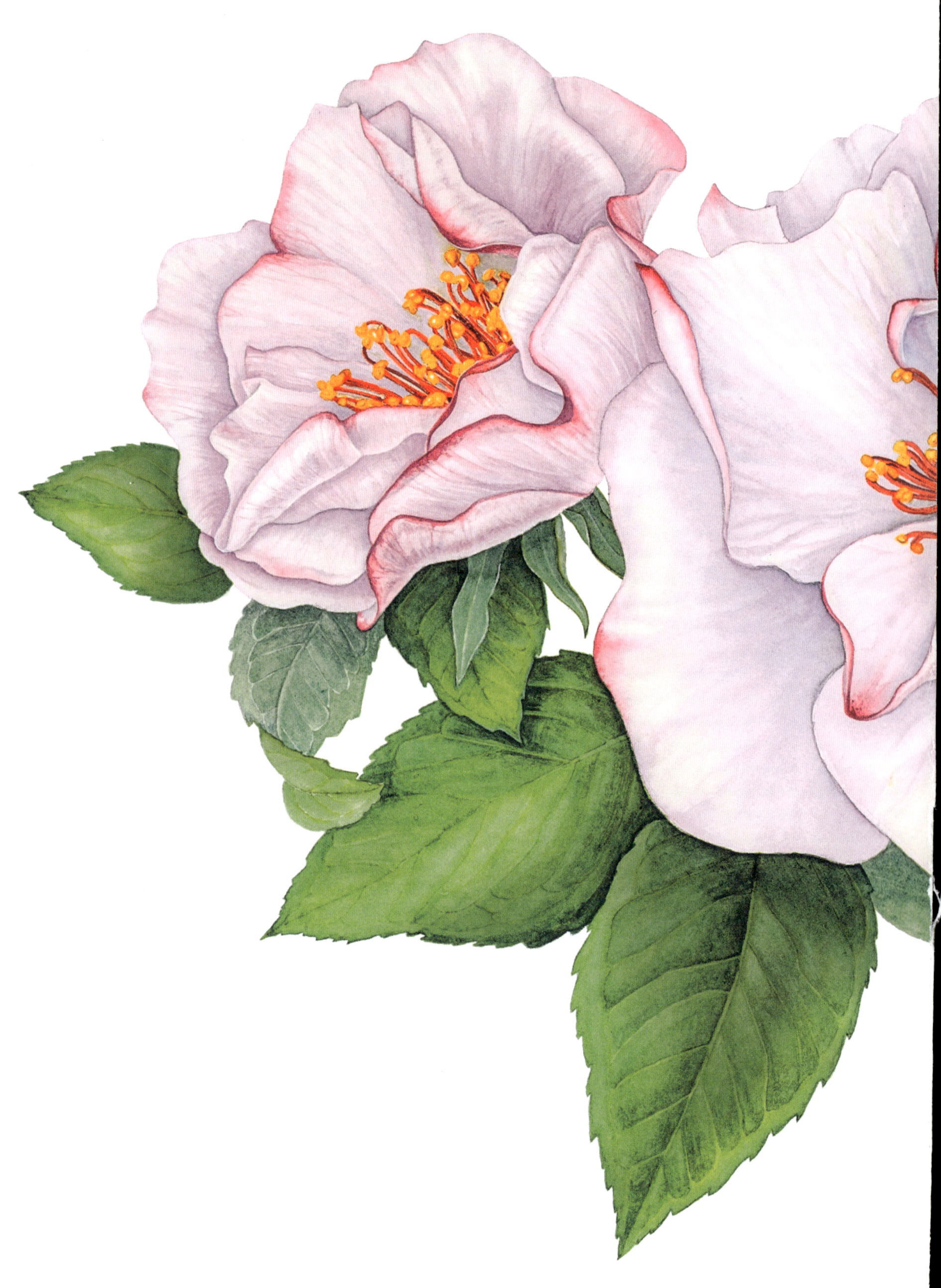